Harvesting Prosperity

Harvesting Prosperity

Technology and Productivity Growth in Agriculture

Keith Fuglie, Madhur Gautam,
Aparajita Goyal, and William F. Maloney

 **WORLD BANK GROUP**

Contents

Preface xiii

Acknowledgments xv

Abbreviations..xvii

Executive Summary: The Elusive Promise of Productivity xxi

1. Sources of Growth in Agriculture..1

    Improving Agricultural Productivity: Traversing the Last Mile toward
        Reducing Extreme Poverty 1

    Poverty Reduction, Productivity Growth, and Economic Transformation 2

    Trends in Land and Labor Productivity...7

    Conceptualizing Sources of Agricultural Growth 8

    The Increasing Importance of TFP in Driving
        Agricultural Output Growth 11

    What Will Accelerate Agricultural TFP? 17

    Annex 1A. Issues in Measuring Agricultural Productivity..........................24

    Notes 37

    References 38

2. Misallocation and Productivity Growth 43

    The Potential for Productivity Gains from Reallocation 43

    Insights on Farm Size and Productivity...44

    Labor Productivity and Structural Transformation 55

    Annex 2A. Microdata Sources for Measuring Labor
        Productivity in China and India...82

    Annex 2B. Distribution of Workdays by Farm and Nonfarm
        Activities in a Typical Month for an Average Adult Worker
        in India 84

    Annex 2C. Labor Productivity Differences by Farm Size...........................85

    Annex 2D. Labor Productivity Differences by Education Level 86

Annex 2E. Drivers of Wage Differentials between Farm and
Nonfarm Work in China 87

Notes 88

References 88

3. Investing in Innovation 95

Agriculture Innovation Policy in a Changing Global Context 95

Agriculture R&D Spending Worldwide: Increasing but Uneven 98

Revitalizing Public Research 105

Providing Incentives for Private Innovation 114

Concluding Remarks 131

Annex 3A. Market Liberalization in Africa's Maize Seed Industry 133

Annex 3B. Do Plant Breeders' Rights Stimulate Investment in
Crop Improvement? 135

Annex 3C. Herbicide Demand and Regional Harmonization of
Regulations in Africa 137

Notes 139

References 140

4. Improving the Enabling Environment for Technology Adoption 147

Removing Constraints and Adopting Policies to Promote
Diffusion of Technology 147

The Technology Adoption Puzzle 148

Removing Policy Bias against Agriculture 151

Closing Education Gaps 153

Securing Land Tenure Rights for Smallholders 156

Providing Information Services 157

Helping Farmers Manage Risk 164

Improving Access to Financial Services 169

Linking Farmers to Markets 174

Concluding Remarks 178

Notes 180

References 180

**5. The Challenge of Agricultural Productivity Policy and the Promise of
Modern Value Chains 187**

The Agricultural Productivity and Innovation System 187

The Productivity Policy Dilemma in Agriculture and the
Modern Value Chain 191

The Emergence of High-Value Markets 195

Value Chains and Agricultural Productivity: Some
    Conceptual Issues.. 198

Models of Value Chain Innovations and Organization...........................205

The Impact of Value Chain Transformations on Productivity.................208

Cultivating Value Chains 214

Concluding Remarks...222

Notes 224

References 225

Boxes

1.1 Decomposing Sources of Agricultural Growth...9

1.2 New Data for Decomposing Agricultural Growth and Measuring
     Total Factor Productivity 12

1.3 Research, Technological Capabilities, and Knowledge Diffusion: Key to the
     Transformation of US Agriculture 21

2.1 Analytically Challenged? The Mechanics of the Agricultural
     Productivity Gap..59

2.2 High-Quality Microdata Sets Provide New Insights on Rural Labor 63

3.1 R&D Capital, R&D Elasticities, and the Rate of Return to Research..................104

3.2 The Expansion of Animal Protein Industries in Nigeria and Bangladesh..........118

3.3 Policies and Innovation in China's Agricultural Machinery Industry...............124

4.1 Farmer Adoption of Flood-Tolerant Rice in Odisha, India 170

4.2 Ethiopia: An Emerging African Success Story in Agricultural-Led
     Development 176

5.1 The Agriculture for Development Sequence...193

5.2 Value Chain Innovations and Farm Productivity in Eastern Europe,
     1990–2005..210

5.3 Farm-Level Productivity Spillovers of Value Chain Innovations in
     Two African Countries in the 2000s..212

5.4 Examples of Multistakeholder Platforms to Stimulate Innovative
     Forms of Value Chain Organization..218

5.5 Blockchain at the Border: Exploring Whether Blockchain Can Help Rural
     Entrepreneurs and SMEs Boost Exports and Get Financing 220

5.6 Pilot of Distributed Ledger Technology for Traceability and Payment
     in Haiti's Fresh Fruits Value Chains..221

Figures

1.1   An Increase in Agricultural Productivity Has Nearly Twice the Impact on Reducing Extreme Poverty as a Comparable Productivity Increase in Industry or Services 3

1.2   Agricultural Output Has Dramatically Outstripped Population Growth, and Its Relative Price Has Fallen 4

1.3   The Volatility of Agricultural Production, after Falling for Decades, Has Begun to Increase, while Food Output per Capita Is Falling 5

1.4   Africa and South Asia Lag in Average Yield of Cereal Grains 6

1.5   Fifty-Year Trends in Agricultural Land and Labor Productivity Reveal the Large Divergence in Regions and Countries, 1961–2015 7

1.6   Decomposing Agricultural Economic Growth 8

1.7   Increases in Total Factor Productivity Have Become an Increasingly Important Source of Global Agricultural Growth 14

1.8   As the Amount of Land and Labor Shrinks in the Agricultural Sector, Growth Has Been Entirely Due to Improved Total Factor Producitivity in Both Developed and Developing Countries 15

1.9   A Framework for Raising Agricultural Productivity 18

B1.3.1 Technology Adoption in US Agriculture 21

B1.3.2 Mechanization in US Agriculture 22

1.10   Half the Countries in Africa Have Zero or Negative Growth in Spending on Agricultural R&D 23

1A.1   FAO versus Satellite-Based Estimates of Cropland 29

1A.2   A Comparison of Estimates of the Global Agricultural Labor Force ...31

1A.3   Estimates of Global Agricultural Capital Based on the Current Inventory Method versus the Perpetual Inventory Method 33

2.1   There Is No Optimal Farm Size: Both Large and Small Farms Can Be Equally Efficient 53

2.2   Across World Regions, Macrostatistics Show That Labor Productivity Is Higher in Industry and Services Than in Agriculture, 2011–15 56

2.3   Different Measures Yield Different Estimates of the Share of Labor in Agriculture and Other Sectors in Four African Countries 64

2.4   Only about One-Third of Rural Households' Total Work Time Is Spent on Farming Activities in China, 2003–13 65

2.5   Distribution of Workdays by Farm and Nonfarm Activities in a Typical Month for an Average Adult Worker in India 67

2.6   The Seasonality of Farm Work Is an Important Factor in the Distribution of Workdays Each Month for Adult Rural Workers between Farm and Nonfarm Work 68

2.7   Across the Six Countries Analyzed, Macrostatistics Show That Labor Productivity Is Higher in Industry and Services Than in Agriculture 69

2.8   Gaps in Labor Productivity Observed across Sectors Diminish When a Measure Based on Hours Worked, Rather Than the Primary Sector of Work, Is Used 69

2.9   Average Labor Productivity in China Is Significantly Higher Using Actual Labor Time Spent on Agriculture Instead of Assuming "Agricultural Workers" Spend All Their Work Time in Agriculture.....................70

2.10   Returns to Labor from Farm and Nonfarm Activities in India Vary by How Labor Is Measured, 2010–14 71

2.11   How Labor Is Measured Completely Changes the Relative Attractiveness of Agriculture Work in India, 2010–14 73

2.12   Trends in Farm and Nonfarm Wages in China: Agricultural Wage Workers Earn a Premium Wage, Which Has Risen over Time..............................77

2.13   Wages for Farm Work Are Higher Than Casual Nonfarm Wages throughout the Year at the Village Level in India...78

2.14   Wages Reported by Households Confirm the Reverse Wage Gap for Male Workers, but Not Female Workers...78

2B.1   Workdays Spent on Different Activities in a Typical Month for an Average Adult Rural Worker 84

2C.1   Average Earnings by Farm Size, India, 2010–15 85

2D.1   Annual Earnings by Education Level, India, 2010–14 86

3.1   Liberalization of Agricultural Input Markets Is Proceeeding in Different Ways in Brazil, India, and China..126

3A.1   Seed Market Reforms Had Different Effects on Maize Yields in Ethiopia, Ghana, Kenya, and Zambia 134

3B.1   One Company Came to Dominate Market Shares of Wheat Varieties Cultivated in South Africa 137

4.1   Evidence That Policies Are Discriminating against Farmers and Lowering the Agricultural Terms of Trade Can Be Found in Negative Nominal and Relative Rates of Assistance...152

4.2   In Many Developing Countries, Gender Gaps Persist in Labor Force Schooling Levels 154

4.3   Agricultural Workers Get Less Schooling Than Nonagricultural Workers 155

4.4   Access to Information and Communication Technologies Is Rapidly Gaining in Developing Countries...161

4.5   In Niger, the Marginal (per Search) Cost of Obtaining Agricultural Information Varies Greatly by Communication Method....................................162

B4.1.1 The Yield Advantage of Swarna-Sub 1 Increases for Up to Two Weeks of Continuous Flooding 170

4.6   High Travel Costs Constrain Crop Production in Sub-Saharan Africa..............174

4.7   High Transport Costs Reduce the Use of Modern Agricultural Inputs in Ethiopia..175

B4.2.1 Ethiopian Agricultural Growth Soared between 2001 and 2015 176

5.1 The Agricultural Productivity and Innovation System 188

5.2 Although Foreign Direct Investment in the Agriculture and Food Sectors
Has Increased Sharply in Asia and Latin America since 1993, It Has Lagged
in Africa...196

5.3 Horticulture Exports from Less-Developed Countries Have
Soared since 1995 197

5.4 The Proliferation of Food Standards Is Illustrated by the Large Increase in
Sanitary and Phytosanitary Notifications to the World Trade Organization.....198

5.5 Food Value Chain with Perfect Markets...200

5.6 Value Chain Innovations Are Likely to Occur When Both the Value of the
Product and the Extent of Market Imperfections Are High 202

B5.2.1 Value Chain Innovation Spurred Large Increases in Production
and Productivity at the Slovak Republic's Biggest Sugar Processor and
Its Supplying Sugar Beet Farms 210

B5.2.2 Milk Productivity in Poland Rose Steeply in the 1990s and Early 2000s...........211

Map

1.1 Gains in Agricultural Total Factor Productivity Varied Greatly across
Countries from 1971 to 2015...16

Tables

1.1 Sources of Growth in Developing Countries, 2001–15 17

1A.1 Alternative Measures of Agricultural Output and Productivity
Growth, 2001–15 35

2.1 Urban-Rural Daily Wage Premiums for Male and Female Workers
and Cost of Living Differences in India 79

2E.1 Regression Results 87

3.1 Spending on Public Agricultural R&D by Developing Countries Tripled
between 1981 and 2011, but Agricultural R&D Investment Remains
Uneven across Regions...99

3.2 Numerous Studies Confirm a Very Strong Relationship between
R&D Investment and Agricultural Total Factor Productivity.............................101

3.3 Nearly 300 Studies Have Shown That Returns to Agricultural Research
Spending in Specific Countries and Commodities Are Exceptionally High,
on Average...106

3.4 The Private Sector's Role in Agricultural R&D Is Increasing
around the World 115

3.5 Private Food and Agricultural R&D Is Spread across Multiple
Industries in Brazil, India, and China 116

3.6   The Use of Agricultural Inputs Has Risen Steadily in India for More Than
        Four Decades 120

3.7   Various Policies Can Support Private Agricultural R&D, Innovation, and
        Technology Transfer 122

3.8   Common Regulatory Practices Regarding Agricultural Production Inputs 129

3C.1   Sources of Pesticide, Fertilizer, and Improved Seed Sold to Farmers in
        Ethiopia in 2011 138

4.1   Use of Modern Agricultural Inputs Varies across Developing Countries 149

4.2   Adoption of Modern Crop Varieties Is Highly Uneven across
        Sub-Saharan Africa, circa 2006–10 150

4.3   Agricultural Extension Workers Are Highly Concentrated in a
        Few Countries 157

B4.2.1 Impacts of Agricultural and Economic Growth in Ethiopia 176

B5.1.1 The Stages and Processes of the Agriculture for Development Sequence 193

Preface

Productivity accounts for half of the differences in gross domestic product per capita across countries. Identifying policies to stimulate it is thus critical to alleviating poverty and fulfilling the rising aspirations of global citizens. Yet productivity growth has slowed globally in recent decades, and the lagging productivity performance in developing countries constitutes a major barrier to convergence with advanced-economy levels of income.

The World Bank Productivity Project seeks to bring frontier thinking on the measurement and determinants of productivity, grounded in the developing-country context, to global policy makers. Each volume in the series explores a different aspect of the topic through dialogue with academics and policy makers and through sponsored empirical work in our client countries. The Productivity Project is an initiative of the Vice Presidency for Equitable Growth, Finance, and Institutions.

Harvesting Prosperity: Technology and Productivity Growth in Agriculture, the fourth volume in the series, argues that there are large potential gains to be made in productivity, and hence income, precisely where the vast majority of the extreme poor are found—in rural areas and engaged in small-scale farming. Thus, increasing agricultural productivity must be central to the growth and poverty reduction agendas. It is also critical to food security and environmental sustainability objectives. This said, recent research suggests some reconsideration of current approaches: the potential gains from reallocating land and labor are probably less promising than previously thought. Hence this volume instead focuses on intensifying the generation and dissemination of new, more productive practices and technologies, as well as removing the barriers farmers face to adopting them. The emergence of value chains and private sector research organizations offers important alternatives to direct public sector approaches to these ends, but their cultivation requires additional reforms, particularly with respect to the overall policy environment and incentives.

This book is a joint effort between the Agriculture and Food Global Practice of the Sustainable Development Vice Presidency and the Equitable Growth, Finance, and Institutions Vice Presidency. It was supported in part by the US Department of Agriculture (USDA) and the US Agency for International Development (USAID).

This volume is dedicated to the memory of Guillermo Perry (1945–2019), former Chief Economist of the World Bank's Latin American and Caribbean region.

William F. Maloney
Chief Economist
Equitable Growth, Finance, and Institutions Vice Presidency
World Bank Group

Other Titles in the World Bank Productivity Project

High-Growth Firms: Facts, Fiction, and Policy Options for Emerging Economies. 2019. Arti Grover Goswami, Denis Medvedev, and Ellen Olafsen. Washington, DC: World Bank.

Productivity Revisited: Shifting Paradigms in Analysis and Policy. 2018. Ana Paula Cusolito and William F. Maloney. Washington, DC: World Bank.

The Innovation Paradox: Developing-Country Capabilities and the Unrealized Promise of Technological Catch-Up. 2017. Xavier Cirera and William F. Maloney. Washington, DC: World Bank.

All books in the World Bank Productivity Project are available free at https://openknowledge.worldbank.org/handle/10986/30560.

Acknowledgments

This book was prepared by a core team of Keith Fuglie (USAID and USDA), Madhur Gautam, Aparajita Goyal, and William F. Maloney (all of the World Bank), with contributions from World Bank and external experts: Mansur Ahmed, Jock R. Anderson, Leah Bridle, Prasana Das, Emiliano Duch, Rob Kuijpers, Jeremy Magruder, Craig McIntosh, Latha Nagarajan, Anwar Naseem, Carl Pray, Nicholas Rada, Tavneet Suri, and Johan Swinnen.

The study was undertaken under the overall guidance of William F. Maloney. Special thanks to Ceyla Pazarbasioglu for her invaluable support. The team benefited greatly from consultations and discussions with, and suggestions from, Juan Buchenau, Mark Cackler, César Calderón, Luc Christiaensen, Andrew Dabalen, Alain de Janvry, Chris Delgado, Felipe Dizon, Simeon Ehui, Ejaz Ghani, Xavi Giné, Doug Gollin, Mary C. Hallward-Driemeier, Ruth Hill, Hanan Jacoby, Ellen McCullough, Rinku Murgai, Toshi Ono, Pierella Paci, William Price, Diego Restuccia, Loraine Ronchi, Mark Rosenzweig, Elisabeth Sadoulet, Carolina Sánchez-Páramo, Rachel Sberro, Robert Townsend, Chris Udry, Dina Umali-Deininger, Felipe Valencia Caicedo, Panos Varangis, Juergen Voegele, Jonathan Wadsworth, Michaela Weber, and Albert Zeufack.

Thanks also to Chao Peng and Chen Zhang for assistance in the access to and analysis of the Research Center for Rural Economy (RCRE) survey data for China, and Bernardo Atuesta for excellent data assistance.

Production of the volume was managed by Susan Mandel of the World Bank's formal publishing program; Patricia Katayama, of the Development Economics unit, was the acquisitions editor. Yaneisy Martinez, also with the World Bank publishing program, was the print coordinator. Nancy Morrison edited the volume.

Abbreviations

AI	artificial intelligence
APG	agricultural productivity gap
APO	Asian Productivity Organization
ARC-SGI	Agricultural Research Council–Small Grains Institute (South Africa)
ARI	agricultural research institute
ASTI	Agricultural Science and Technology Indicators
ATAI	Agricultural Technology Adoption Initiative
AWG	agricultural wage gap
C	Celsius
CABI	Centre for Agriculture and Bioscience International
CARDI	Caribbean Agricultural Research and Development Institute
CGIAR	Consultative Group on International Agricultural Research
CIM	current inventory method
CIMMYT	International Maize and Wheat Improvement Center
COL	cost of living
CORPOICA	Corporación Colombiana de Investigación Agropecuaria (Colombia)
CRADA	Cooperative Research and Development Agreements (United States)
CSP	Comité Sahelien des Pesticides (Sahelian Pesticides Committee)
EATA	Ethiopian Agricultural Transformation Agency
ECOWAS	Economic Community of West African States
EMBRAPA	Empresa Brasileira de Pesquisa Agropecuária (Brazilian Agricultural Research Corporation)
FAO	Food and Agriculture Organization (of the UN)
FDI	foreign direct investment
FFS	farmer field schools
FTE	full-time equivalent
GDP	gross domestic product
GFSAD30	Global Food Security Analysis-Support Data at 30 Meters
GIS	geographic information systems
GLOBALG.A.P.	worldwide standard for Good Agricultural Practices
GM	genetically modified
GPS	Global Positioning System
ha	hectare
ICRISAT	International Crops Research Institute for the Semi-Arid Tropics
ICT	information and communication technology

IFAD	International Fund for Agricultural Development
IFPRI	International Food Policy Research Institute
ILO	International Labour Organization
IoT	Internet of Things
IPCC	Intergovernmental Panel on Climate Change
IPRs	intellectual property rights
IR	inverse relationship
IRR	internal rate of return
ISAAA	International Service for the Acquisition of Agri-biotech Applications
KALRO	Kenya Agricultural and Livestock Research Organization
kg	kilogram
kg/ha	kilograms per hectare
KSC	Kenya Seed Company
LAC	Latin America and the Caribbean
LSMS-ISA	Living Standards Monitoring Surveys–Integrated Surveys on Agriculture
MNCs	multinational corporations
MUV	manufactured exports unit value
NAS	national accounts statistics
NGO	nongovernmental organization
NRA	nominal rate of assistance
NSS	National Sample Surveys
NWLR	New Wave Land Reform
OECD	Organisation for Economic Co-operation and Development
PA	Productive Alliance
PBRs	plant breeders' rights
PIM	perpetual inventory method
PPP	purchasing power parity
PSE	producer support estimate
R&D	research and development
RCRE	Research Center for Rural Economy (China)
RDIP	Rural Development Investment Program (Colombia)
RRA	relative rate of assistance
SAT	semi-arid tropics
SMEs	small and medium enterprises
SOE	state-owned enterprise
SSA	Sub-Saharan Africa
T&V	training and visit
t/ha	tons per hectare
TFP	total factor productivity
TRIPS	Agreement on Trade-Related Aspects of Intellectual Property Rights

UNICEF	United Nations Children's Fund
UPOV	International Union for the Protection of New Varieties of Plants
USAID	US Agency for International Development
USDA	US Department of Agriculture
USDA-ERS	US Department of Agriculture Economic Research Service
USGS	US Geological Survey
VDSA	Village Dynamics in South Asia (India)
WANA	West Asia and North Africa
WDI	World Development Indicators (World Bank)
WFP	World Food Programme
WHO	World Health Organization
WRI	World Resources Institute
WTO	World Trade Organization

Note: All dollar amounts are in US dollars, unless otherwise specified.

Executive Summary: The Elusive Promise of Productivity

Harvesting Agriculture's Promise through Innovation

The history of early human advance is the history of harvesting prosperity from agricultural innovation. In India, the later Vedic texts (c. 3000–2500 BCE) make frequent references to agricultural technology and practices. Jia Sixie, drawing on over one thousand years of Chinese study in his *Qimin Yaoshu*, or *Essential Techniques for the Common People* (535 CE), asserts throughout his work the centrality of agricultural advance for the well-being of the people and the state. He proposed essential techniques to "save labor and increase yields." Giving practical advice for improving farm management, the Roman statesman Cato the Elder in *De Agricultura* (160 BCE) emphasized how a prosperous agricultural system contributes to general welfare and stability. "It is from the farming class that the bravest men and the sturdiest soldiers come, their calling is most highly respected, their livelihood most assured."

Continuing to make improvements to agricultural productivity, especially in low-income nations, is necessary to ensure sufficient food for an increasing global population and to traverse the last mile toward eliminating extreme poverty in developing nations:

- Two-thirds of the global extreme poor earn their livelihood in farming and productivity growth in agriculture has the largest impact of any sector on poverty reduction. Rising agricultural productivity in China and other countries of East Asia has contributed to impressive reductions in poverty, but has been too low to have similar impacts in Africa and in South Asia, precisely where the largest remaining pockets of extreme poverty are to be found. The modest expansion of urban manufacturing and service sectors is unlikely to provide alternative income sources over the medium term.
- Despite increases in world agricultural productivity over the past few decades, global undernourishment remains significant, affecting 821 million people as of 2017, and is on the rise, driven by conflict and worsening climatic evolution.
- Climate change will hit agriculture hard, particularly where large numbers of poor and vulnerable people live. Climate change models suggest warming of 1 to 2 degrees Celsius (C) from the preindustrial level by 2050. For every 1-degree C increase, average global cereal yields are expected to decline 3 percent to

10 percent, the United Nations Food and Agriculture Organization estimates. In addition, a deteriorating natural resource base reduces the resilience of the production system to climate variability and depresses future productivity.

- Agricultural productivity is lower and is growing more slowly in poor countries, impeding their convergence to the advanced economies. Over four decades, crop yields in Sub-Saharan Africa have barely doubled, even as they tripled in South Asia and increased about six-fold in East Asia.

Hence, even after centuries of experimentation and progress, further advances in agricultural productivity remain critical to providing for basic human welfare, reducing extreme poverty, maintaining food security, and achieving social stability. Importantly, public and private investments in technology and innovations to sustain agricultural productivity growth are also central to strategies addressing emerging environmental challenges and achieving a sustainable food future in the face of climate change.

The Rising Importance of Growth in Total Factor Productivity

A deeper understanding of the drivers of agricultural productivity growth, and what is constraining it, hence remains critical. Globally, over the past five decades there has been a major shift in agriculture from resource-led growth to productivity-led growth. Rather than increasing agricultural output by expanding the amount of land, water, and input usage, most agricultural growth today comes from increasing total factor productivity (TFP) of these resources, or the efficiency with which these inputs are combined to produce output by using improved technology and practices. TFP is a more complete measure of technical and efficiency change in an economic sector. It represents how "knowledge capital," or the application of new ideas (embodied in new technologies and production practices), contributes to growth. TFP growth is especially important for agriculture and its sustainability, given that the supply of land is inherently limited and use of labor or further expansion has an enormous environmental footprint, and use of labor and capital face diminishing returns.

Improvement in TFP accounted for over two-thirds of agricultural growth globally from 2001 to 2015 (up from 20 percent in the 1960s), and nearly 60 percent of the agricultural growth in developing countries.

The new data and estimates of TFP offered here suggest that most gains in output are, in fact, driven by productivity, and that rates of productivity growth differ greatly across countries. The exercise reveals the need for continued research in measuring productivity and its drivers. Further, empirical assessments of agricultural productivity should (but rarely do) account for changes in the quality and quantity of natural resources—such as to land, water, biodiversity, and greenhouse gas emissions—that result from agricultural activity. Considering environmental factors in assessments of agricultural productivity is important because these resources have social value and significant impacts on actual productivity that can be achieved in the future. Although there is some evidence that agricultural TFP growth can conserve natural resources in many cases, more research is needed on this issue. Though beyond the scope of this book, sustainability is an important complementary policy objective to increasing productivity.

Transformations under way in market value chains in global food and agricultural products open up broader opportunities for raising productivity. Improving farm productivity entails more than just raising yields or decreasing the use of inputs and costs. It also involves raising food quality and moving into higher-value products, such as from generic maize to specialty crops and exportable food products. Moving toward higher-end products can provide an important growth opportunity for smallholder producers if they can reliably meet the more exacting standards of these markets.

As discussed in a previous volume, *Productivity Revisited*, TFP is generally conceived as the overall efficiency with which inputs are used to produce products of the highest value. Broadly speaking, among the population of firms or farms, this can occur by (1) reallocating factors of production, such as moving land or inputs from lower- to higher-productivity farms, or labor from agriculture to other activities; (2) increasing the productivity of existing farms through adoption of new technology, improved practices, and higher-value commodities; and/or (3) entry of more productive farms and exit of less productive ones. Correspondingly, there have been two broad schools of thought on where policies to raise productivity should focus: (1) removing barriers that prevent the rapid reallocation of factors of production across farms and sectors; and (2) increasing within-farm or potentially new-farm productivity through technological progress.

The Gains from Reallocating Land and Labor Are Not as Large as Once Thought

On the first area of focus—the removal of barriers or distortions that may prevent a reallocation of productive resources across farms to achieve higher productivity and growth—new research finds that potential efficiency gains from removing the ostensible barriers may not be as large as once thought. The principal misallocations are thought to lie in land and labor markets.

Distortions in land markets may prevent resources from being reallocated to the most productive farmers. Evidence of such distortions has come from the commonly observed inverse relationship between farm size and land productivity in developing countries, and economics of scale in mechanization. The inverse relationship has often been used to justify land reform policies that redistributed land to smallholders, but such policies have rarely met with much success. On the other hand, if larger farms were more productive and if land markets functioned well, efficient farms could acquire more land, substitute capital for labor, and capture economies of scale. In this view, a continued preponderance of small farms may indicate that land market distortions constrain overall agricultural growth and competitiveness.

Recent research, however, suggests that there is no optimal farm size and that both small and large farms can be equally efficient. Importantly, recent studies have shown that in developing countries, growth in productivity has not been confined to either very small or very large farms. But, at the same time, the emergence of new technologies especially suited for small farms—labor-intensive horticulture, solar-powered water pumps, minitractors combined with leasing markets—enable the introduction of highly productive farming on small plots of land. Intensification of precision agriculture applying rapidly emerging digital technologies may further reduce any size-based advantages or disadvantages in crop management. When overall input use is considered, it is not clear whether there are systematic differences in economic efficiency by farm size, and any differences may be diminishing with technological advance and movements into higher–value added commodities.

The second potential misallocation is in the labor market since barriers to mobility may prevent workers from moving out of agriculture into other sectors in which labor productivity is higher. This view—that leaving too much labor in agriculture reduces economic output—has been claimed by a long literature based on macroevidence that the average productivity of workers in agriculture is substantially lower than labor productivity in nonfarm sectors.

Again, however, recent work, as well as evidence offered in this volume, call into question whether the potential gains from labor reallocation are all that large. First, at a conceptual level, the differences in average productivity between industrial and agricultural sectors may simply reflect differences in capital per worker, and would be expected even with an efficient labor market that equates marginal productivities (that is, wages) across sectors, implying no misallocation. Second, differences in human capital (education, gender, age) may account for much of the observed differences in respective wages, implying that effective marginal labor productivities are equated. Third, recently generated microdata allow for better accounting of the actual time spent in different activities. These new data find that assuming that all rural labor is occupied full time in agriculture is a vast overestimate, and thus actual daily or hourly productivity in agriculture is higher than previously thought. When properly measured, apparent gaps in labor productivity across sectors are often greatly diminished. Finally, there is an important role for workers selecting into sectors based on preferences and skills. Once more, research using more accurate estimates of hours worked and taking into account personal characteristics and self-selection finds that there is not much difference in either average productivity or, more importantly, marginal productivity across sectors.

These findings reinforce the skepticism as to whether quick and easy productivity gains could be achieved by removing the perceived distortions constraining a reallocation of labor across sectors. Although eliminating barriers to reallocation of resources across sectors remains an important item on the reform agenda in many countries, the evidence suggests that the potential gains in terms of productivity and economic growth from reallocation are likely to be less than previously expected. Achieving faster structural transformation instead requires focusing on achieving productivity growth through technological progress both on and off the farm.

Renewing the Focus on Innovation

This discussion moves the second potential driver of TFP—the invention, adaptation, and dissemination of new technologies to existing firms—to center stage. Sustaining growth in agricultural productivity depends on farmers adopting a steady stream of new farm practices and technologies that enable them to raise yield, manage inputs more efficiently, adopt new crops and production systems, improve the quality of their products, and conserve natural resources. Moreover, these new technologies must be well adapted to local environmental and social conditions and be renewed as environmental conditions change (due to coevolution of pests and diseases, degradation of water and land resources, and climate change, for example). These factors—constraints to direct technology transfer between regions and productivity losses in the face of environmental changes—point to a pressing need to strengthen national agricultural research and development (R&D) and innovation systems. Such localized R&D capacity is essential for adapting technologies in specific areas and for specific needs.

The evidence is strong that investments in agricultural R&D pay off. Across developing countries, social rates of return to agricultural R&D have averaged over 40 percent per year, implying that the economy-wide benefits of R&D greatly exceed its cost. Moreover, high returns to agricultural R&D have all been achieved in all developing regions. But because of significant "knowledge spillovers" from R&D (the profitable use of new technologies by persons other than the inventor), the private sector underinvests in technology development. Thus, there is an essential role for the government in national agricultural R&D systems—both as a direct funder of public agricultural R&D and to create conditions to attract more private investment into agricultural R&D.

Sustained and effective productivity improvement involves a steady supply of new technologies, but it also requires that farmers be willing and able to adopt them. Imperfect information about new technologies, missing markets for insurance and capital, high market transactions costs, and policy biases against agriculture can inhibit adoption and diffusion of new technologies among farms. Policy makers need to give careful attention to the broader "enabling environment" for technology generation and uptake, working on both the supply and demand sides, in order to drive productivity growth.

The Changing Global Context of Agricultural Innovation

Further, policy makers need to consider national innovation systems in the context of twenty-first-century global developments. Important changes are under way in the nature of food and agricultural markets, the global landscape for agricultural research and development, and the emergence of new institutions and means for knowledge transmission:

- Freer international trade in food and agricultural products has created incentives for domestic production to be more closely aligned with comparative advantage.
- The types of technologies needed on the farm are changing because of structural changes in agricultural and food marketing systems, including the rise of supermarkets and vertically coordinated market chains—driven by consumer demands for product diversity, quality, and safety, and by economies of scale in food processing and marketing. Food marketing and processing companies are becoming important players in creating and disseminating technologies to farmers in order to meet higher standards. This, in turn, opens new opportunities for public-private partnerships.
- Around the world, sources of advanced agricultural science and technology are becoming more diverse. Some countries, like Brazil, China, and India, have expanded their capacities in agricultural sciences, and are likely to become increasingly important sources of technology spillovers for global and developing-country agriculture.
- The emergence of an international private agricultural input supply sector as a provider and disseminator of new technologies offers developing countries the possibility of harnessing the private sector to increase international technology transfer and expand the overall national R&D effort. This requires developing effective relationships and networks with these sources, and enacting and enforcing regulations governing intellectual property rights, the movement of genetic material, health and safety of new products, as well as streamlining processes for registering and approving new technology.
- The rapidly expanding access to new digital information and communication technologies around the world offers new modalities for knowledge development and dissemination. Although digital technologies substantially reduce the cost of information, their successful application to improve farm practices and promote technology adoption obviously depends on the quality and local relevance of the messaging.

Agricultural policies, and the incentives they create, must be considered in the context of this evolving global environment.

Elements of a Twenty-First Century Agricultural R&D System

Agriculture has its own version of the innovation paradox. Although studies consistently find that investment in agricultural R&D leads to higher productivity growth, with social returns to public R&D averaging more than 40 percent, investment in agricultural R&D is stagnant or falling in regions where agricultural growth is most needed. Many of the poorest regions of the world, like Africa and South Asia, have an increasingly acute research spending gap. Further, declining capacities, particularly in African agricultural universities, constrain long-term capacity development in human resources and knowledge creation in this region. But it is not only a question of adequate funding for public science institutions. It also depends on how well those funds are used, and on aligning policies and incentives to crowd in private investment. Building an effective agricultural innovation system requires supportive policies that reward performance of public scientists and advisory service providers, build human and knowledge capital, and encourage the private sector to invest in innovation and technology transfer to farmers.

1. Revitalizing Public Agricultural Research Institutes

Even with greater private R&D, strong public R&D institutions are still essential for agricultural growth. In addition to expanding the scientific frontier, public institutions continue to provide most of the new technologies for agriculture, especially in developing countries. Whereas private research is focused on specific crops and on improving specific inputs such as hybrid seed, agrochemicals, machinery, and other inputs that can be sold to farmers, public research addresses a much broader range of scientific and technical issues, commodities, and resource constraints. Public capacity in agricultural science and technology is also needed to support government regulatory actions permitting the use of new technologies, establishing and enforcing sanitary and phytosanitary standards, and assuring safe food products. The fact that social returns to R&D tend to be much higher than private returns to R&D indicates the strong "public good" nature of research benefits. Moreover, the high social rates of return from agricultural R&D provide direct evidence of persistent societal underinvestment in this public good, and imply that valuable opportunities for economic growth and poverty reduction are being missed.

Successful public research institutions foster a climate of innovation in which creativity and collaboration are encouraged and performance is recognized and rewarded. International best practice suggests that several factors contribute to high-performing public research institutes:

- *Institutional autonomy*. Many public research institutes are located within ministries of agriculture. They are thus subject to government-wide budgetary and human resource rules and regulations that are designed to assure hierarchical control of policies or programs but often interfere with the incentives necessary to encourage high performance in research programs. Granting greater autonomy within the context of a clear mission statement and well-designed incentives is necessary to encourage high performance in research programs.

- *Performance incentives for scientists.* As in any research institute, the attraction and motivation of staff is perhaps the central challenge for management. Hence, a modern human resource policy with performance rewards is critical. Some institutions provide bonuses and promotions to staff whose research has led to demonstrable outputs and impact. Plant breeders, for example, might be remunerated on the basis of area adopted to varieties they develop. Another important source of staff remuneration is to provide opportunities for further education, training, and career advancement for staff who consistently perform at a high level. Institutes should avoid pressures to expand staff numbers if it means diluting resources for research and staff development (that is, if expenditure per scientist declines). In Sub-Saharan Africa, low staff retention, high absenteeism, and salary structures that do not reward performance or are competitive with the private sector are depleting human resources at many public agricultural research institutes.

- *Stable and diversified financing.* Public agricultural research institutions have historically depended on general government revenues or aid programs for funding. Lack of diverse funding sources can leave them vulnerable to low and unstable funding. One potential source of supplementary funding for research is through producer levies. Levies are assessments made on the value of commodity sales or exports. Revenues from levies may be channeled through producer organizations and used to fund a range of cooperative activities, including research, extension, and market promotion. Governments may give statutory authority to producer associations to impose mandatory levies on all their members when a majority of members are in favor. Levies are mostly used for commodities that are grown commercially and for export, and that are marketed through a limited number of outlets, such as processing mills or ports (which reduces the transaction cost of collecting the levy). Another potential source of research funding is by charging fees for technology products and services.

- *Programs aligned with client needs through public-private partnerships.* One way of improving alignment with local farmer needs and to facilitate dissemination of agricultural innovations to farmers is through partnerships with producer groups and the private sector. Funding of public research through producer associations, as described in the previous bullet, ensures that producers have a direct stake (and say) in R&D program orientation. Joint R&D ventures, whereby public institutes and private companies share in the development costs, also help ensure alignment of research with client needs.

- *International R&D links.* Although agricultural technologies need to be tailored to location-specific conditions, much of the pool of knowledge and genetic resources that scientists draw upon to make these adaptions are supplied by universities and research institutes in developed countries or through the 15 affiliated research centers of the global agricultural innovation network, CGIAR. Over the past few decades, for example, major advances have been made in the science of crop and animal breeding. Follower countries can gain rapid access to these scientific developments through research partnerships with foreign and international institutes. This is especially important for small countries whose own research institutes lack the scale to replicate these advances. Agricultural scientists in developing countries need to form networks and collaborative relationships with scientists from foreign and international centers through attendance at conferences, study leaves abroad, and collaborative research. Research budgets and human resource policies need to accommodate and encourage this.

2. Strengthening Agricultural Universities

An additional characteristic of a viable agricultural research system is integral involvement of higher education in research. This is essential if developing countries are to remove the constraints to scientific knowledge and expertise that limit their capacity to move toward productivity-based agricultural growth. Graduate-level education in agricultural sciences is most effective when it occurs in association with a significant research program. Thus, universities play a fundamental role in agricultural research systems. Agricultural universities are home to some of the most highly skilled scientists, who have the essential task of training the researchers and technicians that staff research and development organizations in both the public and private sectors. However, there has been a serious decline in the quality of graduate training programs at many African agricultural universities, due primarily to declining public investment. This is crippling the ability of these institutions to train scientists and create sufficient agricultural research capacity in this region. Most of the reforms mentioned in the case of public research institutes also apply to research at agricultural universities.

3. Encouraging Private R&D

Governments need to consider both public and private research and technology transfer as they strengthen their overall innovation systems. Private R&D can help close the R&D funding gap and stimulate more rapid access to new technologies for farmers. In developed countries, private companies contribute about half the total R&D spending targeting the needs of farmers, and in large emerging economies like Brazil, India, and China, as much as 25 percent. Governments can employ several policy tools to encourage more private R&D in agriculture:

- Expand the market size for agricultural inputs by reducing restrictions on market participation, encouraging competition, and leveling the playing field.

Countries can liberalize markets for seed, chemicals, and farm machinery to increase (foreign and domestic) participation and competition in these markets, including by eliminating monopolies held by state-owned enterprises. Reducing input subsidies that favor existing products and are not available for new products or that channel input sales through government tenders rather than markets could also provide more opportunity for private input suppliers. Eliminating government monopolies in agricultural input markets and permitting private companies to operate in these markets is a prerequisite for private investment in agricultural research and innovation. However, studies have shown that market liberalization alone may not lead to greater private research unless other conditions are in place, such as protection for intellectual property and clear regulatory pathways for licensing new technology. Reducing tariff and nontariff barriers to trade in seed, breeding stock, and other agricultural inputs can encourage research and technology transfer in countries with small domestic markets.

- Provide incentives to firms to invest more in R&D by removing onerous or duplicative regulations. The commercialization of new technologies for agriculture often involves lengthy and costly regulatory protocols that require substantial data to be collected and submitted to government regulators on a product's safety and performance. Streamlining and eliminating duplicative regulations can reduce their costs and thus make technology development more profitable for private firms. For instance, relaxing duplicative environmental, health, and efficacy testing for new technologies that have already passed these requirements in another country with similar growing conditions or moving toward regional harmonization of regulatory norms can promote technology transfer. Establishing regulatory protocols allowing the use of safe genetically modified (GM) crops could induce more research and technology transfer by seed and biotechnology companies.

- Strengthen intellectual property rights (IPRs) over new technology. IPRs enable firms to appropriate some of the gains from new technologies they develop, which is essential if companies are to earn a positive return on their R&D investments. Although the evidence of the positive impact of IPRs on private R&D from middle-income countries is robust, results from low-income countries are mixed. Stronger IPRs alone may be insufficient if market size is small or regulatory regimes are too onerous.

- Support public institutes and universities. These centers provide complementary inputs for private sector research, supply advanced scientific personnel and resources, and expand the set of technological opportunities available for commercialization. These public investments are implicitly another form of subsidy that evidence suggests creates positive knowledge spillovers and stimulates more R&D by the private sector. However, public research may also crowd out private research if it duplicates activities that could profitably be undertaken by private firms.

Facilitating Adoption of New Technologies by Farmers

In addition to low investment in high-payoff R&D, the second but related aspect of the agricultural innovation paradox is that farmers often do not adopt the technologies that are available. This demand side of the innovation dynamic is as central for policy makers to address as the supply of new technologies. It involves remedying numerous types of market distortions and failures. Clear identification of these constraints and appropriate design of policy remedies are essential for an innovation system to perform well. Key policy elements needed to strengthen the enabling environment for technology adoption include the following:

- *Remove policy biases against agriculture.* Policies in many developing countries have discriminated against agriculture, effectively taxing agriculture to provide subsidies to urban dwellers or nonagricultural sectors. Such policies lower returns to agricultural investment, discourage technology adoption, and lead to inefficient use of economic resources. For instance, reforms allowing agricultural prices to reflect market forces and permitting farmers to reap rewards from their efforts have led to large increases in productivity. Conversely, overvalued exchange rates that provide cheaper imports to consumers or trade policies that protect manufacturers impose implicit taxes on the agricultural sector. It is essential to stress that even the most energetic innovation policies will fail if policy biases make it unprofitable for farmers to expand or experiment with new technologies.
- *Increase the capabilities of farmers.* Raising the human capital of farmers allows them to better evaluate technological opportunity and manage technology-related investments. In line with findings from the World Bank's Human Capital Project, both the average attainment levels and the quality of rural schooling trail that of urban areas. This is particularly the case for women, who form a major part of the agricultural workforce and often manage their own farms. Unsurprisingly, the returns to education increase when there are greater opportunities for new technological adoption.
- *Increase the flow of information to smallholder farmers.* The traditional argument for agricultural extension services linked to research centers is that farmers are not aware of new technologies or their optimal usage. The success of extension and advisory services clearly depends on the quality of the knowledge being diffused. In addition, the performance of extension services can be greatly improved through institutional reforms that include embracing nongovernment actors; increasing the accountability to farmers and local

authorities; and improving the knowledge, networking, and coordination skills of agents. Finally, new information and communication technology (ICT), often combining voice, text, videos, and Internet to interact with farmers, offers the potential for communicating tailored information at lower cost. ICT also opens the door to more sophisticated precision farming systems involving sensing data and satellite imagery to provide precise and real-time crop management advice that is more commonly applied on technologically advanced farms and plantations. Some of the world's newest industries have started to put money and tech talent into farming—the world's oldest industry. Digital soil maps, remote sensing, and Global Positioning System (GPS) guidance are critical tools for modern farmers. "Big data" for precision agriculture increase yields and efficiency. These high-tech tools mostly benefit big farms that can make large investments in technology. But there are also many innovative ways in which poorer and otherwise disadvantaged people use digital technologies, such as basic mobile phones. Greater efforts to close the digital divide in rural areas can have great payoffs.

- *Improve access to financial services.* Formal banking institutions are hampered in servicing smallholder farmers, given high transaction costs and lack of acceptable forms of collateral. Improving financial services, particularly by offering low-cost and reliable means for poor households to accrue savings, can help smallholder farmers stabilize household expenditures and lessen their aversion to risk taking and technology adoption. Utilizing ICT to create new instruments like digital finance and mobile money can dramatically lower the cost of financial transactions. These financial innovations offer new opportunities to extend financial services to better serve smallholder agriculture. Facilitating the establishment of credit histories, developing flexible collateral arrangements, and accounting for seasonality in repayment schedules all offer ways of tailoring financial services to smallholders' needs and, again, all are facilitated by ICT.

- *Help farmers manage risk.* Adopting an unfamiliar new technology fundamentally entails placing an informed bet that potentially poses risks to family income. Insurance institutions can help manage risk, but like financial services, they are hampered in servicing smallholder farmers because of market failures. Innovations like weather index insurance significantly reduce transaction costs and avoid pitfalls from moral hazard (whereby only the riskiest seek insurance) and adverse selection (whereby the insured take less care of their crops). But they have suffered from insufficient targeting of payouts, lack of trust in the provider, and weak financial literacy among clients. Again, technological advances such as satellite-based remote sensing and improvements in agronomic crop models offer potential to improve insurance products and lower risks faced by farmers. Alternatives should be tested, such as developing more sophisticated indexes, providing subsidized policies as a form of social protection, and expanding the market for reinsurance among financial institutions. Importantly, agricultural R&D can be directed toward developing technologies that reduce risk, such as crop varieties that tolerate drought or resist pests and diseases.

- *Enhance security of land tenure.* Providing secure tenure to land creates the incentives needed for farmers to invest in land-improving practices, a key element for sustainable and productive land use. It can often help farmers obtain better credit, provide an insurance substitute in the event of an income shock, and enhance the asset base of those, such as women, whose land rights are often neglected. Land policies need to be attuned to local conditions. Providing formal title is only one means of increasing tenure security; legal recognition of existing customary rights, with codification of internal rules and mechanisms for conflict resolution, can also greatly enhance occupants' security and lead to better outcomes for economic efficiency and equity.

- *Improve rural infrastructure.* Remoteness from markets is often more a function of the quality of roads than actual distances travelled. The set of technologies that producers in remote locations can profitably adopt is often restricted because of high transport costs resulting from poor infrastructure, which drive up the prices paid for modern inputs and force down the prices received for farm commodities. Investments that improve rural roads and related transport infrastructure can yield high returns by stimulating profitable adoption of agricultural technology and productivity growth in rural areas.

Each of these represents a component of the enabling environment whose healthy functioning is an essential complement to investment in R&D. Eliminating distortions and resolving market failures that constrain technology adoption is an essential part of any productivity program. However, agricultural policy faces the same productivity policy dilemma faced elsewhere: that simultaneously resolving multiple market failures is often challenging given limited government resources and capabilities to diagnose problems and implement successful reforms. One way of reducing the dimensionality of the problem is to identify the most binding constraints in the local context and focus attention on these first. For instance, in many regions that rely on rainfed agriculture, inability for farmers to adequately manage risk may be a more significant constraint to technology adoption than lack of access to financial services per se. In addition, drawing more heavily on the private sector when possible—for instance, in undertaking R&D—reduces the demands on the capabilities of the public sector.

The Promise of Modern Value Chains

In recent decades, value chains connecting stages of production from farm to fork—particularly those selling to high-end markets—have surged. Technical and institutional innovations in these value chains offer new tools to approach the coordination challenges between the different stages of production, processing, and trade.

A high-value chain can offer an incentive to a lead firm to develop interlinked contracts whereby they resolve the market failures particular to their business, such as providing farmers with information, new technologies, credit, insurance, and guaranteed access to larger or international markets. The particular institutional structure the chains take varies from the most common vertical farmer/retailer relationships, to more complex contracts (including leasing possibilities that reduce collateral issues) and triangular structures and special-purpose vehicles that link third-party financial institutions to supply credit to chain suppliers, to fully vertically integrated models that incorporate the farmer within the company. The available evidence, though scarce, suggests that farm productivity rises and the prices received for output are higher as a result of being part of a value chain. In addition, there are spillovers to members beyond the chain in the form of a demonstration effect by incentivizing similar contracting mechanisms in other crops and value chains. Though working with larger farmers clearly reduces transaction costs, smallholders dominate value chains, particularly in Asia.

Attracting private investment in value chains requires many of the characteristics of the enabling environment already discussed, although with some additional considerations. Specific policy actions that can support the development of value chains include the following:

- *Encourage competition and reduce distortions.* Allowing market prices to reflect the true value of the product in the relevant market is critical for the establishment of globally competitive value chains, as is ensuring competition at the various stages of the chain. Governments need to be aware of how their own actions can distort prices and create an uneven playing field, such as input subsidies, support of state-owned enterprises, or selective support to companies.
- *Facilitate deeper international integration.* For export-oriented value chains, easy access to external markets and necessary inputs is essential. In addition, given that domestic prices reflect external prices filtered through exchange rates, preventing overvaluation remains critical to ensuring the profitability of potential value chains.
- *Establish a credible contracting environment.* Interlinked contracts depend on credible commitments along the chain. For instance, farmers under contract who receive proprietary technologies do not pass them along to others outside the chain; after inputs or credit are offered, the crop is not sold to a third party; and private companies establish transparent pricing mechanisms and assure timely service delivery and payments.
- *Extend essential infrastructure.* Though clearly important in delivering inputs and information, infrastructure deficiencies in roads, electrification, rail, cold-chain facilities, designated trading areas, and ICT are particularly binding in the last mile to market.

- *Ensure shared benefits of value chains.* Governments need to be vigilant to ensure that the cultivation of large lead firms and the bargaining power they have serves the interests of farmers. Some private development programs demand the involvement of a nongovernmental organization (NGO) such as an association or union to represent the interests of farmers and wage laborers to ensure the inclusiveness of the initiatives.

In cases in which a clear market failure is identified—for instance, when a value chain is expected to produce large spillovers (benefits beyond what participants in the chain can profit in, say through demonstration effects to other farms and value chains)— direct support to enable lead companies to start and develop a value chain may be considered. It might include offering cofinancing or concessional loans, or providing complementary state-provided R&D or infrastructure. Policy can also target particular links of the value chain. For instance, traders, processors, and retailers might commit to engage in buyer agreements if public investment projects help farmers comply with product and processing requirements. Traditional areas of public investment, such as research and extension, market information systems, and veterinary services, can be refocused to facilitate the establishment of the chain. In general, to prioritize government actions, ongoing dialogue between public and private actors is necessary to identify key constraints that are binding to the development of the value chain.

Value chains offer an important tool but cannot be expected to encompass the entire rural or agricultural sectors, in particular those parts engaged in low-value crops that offer little incentive to engage in the interlinked contracts that would resolve market failures. Most bulk commodities fit this description. As in the case of research, a division of labor may emerge whereby private-led value chains focus on areas where high-value crops are concentrated and the public sector focuses on more traditional commodities and farmers.

Concluding Remarks

The focus of this volume is deliberately confined to the question of how to raise productivity in agriculture. Clearly, harvesting agricultural prosperity for rural economic growth will require a more comprehensive vision that goes beyond improving efficiency, shifting to high-value crops and diversification, discussed here, to the larger transformation of the rural economy. This lies beyond the scope of this analysis, but clearly merits a complementary effort, as does the looming issue of climate change that threatens to undermine rural prosperity and will condition future agricultural research and policy in many important ways.

This said, the aspirations of this work are metaphorically captured by the painting displayed on the front cover, "Rebellious Plant," by the Spanish-Mexican surrealist

Remedios Varo. The miracle of agricultural productivity has nourished people and lifted people out of poverty to a degree unimaginable to our ancestors. However, adapting agriculture to new and possibly dramatically changing contexts requires a sustained process of experimentation and scientific inquiry. Continuing this trend is vital in the final push to end global poverty and create fulfilling livelihoods for all.

1. Sources of Growth in Agriculture

Improving Agricultural Productivity: Traversing the Last Mile toward Reducing Extreme Poverty

The history of early human advance is the history of harvesting prosperity from agricultural innovation.[1] In India, the later Vedic texts (1100 BCE) make frequent references to agricultural technology and practices (Tauger 2010). Jia Sixie, drawing on over one thousand years of Chinese study in his *Qimin Yaoshu*, or *Essential Techniques for the Common People* (535 CE), asserted throughout his work the centrality of agricultural advance for the well-being of the people and the state and proposed techniques to "save labor and increase yields."[2] Giving practical advice for improving farm management, the Roman statesman Cato the Elder in *De Agricultura* (160 BCE) emphasized how a prosperous agriculture contributes to general welfare and stability. "It is from the farming class that the bravest men and the sturdiest soldiers come, their calling is most highly respected, their livelihood most assured..."

Today, increasing output from finite resources remains critical to ensuring sufficient food for an expanding global population and to traverse the last mile toward eliminating extreme poverty in developing nations. For the third consecutive year since reaching its nadir in 2015, global undernourishment is on the rise, reaching 821 million people in 2017 (FAO et al. 2018), driven by conflict and worsening climatic evolution. Two-thirds of the global extreme poor who are working earn their livelihoods in agriculture. More generally, the lack of income convergence of most follower countries toward the advanced countries is exacerbated by a very clear divergence in agricultural productivity. Hence, even after centuries of experimentation and progress, further advances in understanding agricultural productivity remain critical to advancing human welfare, meeting new environmental challenges, and to driving down widespread extreme poverty.

This volume builds on the now vast literature on agricultural productivity in several ways. First, drawing upon the international agricultural productivity data set developed by the US Department of Agriculture's Economic Research Service (USDA-ERS 2018), it offers the first consistent estimates of the sources of agricultural output and productivity growth to date globally and by region.

Second, it locates research on agriculture productivity in the larger evolution of thinking on productivity generally that was discussed in an earlier volume of this series,

Productivity Revisited (Cusolito and Maloney 2018). In particular, it argues that the diagnostics pointing to the productivity gains that could be realized from reallocating factors of production have probably been overemphasized: Studies of optimal firm size have become more agnostic as to whether there are large gains to be had by redistributing factors of production; and arguments that large distortions prevent the movement of labor and hence structural transformation are less convincing.

Third, with the deemphasis on reallocation, the focus necessarily shifts to within-farm improvements as the driver of productivity and, in turn, the centrality of research and technological diffusion. Yet, despite documented very high rates of return to agricultural research, the volume finds that both spending and the efficiency of that spending have been atrophying, particularly in Africa, over the last few decades. That is, although evidence suggests that agricultural research is a powerful weapon for attacking the most resistant areas of extreme poverty, the effort in this area is waning. Fortunately, there are more tools available to close the agricultural research gap than in past decades. The rise of private companies with research and international marketing arms leads to a reconsideration, here, of the relative roles of public versus private investments in research and technology transfer, as well as the framework conditions necessary to attract these new players.

Fourth, an exploding literature using a variety of measurement techniques has shed increased light on the agricultural analogue to the *innovation paradox* described earlier in this series (Cirera and Maloney 2017): why, if returns to adoption of new technologies are so high, do so few farmers adopt them? Recent thinking on the barriers posed by problems of information, finance, risk, and market access suggests that no single constraint can explain the lack of adoption, and multipronged approaches may be necessary to accelerate updates of new technologies so that increased research spending is not to be pushing on a string.

Fifth, the rise of value chains in agriculture radically changes that landscape of global agricultural production and marketing and offers new tools to resolve the various market failures impeding research and adoption of new technologies. The volume explores the roles of linked contracting necessary to the establishment of value chains and of the conditions necessary to attract and cultivate them.

Finally, throughout, the volume highlights how the advent of new digital technologies permits new forms of global coordination of research, less expensive and more tailored modalities of extension, flexible and low-cost financial instruments that can extend credit to heretofore unreachable small farmers, and more effective ways of managing and hedging risk.

Poverty Reduction, Productivity Growth, and Economic Transformation

Economic development, structural transformation, and productivity growth are intricately linked, although thinking on how they interact continues to change. For the early thinkers on economic development, agriculture—unlike more "modern" sectors—was identified with low productivity. It was a deep pool of cheap labor, and as an economy's structure transformed, labor would flow from agriculture into more productive manufacturing (and later services) sectors (see, for example, Clark 1951; Lewis 1954; Kuznets 1955; Chenery and Syrquin 1975). Since then, however, agricultural productivity has come to be understood to be a powerful driver of growth that raises people out of poverty and contributes to overall development (Christiaensen, Demery, and Kuhl 2011). Three-quarters of the world's poor are rural people, and most derive their livelihoods from farming. Clearly, if any development strategy is to "move the needle" toward the twin goals of reducing poverty and boosting shared prosperity, it must catalyze growth where the majority of poor people live and work.[3] Over the near term, it does not appear that the manufacturing and modern services sectors can absorb the agricultural population.

In fact, growth in agriculture reduces poverty more than growth elsewhere in an economy, especially in the earlier stages of structural transformation (Ligon and Sadoulet 2018). As figure 1.1 suggests, a 1 percent increase in agricultural gross domestic product (GDP) per worker yields roughly double the impact on extreme poverty as a comparable increase in labor productivity in industry or services (Ivanic and Martin 2018). Agriculture's poverty-reducing advantage disappears as countries (and people)

FIGURE 1.1   An Increase in Agricultural Productivity Has Nearly Twice the Impact on Reducing Extreme Poverty as a Comparable Productivity Increase in Industry or Services

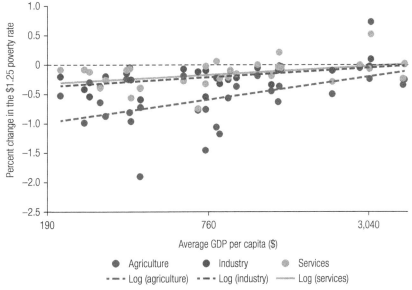

Source: Ivanic and Martin 2018.

Note: The y-axis represents the percent change in the US$1.25 poverty rate given a 1 percent increase in total factor productivity of a sector. GDP = gross domestic product.

grow richer—but the evidence affirms that improvements in agricultural productivity are vital for structural transformation and a smooth transition toward more urbanized economies because growth in agricultural productivity leads to higher incomes, promotes nonfarm jobs, and enables people to move out of agriculture over time (Gollin, Parente, and Rogerson 2002; McMillan and Harttgen 2014). In countries where rural populations are still rising, technical change in agriculture can also help absorb the rapidly growing youth labor force at the same time as raising farm wages (Filmer and Fox 2014). Investments and policies to stimulate growth in the agricultural economy are critical for accelerating the transition out of poverty and fostering inclusive growth.

Besides fostering structural transformation, long-term improvement in agricultural productivity has helped ward off the Malthusian catastrophe predicted in the 1960s, when world population growth accelerated. As figure 1.2 shows, agricultural production began to outstrip population growth as "Green Revolution" technologies spread across many parts of the world. Real agricultural prices fell as commodities became cheaper to produce (although with significant price shocks in the 1970s and again in 2003–14). This all occurred without a corresponding expansion of land in agriculture: The seven-fold increase in output since 1900 occurred with little over a

FIGURE 1.2 Agricultural Output Has Dramatically Outstripped Population Growth, and Its Relative Price Has Fallen

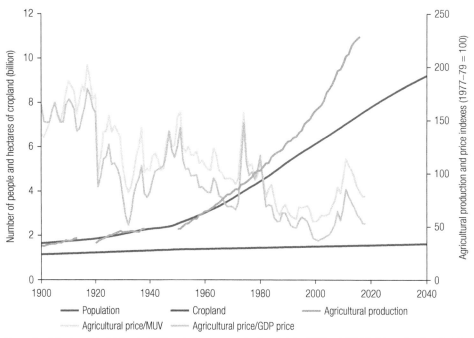

Source: Population from Oxford University (2017); agricultural output index from Federico (2005) and FAO (2018a); cropland from Federico (2005); agricultural price indexes from Pfaffenzeller, Newbold, and Rayner (2007) and extended with IMF commodity price data.

Note: Agricultural price/MUV (manufactured exports unit value) is the ratio of price indexes of agricultural commodities and manufactured goods. Agricultural price/GDP price compares agricultural prices with the US GDP price index, which includes a broader set of goods and services. GDP = gross domestic product; IMF = International Monetary Fund.

50 percent increase in cropland. Countries that were most able to benefit from this agricultural technology revolution, such as in East and Southeast Asia, enjoyed dramatic declines in extreme poverty and an acceleration in the structural transformation of their economies (Timmer 2002; Gollin 2010).

Equally importantly, as figure 1.3 shows, at the global level, the overall volatility of agricultural output has fallen. This is partly due to the spread of irrigation, which reduced volatility in food production by making it less sensitive to rainfall. But most global agricultural land is still rainfed. And in rainfed areas, it is innovation—especially the spread of varieties and crops bred to withstand various forms of biotic and abiotic stress—that has expanded food production and reduced its volatility.

Despite the gains in productivity achieved so far, recent trends strongly caution against complacency and highlight the need to push for faster growth in agricultural productivity in the regions that are still lagging. Further the trend toward reduced volatility has reversed. Conflicts in various parts of the world have contributed to this problem, but a more widespread contributor is climate change. Even as the impacts of climate change are felt worldwide, the Intergovernmental Panel on Climate Change (IPCC 2018) released further sobering news: climate models suggest warming of 1 to 2 degrees Celsius by 2050 from the pre-industrial levels and the United Nations Food and Agriculture Organization (FAO) estimates a 3 percent to 10 percent decline in average global cereal yields for every 1-degree Celsius increase (FAO 2018b). These impacts, together with a deteriorating natural resource base, will hit agriculture especially hard. As it is, food security remains a persistent concern for policy makers, not only in rural Africa—where the recent rise in the absolute number of undernourished people is

FIGURE 1.3 **The Volatility of Agricultural Production, after Falling for Decades, Has Begun to Increase, while Food Output per Capita Is Falling**

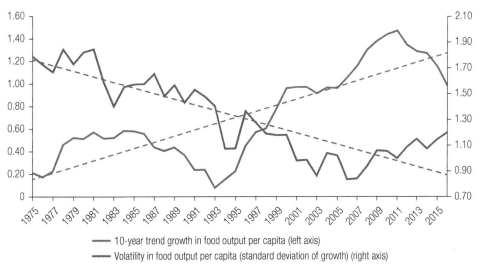

— 10-year trend growth in food output per capita (left axis)
— Volatility in food output per capita (standard deviation of growth) (right axis)

Source: FAOSTAT.

concentrated, and where agricultural growth remains driven mostly by factor accumulation—but also in South and East Asia, and parts of Latin America and the Caribbean, where the effects of climate change are expected to be felt most severely and large numbers of poor and vulnerable people still remain. In West Africa and India farming yields could fall by as much as 2.9 percent and 2.6 percent respectively by 2050, the FAO (2018b) predicts. All these trends speak to the compelling need for policies and options to accelerate agricultural productivity growth, in the interest not only of food security and incomes, but also of sustainability and social stability. Investments in research and development to generate new technologies and appropriate incentives for the private sector to innovate will be key to creating a sustainable food future (World Resources Institute 2019).

An important factor behind the large divergence in standards of living across countries, and across sectors within countries, is that agriculture in poor countries appears to be much less productive and has grown more slowly in lagging countries. As an example, the Green Revolution that boosted yields in so many countries largely bypassed Africa. Since the 1960s, cereal yields in Sub-Saharan Africa have lagged increasingly behind yields in all other regions. Since 1961, the average yield of cereal grain crops in Sub-Saharan Africa has barely reached 1.5 tons per hectare (t/ha), even as they tripled to 3 t/ha in South Asia and increased to 6 t/ha in East Asia (figure 1.4). This pattern will hold more generally with broader measures of productivity (total factor productivity, or TFP) discussed below.

FIGURE 1.4   **Africa and South Asia Lag in Average Yield of Cereal Grains**

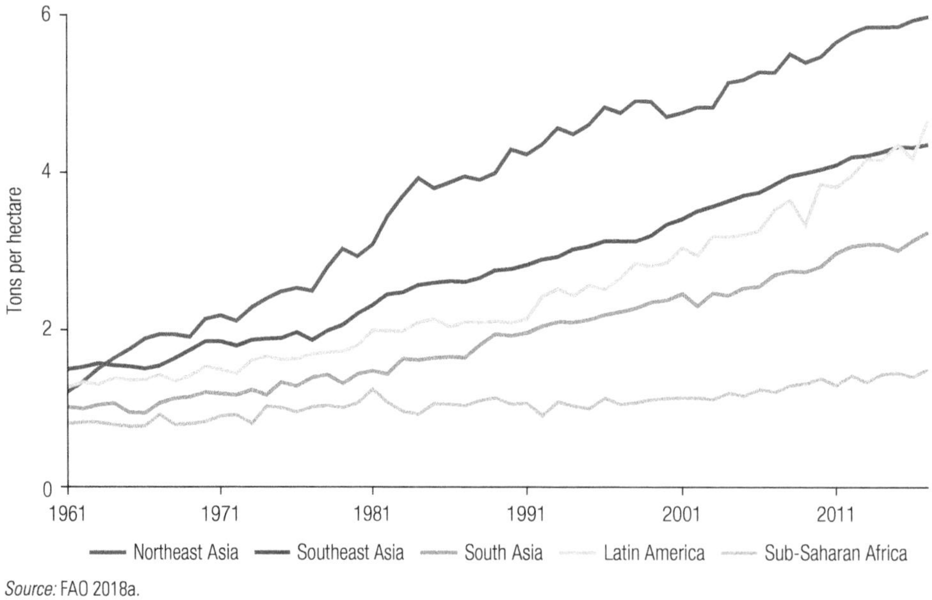

Source: FAO 2018a.

Trends in Land and Labor Productivity

Figure 1.5 offers a more general view of the evolution of aggregate agricultural productivity measured in constant dollars on a log scale as output per hectare (vertical axis) or per worker (horizontal axis). The colored lines represent the progress each region has made across these dimensions over 1961–2015. By far, the world's highest yields—gross output of crops and livestock per hectare of farmland—are found in the developed countries of northeast Asia (Japan and the Republic of Korea). More relevant from the point of view of worker income, the highest output per agricultural worker is in North America (the United States and Canada) and Oceania (Australia and New Zealand) followed by Europe and Japan and Korea. In addition, these areas have grown at the fastest rate measured by the horizontal travel along the 50-year curve while Sub-Saharan Africa and to a degree, South Asia have moved little. Southeast Asia has progressed somewhat faster and China has moved from African levels of productivity to almost catch up with Latin America. Overall, however, the limited progress in Africa and South Asia graphically dramatically illustrates the

FIGURE 1.5   Fifty-Year Trends in Agricultural Land and Labor Productivity Reveal the Large Divergence in Regions and Countries, 1961–2015

Agricultural land and labor productivity by region

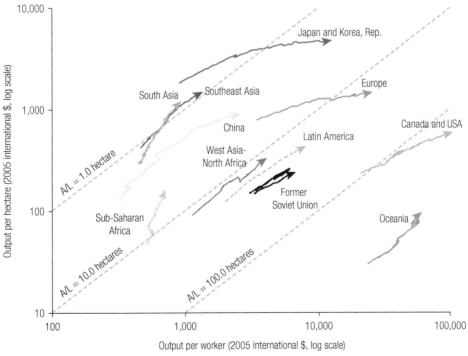

Source: Derived from FAO (2018a) data.

Note: The diagonal lines represent constant land-labor (A/L) ratios.

divergence in agricultural productivity that contributes to the overall lack of country convergence across countries already discussed.

These measures, however, may overstate the gains to workers because they include the contribution coming from more intensive use of other inputs—such as fertilizers, machinery, energy, and irrigation— which add to costs. Ideally, we would like to decompose output growth into the contribution arising from using more land and other inputs versus increasing the total productivity of those inputs. Total factor productivity (TFP) is the efficiency with which these inputs are combined to produce output. TFP is a more complete measure of technical and efficiency change in an economic sector. It represents how "knowledge capital," or the application of new ideas (embodied in new technologies and production practices) contributes to growth. TFP growth is especially important in agriculture since the supply of land is inherently limited and hence the use of labor and capital face diminishing returns.

Conceptualizing Sources of Agricultural Growth

Figure 1.6 graphically depicts the decomposition of agricultural growth, with the size of the stacked bars indicating the contribution of various factors to the growth in total value of output. Note that changes in the real value of agricultural output is due to changes in the volume of supply (labeled "real output growth" in figure 1.6) and changes in the agricultural terms of trade (or the price of agricultural commodities relative to the overall GDP price level). During periods of commodity price booms, agricultural GDP may rise, even if the volume of production remains unchanged. Conversely, it may decline during periods of price busts due to these terms-of-trade effects.

FIGURE 1.6 Decomposing Agricultural Economic Growth

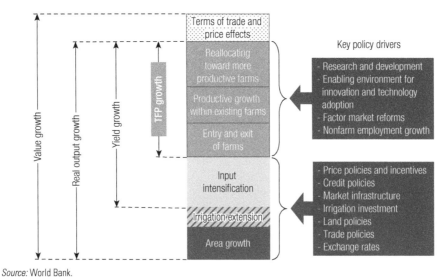

Source: World Bank.

Note: TFP = total factor productivity.

The top box depicts terms-of-trade effects. Because the focus of this volume is in the long-term performance of the sector and not short-term cyclical movements in prices or terms of trade, the analysis focuses on the components that contribute to real output growth—increases in the total volume of commodities produced.

The bottom component (red box) captures the contribution to growth of land expansion (including augmentation of land quality through irrigation). The middle component (yellow box) captures growth due to input intensification on existing land (for example, the use of more capital, labor, and fertilizer per hectare). The upper component (green boxes) represents TFP growth, where TFP reflects the average efficiency with which all inputs are transformed into outputs. For a mathematical description of this growth decomposition, see box 1.1.

BOX 1.1

Decomposing Sources of Agricultural Growth

A basic framework for decomposing sources of growth into resource-led growth and productivity-led growth (that is, growth led by total factor productivity, TFP) is given in equations (1) through (4). The first equation is a basic production function, whereby aggregate output Y at time t is a function of inputs X (composed of land, labor, capital, and intermediate inputs) used in production and a factor-neutral technology index TFP:

$$(1) \quad Y_t = TFP_t * f(X_t).$$

Expressed as logarithms, changes in equation (1) over time can be written as

$$(2) \quad \sum_{j=1}^{J} R_j ln\left(\frac{Y_{j,t}}{Y_{j,t-1}}\right) = ln\left(\frac{TFP_t}{TFP_{t-1}}\right) + \sum_{i=1}^{I} S_i ln\left(\frac{X_{i,t}}{X_{i,t-1}}\right),$$

in which R_j is the revenue share of the j-th output, S_i is the cost share of the i-th input, and

$$\sum_{j=1}^{J} R_j = \sum_{i=1}^{I} S_i = 1.$$ In other words, aggregate growth in total agricultural output is found

by summing the growth rate of each commodity, weighted by its share of total revenue. Total input growth is found by summing the growth rate of each factor of production, weighted by its share of total costs. TFP growth is then the difference between the growth of total output and total input. Equation (2) shows that the growth in output can be decomposed into a part due to changes in resources used in production and a part due to changes in the total productivity of those resources.

One difference among growth accounting methods is whether the revenue and cost share weights are fixed or vary over time. Paasche and Laspeyres indexes use fixed weights, whereas the Tornqvist-Thiel and Fisher chained indexes use variable weights. Allowing the weights to vary reduces potential "index number bias," which can arise when producers substitute among outputs and inputs depending on their relative profitability or cost. In other words, the growth rates in X_i

(Box continues on the following page.)

BOX 1.1

Decomposing Sources of Agricultural Growth (*continued*)

are not independent of changes in S_i. For example, if labor wages rise relative to the cost of capital, producers are likely to substitute more capital for labor, thereby reducing the growth rate in labor and increasing growth in capital. For agriculture, index number bias in productivity measurement appears to be more significant for inputs than outputs. Cost shares of agricultural capital and intermediate inputs tend to rise in the process of economic development, while the cost share of labor tends to fall. Commodity revenue shares, on the other hand, generally show less change over time. Crop and livestock shares of global agricultural output have remained fairly stable since the 1960s, for example (although an increasing share of crop production is being used for feed instead of consumed directly as food).

For these reasons, and as a practical matter, most measures of international agricultural growth decomposition use fixed output prices to aggregate output while allowing input cost shares to vary over time and by country. To measure gross agricultural output, the Food and Agriculture Organization (FAO) uses global average prices from a base year (derived using the Geary-Khamis method; see Rao 1993) to estimate the annual volume of agricultural output for each country of the world since 1961. The current base period used by FAO in valuing gross agricultural output is 2004–06, and output for each country is measured in constant 2005 US dollars.

It is also possible to extend the growth decomposition of equation (2) by focusing on a particular input, say land or labor (which can be named as X_1). To illustrate, equation (2) can be simplified by representing an element's value by a capital letter and its annual growth rate by a small letter (for example, X for level and x for growth rate). Then breaking out X_1 separately from the other inputs, the rate of total output growth y can be decomposed into a component due to expansion of the use of resource X_1 and the change in the productivity of this resource:

$$(3) \quad y = x_1 + (y - x_1) = x_1 + \sum_{i=2}^{I} S_i (x_i - x_1) + tfp$$

Equation (3) decomposes output growth first into changes in the amount of the resource X_1 used and changes in average output per unit X_1 (note that the growth in yield (Y/X_1) = $y - x_1$), and then further decomposes the growth in yield of X_1 into changes in the intensity with which other inputs (labor, capital, fertilizer, and so on) are used per unit of X_1 [growth in (X_i/X_1) = $x_i x_1$] and growth in TFP. If X_1 represents land, this decomposition corresponds to what is commonly referred to as *extensification* (land expansion) and *intensification* (land yield growth), with intensification arising from increased input use per hectare and from technical or efficiency changes, represented by growth in TFP. Bringing X_1 to the left-hand-side of equation (3) shows that this decomposition links the partial productivity of an input (Y/X_1) to the intensification of other inputs and *TFP*:

$$(4) \quad (y - x_1) = \sum_{i=2}^{I} S_i (x_i - x_1) + tfp$$

If X_1 represents labor, then equation (4) describes changes in labor productivity as partially due to "capital deepening" (or the use of capital, land, and intermediate inputs per worker) and partially due to gains in *TFP*.

TFP growth is the sum of all the productivity changes taking place on individual farms. It, in turn, can be decomposed in a standard fashion into three effects (see Cusolito and Maloney [2018] for an extensive discussion): (1) reallocation of factors of production: this could be reallocating land or inputs from lower- to higher-productivity farms, or even labor from agriculture to other activities; (2) increasing productivity among existing farms due to technical and managerial improvements; and (3) entry of higher-productivity farmers and exit of less productive farmers.

The decomposition conveys a critical message: without land expansion, all increases in agricultural output will be due to more intense use of inputs and growth in TFP. Both can be affected by changes in commodity or input prices. For example, higher crop prices or real wages will induce more intensive use of existing farmland and investment in land improvement. But, in the short term, the ability to raise yields through intensification is largely confined to existing technology and subject to diminishing returns. Changes in TFP, on the other hand, are driven by innovations and changes in technology. Moreover, through investment in research and development (R&D), incremental improvements to productivity can be sustained over the long term. Policies that provide a constructive "enabling environment" can stimulate investment in innovation and adoption. Improved market integration and trade liberalization can raise TFP by enabling farmers to specialize in commodities in which they have a comparative advantage and thereby improve efficiency.

The Increasing Importance of TFP in Driving Agricultural Output Growth

The growth decomposition depicted in figure 1.6 can in principle be implemented empirically to identify the sources of output growth and the contribution of TFP. To date, however, such exercises at the global level have been constrained by a lack of comprehensive data on inputs and their costs that is comparable across many countries. An innovative approach developed by USDA-ERS attempts to surmount these issues by drawing on a wide range of data and economic research and develop comprehensive, though approximate, measures of output, input, and TFP change (see box 1.2). In practice, measuring TFP is a data-intensive exercise requiring detailed historical data on the quantities and prices of outputs and inputs, and the use of appropriate index methods to account for input and output substitution possibilities as relative prices change. Annex 1A contains a discussion of some of the conceptual and data issues in measuring agricultural TFP in developing countries.

Empirical measures of agricultural TFP are based on market values of outputs produced and inputs used. The market prices used to value the quantities are assumed to signal the relative scarcity of these goods and services. However, agricultural production also involves the use of factors whose scarcity is not fully reflected in market prices. Use of water for irrigation, for example, is often not priced at its full market value.

New Data for Decomposing Agricultural Growth and Measuring Total Factor Productivity

Decomposing output growth in agriculture requires accurately quantifying the value of each input. The US Department of Agriculture Economic Research Service (USDA-ERS) has developed a system of international agricultural productivity accounts that has gone furthest toward this goal. These accounts draw on data from United Nations agencies on the amounts of land, labor, capital, and major intermediate inputs employed in agriculture. To overcome a general lack of price information in these inputs, USDA-ERS assembled a set of estimates of agricultural cost shares for various countries and regions of the world, drawing upon more than 20 studies of national agricultural total factor productivity (TFP) (conducted for countries representing more than two-thirds of global agricultural output) as well as econometrically estimated production elasticities for Sub-Saharan Africa and the (formerly) centrally planned economies. For the remaining countries, representing about one-fourth of global agricultural output, cost shares were approximated by applying observed cost shares from a "similar" country.

Measuring land quality is a particular challenge. The analysis of agricultural growth often focuses on the role of land because land represents not only the fertility of soil but also other natural resource inputs related to location, such as rainfall, climate, and topography, which vary greatly across contexts. Hence, it is necessary to adjust for quality to get an accurate measure of its contribution to output.

One important quality distinction is between cropland and permanent pastures. Globally, permanent pasture represents about two-thirds of all agricultural land, although much of this land is very marginal and supports few livestock (Mottet et al. 2017). For cropland, an important distinction is drawn between rainfed and irrigated areas. In 1998–2002, about 43 percent of global production of cereal crops was on irrigated land, and without irrigation this cereal production would fall by about 20 percent, Siebert and Döll (2010) estimate.

By assigning quality weights to different types of agricultural land, it is possible to parcel out the contributions to agricultural growth of changes in particular kinds of land. An increase in the share of agricultural land that is equipped for irrigation, then, could be viewed as an augmentation in the land input, even if the area of total agricultural land remains unchanged.

USDA-ERS uses this approach, assigning different quality weights to pastures, rainfed cropland, and irrigated cropland, and varying these weights for different regions of the world. For a full description of methods and data sources for estimating international agricultural TFP, see Fuglie (2015).

Agricultural activity also contributes greenhouse gas emissions, may reduce biodiversity, and may degrade land and water quality. The social costs of these inputs (or bad outputs) are not included in market-based TFP. Thus, if productivity growth involves increased use of underpriced resources, then the measured rate of TFP growth would be overstating the true gain in production efficiency. On the other hand, efficiency gains from TFP may enable outputs to be produced using fewer natural resource inputs, especially when measured on a per unit basis (for example, innovations that result in less water used per ton of crop production). In this case, measured TFP growth would be understating the full gain in efficiency.

Whether productivity growth in agriculture has come at a cost to natural resources is not well understood. Some studies suggest that productivity improvement has significantly reduced negative environmental externalities from agriculture, for instance by preventing forests from being converted to cropland (Byerlee, Stevenson, and Villoria 2014; Villoria 2019) and by reducing greenhouse gas emissions per unit of meat and milk produced from ruminant livestock (Burney, Davis, and Lobell 2010). On the other hand, the high levels of fertilizer use and concentration of animal feeding operations that are often associated with rising productivity may exacerbate nutrient runoff into water bodies and reduce air quality (Key et al. 2011). In Pakistan's Punjab, for instance, even though widespread adoption of "Green Revolution" technologies raised TFP, soil and water quality suffered, Mubarik and Byerlee (2002) found. Worldwide, evidence from satellite observations shows alarming rates of depletion of groundwater aquifers in several major food-producing regions, such as northwestern India, the North China Plain, and the central United States and California (Dalin et al. 2017).[4] This degradation of natural resources has likely partially offset the productivity gains from adoption of new technology. In fact, in the presence of technological stagnation, resource degradation would result in declining TFP. Some researchers—such as Lynam and Herdt (1989) and Coomes et al. (2019)—argue that positive agriculture TFP growth provides a good indicator of agricultural sustainability because it indicates that technological improvements are sufficiently robust to offset the negative effects of natural resource degradation. However, they also acknowledge that direct measures on the quantity and quality of natural resources used in agriculture are needed to assess long-term sustainability, and policy reforms and other incentives may be necessary to encourage farmers to conserve natural resources. For example, to increase crop yield and reduce environmental pollution from nutrient runoff, China made a major effort over 2005–15 to train farmers to manage fertilizer better (Cui et al. 2018). In the European Union, reforms to the Common Agricultural Policy decoupled agricultural subsidies from farm production and introduced cross-compliance, whereby farmers receive payments only if they abide by a series of environmental and other regulations (OECD 2011).

Another issue of interpretation of TFP arises with accounting for the effect of innovation on improving the quality of output. This may lead to higher prices commanded and perhaps higher product rents from branding, which has the same effect of a fall in costs (increase in efficiency) in raising value added per worker or per total inputs. For example, higher quality wines earn a corresponding increase in market price, which the history of fine French wine suggests can eventually reach thousands of dollars per bottle. Organic produce commands around a 30 percent premium over conventional produce so "upgrading" out of traditional produce raises revenue. However, such improvements in quality may cause quantity-based measures of efficiency to fall if greater effort or skill is required to produce the higher quality, Cusolito and Maloney (2018) show. In Chile, for example, higher quality wine requires more space per vine, which is associated with fewer bottles produced per worker. This suggests that improving productivity entails more than just decreasing unit costs. Raising quality and moving into higher value products—for instance, from maize to cut flowers—is a central theme associated with the emergence of modern value chains, discussed in chapter 5.

Using the USDA-ERS data, the empirical decomposition of global agricultural output growth into contributions from land (including augmentation of land quality through irrigation), input intensification, and TFP is depicted in figure 1.7. Consistent with figure 1.6, the height of each column gives the average annual growth rate of agricultural output by decade since 1961, with the last column covering 2001–15. Over the entire 1961–2015 period, total inputs (including land and irrigation) grew 56 percent as fast as output, implying that improvement in TFP accounted for about 44 percent of new output. However, the rate of input growth declined over time, while TFP's contribution to output growth has steadily increased. During 2001–15, TFP accounted for two-thirds of the growth in global agricultural production. From a global point of view, TFP is the primary driver of output growth.

Figure 1.8 decomposes agricultural growth for developed and developing countries separately. In developed economies, the average annual rate of output growth fell from

FIGURE 1.7 **Increases in Total Factor Productivity Have Become an Increasingly Important Source of Global Agricultural Growth**

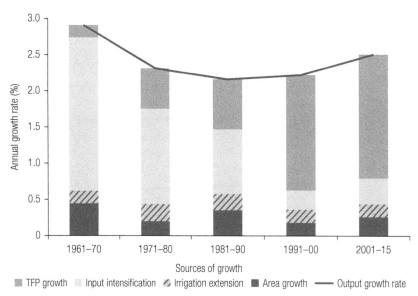

Source: Derived from USDA-ERS (2018).

Note: TFP = total factor productivity.

FIGURE 1.8 **As the Amount of Land and Labor Shrinks in the Agricultural Sector, Growth Has Been Entirely Due to Improved Total Factor Producitivity in Both Developed and Developing Countries**

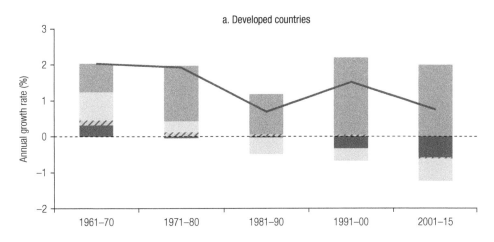

a. Developed countries

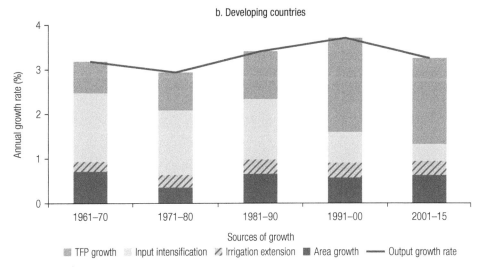

b. Developing countries

Sources of growth

TFP growth Input intensification Irrigation extension Area growth — Output growth rate

Source: USDA-ERS 2018.

Note: TFP = total factor productivity.

around 2 percent in the 1960s and 1970s to about 1 percent since the 1980s. This slow-down in agricultural growth partly reflects Engel's Law, which posits that as incomes rise, the proportion of income spent on food falls, even if absolute expenditure on food rises and the growth in food demand reflects the growth in population, which has slowed markedly in developed countries. Labor and land are being withdrawn from the agricultural sector. The fact that output is able to continue to expand in the face of these resource withdrawals is entirely due to TFP. In fact, TFP has grown fast enough to offset the decline in the amount of resources used, enabled the agricultural sectors of these countries to remain internationally competitive, and made developed countries as a whole net exporters of food.

For developing countries, improved TFP growth since the 1990s was the proximate cause of the acceleration in global agricultural TFP growth apparent in figure 1.7. During the 1960s and 1970s, annual TFP growth in developing countries averaged less than 1 percent per year, but since 1990 their agricultural TFP growth has doubled to nearly 2 percent per year (figure 1.8).

For developing countries as a group, agricultural labor declined in absolute numbers over 2001–15, primarily because nearly 100 million Chinese farm workers exited to the nonfarm sector. This trend is likely to continue in the coming decade, not only in China but in other developing countries, as structural transformation moves workers out of agriculture. In contrast, the agricultural labor force in Sub-Saharan Africa is expected to grow at least through 2020, according to International Labour Organization (ILO 2017) projections.

This said, the acceleration in TFP growth in developing countries has been geographically very uneven. Map 1.1 shows average annual TFP growth by country over 1971–2015. Emerging economies like Brazil and China sustained agricultural TFP growth of over 2 percent per year over this period, while most countries in Sub-Saharan Africa achieved TFP growth rates of less than 1 percent per year.

Table 1.1 offers more detail, decomposing growth in output per farm worker for various geographical regions into "capital deepening" (more land, capital, and other

MAP 1.1 Gains in Agricultural Total Factor Productivity Varied Greatly across Countries from 1971 to 2015

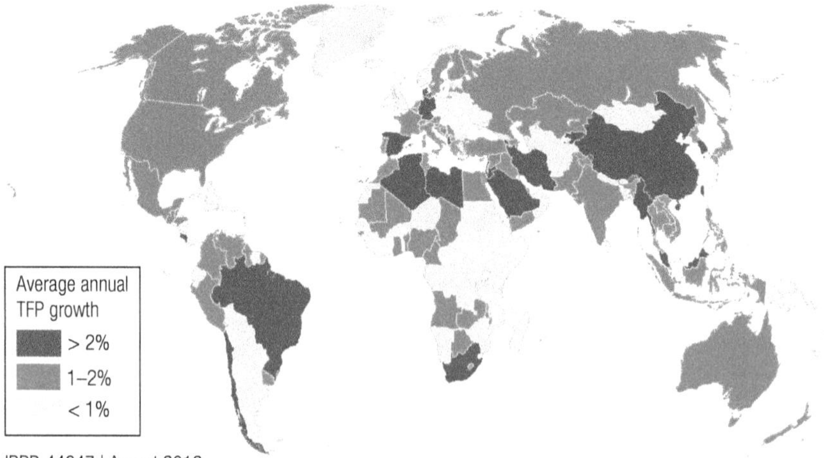

Average annual TFP growth
- > 2%
- 1–2%
- < 1%

IBRD 44647 | August 2019

Source: USDA-ERS 2018.
Note: TFP = total factor productivity.

TABLE 1.1 Sources of Growth in Developing Countries, 2001–15

Region	Output per worker	Capital deepening	TFP	Share of growth in output/worker due to TFP
	(average annual percent growth over period)			(percent)
Latin America	3.67	1.75	1.92	52.3
Central America	2.64	0.78	1.86	70.4
Brazil	6.00	3.20	2.80	46.7
Andean countries	2.13	0.79	1.35	63.1
Southern Cone	2.71	1.22	1.49	54.9
Asia (except West Asia)	4.23	1.63	2.61	61.6
China	7.14	3.67	3.47	48.6
South Asia	2.52	0.47	2.05	81.5
Southeast Asia	3.05	0.98	2.07	67.9
West Asia–North Africa	2.39	0.48	1.91	80.0
Sub-Saharan Africa	0.74	0.34	0.39	53.4
All developing countries	*3.49*	*1.56*	*1.93*	*55.2*
World	**2.83**	**1.13**	**1.71**	**60.4**

Source: USDA-ERS 2018.

Note: Growth in output per worker is the sum of the growth in capital deepening (changes in land/worker, capital/worker, and materials/worker) and total factor productivity (TFP).

inputs per worker) and TFP. For developing countries as a group, agricultural labor productivity rose by an average of 3.49 percent per year over this period. In nearly all regions, TFP accounted for half or more of the growth in agricultural labor productivity. However, these growth rates ranged from over 6 percent per year in Brazil and China to less than 1 percent per year in Sub-Saharan Africa. The contrast between South Asia and Sub-Saharan Africa is particularly striking. Currently, these regions account for most of the world's extreme poor. In both regions, continued growth in the rural and farm population has limited the role of capital deepening to raise output per worker (as existing resources are shared among more workers). But in South Asia, TFP grew by an average of over 2 percent per year during 2001–15, compared with merely 0.39 percent per year in Sub-Saharan Africa. This difference largely explains why output per farm worker grew more than three times as fast in South Asia as in Sub-Saharan Africa. If these trends persist, it is likely that extreme poverty in South Asia will fall rapidly in the coming years, while it will persist in Sub-Saharan Africa.

What Will Accelerate Agricultural TFP?

Figure 1.9 provides a schematic roadmap of this volume's approach to increasing agricultural TFP growth that will be expanded on in the final chapter. Consistent with figure 1.6, raising the productivity of a sector involves raising productivity of existing farms, reallocating factors of production to the most productive farms, and the entry or productive farms and exit of unproductive ones. In each case, this involves the accumulation or reallocation of factors of production depicted in the center panel of figure 1.9. Broadly speaking, innovation or technological adoption can be thought of as the accumulation of knowledge capital, in the same way that farms and firms accumulate land, physical capital, or human capital (Cirera and Maloney 2017). In this sense, innovation needs to be seen as part of a joint decision to accumulate factors of production and not a free-floating activity separate from the optimizing decisions of the farmer.

Conceived this way, productivity growth requires that there needs to be a demand for new factors of production, including technologies, on the part of farmers that depends both on their incentives to expand and become more productive and their abilities to recognize opportunities and implement necessary changes. On the supply side are a relatively fixed supply of land, sources of physical capital and inputs, and institutions that train human capital and generate or collect new ideas. In the middle of the figure are barriers either to reallocating factors of production or their accumulation.

There are broadly two schools of thought regarding where substantial TFP gains are more likely to emerge in developing-country agriculture: (1) from removal of distortions that prevent the reallocation of factors of production across farms or (2) by increasing within-farm or potentially new farm productivity through technological progress. Chapter 2 reviews two related and long-standing concerns about the reallocation of land and labor.

Land

For low-income countries, where most farms are less than 5 hectares, a common empirical finding has been that among nonmechanized farms there is an inverse relationship (IR) between farm size and productivity (for reviews of this literature, see Berry and Cline 1979; Binswanger, Deininger, and Feder 1995; and Eastwood, Lipton, and Newell 2010). This relationship between farm size and productivity has lent support to policies that target aid or land redistribution to smallholders. However, such policies have rarely met with much success (de Janvry 1981; Berry and Cline 1979).

FIGURE 1.9 A Framework for Raising Agricultural Productivity

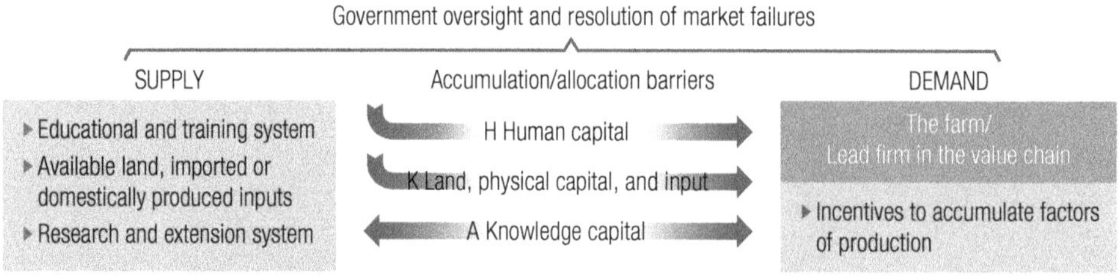

Source: World Bank.

In high-income or developed countries, where farm sizes range much larger (from tens of hectares to several thousand), and where mechanization is substituted for labor, the evidence has tended to show either constant or increasing returns to scale, with changes in relative prices of labor and capital playing an important role in the growth of farm size (Kislev and Peterson 1982, 1996; Morrison-Paul et al. 2004; MacDonald and McBride 2009). These findings suggest that land reforms to reallocate land to small farmers in developing countries, and well-functioning land and labor markets that permit gradual consolidation of farms into larger holdings as economies grow, would be a path for generating future productivity gains.

However, some recent research has challenged the old assumptions of an inverse relationship. Agricultural "land grabs" in many countries, the emergence of mega-farms in middle-income countries like Brazil and Ukraine, and efforts in China and elsewhere to consolidate small farms into larger ones suggest that new technologies and institutional arrangements may be giving rise to significant farm economies of size (Deininger and Byerlee 2012; Foster and Rosenzweig 2017). Some literature even suggests that a continued preponderance of small farms constrains agricultural growth and competitiveness (Collier and Dercon 2014; Adamopoulos and Restuccia 2014; Otsuka, Liu, and Yamauchi 2016).

On the other hand, as figure 1.5 suggests, farming in Asia, dominated by tiny 1-hectare farms, has experienced rates of productivity gain similar to the 10-hectare farms of Europe and the 100-hectare-plus farms of North America and Oceania. Even in high-income countries, many small farms persist. The emergence of new technologies, and innovations such as minitractors combined with leasing markets for machinery services, enable the introduction of very high-tech farming on small plots of land and further diminish any returns to scale.

Chapter 2 brings together new literature on farm size and the productivity debate and explores evidence from a set of novel case studies spanning both high- and low-income countries. Much previous work on productivity and farm size has been limited by a focus on single factor productivity, such as land yield. Even if land productivity is higher on small farms, labor productivity is often lower, and the use of other inputs frequently differs by farm size. To test how productivity changes with farm size, each case study described in chapter 2 uses total factor productivity (TFP) as the primary measure of performance. A second feature is that the case studies draw on panels or pseudo-panels of farms to better understand the dynamics of farm productivity. When overall input use is considered, it is not clear whether small farms are in fact more efficient than large farms or the reverse and whether any differences may be diminishing with technological advance and movements into higher–value added crops. In a non-trivial way, economies of scale are endogenous. A rise in the value of crops may make it worthwhile to adapt technologies to smaller farm size, such as the compact tractors that Mahindra developed in response to the green revolution in India, or the hand tractors now ubiquitous in East and Southeast Asia.

Labor

The second distortion is the inability of labor to move out of agriculture into new sectors with potentially higher productivity, thus leaving too much labor in the agricultural sector and impeding structural transformation. Returning to figure 1.5, the diagonal lines represent constant land-labor ratios. Growth paths that run parallel to the diagonals indicate that land and labor productivity are rising at about the same rate and that average farm size is staying roughly the same. In low-income countries, this growth path often bends to the left, meaning that population growth is causing land per worker to decline. Once industrialization is well under way and workers begin to leave agriculture, the growth path starts to bend to the right, indicating that land per worker is increasing over time. In Asia, land-labor ratios declined until the 1990s but have since begun to rise. In Sub-Saharan Africa, the land-labor ratio is still falling. This is also the region where agricultural labor productivity has risen the least over the past half-century.

The withdrawal of labor from agriculture is a fundamental part of the growth process. It has long been observed that as countries develop, the shares of GDP and employment in agriculture fall, with the GDP share falling faster than the employment share in the initial stages of structural transformation. This tendency has supported a long literature suggesting that the average productivity of workers in agriculture is substantially lower than labor productivity in nonfarm sectors, and that encouraging more rapid migration of workers out of agriculture could be an avenue toward faster GDP growth (Caselli 2005; Restuccia, Yang, and Zhu 2008). However, recent work (Herrendorf and Schoellman 2018; Hicks et al. 2017) calls into question whether the potential gains are as large as imagined. Chapter 2 further pursues the "agriculture labor productivity gap" both conceptually and empirically. In particular, it argues that, in fact, rural households hold a portfolio of income-earning opportunities. The chapter presents microdata on true labor commitment to farming per se. When used in labor productivity or earnings calculations, these data dramatically reduce the measured gap and, correspondingly, the likely productivity gains to removing barriers to mobility across sectors.

This does not obviate concerns with eliminating distortions and remedying market failures. However, with a deemphasis on the potential gains from reallocation, the volume focuses on the importance of technological progress for raising agricultural TFP and reducing poverty.

Knowledge Capital

Historically, there has been a close connection between R&D investment and TFP growth. Localized agricultural research stations and extension services have been important elements in the recipe for transformation of the agricultural sector (see box 1.3). However, in many developing countries, particularly in Africa, investments in agricultural R&D have been declining or stagnant. Very few African countries have achieved an expenditure growth rate of 5 percent or more (figure 1.10), an essential target if R&D capacity in these countries is going to substantially improve. In addition, recent studies suggest that diffusion of new technologies to poor farmers has been exceptionally slow in this region (Fuglie and Marder 2015), and as discussed, so have rates of growth in crop yield and agricultural TFP. If, in fact, the gains from future reallocation are not as large as expected, and the key to agricultural transformation and poverty reduction is the generation and diffusion of knowledge, then many developing countries face a crisis in the systems that generate it.

BOX 1.3

Research, Technological Capabilities, and Knowledge Diffusion: Key to the Transformation of US Agriculture

One of the best-known examples of agriculture research and dissemination were the land grant colleges established in the United States in the mid-nineteenth century. Researchers at experiment stations established at land-grant colleges discovered biological innovations (new and improved crop varieties) and diffused advanced farming practices (appropriate fertilizer intensity and crop rotations) that powered productivity growth in agriculture.

Using the establishment of agricultural experiment stations at preexisting land-grant colleges across the United States in the late nineteenth century, Kantor and Whalley (2019) estimate the importance of proximity to research centers for productivity growth. They find that farms located closer to newly opened experiment stations achieved higher rates of growth in land productivity for about 20 years after the stations were founded.

FIGURE B1.3.1 Technology Adoption in US Agriculture

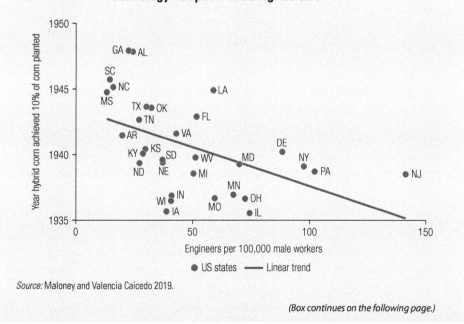

Source: Maloney and Valencia Caicedo 2019.

(Box continues on the following page.)

Research, Technological Capabilities, and Knowledge Diffusion: Key to the Transformation of US Agriculture (*continued*)

More generally, higher levels of technical capabilities and research centers within a society are highly correlated with the adoption of new technologies. Maloney and Valencia Caicedo (2019) compared one measure of these capabilities—the number of engineers per 100,000 male workers in the 1880s—against two iconic measures of technology adoption in agriculture. The first is the year in which hybrid corn adoption reached 10 percent of corn cropland seed, studied in Griliches' celebrated 1957 paper on technological diffusion. The second is the mechanization of agriculture, as proxied by year in which 10 percent of farmers employed tractors. In both cases, the relation is strongly significant.

FIGURE B1.3.2   Mechanization in US Agriculture

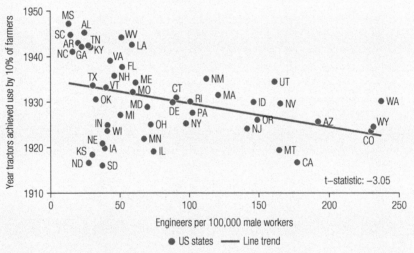

Source: Maloney and Valencia Caicedo 2019.

Kantor and Whalley (2019) find that proximity effects subsequently declined until becoming largely absent today. They conclude that the spatial frictions of the time—poor information flow and difficult transport—substantially reduced the social rate of return to public research spending by a factor of 6 in the late nineteenth and early twentieth centuries, but that such frictions significantly diminished as extension programs, automobiles, and telephones made it easier for discoveries to reach farther farms. As discussed later, the same effect is at work today with the introduction of new digital technologies. These new technologies can substantially increase the social returns of R&D.

This, at very least, demands a reconsideration of government spending priorities and a reexamination of Agricultural Innovation Systems, including the institutional and market failures that prevent accumulation and reallocation and can reduce the impact of public investments in R&D. However, on the positive side, both the

FIGURE 1.10   **Half the Countries in Africa Have Zero or Negative Growth in Spending on Agricultural R&D**

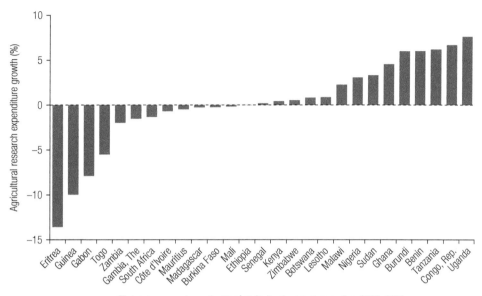

■ Average annual growth rate of agricultural research spending, 2000–2011

Source: Goyal and Nash (2017), based on data from Agricultural Science and Technology Indicators.

Note: The figure excludes Cabo Verde, Central African Republic, Chad, Democratic Republic of Congo, Eswatini, Guinea-Bissau, Liberia, Mauritania, Mozambique, Namibia, Rwanda, and Sierra Leone because time-series data did not date back to 2000.

emergence of private global research entities and the new opportunities offered by digital technologies offer governments new sources of expertise and ways to leverage their limited resources. The remaining chapters of the book explore the possibilities offered by these developments and the conditions countries need to establish to take advantage of them.

Chapter 3 explores the supply side of the technology equation. It establishes the importance of investment in agricultural research, identifies its potentially high social returns, and considers the relative roles of public and private research services. It explores how the enabling environment—again, broadly the factors included in the middle panel of figure 1.9, and including regulations related to technology, trade and intellectual property rights—induces or precludes the appearance of new sources of innovation.

Chapter 4 turns to the demand side of the technology equation. It analyzes factors underlying the resistance of farmers across the developing world to adopt new practices and technologies, the agricultural analogue to the innovation paradox discussed in the first volume in this series (Cirera and Maloney 2017). The discussion synthesizes emerging empirical evidence on constraints to technology adoption in a wide number of countries and settings. To begin, it stresses that even the most energetic innovation policies will fail if policy biases make it unprofitable for farmers to expand or experiment with new technologies. This ranges from distortionary commodity boards to overvalued exchange rates. Beyond such biases, it examines how information and learning, access to credit, management of risk, security of land tenure, and access to input and output markets contribute to farm investment and the rapid adoption of productivity-enhancing technologies. It discusses how new information and communication technologies (ICT) offer potential to facilitate the flow of tailored information, financial services, and risk management. However, the simultaneous resolution of multiple barriers to technology adoption poses a challenge to developing-country governments that may be lacking in the capability to design, implement, and coordinate the necessary policies.

Chapter 5 brings the various chapters together and fleshes out the framework in figure 1.9 in more detail. It also revisits the "productivity policy dilemma": that as countries fall further behind the technological frontier, the number of market failures and distortions increases while government capabilities to redress them diminish (Cirera and Maloney 2017). The discussion moves to ways of identifying key bottlenecks, setting priorities for needed interventions, and enlisting the private sector in the effort. In this context, the chapter discusses developments in agricultural value chains that contribute to raising productivity. Enabling smallholders to participate in market value chains has the potential to both mitigate bottlenecks on the knowledge supply side and simulate solutions to the missing markets or factors impeding technology adoption by farmers on the demand side. Here again, successful insertion in these value chains requires supportive enabling conditions. The chapter gives attention to the new institutional arrangements that are being developed to include smallholder farmers in high-value markets.

Each chapter presents policy recommendations.

Annex 1A. Issues in Measuring Agricultural Productivity

Constructing consistent indexes of agricultural total factor productivity (TFP) is challenging for three main reasons. First, measured inputs of land, labor, and capital are often imprecise. Second, since many of these inputs are supplied internally by farms rather than purchased in the market, information about the value or prices of their services is often sparse or incomplete. Third, inputs, particularly land, may vary considerably in quality. Recent efforts to improve the measurement of resources employed in agriculture have included the use of technology such as satellite remote sensing to determine the extent of cropland. United Nations agencies have released new estimates of agricultural labor and capital. This annex examines some of these new measures and how they might affect estimates of TFP growth in agriculture. But first, it describes two distinct but related concepts of TFP: one based on gross output and one based on value added output.

Variants of TFP: Gross Output and Value Added

When TFP is measured on the basis of gross output (labeled as TFP_G), intermediate inputs are included in the set of inputs along with labor, capital, and land. Value added TFP (TFP_V), on the other hand, is the ratio between value added output (gross output minus the cost of intermediated inputs) and only labor, capital, and land inputs. The growth in TFP_V is estimated as the difference between growth in agricultural value added (or agricultural gross domestic product, GDP) and growth in labor, capital, and land services used in production (intermediate inputs excluded). The difference between TFP_G and TFP_V can be substantial if intermediate inputs make up a large share of total costs. Because new agricultural technology is often embodied in improved intermediate inputs such as seeds and chemicals, TFP_V may understate the contribution of these inputs to growth and exaggerate the role of new technology. For this reason, TFP_G may give a better indication of the rate of technical change in agriculture than TFP_V.

The links between growth accounting with these two variants of TFP can be illustrated by extending the model developed in box 1.1. Recall equation (2) from box 1.1:

$$(2) \qquad \sum_{j=1}^{J} R_j ln\left(\frac{Y_{j,t}}{Y_{j,t-1}}\right) = ln\left(\frac{TFP_t}{TFP_{t-1}}\right) + \sum_{i=1}^{I} S_i ln\left(\frac{X_{i,t}}{X_{i,t-1}}\right).$$

in which the left-hand-side is the revenue share-weight output index and the right-hand-side is the TFP index plus the cost share-weighted input index. Letting aggregating output be Y and breaking out the input vector X into land, labor, capital, and intermediate inputs, representing these by A, L, K, and M (and their growth rates by small letters y, a, l, k, and m), respectively, equation (2) can be rewritten as

$$(5) \qquad y = s_L l + s_K k + s_A a + s_M m + \text{tfp}_G,$$

in which the costs shares $S_L + S_K + S_A + S_M = 1$.

Defining value added output by $V = Y - M$ and its value share relative to gross output as $S^V = \dfrac{V}{Y}$, then value added growth can be decomposed as

$$(6) \qquad v = s_L^V l + s_K^V k + s_A^V a + \text{tfp}_V,$$

in which $S_L^V + S_K^V + S_A^V = 1$ and $S_i^V = \dfrac{S_i}{S^V}$ for $i = L, K,$ and A.

Schreyer and Pilat (2001) show that growth in TFP_V is proportional to growth in TFP_G in the following manner:

$$(7) \qquad \text{tfp}_V = \frac{\text{tfp}_G}{S^V}.$$

Note that since $S^V < 1$, tfp_V is unambiguously larger than tfp_G, it could be substantially larger if intermediate inputs make up a significant share of total costs.

Finally, a commonly used indicator of agricultural productivity, agricultural value added per worker, can be derived from equation (6) as follows:

$$(8) \qquad (v - l) = s_K^V (k - l) \ + \ s_A^V (a - l) \ + \ \text{tfp}_V.$$

Again, this decomposition shows that the growth in agricultural value added per worker $(v - l)$ is partly due to capital per worker $(k - l)$, changes in average farm size $(a - l)$, and growth in value added TFP $(\textit{tfp}_v)$.

Measuring Agricultural Output

Corresponding to the TFP variants discussed in the previous section, there are two main sources of information on national agricultural output and its growth over time: Food and Agriculture Organization (FAO) gross output and World Bank value added output. FAO publishes estimates of the quantities of 198 crop and livestock commodities produced annually by country since 1961, and it aggregates them into a measure of the gross value of agricultural output using a common set of global average farm gate prices. It currently uses prices from 2004–06 to calculate gross output and expresses it in constant 2005 international dollars. Forestry and fisheries output (including farm-raised fish) are not included in FAO gross agricultural output, and the value of hay and fodder crops is excluded as well. FAO also estimates the value of gross output net of farm-grown feed and seed (which it calls net output). However, the FAO net output value still includes crops that are sold but used for feed or seed (perhaps after conditioning or processing) on other farms. The growth rates in the FAO gross and net value of output are virtually identical because the proportions of these crops assumed to be retained on the farm for use as feed and seed hardly change over time.

Because current (or near-current) prices are held fixed over time, FAO gross agricultural output is equivalent to a Paasche quantity index.[5] The set of common commodity prices is derived using the Geary-Khamis method. This method determines an international price p_i for each commodity as an international weighted average of the prices of the i-th commodity in different countries, after national prices have been converted into a common currency using a purchasing power parity (PPP$_j$) conversion rate for each j-th country. The weights are the quantities produced by the country. The computational scheme involves solving a system of simultaneous linear equations that derives both the p_i prices and PPP$_j$ conversion factors for each commodity and country. The FAO updates these prices every few years and recalculates its index of gross production value back to 1961 using its most recent set of international prices. For a thorough description and assessment of these procedures, see Rao (1993).

The second measure of agricultural output is agricultural value added (or agricultural GDP), derived from the national economic accounts of each country and reported by the World Bank in constant US dollars. This measure uses national prices to aggregate domestic production and subtracts the value of intermediate inputs.

For international comparisons of real growth over time, nominal currencies are first deflated by the national GDP price index and then converted to constant dollars using either a PPP or market exchange rate for a particular year. In the World Development Indicators (WDI) database of the World Bank, agricultural value added includes crops, livestock, forestry, and fisheries. Note that FAO reports this measure of agricultural value added, and for a smaller set of countries, FAO gives the value added of just the crop-livestock sector.

Given the differences already discussed, the levels or even the growth rates of FAO gross output and the WDI value added output are not expected to be the same. In fact, significant differences emerge between the FAO and national accounts estimates of agricultural output, partly because of the differences in prices (global average or national) used to weight outputs. For many European countries, Japan, and the Republic of Korea, where government policies have historically supported agricultural prices above border prices, the value of gross agricultural output from the national accounts appears to be about twice that estimated by FAO. Many countries display significant differences in output growth patterns, which may be partly explained by terms-of-trade effects (absent in the FAO estimate because constant prices are used, but present in national accounts because a general price index is used to deflate the value of production of all sectors). A few countries present large differences in levels and growth that are difficult to explain. For example, FAO estimates that the gross agricultural output of Nigeria increased by an average of 2.18 percent during 2001–15, but the WDI indicates that (constant dollar) agricultural value added output for Nigeria increased by 6.62 percent per year over this same period. Given that Nigeria's agricultural imports surged during this period, the high rate of growth in domestic value added seems hard to believe. Generally, the FAO gross agricultural output measure seems to provide a more consistent basis for making international comparisons of productivity.

Measuring Agricultural Inputs

Land and Land Quality

The agricultural productivity estimates presented in this chapter use FAO estimates of agricultural cropland (irrigated and rainfed) and permanent pastures, which are derived from national agricultural surveys and censuses. See et al. (2015) argue that for many countries of the world, particularly in Africa, the accuracy of these data is questionable, and they suggest using high-resolution remote sensing data from satellites for constructing consistent estimates of global agricultural land area. For example, the US Geological Service (USGS) has published global cropland maps based on high-resolution (30 meters per pixel) Landsat data from the Global Food Security Analysis-Support Data at 30 Meters (GFSAD30) Project. The November 2017 update of these maps (USGS 2017) estimates that the world had 1,870 million hectares of cropland in 2015—nearly 300 million hectares more than the FAO estimate of 1,594 million hectares for the same year. These measures of cropland include land in short-term fallow and cultivated pastures, and count multicropped areas only once. FAO estimates that the total crop area harvested (excluding fallow and pastures but including multiple cropping) was 1,478 million hectares in 2014. In addition to cropland, FAO estimates that about 3,275 million hectares is permanent pasture, although Mottet et al. (2017) suggest that about 1,500 million hectares of that land consists of very marginal rangeland capable of supporting very few livestock.

To assess and compare these various measures of agricultural land, it is useful to define agricultural land and its components:

1. FAO defines cropland to include arable land and land in permanent crops. Arable land is the land under seasonal crops (multicropped areas are counted only once), cultivated land that is temporarily fallowed (less than five years), and land cultivated with forage crops for mowing or pasture (cropland pastures). Cropland pastures must be cultivated at least every five years; otherwise this land is classified as permanent pasture. Permanent crops are long-term crops that do not have to be replanted for several years (such as coffee or oil palm, but not plantation timber).
2. FAO defines permanent pasture to be land used permanently (five years or more) to grow herbaceous forage crops, either sown or growing wild (for example, grazing land).
3. FAO defines agricultural land as the sum of cropland and permanent pasture.
4. Crop area harvested includes the total harvested area of seasonal and permanent crops, excluding harvested fodder, silage, and hay crops. Each harvest from multicropped areas is included in the total, although harvests from permanent crops are counted only once.

The GFSAD30 defines cropland similarly to FAO but does not distinguish between temporary and permanent cultivation. It defines cropland as "lands cultivated with plants for food, feed, and fiber, including both seasonal crops (such as wheat, soybeans, cotton, vegetables), and continuous plantation (such as coffee, oil palm, rubber, fruit trees). Cropland fallows are land uncultivated during a season or year but equipped for cultivation, including plantations. Croplands include all planted crops plus cropland fallows." Note that the GFSAD30 definition includes cropland pastures (cultivated plants for feed), but it does not specify how often these pastures should be cultivated or reseeded. In practice, it may be difficult to differentiate between temporary and permanent fodder crop and pasture areas. In the 2007 United States agricultural census, for example, the National Agricultural Statistical Service reclassified around 20 million hectares of cropland pasture as permanent pasture because it was primarily used for grazing with infrequent reseeding.

Another issue is the treatment of mixed cropping and agroforestry systems. In principle, for fields planted with several crops simultaneously, the area assigned to each crop should be proportional to the crop's significance in the field. In practice, this may be difficult to do. Satellite remote sensing in particular may have difficulty identifying cropland that is part of mixed agroforestry systems (See et al. 2015).

Figure 1A.1 compares, for each country, FAO cropland estimates (averaged over 2012–14) with cropland estimates for 2015 from high-resolution remote sensing from the Landsat satellite produced by the GFSAD30 project (USGS 2017). As noted, the

FIGURE 1A.1 FAO versus Satellite-Based Estimates of Cropland

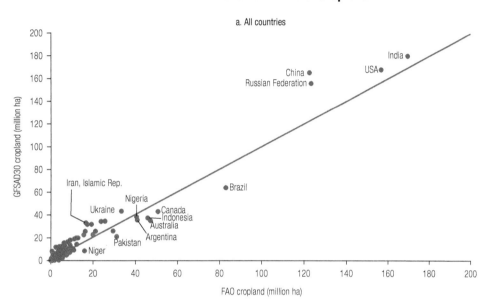

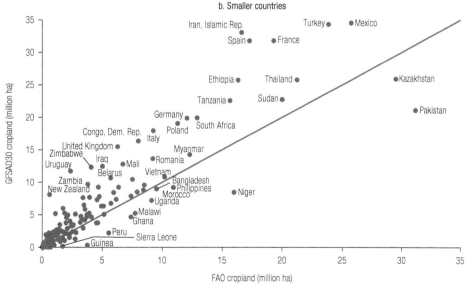

Sources: USGS 2017; FAO 2018a.

Note: FAO = Food and Agriculture Organization; GFSAD30 = Global Food Security Analysis-Support Data at 30 Meters; ha = hectares.

GFSAD30 cropland estimates are nearly 20 percent higher (300 million hectares world-wide) than the FAO cropland estimates. GFSAD30 estimated significantly more crop-land in China (43 million hectares, or 35 percent more than FAO), the Russian Federation (33 million hectares, or a 26 percent increase), the United States (11 million hectares), and India (10 million hectares). GFSAD30 also estimates that there was an additional 68 million hectares of cropland in Western Europe—86 percent more than FAO. It appears, however, that these differences are primarily due to how cultivated grasslands are classified. The GFSAD30 data appear to be counting as cropland any grassland that has ever been seeded to exotic varieties, whereas FAO uses a narrower definition, limiting cropland pastures only to those that have been reseeded within the past five years. These differences in definition are starkly illustrated in the case of New Zealand, where FAO reports about 0.6 million hectares of cropland, whereas GFSAD30 reports more than 8.1 million hectares of cropland. GFSAD30 is apparently counting 7.5 million hectares of exotic grasslands (which at some point in the past were seeded with introduced grasses) as cropland, whereas FAO classifies these areas as part of permanent pasture.

For some other countries, GFSAD30 reports significantly less cropland than FAO. GFSAD30 estimated 23 percent less cropland for Brazil than FAO (64 million hectares versus 83 million hectares by FAO), 25 percent less for Australia (35 million hectares versus 47 million hectares), and 32 percent less for Pakistan (21 million hectares versus 31 million hectares), and only a small fraction of the FAO cropland estimates for several countries in West and Central Africa. For Guinea, for example, FAO reports 3.8 million hectares of cropland compared with only 0.3 million hectares by GFSAD30. As mentioned, satellite imagery often fails to pick up crop area in extensive agroforestry systems (See et al. 2015), which are common in many parts of Africa.

In conclusion, it seems that GFSAD30 has not "found" more land in agriculture but rather has classified several hundred million hectares of grasslands as cropland—land that FAO counts as permanent pasture. It would be valuable to be able to compare these sources for what they imply about changes in land use over time, when time-series estimates of agricultural land from GFSAD30 become available.

Labor

For agricultural labor, FAO previously published modeled estimates of the number of adults by country whose primary economic activity was in agriculture, but FAO discontinued this series in 2015. The last version of the FAO labor data provided annual estimates from 1980 and projected out to 2020, but earlier versions reported the series back to 1961. Since then, the International Labour Organization (ILO) has continued to publish revised annual estimates of the number of adults economically active in agriculture from 1990 to 2020 and beyond. These labor series are modeled estimates informed by national population censuses and labor force surveys. They use United

Nations projections of age-specific populations as a base, and then make assumptions about labor force participation rates and the share of the labor force employed in manufacturing, services, and primary sectors (which include agriculture, forestry, and fisheries).

The US Department of Agriculture Economic Research Service (USDA-ERS) international productivity accounts have spliced together old FAO series (FAO 2006, 2015) to construct agricultural labor series from 1961 to 2015. For some countries—namely, China, Nigeria, and the transition economies of the former Soviet Union and Eastern Europe—USDA-ERS (2018) replaced these FAO estimates with national labor force estimates, due to significant discrepancies in the old FAO agricultural labor estimates for those countries.[6] Figure 1A.2 compares the ILO (2017), old FAO, and USDA-ERS (2018) estimates of global agricultural labor. The ILO estimate suggests that global employment in agriculture has peaked and is now declining in absolute numbers. The old FAO and USDA-ERS series differ primarily because of China, where national labor force statistics indicate a smaller and more rapidly shrinking work force in agriculture.

FIGURE 1A.2   A Comparison of Estimates of the Global Agricultural Labor Force

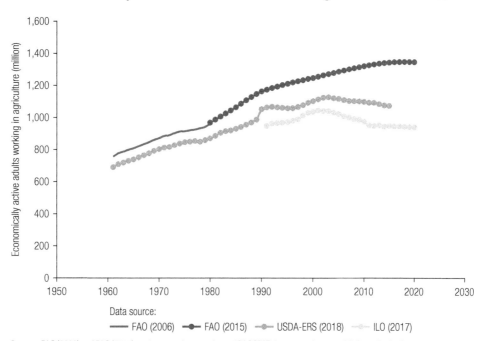

Sources: FAO (2006) and FAO (2015) are from previous versions of FAOSTAT that are no longer publicly available. The USDA-ERS (2018) series is based primarily on old FAO data but uses national estimates of agricultural labor for China, transition economies, and Nigeria. The ILO (2017) series is a new annual (modeled) estimate of agricultural labor that covers the period 1990–2020.

Note: FAO = Food and Agriculture Organization; ILO= International Labour Organization; USDA-ERS = US Department of Agriculture Economic Research Service.

Capital: The Perpetual Inventory Method versus the Current Inventory Method

Capital includes long-lived inputs that are used for more than one year. In agriculture, capital can take several forms, such as machinery, structures, land improvements, breeding stock, and fruit trees. These items may become less productive over time through depreciation (the wear and tear on capital items as they age), also known as capital consumption. It is difficult to measure current effective capital stock because of the heterogeneous nature of capital and its variable productivity with age. Two general approaches have been used. The first is the current inventory method (CIM), which is a count of the number of capital items in use on farms (number of breeding stock, number of tractors, and so on), with values (such as a purchase price) assigned to each. These values are then added up to get a total stock of capital. The second approach is based on the perpetual inventory method (PIM). This method adds up past spending on capital items in order to get the cumulative gross value of capital stock held on farms. The PIM includes information on when capital was purchased, so older capital can be discounted by its rate of depreciation to derive net capital stock (that is, gross capital stock net of capital consumption). The PIM is considered to be a better measure of capital stock because it includes investment in all types of capital (not just large items included in an inventory) and takes depreciation into account. At the same time, the PIM is sensitive to assumptions about how long a capital asset lasts and how quickly it wears out.

Building on earlier work by Larson et al. (2000), FAO recently released new national and global estimates of agricultural capital stock based on the PIM, expressed in constant 2005 international dollars, for the period from 1990 to 2015 (FAO 2018a). Previously, FAO used the CIM method to estimate agricultural capital over 1975–2007 (FAO 2015). The USDA-ERS (2018) international agricultural productivity accounts use the CIM to develop a capital index spanning 1961–2015. The USDA-ERS (2018) capital stock consists of agricultural machinery (measured in total horsepower, based on numbers and sizes of tractors, combine-harvesters, threshers, milking machines, and water pumps in use on farms) and livestock inventories (measured in cattle-equivalents, which aggregate animals of different species based on relative size weights). These estimates of machinery and livestock capital can be aggregated into a single capital index to indicate the growth in capital stock relative to the base year of the index.

The new FAO (2018a) PIM measure shows faster growth in global agricultural capital than either the old FAO (2015) CIM or USDA-ERS (2018) CIM estimates of capital. According to the FAO (2018a) PIM, world agricultural capital stock (gross or net) increased by 58 percent between 1995 and 2015, compared with 29 percent according to the USDA-ERS (2018) CIM estimate. The FAO PIM estimate is sensitive to assumptions about capital life and rates of depreciation, which can vary markedly between countries, over time, and by type of capital. Lacking detailed information, FAO assumes that all capital assets last 25 years and depreciate at an annual rate of

6 percent (Dubey 2017), even though different types of capital may have different life spans and depreciation rates.

Capital life span and depreciation rates may also be influenced by economic conditions. In situations when capital investment is growing rapidly, a more rapid rate of replacement (or shorter capital life) may be expected to prevail and older equipment is updated more frequently. In China, agricultural capital investment grew at a very rapid annual rate of 8.5 percent over 1995–2015. Using the FAO PIM assumptions, this implies that net capital stock in China increased by 375 percent between 1991 and 2008, and that by 2015 it was 635 percent above 1991 levels. Using the same capital investment data but assuming a depreciation rate of 8 percent for structures and 17 percent for machinery and livestock, Wang et al. (2013) estimate that China's agricultural capital stock grew by only 181 percent between 1991 and 2008, slightly higher than the USDA-ERS (2018) CIM estimate of 168 percent. These differences illustrate the sensitivity of estimates of capital stock to assumptions about life span and rate of depreciation.

Figure 1A.3 compares FAO PIM, FAO CIM, and USDA-ERS CIM estimates of global agricultural capital. According to the FAO PIM, global agricultural gross capital stock increased from about $4,300 billion to over $7,000 billion (in constant 2005

FIGURE 1A.3 **Estimates of Global Agricultural Capital Based on the Current Inventory Method versus the Perpetual Inventory Method**

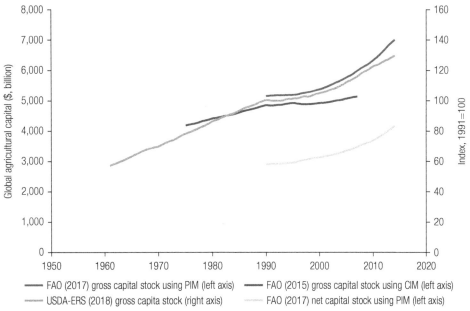

Sources: FAO 2015, 2018a; USDA-ERS 2018.

Note: CIM = current inventory method; FAO = Food and Agriculture Organization; PIM = perpetual inventory method; USDA-ERS = US Department of Agriculture Economic Research Service; $ = 2005 international dollars.

international dollars), while net capital stock (taking into account capital consumption) increased from $2,850 billion in 1995 to more than $4,520 billion by 2015. The USDA-ERS (2018) CIM shows growth similar to the FAO PIM between 1990 and 2009, but then the two series diverge. All series show relatively slow capital accumulation in the early 1990s, a period when agriculture and agricultural capital were sharply contracting in many transition economies.

Alternative Estimates of Agricultural TFP

Given the variants in international measures of agricultural output (especially FAO gross output at international prices and the World Bank's value added output reported in the WDI), and uncertainties in input measures, this section compares alternative configurations of trends in agricultural productivity. Three alternative estimates of the growth rates in agricultural labor productivity and TFP are derived as follows:

1. USDA-ERS. Labor, capital, land, and material inputs from USDA-ERS and FAO gross value of output (same as TFP reported in the main text of this chapter).
2. FAO-ILO. Newly revised estimates of ILO agricultural labor and FAO agricultural capital and gross output (with USDA-ERS estimates of land and intermediate inputs).
3. WDI-ILO-FAO. World Bank value added agricultural output and for inputs, ILO labor, FAO capital, and USDA-ERS land.

For each case, agricultural land is the USDA-ERS estimate of quality-weighted agricultural land (the sum of rainfed cropland, irrigated cropland, and permanent pasture, quality-weighted in rainfed-equivalent cropland hectares). For the purpose of estimating TFP_g, intermediate inputs include fertilizer and animal feed and are from USDA-ERS.

The results are presented in table 1A.1. The estimates show average annual growth rates in agricultural output, labor, labor productivity, and TFP over 2001–15 for major developing-country regions. The table also decomposes the growth in labor productivity into capital deepening and TFP. The decomposition shows how changes in inputs employed per worker and growth in TFP contribute to changes in labor productivity.

The first two columns in table 1A.1 show the growth rates in agricultural output and the agricultural labor force, respectively. The third column shows the growth in agricultural labor productivity (which is simply the difference between the data in the first two columns). For developing countries as a whole, the growth in gross and value added agricultural output are similar (3.25 percent per year versus 3.59 percent per year), although large differences in these measures of output growth emerge for some regions. In particular, in Sub-Saharan Africa and China, World Bank value added growth is significantly higher than FAO gross output growth. Much of the difference in Sub-Saharan Africa

TABLE 1A.1 **Alternative Measures of Agricultural Output and Productivity Growth, 2001–15**
Average annual growth

Region	a. USDA-ERS: Based on FAO agricultural gross output, USDA-ERS labor and capital						
	Output	Labor	Output/ worker	Land/ worker	Capital/ worker	Materials/ worker	*TFPg*
Latin America	3.04	−0.63	3.67	1.67	1.83	3.74	1.92
Asia (except West Asia)	3.33	−0.90	4.23	3.19	1.61	4.01	2.61
China	3.37	−3.77	7.14	5.98	4.67	6.09	3.47
South Asia	3.61	1.09	2.52	3.07	−0.66	2.58	2.05
Southeast Asia	3.53	0.47	3.05	1.93	0.70	3.39	2.07
West Asia–North Africa	2.27	−0.12	2.39	1.46	−0.06	0.52	1.91
Sub-Saharan Africa	3.11	2.37	0.74	0.36	−0.15	2.59	0.39
Nigeria	2.18	1.94	0.24	−0.57	0.53	3.18	−0.08
Rest of Sub-Saharan Africa	3.43	2.41	1.02	0.06	0.35	2.77	0.60
All developing countries	**3.25**	**−0.23**	**3.49**	**3.13**	**1.18**	**3.29**	**1.93**
World	*2.51*	*−0.32*	*2.83*	*1.92*	*0.76*	*2.18*	*1.71*

Region	b. FAO-ILO: Based on FAO agricultural gross output, ILO labor, and FAO capital						
	Output	Labor	Output/ worker	Land/ worker	Capital/ worker	Materials/ worker	*TFPg*
Latin America	3.04	−0.73	3.77	1.93	2.36	3.83	1.79
Asia (except West Asia)	3.33	−2.19	5.53	2.90	7.07	5.30	2.60
China	3.37	−5.10	8.47	6.00	15.28	7.43	1.81
South Asia	3.61	−0.52	4.13	0.94	6.77	4.19	2.62
Southeast Asia	3.53	−0.72	4.24	1.89	4.49	4.58	2.36
West Asia–North Africa	2.27	0.08	2.19	−0.26	2.53	0.32	1.57
Sub-Saharan Africa	3.11	2.02	1.09	0.21	0.92	2.94	0.41
Nigeria	2.18	−1.77	3.95	3.14	9.99	6.89	−1.07
Rest of Sub-Saharan Africa	3.43	2.50	0.93	−0.03	−0.84	2.68	0.94
All developing countries	**3.25**	**−1.21**	**4.46**	**2.15**	**6.60**	**4.26**	**1.71**
World	*2.51*	*−1.26*	*3.77*	*1.70*	*3.98*	*3.12*	*1.76*

(Table continues on the following page.)

Alternative Measures of Agricultural Output and Productivity Growth, 2001–15 (*continued*)

Average annual growth

Region	Output	Labor	Output/ worker	Land/ worker	Capital/ worker	Materials/ worker	TFPv
c. WDI-ILO-FAO: Based on WDI agricultural value added, ILO labor, and FAO capital							
Latin America	2.56	−0.73	3.29	1.93	2.36	n.a.	2.06
Asia (except West Asia)	3.40	−2.19	5.60	2.90	7.07	n.a.	3.05
China	4.22	−5.10	9.32	6.00	15.28	n.a.	2.79
South Asia	3.36	−0.52	3.88	0.94	6.77	n.a.	2.71
Southeast Asia	3.21	−0.72	3.93	1.89	4.49	n.a.	2.49
West Asia–North Africa	3.20	0.08	3.11	−0.26	2.53	n.a.	2.34
Sub-Saharan Africa	4.44	2.02	2.42	0.21	0.92	n.a.	2.00
Nigeria	6.62	−1.77	8.39	3.14	9.99	n.a.	3.58
Rest of Sub-Saharan Africa	3.16	2.50	0.66	−0.03	−0.84	n.a.	0.98
All developing countries	**3.59**	**−1.21**	**4.80**	**2.15**	**6.60**	n.a.	**2.38**
World	*2.88*	*−1.26*	*4.14*	*1.70*	*3.98*	n.a.	*2.51*

Source: USDA-ERS 2018.

Note: Agricultural gross output is the value of commodities produced at 2005 global average prices (FAO 2018a). Agricultural value added output is from national accounts and converted to 2010 US$ (World Bank). Labor is the number of adults economically active in agriculture (USDA-ERS [2018] or ILO [2017]; see text). USDA-ERS capital is an index of the current inventory of agricultural machinery and livestock held on farms (USDA-ERS 2018). FAO capital is derived from national accounts using the perpetual inventory method in constant 2005 US dollars (FAO 2018a). Materials are intermediate inputs consisting of synthetic fertilizers and animal feeds (USDA-ERS 2018). *TFPg* and *TFPv* are total factor productivity based on gross output and value added output, respectively. FAO = Food and Agriculture Organization; ILO= International Labour Organization; n.a. = not applicable; USDA-ERS = US Department of Agriculture Economic Research Service; WDI = World Development Indicators (World Bank).

appears to be due to Nigeria, which reports very rapid value added growth (6.62 percent per year) but, according to FAO, much slower growth in gross output (2.18 percent per year) over 2001–15. For China, part of the higher growth in value added is likely due to the fact that it includes fisheries, a subsector that has grown very rapidly in recent decades. Fisheries are not included in FAO's gross agricultural output.

The ILO modeled estimates of agricultural labor show a more rapid rate of decline during 2001–15 across all developing countries (−1.21 percent per year) than the USDA-ERS estimates (−0.23 percent per year), and for all regions except West Asia–North Africa. As a result, the growth rates in agricultural labor productivity estimated by USDA-ERS are generally lower than the growth rates estimated using ILO labor data. Although all sets of estimates in table 1A.1 show that Asia experienced the fastest growth in agricultural labor productivity, the WDI-ILO-FAO estimates accentuate this regional exceptionalism. For Sub-Saharan Africa, the WDI-ILO-FAO estimates suggest that agricultural labor productivity grew quite strongly (2.42 percent per year) over 2001–15, whereas the USDA-ERS estimates suggest much more modest growth (0.74 percent per year). Again, the difference is primarily due to Nigeria. Once this country is excluded, the WDI-ILO-FAO estimate also shows that growth in labor productivity has been slow (0.66 percent per year) in Sub-Saharan Africa.

The estimates of TFP growth are higher when value added output is used versus when gross output is used, as predicted in the model previously discussed. For developing countries as a whole, agricultural TFP grew by 1.93 percent per year using USDA-ERS data, 1.71 percent per year using gross output and ILO-FAO data, and 2.38 percent per year using WDI-ILO-FAO data (which uses value added output instead of gross output). Despite these differences, each of the three sets of measures show that growth in TFP accounted for roughly half the growth in output per worker in developing countries.

In other words, technical and efficiency changes, rather than factor accumulation per worker, have been the primary drivers of agricultural labor productivity in developing countries. China may be an exception; the very rapid reduction in the agricultural labor force is raising the amounts of land, capital, and material inputs available to each worker remaining in the sector. Using the ILO-modeled estimates of China's labor force, agricultural value added per worker grew by 9.32 percent per year over 2001–15, with about 70 percent of this growth due to increased inputs per worker, and the rest to TFP. Using the USDA-ERS estimate of China's agricultural labor force, which is based on Chinese government labor statistics, agricultural labor productivity rose by 7.14 percent per year and TFP accounted for about half of this growth.

For Sub-Saharan Africa, the high rate of value added growth for Nigeria inflates the estimate of the region's TFP_v growth. Excluding Nigeria, agricultural TFP growth in Sub-Saharan Africa averaged less than 1 percent over 2001–15 (by all three estimates of TFP in table 1A.1)—less than half the rate for developing countries on average. The slow rate of improvement in technical and efficiency changes in Sub-Saharan Africa represents a major constraint to raising agricultural productivity and reducing poverty in this region.

Notes

1. This chapter draws from a 2019 background paper entitled "Sources of Growth in Agriculture" by Keith Fuglie.

2. A successful farmer, Jia Sixie says, "would not only mechanically do his work, but would critically observe the seasons, weather, and the quality of the soil, in order to adapt his work to these factors. Such a method would save labor and increase yields" (*yong li shao er cheng gong duo* 用力少而成功多). http://www.chinaknowledge.de/Literature/Science/qiminyaoshu.html.

3. For a still very relevant and thorough treatment of these themes in the Latin American context, see de Ferranti et al. (2005).

4. Observations from the GRACE satellite program use minute changes in the Earth's gravitational field to measure changing water volumes below the surface. Although GRACE can measure changes in volumes, it is not able to measure the volumes of water remaining in the world's aquifers (Dalin et al. 2017).

5. A Paasche quantity index uses end-period prices as weights on quantities to measure changes in aggregate quantity over time. A Laspeyres quantity index uses beginning-period prices as weights.

6. Modeled estimates of agricultural labor may fail to keep pace with the structural changes occurring in countries undergoing significant economic reforms. Since Fan (1991) and Lin (1992) initiated the first reform-era studies of agricultural productivity in China, virtually all studies of China's agricultural productivity have preferred national statistics on land and labor to FAO estimates. Similarly, Macours and Swinnen (2002) use national labor force estimates in place of FAO estimates in their study of agricultural productivity in transition economies. Fuglie and Rada (2013) identify major inconsistencies in FAO agricultural labor data for Nigeria. The new ILO modeled estimates are more consistent with current national labor force estimates but are available only for 1990 and onward.

References

Adamopoulos, T., and D. Restuccia. 2014. "The Size Distribution of Farms and International Productivity Differences." *American Economic Review* 104 (6): 1667–97. doi: 10.1257/aer.104.6.1667.

Berry, R., and W. Cline. 1979. *Agrarian Structure and Productivity and Developing Countries.* Baltimore, MD: Johns Hopkins University Press.

Binswanger, H. P., K. Deininger, and G. Feder. 1995. "Power, Distortion, Revolt, and Reform in Agricultural Land Relations." In *Handbook of Development Economics*, Vol. 3, edited by J. Behrman and T. N. Srinivasan, 2659–2772. Amsterdam: Elsevier.

Burney, J., S. J. Davis, and D. B. Lobell. 2010. "Greenhouse Gas Mitigation by Agricultural Intensification." *PNAS* 107 (26): 12052–57. https://doi.org/10.1073/pnas.0914216107.

Byerlee, D., J. Stevenson, and N. Villoria. 2014. "Does Intensification Slow Crop Land Expansion or Encourage Deforestation?" *Global Food Security* 3 (2): 92–98. https://doi.org/10.1016/j.gfs.2014.04.001.

Caselli, F. 2005. "Accounting for Cross-Country Income Differences." Chapter 9 in *Handbook of Economic Growth*, Vol. 1A, edited by P. Aghion and S. N. Durlauf, 679–741. Amsterdam: Elsevier.

Chenery, H., and M. Syrquin. 1975. *Patterns of Development: 1950–1970.* London: Oxford University Press.

Christiaensen, L., L. Demery, and J. Kuhl. 2011. "The (Evolving) Role of Agriculture in Poverty Reduction—An Empirical Perspective." *Journal of Development Economics* 96 (2): 239–54. https://doi.org/10.1016/j.jdeveco.2010.10.006.

Cirera, X., and W. Maloney. 2017. T*he Innovation Paradox: Developing-Country Capabilities and the Unrealized Promise of Technological Catch-Up.* Washington, DC: World Bank. https://openknowledge.worldbank.org/handle/10986/28341. License: CC BY 3.0 IGO.

Clark, C. C. 1951. *The Conditions of Economic Progress.* London: Macmillan & Co LTD.

Collier, P., and S. Dercon. 2014. "African Agriculture in 50 Years: Smallholders in a Rapidly Changing world?" *World Development* 63 (C): 92–101. doi: 10.1016/j.worlddev.2013.10.001.

Coomes, O., B. Barham, G. MacDonald, N. Ramankutty, and J.-P. Chavas. 2019. "Leveraging Total Factor Productivity Growth for Sustainable and Resilient Farming." *Nature Sustainability* 2 (2019): 22–28.

Cui, Z., et al. 2018. "Pursuing Sustainable Productivity with Millions of Smallholder Farmers." *Nature* 555 (15 March): 363–66.

Cusolito, A., and W. Maloney. 2018. *Productivity Revisited: Shifting Paradigms in Analysis and Policy.* Washington, DC: World Bank.

Dalin, C., Y. Wada, T. Kastner, and M. J. Puma. 2017. "Groundwater Depletion Embedded in International Food Trade." *Nature* 543 (7647): 700–04. doi:10.1038/nature21403.

De Ferranti, D., G. E. Perry, D. Lederman, A. Valdes, and W. Foster. 2005. *Beyond the City: The Rural Contribution to Development.* Washington, DC: World Bank. https://elibrary.worldbank.org/doi/abs/10.1596/0-8213-6097-3.

de Janvry, A. 1981. "The Role of Land Reform in Economic Development: Policies and Politics." *American Journal of Agricultural Economics* 63 (2): 384–92.

Deininger, K., and D. Byerlee. 2012. "The Rise of Large Farms in Land Abundant Countries: Do They Have a Future?" *World Development* 40 (4): 701–14. https://doi.org/10.1016/j.worlddev.2011.04.030.

Dubey, S. 2017. "Metadata: Agricultural Capital." Food and Agriculture Organization, Rome (accessed December 2017), http://www.fao.org/faostat/en/#data/CS.

Eastwood, R., M. Lipton, and A. Newell. 2010. "Farm Size." In *Handbook of Agricultural Economics*, Vol. 4, edited by P.L. Pingali and R. E. Evenson, 3323–97. North Holland: Elsevier.

Fan, S. 1991. "Effects of Technological Change and Institutional Reform on Production Growth in Chinese Agriculture." *American Journal of Agricultural Economics* 73 (2): 266–75. https://doi.org/10.2307/1242711.

FAO (Food and Agriculture Organization). 2006. FAOSTAT Online Database, FAO, Rome (accessed October 2006), http://www.fao.org/faostat/en/#data.

———. 2015. FAOSTAT Online Database, FAO, Rome (accessed October 2017), http://www.fao.org/faostat/en/#data.

———. 2018a. FAOSTAT Online Database, FAO, Rome (accessed April 2018), http://www.fao.org/faostat/en/#data.

———. 2018b. *State of Agricultural Commodity Markets: Agricultural Trade, Climate Change and Food Security.* Rome: FAO.

FAO, IFAD, UNICEF, WFP, and WHO (Food and Agriculture Organization, International Fund for Agricultural Development, United Nations Children's Fund, the World Food Programme, and the World Health Organization). 2018. *The State of Food Security and Nutrition in the World 2018: Building Climate Resilience for Food Security and Nutrition.* Rome: FAO, IFAD, UNICEF, WFP, and WHO. License: CC BY-NC-SA 3.0 IGO.

Federico, G. 2005. *Feeding the World: An Economic History of Agriculture: 1800–2000.* Princeton, NJ: Princeton University Press.

Filmer, D., and L. Fox. 2014. *Youth Employment in Sub-Saharan Africa: Overview.* Washington, DC: World Bank.

Foster, A., and M. Rosenzweig. 2017. "Are There Too Many Farms in the World? Labor-Market Transaction Costs, Machine Capacities, and Optimal Farm Size." NBER Working Paper 23909, National Bureau of Economic Research, Cambridge, MA.

Fuglie, K. 2015. "Accounting for Growth in Global Agriculture." *Bio-based and Applied Economics* 4 (3): 221–54. doi: http://dx.doi.org/10.13128/BAE-17151.

———. 2019. "Sources of Growth in Agriculture." Background paper for *Harvesting Prosperity: Technology and Productivity Growth in Agriculture*, World Bank, Washington, DC.

Fuglie, K., and J. Marder. 2015. "The Diffusion and Impact of Improved Food Crop Varieties in Sub-Saharan Africa." In *Crop Improvement, Adoption and Impact of Improved Varieties in Food Crops in Sub-Saharan Africa*, edited by Thomas Walker and Jeffrey Alwang, 338–69. Wallingford, UK: Centre for Agriculture and Bioscience International (CABI).

Fuglie, K., and N. Rada. 2013. *Resources, Policy, and Agricultural Productivity in Sub-Saharan Africa.* Economic Research Report 145, Economic Research Service, US Department of Agriculture, Washington, DC.

Gollin, D. 2010. "Agricultural Productivity and Economic Growth." In *Handbook of Agricultural Economics*, Vol. 4, edited by R. E. Evenson and P. Pingali, 3825–66. Amsterdam: Elsevier.

Gollin, D., S. Parente, and R. Rogerson. 2002. "The Role of Agriculture in Development." *The American Economic Review* 92 (2): 160–64. https://www.jstor.org/stable/3083394.

Goyal, A., and J. Nash. 2017. *Reaping Richer Returns: Public Spending Priorities for African Agriculture Productivity Growth*. Washington, DC: World Bank.

Griliches, Z. 1957. "Hybrid Corn: An Exploration in the Economics of Technological Change." *Econometrica* 25 (4): 501–22.

Herrendorf, B., and T. Schoellman. 2018. "Wages, Human Capital, and Barriers to Structural Transformation." *American Economic Journal: Macroeconomics* 10 (2): 1–23. doi: 10.1257/mac.20160236.

Hicks, J. H., M. Kleemans, N. Y. Li, and E. Miguel. 2017. "Reevaluating Agricultural Productivity Gaps with Longitudinal Microdata." NBER Working Paper 23253, National Bureau of Economic Research, Cambridge, MA. doi: 10.3386/w23253.

ILO (International Labour Organization). 2017. ILOSTAT, online database, Geneva (accessed October 2017), http://www.ilo.org/global/statistics-and-databases/lang--en/index.htm.

IPCC (Intergovernmental Panel on Climate Change). 2018. "Global Warming of 1.5°C. An IPCC Special Report on the Impacts of Global Warming of 1.5°C above Pre-Industrial Levels and Related Global Greenhouse Gas Emission Pathways, in the Context of Strengthening the Global Response to the Threat of Climate Change, Sustainable Development, and Efforts to Eradicate Poverty." Geneva: IPCC. Version http://www.ipcc.ch/report/sr15/ (accessed November 2018).

Ivanic, M., and W. Martin. 2018. "Sectoral Productivity Growth and Poverty Reduction: National and Global Impacts." *World Development* 109 (September): 429–39.

Kantor, S., and A. Whalley. 2019. "Research Proximity and Productivity: Long-Term Evidence from Agriculture." *Journal of Political Economy* 127 (2): 819–54. https://www.journals.uchicago.edu/doi/abs/10.1086/701035?mobileUi=0.

Key, N., W. McBride, M. Ribaudo, and S. Sneeringer. 2011. "Trends and Developments in Hog Manure Management: 1998–2009." Economic Information Bulletin 81, Economic Research Service, US Department of Agriculture, Washington, DC.

Kislev, Y., and W. Peterson. 1982. "Prices, Technology, and Farm Size." *Journal of Political Economy* 90 (3): 578–95.

———. 1996. "Economies of Scale in Agriculture: A Reexamination of the Evidence." In *The Economics of Agriculture: Papers in Honor of D. Gale Johnson*, edited by J. Antle and D. Sumner, 156–70. Chicago: University of Chicago Press.

Kuznets, S. 1955. "Economic Growth and Income Inequality." *American Economic Review* 45 (March): 1–28.

Larson, D., R. Butzer, Y. Mundlak, and A. Crego. 2000. "A Cross-Country Database for Sector Investment and Capital." *World Bank Economic Review* 14 (2): 371–91.

Lewis, W. A. 1954. "Economic Development with Unlimited Supplies of Labour." *The Manchester School* 22 (2): 139–91.

Ligon, E., and E. Sadoulet. 2018. "Estimating the Relative Benefits of Agricultural Growth on the Distribution of Expenditures." *World Development* 109 (September): 417–28. https://doi.org/10.1016/j.worlddev.2016.12.007.

Lin, J. Y. 1992. "Rural Reforms and Agricultural Growth in China." *American Economic Review* 82 (1): 34–51.

Lynam, J. K., and R. W. Herdt. 1989. "Sense and Sustainability: Sustainability as an Objective in International Agricultural Research." *Agricultural Economics* 3 (1989): 381–98.

MacDonald, J. M., and W. D. McBride. 2009. "The Transformation of U.S. Livestock Agriculture: Scale, Efficiency, and Risks." Economic Information Bulletin 43, Economic Research Service, US Department of Agriculture, Washington, DC.

Macours, K., and J. F. M. Swinnen. 2002. "Patterns of Agrarian Transition." *Economic Development and Cultural Change* 50 (2): 365–94. https://doi.org/10.1086/322883.

Maloney, W., and F. Valencia Caicedo. 2019. "Engineering Growth." Unpublished.

McMillan, M. S., and K. Harttgen. 2014. "What Is Driving the 'African Growth Miracle'?" NBER Working Paper 20077, National Bureau of Economic Research, Cambridge, MA. doi: 10.3386/w20077.

Morrison-Paul, C., R. Nehring, D. Banker, and A. Somwaru. 2004. "Scale Economies and Efficiency of U.S. Agriculture: Are Traditional Farms History?" *Journal of Productivity Analysis* 22 (3): 185–205. doi: 10.1007/s11123-004-7573-1.

Mottet, A., C. de Hann, A. Falcucci, G. Tempio, C. Opio, and P. Gerber. 2017. "Livestock: On Our Plates or Eating at Our Table? A New Analysis of the Feed/Food Debate." *Global Food Security* 14 (September): 1–8. https://doi.org/10.1016/j.gfs.2017.01.001.

Mubarik, A., and D. Byerlee. 2002. "Productivity Growth and Resource Degradation in Pakistan's Punjab: A Decomposition Analysis." *Economic Development and Cultural Change* 50 (4): 839–63.

OECD (Organization for Economic Co-operation and Development). 2011. *Evaluation of Agricultural Policy Reforms in the European Union.* Paris: OECD Publishing. http://dx.doi.org/10.1787/9789264112124-en.

Otsuka, K., Y. Liu, and F. Yamauchi. 2016. "Growing Advantage of Large Farms in Asia and Its Implications for Global Food Security." *Global Food Security* 11 (December): 5–10. http://dx.doi.org/10.1016/j.gfs.2016.03.001i.

Oxford University. 2017. "World Population Growth." Our World in Data. Oxford University, Oxford, UK.

Pfaffenzeller, S., P. Newbold, and A. Rayner. 2007. "A Short Note on Updating the Grilli and Yang Commodity Price Index." *World Bank Economic Review* 21 (1): 151–63.

Rao, D. S. P. 1993. "Intercountry Comparisons of Agricultural Output and Productivity." FAO Economic and Social Development Paper, Food and Agriculture Organization, Rome.

Restuccia, D., D. T. Yang, and X. Zhu. 2008. "Agriculture and Aggregate Productivity: A Quantitative Cross-Country Analysis." *Journal of Monetary Economics* 55 (2) 234–50. https://doi.org/10.1016/j.jmoneco.2007.11.006.

Schreyer, P., and D. Pilat. 2001. "Measuring Productivity." OECD Economic Studies 33, 2001/II. Organisation for Economic Co-operation and Development, Paris.

See, L., S. Fritz, L. You, N. Ramankutty, M. Herrero, C. Justice, I. Becker-Reshef, P. Thorton, K. Erb, P. Gong, H. Tang, M. van der Velde, P. Ericksen, I. McCallum, F. Kraxner, and M. Obersteiner. 2015. "Improved Global Cropland Data as an Essential Ingredient for Food Security." *Global Food Security* 4 (March): 37–45. https://doi.org/10.1016/j.gfs.2014.10.004.

Siebert, S., and P. Döll. 2010. "Quantifying Blue and Green Virtual Water Contents in Global Crop Production as well as Potential Production Losses without Irrigation." *Journal of Hydrology* 384 (3–4): 198–217. https://doi.org/10.1016/j.jhydrol.2009.07.031.

Tauger, M. 2010. *Agriculture in World History.* Taylor and Francis Group.

Timmer, C.P. 2002. "Agriculture and Economic Development." In *Handbook of Agricultural Economics,* Vol. 2A, edited by B. Gardner and G. Rausser, 1487–1546. Amsterdam: North-Holland.

USDA-ERS (US Department of Agriculture Economic Research Service). 2018. International Agricultural Productivity. Online database. Washington, DC (accessed September 2018), https://www.ers.usda.gov/data-products/international-agricultural-productivity/.

USGS (US Geological Service). 2017. Global Food Security Analysis-Support Data at 30 Meters (GFSAD30) Project. Washington, DC (accessed December 2017), https://geography.wr.usgs.gov /science/croplands/index.html.

Villoria, N. 2019. "Technology Spillovers and Land Use Change: Empirical Evidence from Global Agriculture." *American Journal of Agricultural Economics* 101 (3): 870–93.

Wageningen Economic Research. 2018. "Climate Change and Global Market Integration: Implications for Global Economic Activities, Agricultural Commodities, and Food Security." SOCO (State of Agricultural Commodity Markets) 2018 Background Paper, Food and Agriculture Organization (FAO), Rome.

Wang, S. L., F. Tuan, F. Gale, A. Somwaru, and J. Hansen. 2013. "China's Regional Agricultural Productivity Growth in 1985–2007: A Multilateral Comparison." *Agricultural Economics* 44 (2): 241–51. https://doi.org/10.1111/agec.12008.

World Bank. World Development Indicators (WDI) online database. Washington, DC. http:// databank.worldbank.org/data/reports.aspx?source=World-Development-Indicators.

World Resources Institute. 2019. *The World Resources Report: Creating a Sustainable Food Future.* Washington, DC: World Resources Institute.

2. Misallocation and Productivity Growth

The Potential for Productivity Gains from Reallocation

Barriers to factor mobility as a drag on productivity growth have long been a concern.[1] Economists have long been concerned with the ease with which the means of production (that is, land, labor, and capital) can move between different uses or productive activities. At the center of this concern is the potential misallocation of the two main factors of production in agriculture, land and labor, as a result of distortions preventing them from moving to their most productive use, as discussed in chapter 1.

How large are the potential gains from removing barriers and enabling such a reallocation? New and emerging evidence sheds light on the contemporary debates relating to land and labor employed in agriculture. The first section of this chapter addresses the question of farm size and productivity, and discusses new evidence based on total factor productivity (TFP), a more relevant measure than the commonly used measure of yields (which measures partial factor productivity). The second section looks at the potential misallocation of labor. Two questions relating to labor productivity are addressed. The first is the magnitude of the difference in average labor productivity across sectors, commonly referred to as the agricultural productivity gap (APG). This discussion examines the role of the APG in structural transformation—defined as the reallocation of productive resources across economic activities, typically characterized under three broad sectors (agriculture, manufacturing, and services)—that accompanies the process of modern economic growth. The second question is the potential misallocation of labor across sectors and the significance of barriers to labor mobility. This discussion focuses on wage gaps (as a proxy for marginal productivity of labor) across sectors.

The main conclusion emerging from these analyses is that potential gains from reallocation may be significantly less than formerly thought. On the relationship between farm size and productivity, evidence from novel case studies suggests that there is no economically optimal agrarian structure, although some farm sizes may face productivity disadvantages depending on their country's level of economic development and circumstances. With rising population pressure (as in Sub-Saharan Africa), farm size will likely continue to fall. The consistent evidence on the existence of the inverse farm-size–productivity relationship in these countries suggests that smaller farms will likely be able to accommodate—at least in part—the rising population pressure and provide a subsistence livelihood. But without an increase in per capita productivity, the result could simply be "agricultural involution" (Geertz 1968), whereby agriculture absorbs more workers but output per capita never rises above subsistence requirements. These analyses suggest that in addition to land policies, technology policy is key to influencing how smallholders compete during the processes of economic development and structural transformation.

As to APG, microdata suggest that the gap in average labor productivity between agricultural and nonagricultural workers either disappears or is significantly lower than the APG derived from macrodata. In other words, agriculture may not be as inherently unproductive as macrostatistics suggest. This finding is robust across the range of development settings considered, from low-income countries in Africa (Ethiopia, Malawi, Tanzania, and Uganda) to lower-middle-income India in South Asia, to upper-middle-income China in East Asia. The differences are found to be purely a matter of measurement, pertaining to the way labor input is measured. Labor use in agriculture is typically overestimated—so labor productivity in agriculture is systematically underestimated—when measured using sectoral labor data from macrostatistics.

Second, the existence (or lack) of an APG provides little insight as to the extent of labor misallocation across sectors. Establishing labor misallocation requires an analysis of the gap in the marginal productivity of labor, or wages, across sectors. In explaining observed wage gaps across sectors, findings spanning a wide range from high-income to low-income countries (United States, Brazil, Indonesia, and Kenya) point to the strong role of self-selection based on worker skills and ability. The evidence from China similarly indicates that workers are self-selecting across activities (or sectors) based on their capability or skills. The equalization of wages, or marginal productivities, despite the labor market distortions in China (embodied in the *hukou* system, which restricts rural-to-urban migration) reinforces the skepticism raised by other studies on quick and easy productivity gains from a reallocation of labor across sectors. The findings from India on wage differentials in local labor markets also do not support the notion of any major wedges holding back reallocation of labor from one sector to another. Instead, findings from both settings (India and China) put the onus of productivity growth back on supporting innovation and productivity-enhancing investments (in both on- and off-farm activities) and deepening human capital to accelerate structural transformation and spur aggregate productivity growth.

Insights on Farm Size and Productivity

This section offers new perspectives on the debate about the relationship between farm size and productivity by bringing together evidence from a set of novel case studies spanning both high- and low-income countries. Much previous work on productivity and farm size has been limited by a focus on single factor productivity.

Even if land productivity is higher on small farms, labor productivity is often much lower, and the use of other inputs frequently differs by farm size. When overall input use is considered, it is not clear whether small farms are in fact more efficient than large farms. To test how productivity changes with farm size, each case study described here uses total factor productivity (TFP) as the primary measure of performance. A second feature is that they all draw on panels or pseudo-panels of farm households in order to better understand the dynamics of farm productivity. Even if small farms exhibit relatively high productivity at present, some indication of whether their productivity is growing or stagnant is likely to shed considerable light on the evolution of agrarian structure.

An Evolution of Thought on Farm Size and Productivity

In the early 1960s, Sen (1962) noted that smaller farms employed more family labor per hectare, and that average labor productivity on these small farms was lower than on larger farms. This finding seemed to imply an inefficiency. Smaller farms could profitably rent in land or hire out labor to larger farms, thereby increasing the incomes of both—if factor markets allowed them to do so. Sen speculated that difficulties in finding alternative employment led smallholders to allocate much of their household's labor to their own farms.

In the mid-1980s, Feder (1985) and Eswaran and Kotwal (1986) put forth theoretical models that show how imperfections in factor markets could lead to higher crop yields on smaller farms. Their models assume that due to agency[2] or incentive problems hired laborers require more supervision by the farm manager, and hired labor is therefore less efficient than family labor. They also assume that access to working capital is constrained by land ownership, as land provides collateral for loans. Imperfections in at least two factor markets resulted in higher labor inputs and outputs per hectare on smaller farms, but higher output per worker on larger farms. Barrett (1996) adds that to achieve food self-sufficiency and avoid market risk in the price of food, risk-averse farm households facing credit constraints may oversupply family labor to their own farms and undersupply labor to the market.

These models, however, do not allow for larger farms to substitute machinery for labor and thereby continue to use family labor instead of hired labor on their farms. Kislev and Peterson (1982) show that in the United States, as nonfarm wages rose, farms expanded in size and substituted capital for labor to keep total labor per farm about the same, enabling larger farms to continue to rely primarily on family labor and obtain remuneration comparable with nonfarm opportunities. On southern cotton farms, agricultural mechanization replaced labor that was largely being "pulled" away from the farm sector by rising nonfarm wages, rather than being "pushed" out by labor-saving technological innovations (Peterson and Kislev 1986).

Recent work by Foster and Rosenzweig (2017) proposes a theoretical model that incorporates imperfect factor markets and economies of size in the use of farm machinery. Their model generates a U-shaped land productivity pattern, with the highest levels being achieved by the smallest and largest farms. Farms in the middle are too large to rely solely on family labor (and thus incur agency costs associated with the use of hired labor) and are not large enough to efficiently adopt labor-saving machinery.

Challenges to the Inverse Relationship Hypothesis

An important point illustrated by figure 1.5 in chapter 1 is that a prevalence of small farms has not deterred growth in productivity—the tiny 1-hectare farms in Asia have performed about as well as the 10-hectare farms of Europe or the 100-hectare-plus farms of North America and Oceania in achieving sustained growth in agricultural land and labor productivity.

One prominent challenge that has been made to the inverse relationship (IR) hypothesis is that farm size endogenously reflects land quality. Higher-quality cropland would, over time, be subdivided among more heirs and become more densely populated. Thus, smaller farms would tend to occupy higher-quality cropland where they would obtain higher average yields. Yet even when cropland quality characteristics have been carefully measured at the plot level, the inverse relationship seems to persist (Barrett, Bellemare, and Hou 2010; Julien, Bravo-Ureta, and Rada 2019; Gautam and Ahmed 2019b).

Another criticism is that land productivity measures may be biased. Because most studies have based their IR findings on farm surveys, yield could be overstated if small farms tended to underestimate their area or overstate their production (or if large farms did the opposite). Recent studies using Global Positioning System (GPS) measures of farm and plot size rather than survey responses have shown that the IR persists, however (Carletto, Gourlay, and Winters 2015; Julien, Bravo-Ureta, and Rada 2019).

Yields could also be biased if output is mismeasured. Two recent studies comparing output reported through farmer interviews and crop-cut surveys find that smaller farms may systematically overreport crop output (and therefore yield), at least in Africa (Desiere and Jolliffe 2018; Gourlay, Kilic, and Lobell 2017). These studies find that when crop cuts physically measure output, differences in harvested yield among farm sizes disappear. Yet small farms raise output on their plots not only by raising harvested yield of specific crops, but also, and perhaps more importantly, by increasing cropping intensity and changing the crop mix (Binswanger, Deininger, and Feder 1995). Ali and Deininger (2015) show, for example, that in Rwanda smaller farms devoted a greater share of their land to growing high-value and nutrient-dense vegetables, fruits, and root crops, compared to larger farms that devoted more land to grains.

Recent Evidence on the Inverse Relationship Hypothesis

In Asian countries undergoing rapid economic and wage growth, the IR may be disappearing, according to a recent review by Otsuka, Liu, and Yamauchi (2016). Economic growth appears to be creating improved labor market dynamics, allowing farm family labor to be reallocated to nonfarm jobs. Capital and land markets also may be evolving to allow more successful farms to expand in size and substitute machinery for labor.

Institutional and legal restrictions on labor and land market transactions could also be constraining the optimal growth of farm size. Adamopolous and Restuccia (2014) claim that in many developing countries, land tenure policies, such as area ceilings and rental restrictions, have prevented the most capable farmers from expanding their farm sizes and that such restrictions have become a significant constraint on agricultural growth. Previously, however, Vollrath (2007) came to the opposite conclusion, finding that countries with a more equitable distribution of farmland achieved higher levels of productivity. The difference between these results hinges critically on the metric of productivity used. Whereas Adamopolous and Restuccia (2014) focus on labor productivity (which is higher on large farms), Vollrath (2007) compares land productivity (which tends to be higher on small farms). These seemingly contradictory results illustrate the need to move to multifactor productivity measures to better understand productivity differences among farms and countries.

In high-income countries, findings by Kislev and Peterson (1982, 1996) that agriculture was likely to exhibit near-constant returns to scale have been challenged by studies using more recent data. MacDonald and McBride (2009) survey studies on the livestock sector in the United States, and they find strong evidence of size economies, at least up to a point, in confined livestock operations like poultry, hogs, and dairy. These economies are driven not only by technology but also by new institutional arrangements for financing and marketing, such as contract growing with vertically integrated agroprocessors. Evidence is emerging that economies of size have become pronounced in grain production as well (MacDonald, Korbe, and Hoppe 2013; Sheng et al. 2014; Key 2019), and advances in information-technology farming (precision agriculture) may favor this trend (Schimmelpfennig 2016). Nonetheless, even in these cases, size economies are not unlimited, and average firm sizes are likely to remain far lower in agriculture than in industry.

Modern value chains and information technologies may increasingly erode the productivity advantages of small farmers in developing countries as well. Henderson and Isaac (2017) develop a model in which modern value chains, typified by contractual arrangements between agroprocessors and growers to meet more exacting quality standards, attenuate the IR of smallholders. The reason is that processors, which control a growing share of commodity marketing, face higher transaction costs in dealing with many smallholders compared with a few large farms. Collier and Dercon (2014) and Deininger and Byerlee (2012) point to size economies in acquiring information and accessing services for farm, financial, risk, and marketing management as factors favoring the growth of mega-farms in some developing and transition countries. These findings from theoretical and empirical research point to the need for new research on the economies of size in agriculture.

The Relationship between Farm Size and Total Factor Productivity

A recent issue of *Food Policy* brought together new evidence on farm size and productivity from five case studies spanning both high- and low-income countries.[3] These countries represent highly different levels of development and agrarian structures and the case studies share common methodological features. First, they all use TFP as the primary metric for productivity comparisons among farms. Second, they attempt to control for variations that do not change over time (time-invariant heterogeneity), such as the quality of natural resources. Third, when possible, they compare not only TFP levels but also TFP growth (except for the African cases where the panels were too short to allow reasonable estimates of growth over time).

The first case study, by Julien, Bravo-Ureta, and Rada (2019), uses multiple rounds of a nationally representative survey administered by the World Bank, the Living Standards Monitoring Surveys–Integrated Surveys on Agriculture (LSMS-ISA), from three African countries (Malawi, Tanzania, and Uganda),[4] where most farms operate less than 5 hectares (ha) of cropland. In the second study, Gautam and Ahmed (2019b) use three rounds (2000, 2004, and 2008) of nationwide farm household surveys from Bangladesh, one of the most densely populated countries in the world, where farms average less than 2 ha and where farm size has declined over time. The third case study, by Rada, Helfand, and Magalhães (2019), looks at Brazil using agricultural census data from 1985, 1995/96, and 2006. Brazil represents a particularly interesting case because it includes significant numbers of very small and very large farms. The final two case studies focus on the performance of relatively large farms in developed countries. Key (2019) examines changes in farm structure and productivity on grain-producing farms in the United States Corn Belt, drawing on agricultural census data between 1982 and 2012, whereas Sheng and Chancellor (2019) focus on grain farms in Australia using a farm survey spanning 1979 to 2004.

Africa
The African data used by Julien, Bravo-Ureta, and Rada (2019) includes at least two LSMS-ISA survey rounds for each country (Malawi in 2010 and 2013; Tanzania in 2008, 2010, and 2012; and Uganda in 2010 and 2011). Average farms in these East African countries are small, ranging from 0.1 ha to 1.8 ha in Malawi, 0.2 ha to 30.3 ha in Tanzania, and 0.1 ha to 6.6 ha in Uganda. The authors estimate a stochastic production function using a random parameters model with random effects. Each farm gets

its own "estimated intercept," controlling for differences in temperature, rainfall, slope, elevation, soil quality, farmer experience, number of plots, gender of the household head, distance to roads, and frequency of contact with extension services. Their results show widely varying levels of productivity among farms in the samples (low levels of technical efficiency, measured by the TFP of any given farm, compared to the level of the best-practice farm in that country). The average Malawian farm produced, on average, only 45 percent of the output of the best-practice farms in the Malawian sample. That estimate is 40 percent in the Tanzanian sample, and 64 percent in Ugandan sample. These estimates point to very low average managerial skill, weighing down agricultural growth.

Across these African countries, Julien, Bravo-Ureta, and Rada (2019) find higher TFP for smaller farms and pervasive imperfections in land and labor markets. Limited economic growth in the nonfarm economy has likely contributed to a low opportunity cost of labor and high opportunity cost of land on smaller farms. Although managerial skill (technical efficiency) did not appear to vary by farm size, there was large variation within each size class. Declining TFP amid constant technical efficiency over farm sizes suggests a consistent performance gap, with a few farms in each size class setting the technological, best-practice frontier and the average-performing farms lagging far behind. The authors point to greater public investment in extension services as one way to improve managerial skill and thus farm performance, regardless of size. In sum, and consistent with much of the development economics literature, within a range of 0 to about 10 ha, larger farm sizes in these East African countries continue to underperform relative to their smaller counterparts.

The evidence on decreasing returns to size in African agriculture remains far from definitive, however. Gollin and Udry (2019) suggest that apparent large dispersion in productivity among farms included in the LSMS may simply reflect measurement errors, unaccounted-for heterogeneity in land quality, and random production shocks. They suggest that even though the quality of the data on African farms from LSMS has greatly improved, these measurement factors may overstate actual differences in levels of productivity among farms. Another criticism of the LSMS data is that they underrepresent medium-sized and large farms, which now produce a significant share of output in a number of African countries (Jayne et al. 2016). With relatively small numbers of medium and large farms in the LSMS surveys, estimated variances are simply too large to draw strong conclusions. In a recent paper, Muyanga and Jayne (2019) combine a population-based survey of 1,300 Kenyan farms from 2010 with a specially commissioned 2012 survey of 200 medium-scale farms to test the IR relationship over a larger range of size classes. They find a U-shaped relationship between TFP and farm size: the IR holds for farms cultivating 3 hectares or less; TFP is relatively flat for farms between 3 and 5 hectares; and TFP then rises for farms within the 5- to 70-hectare range. They find TFP to be largest among the farms in the 20- to 70-hectare range. Although these results are intriguing, limitations of the study are that the surveys came from different years, analysis was confined to a single crop (maize), and only the cultivated area was considered as the land input. Given that small farms tend to use cropland more intensively (more harvests per hectare of land holdings) and often alter their crop mix (planting crops with greater harvest value per hectare), the apparently higher TFP of the larger farms in this study may be overstated. More research, and better measures, are needed to explain the apparent differences in farm-to-farm productivity in the African context.

Bangladesh

Some of the first systematic observations of the IR come from South Asia (Sen 1962). However, recent studies have pointed to an apparent erosion of the IR in a number of Asian countries, especially ones undergoing rapid economic growth, such as China (Rada, Wang, and Qin 2015; Wang et al. 2016); India (Deininger et al. 2018); Indonesia (Yamauchi 2016); and Vietnam (Liu, Violette, and Barrett 2016). These studies point toward the emergence of more dynamic rural labor markets as reducing imperfections in factor markets and providing more nonfarm employment opportunities for family labor. Bangladesh has also experienced robust economic growth over the past decade. Its gross domestic product (GDP) per capita growth rate nearly doubled, rising from an annual average of 3.20 percent in 1996–2006 to 5.05 percent in 2006–2016, and it is now classified as a lower-middle-income country (World Bank 2018). Nonetheless, agricultural employment on microfarms still dominates the Bangladeshi economy. Between 2000 and 2008, the mean and median farm sizes declined and by 2008 were below 1 ha, as Gautam and Ahmed (2019b) show. However, Bangladeshi farmers also rapidly acquired more capital. Over this period, the share of total area under irrigation rose from 66 percent to 80 percent, and the share of farms using some mechanization increased from 66 percent to 89 percent. Innovations in mechanization (in the form of smaller or scalable machinery) enabled small farms to substitute capital for labor amid rising wages.

With three rounds (2000, 2004, and 2008) of a large panel survey of Bangladeshi farms, Gautam and Ahmed (2019b) estimate a stochastic production function using a correlated random effects model in which time-averages of the production inputs are included in the specification to account for time-invariant heterogeneity across farm households. They find clear evidence of an IR: TFP declined with size. However, between 2000 and 2008, the IR decreased, indicating a convergence of TFP between large and small farms. Although all farm size classes achieved TFP growth over the study period, TFP of larger farms grew somewhat faster. In 2000, Bangladesh's larger farms were only 74 percent as productive as its smaller farms, but by 2008, they were 93 percent as productive. The rapid improvement by larger farms and absolute improvement of all farms suggest that robust off-farm economic growth facilitated active agricultural factor markets, which in turn contributed to raising the productivity of all farms and alleviating the productivity disadvantage of larger farms. This evidence from Bangladesh is consistent with the findings from other rapidly growing Asian countries cited earlier.

Brazil

Brazil contains a very large share of small, labor-intensive farms (reflective of a developing country), paired with a small share of land-intensive farms that produce a large share of national agricultural output (reflective of a developed country). In Brazil's latest (2006) agricultural census, 36 percent of its 4.17 million farms operated less than 5 ha and produced 7 percent of total agricultural output value, whereas 2 percent of farms operated over 500 hectares and produced 36 percent of total output. Unlike Africa and South Asia, Brazil offers an opportunity to test the IR hypothesis over a much larger range in farm sizes.

Drawing on 1985, 1995/96, and 2006 farm census data, Rada, Helfand, and Magalhães (2019) construct a pseudo-panel of farms, in which each observation is a "representative farm" for farm size classes in each of roughly 3,800 municipalities. With five farm size classes defined, they estimate a production function for each size class taking into account municipality fixed effects and a number of control variables. From their econometric estimates they are able to derive average TFP for each size class and for each census round.

In the initial year (1985) of the study, TFP levels were somewhat higher on larger farms. The output produced by farms operating over 500 ha was achieved with TFP that was on average 20 percent greater than the average TFP of farms under 5 ha. But between 1985 and 2006, TFP of both very small and very large farms grew rapidly. By 2006 that TFP disparity had been reduced to 9 percent, and mid-sized farms had become the least productive farm size class. Moreover, by 2006 a U-shaped pattern of the TFP–farm size relationship had emerged, similar to what Muyanga and Jayne (2019) find for Kenya, with the smallest and largest farm size classes achieving the highest TFP. These are not the first instances where such a farm-performance relationship has been observed. A U-shaped relationship was found in Kenya's Njoro region by Carter and Wiebe (1990); in Brazil's Center-West by Helfand and Levine (2004); among a sample of Pakistani farmers by Heltberg (1998); and in semi-arid India (Foster and Rosenzweig 2017) in recent rounds of the International Crops Research Institute for the Semi-Arid Tropics (ICRISAT) farm survey. Foster and Rosenzweig (2017) attribute the emergence of this pattern to factor market transaction costs coupled with economies of size in farm mechanization.

The fact that the U-shaped pattern emerged in Brazil only recently, however, suggests that more may be going on. Rada, Helfand, and Magalhães (2019) examine a number of factors that may explain the pattern of TFP growth in Brazil, including the role of commodity specialization and policy. Brazil is perhaps unique in that it has developed separate policies (and separate government ministries) for its small and large farm sectors. The authors find that regardless of farm size, specialization in annual crops was associated with faster TFP growth, whereas greater perennial crop specialization was associated with faster TFP growth for the smallest farms. Public education investments had a positive effect for most farm sizes, but the positive TFP effect of technical assistance was associated only with larger farm sizes.

United States and Australia

In high-income countries, large farms tend to dominate production. Nonetheless, they continue to coexist with millions of relatively small farms. If returns to size are roughly constant, then such coexistence does not imply any drag on efficiency. Even if some farms are not large enough to provide year-round employment or income comparable with nonfarm occupations, they can be an efficient mode of production if operated on a part-time basis. On the other hand, if larger farmers achieve significantly higher TFP (and thus lower unit costs and higher profitability), economic pressures can be expected to favor consolidation in the sector over time.

The two case studies reviewed here focus on farms specializing in grain production. Over the past few decades there has been considerable consolidation in this sector of agriculture in both the United States (MacDonald, Korbe, and Hoppe 2013) and Australia (Sheng et al. 2014). In the case of grain production in the US Corn Belt over 1982–2012, Key (2019) finds that across five farm size classes, not only are larger farms operating at higher TFP levels, but a clear productivity disadvantage emerges when grain operations fall under 100 acres (40 ha). Above that threshold, though, productivity improvements have been rather uniform among grain farms; that is, medium-sized grain farms have been able to increase their TFP levels but have not closed the productivity gap with larger farms. In fact, the largest farm size class appears to be increasing TFP at a slightly faster rate compared to other farms.

Key (2019) further shows that farm consolidation (represented by the growing output share of larger farms) accounted for 16 percent of aggregate TFP gains, and factor productivity improvements within a size class accounted for the remaining 84 percent. He contends that the widening disparity between unit costs faced by smaller farms relative to larger farms may be a result of technological advances favoring mechanization gains that are dependent on farm size.

Like the US case, Sheng and Chancellor (2019) find that larger Australian grain producers operate at higher levels of TFP than smaller grain farms. This study examines whether the asymmetric budget constraints between farms of different sizes are restricting small farms' ability to adopt technology embodied in new plant and machinery.

Lags in adoption of new technology could be contributing to the TFP gap between large and small farms. Sheng and Chancellor suggest that machinery outsourcing could be an option to help smaller farms make efficient use of capital. They find that renting in machinery services helped narrow but did not close the TFP gap between smaller and larger farms.

Figure 2.1 provides a stylized summary of the findings on farm size and productivity from the five case studies discussed. The lines compare productivity among farms of different sizes, and how those productivity differences have evolved over time, within a country. However, the lines should not be interpreted as comparing TFP across countries (they do not compare agricultural TFP between Bangladesh and Brazil, for example). In the case of developing countries, consistent with the inverse relationship, the smallest farms achieve higher TFP than slightly larger ones. However, with mechanization significantly larger farms appear to benefit from economies of size, particularly in grain production, suggesting a possible U-shape to the farm size-productivity relationship. In the case of Africa, a dashed line with a question mark ("?") extends the IR of small farms to possibly constant or increasing returns for larger farms. But whether larger farms in Africa achieve higher levels of productivity remains an issue that needs to be tested against more and better data.

FIGURE 2.1   There Is No Optimal Farm Size: Both Large and Small Farms Can Be Equally Efficient

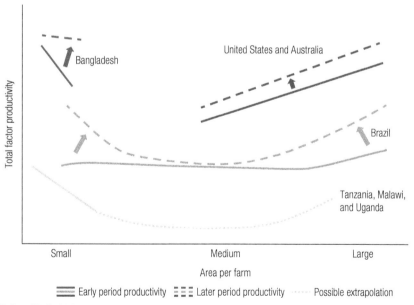

Source: Rada and Fuglie 2019.

Note: The lines compare productivity among farms of different sizes, and how those productivity differences have evolved over time, within a country. However, the lines should not be interpreted as comparing total factor productivity (TFP) across countries (they do not compare agricultural TFP between Bangladesh and Brazil, for example).

Implications of Recent Findings on Farm Size and Productivity

Optimum Farm Size

The evidence highlighted above and depicted in figure 2.1 suggests that there is no economically optimal farm size—although some farm sizes may face productivity disadvantages depending on their country's level of economic development and circumstances. Low-income countries facing significant rural demographic pressure (as in Sub-Saharan Africa) will likely experience falling average farm size as family and communal lands are further subdivided to provide livelihoods for expanding populations. Given the IR in these countries, smaller farms should be able to accommodate—at least in part—the rising population pressure and provide a subsistence livelihood. But without an increase in per capita productivity, the result could simply be "agricultural involution"—a pattern Clifford Geertz (1968) first described to characterize Indonesia's agricultural stagnation in the early twentieth century, in which agriculture absorbs more workers but output per capita never rises above subsistence requirements.

Access to Land

An important dimension for policy in such an environment is to enable newly forming households to gain access to land. In many parts of Africa, traditional tenure systems in which local inhabitants have user rights to communally owned land are giving way to formal titling systems (Jayne et al. 2016). Land policies that facilitate the emergence of land rental arrangements can provide a means for poor households to gain access to such land (Deininger, Savastano, and Xia 2017; Eastwood, Lipton, and Newell 2010). As countries move beyond stagnant per capita GDP to reach a point at which the nonfarm sector is growing fast enough to create employment opportunities for rural labor, farm households can begin to transit out of agriculture, either part-time or permanently. As labor begins to exit the sector, there is a need for land policies that permit or facilitate the consolidation of farmland so that the most successful farmers can expand their operations. Emerging medium-sized farms can also be expected to substitute capital for labor as wages rise and farm labor leaves the sector. Small, part-time farmers may persist (and be efficient) for a long time, especially if new technologies exhibit constant returns to scale. Public services to support agriculture should not ignore small farms, as they can continue to be a dynamic source of growth. There may be opportunities to extend these supporting services into the marketing sector, to reduce the transaction costs associated with small farms accessing new technology in plant and machinery services and participating in modern agri-food value chains. In high-income countries with an already high degree of farm mechanization and few constraining market imperfections, sustaining small farms may be an important social objective. It is unlikely to contribute much to the aggregate growth of the farm sector, however, because the agricultural value added of small farms becomes negligible overall. The issues of smallholder access to land tenure security and market value chains are taken up again in chapters 4 and 5, respectively.

Technology Policy

Beyond land and market policies, technology policy is key to influencing how smallholders compete during the processes of economic development and structural transformation. In economies with scarce land and abundant labor, technologies need to evolve that are land-saving and labor-using, such as those that characterized the Asian Green Revolution. As the cost of labor rises relative to capital and intermediate inputs, labor-saving innovations will emerge, mostly from the private sector. However, if countries fail to develop strong agricultural research and development (R&D) systems that are linked to the needs of local farmers, then the technology options available to these farmers may not reflect the relevant factor scarcities facing them.

The case studies present important insights on the relationship between agrarian structure and productivity growth. The IR appears to have provided African communities facing demographic pressure a means to increase food production despite limited technical change. The smallholder dynamism documented by the studies of Bangladesh and Brazil should help allay concerns that smallholders in developing countries are a drag on growth. For high-income countries like the United States and Australia, the persistent higher productivity among the largest farms suggests that the process of structural change in agriculture is not yet over.

Labor Productivity and Structural Transformation

Labor productivity is directly related to labor incomes, and ultimately to poverty reduction, thus making it of great interest to policy makers. The fact that labor productivity differs across sectors, and the way these differences are resolved, are central to the process of structural transformation and the nature of growth in an economy. The discussion on structural transformation has thus long focused on the large gaps observed in labor productivity across sectors, typically measured as the average sectoral value added per worker. National accounts statistics (NAS) on sectoral value added and sectoral employment, such as from the World Bank's World Development Indicators database, show that the average labor productivity in industry or services is multiples of the average labor productivity in agriculture—suggesting a large "agriculture productivity gap" (APG) in developing countries. Figure 2.2 shows the average APG for the major regions of the world.

Because agriculture commands a large share of labor in poor countries, and because average labor productivity in agriculture is typically measured to be low, moving labor from agriculture to other sectors would seem to offer a straightforward path toward

FIGURE 2.2 Across World Regions, Macrostatistics Show That Labor Productivity Is Higher in Industry and Services Than in Agriculture, 2011–15

Average ratio

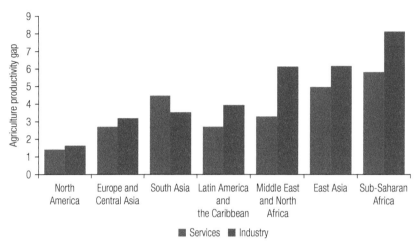

Source: World Development Indicators, World Bank, https://data.worldbank.org/products/wdi.

Note: The agriculture productivity gap is the ratio of average labor productivity in industry or services to the average labor productivity in agriculture.

economy-wide growth in productivity (McMillan and Rodrik 2011; Collier and Dercon 2014; Gollin, Lagakos, and Waugh 2014; McMillan and Headey 2014).

The large and persistent gap in average labor productivity across sectors has spawned a large body of literature in recent years, attempting to resolve the puzzle of why so much labor remains in agriculture, generally tending small plots of land. Alternative interpretations of the APG offered by this research and their implications for the misallocation of labor across sectors are briefly discussed in the next subsection. Importantly, the magnitude of the APG estimated from NAS has been questioned because of likely mismeasurement in the effective supply of labor to different sectors. Microevidence on the actual time individuals spend on specific activities (farming, nonfarm work, domestic work, and so on) paints a vastly different picture from data at the national level. Importantly, although the magnitude of the APG suggests that productivity differences across sectors may not be as large as generally believed, the APG does not speak to the issue of misallocation, which requires a focus on the marginal productivity of labor or wages.

The rest of this section pursues this line of investigation, seeking empirical insights on three core questions: (1) How do farm workers allocate their labor? Specifically, how much labor do they actually spend on agriculture? (2) How large is the APG? Specifically, what is the difference in average labor productivity across the particular farm and nonfarm activities that each household engages in, using more accurate estimates of actual labor supplied to these activities? (3) How large is the wage gap across different types of activities that might be indicative of barriers to labor mobility, and hence misallocation of labor? Based on these findings, the implications for policy and strategy to promote faster productivity growth and structural transformation are drawn.

These questions are addressed using micro-level data from three important settings. The first set of results are from a study of four African countries using the World Bank's LSMS-ISA household surveys by McCullough (2017). These microdata provide a very different perspective on structural transformation than macrodata, even for economies in the early stages of their structural transformation process. And although these findings are insightful, McCullough's paper does not look at the wage gaps and as such does not address the issue of any potential misallocation of labor. Another outstanding question is whether the findings are transferable to other economies at different stages of structural transformation.

These issues are addressed using new empirical evidence from two large economies: China, an upper-middle-income country; and India, a lower-middle-income country. Besides their distinct geographies, income levels, and levels of transformation, these two countries are important case studies because they are often cited as outstanding examples with barriers to factor mobility—because of the *hukou* (residential permit) system in China (Adamopoulus et al. 2017; Restuccia and Rogerson 2008) and the caste system in India (Hsieh and Klenow 2009; Herrendorf and Schoellman 2018).

A major strength of all these analyses is that they exploit rare microdata on individual households' labor use in agricultural and nonagricultural activities from detailed household surveys. These data are well placed to answer the three core questions posed above based on observed labor productivity and wage gaps resulting from households' choice to participate in multiple sectors.

Interpreting the Agriculture Productivity Gap

Interest in the APG has been rekindled recently, following Caselli (2005), as growth economists search for an explanation for the large divergence in standards of living across countries, and across sectors within countries (Gollin, Parente, and Rogerson 2007; Cordoba and Ripoll 2009; Restuccia, Yang, and Zhu 2008; Vollrath 2009, among others). Consistent with the insights of Schultz (1964) that smallholder farmers are constrained optimizers—"efficient but poor"—the core of this research is to solve the puzzle of why labor does not move away from agriculture to sectors with higher productivity that should offer higher returns to labor. The emerging literature has sought to understand how wide the APG really is, and what might explain its persistence (Caselli and Coleman 2005; Herrendorf and Schoellman 2018; Hicks et al. 2017; Rogerson 2017). This growing literature provides alternative interpretations of the measured APG that can be clustered into two broad categories: misallocation and measurement errors.

Misallocation

One popular interpretation of the APG is that it reflects *wedges*, or barriers created by policies hindering a smooth reallocation of factors across sectors. Assuming that different sectors use a common technology, both the average and marginal productivities would equalize across sectors in a competitive equilibrium. The existence of an APG would thus suggest a wedge preventing labor mobility. The key to aggregate productivity growth and poverty reduction is arguably to remove the underlying distortion and allow labor to exit agriculture (Hsieh and Klenow 2009; Restuccia and Rogerson 2008). Following this line of reasoning, several recent papers have suggested large potential productivity gains from addressing the policies driving the apparent misallocation of factors (Adamopoulos and Restuccia 2014; Adamopoulos et al. 2017; Restuccia and Santaeulalia-Llopis 2017).

To put this interpretation of APG in context, it is important to note the analytical benchmark used in much of this macrogrowth literature. The workhorse model in growth diagnostics is the two-factor Cobb-Douglas transformation function. One key assumption maintained in this benchmark model is that the labor-share parameter, which characterizes the technology, is the same across the sectors (as elaborated, for example, in Gollin, Lagakos, and Waugh 2014). The second key assumption is that labor is fully fungible—that is, perfectly substitutable—across sectors.

Relaxing the first assumption of a common technology across sectors, the interpretation of an APG as reflecting misallocation is not obvious. Rogerson (2017) shows that different factor shares in sector value added, or the technology parameters in a standard Cobb-Douglas model, would result in differences in average productivity across sectors even if factor allocation is efficient (see box 2.1). In other words, the existence of APG in itself is not sufficient evidence of misallocation because with labor productivity equalized at the margin, reallocation across sectors per se offers no scope for aggregate productivity gains.

The key question for ascertaining misallocation is whether labor markets function efficiently. On this question, evidence from studies indeed suggests a significant and persistent gap between average agricultural and nonagricultural wages, or an agricultural wage gap (AWG), with nonagricultural wages typically found to be significantly higher than agricultural wages (Vollrath 2009, 2014; Herrendorf and Schoellman 2018).

Explaining the persistence of AWGs has also attracted considerable attention. Studies looking at labor market efficiency have pointed to adjustment frictions that might prevent labor from flowing from one activity to another as potential explanations for the persistence of AWGs.[5] These studies suggest a number of likely culprits, including the disutility associated with certain types of work; insufficient information

Analytically Challenged? The Mechanics of the Agricultural Productivity Gap

Consider a two-sector world characterized with a transformation function for sector i (=1,2):

$$Y_i = A_i K_i^{\alpha_i} L_i^{(1-\alpha_i)}. \tag{1}$$

For each sector i, average productivity of labor is

$$AP_i = \frac{Y_i}{L_i} = A_i \left[\frac{K_i}{L_i} \right]^{\alpha_i}, \tag{2}$$

and marginal productivity of labor, using (2), is

$$MP_{L_i} = (1-\alpha_i) A_i \left[\frac{K_i}{L_i} \right]^{\alpha_i} = (1-\alpha_i) AP_i. \tag{3}$$

At equilibrium (from the first order condition):

$$MP_{Li} = w_i. \tag{4}$$

With functioning labor markets, free of any barriers, wages would equalize across sectors:

$$w_1 = w_2 = w. \tag{5}$$

Making the appropriate substitutions, equilibrium can thus be characterized as

$$\frac{AP_1}{AP_2} = \frac{(1-\alpha_2)}{(1-\alpha_1)}. \tag{6}$$

With functioning and efficient labor markets, $AP_1 = AP_2$ only if $\alpha_1 = \alpha_2$, or technologies in the two sectors are the same. However, there is no a priori reason to believe that this should be the case.

flows (on available opportunities); job search costs; amenity differences; familiarity (such as uncertainty associated with an unknown place); credit or financial constraints; or lack of insurance to compensate for informal networks to cope with livelihood risks (Baysan et al. 2019; Bazzi 2017; Bryan, Chowdhury, and Mobarak 2014; Bryan and Morten 2017; Ingelaere et al. 2018; Munshi and Rosenzweig 2016).

An important body of work on wage gaps and implications for labor market efficiency challenges the second key assumption of the benchmark model noted earlier: the fungibility of labor (Young 2013; Herrendorf and Schoellman 2018). The presumption of a homogenous quality of workers—whereby quality reflects the ability, skills, or motivation of workers and is typically unobserved (Gollin, Lagakos, and Waugh 2014; Rogerson 2017)— introduces a bias in measured productivity, as effective labor input is not properly accounted for.

Recognizing the heterogeneity of workers in terms of ability, Hicks et al. (2017) argue that rather than a "causal impact" (that is, a worker is inherently more productive in the nonagricultural sector than the same person in the agricultural sector), the productivity gap (measured in terms of earnings per worker) better reflects "worker selection" (that is, the differences in ability or skill, which may not be fully accounted for by standard adjustments in terms of observed human capital, typically years of schooling), as workers of varying ability and skill self-select into specific sectors. Selection of workers into activities by skills would explain observed average earnings gaps across sectors.[6] This view is supported by the finding by Hicks et al. (2017) that "switchers" (individuals who switch from agricultural to nonagricultural work in Indonesia and Kenya) experienced insignificant gains in earnings. The importance of selection is highlighted analytically by Rogerson (2017), and further supported by the empirical findings from Young's (2013) analysis of rural-urban (and reverse) migration across 63 countries, and the findings in Herrendorf and Schoellman (2018) using data from 13 countries (ranging from rich to poor). Another important insight is provided by Baysan et al. (2019), using data on a sample of rice farmers from a poor state in East India. Baysan et al. find that that for individuals working in multiple sectors, selection on unobservable worker quality does not fully explain the wage gap. They argue that a more likely explanation is the disutility associated with the available but physically harder nonfarm work (commonly in construction), with the gap reflecting a compensating wage differential. The main implication of these findings is that labor markets do not appear to reflect any obvious distortions.

Measurement Errors

An alternative interpretation of the APG, remaining agnostic on the assumptions on technology and labor fungibility, is that the observed gaps in productivity—within and across sectors and countries—reflect measurement errors, raising more fundamental concerns about how large the APG really is and the likely gains from reallocation. One potential source of error is the presumption of homogeneity in the physical production environment, particularly as it pertains to spatial comparisons of productivity across countries or between agriculture and other sectors. Gollin and Udry (2019) stress the importance of carefully accounting for the sources of heterogeneity to explain the differences across production units (such as idiosyncratic production shocks, measurement errors, and/or unobserved land quality) in order to assess the real potential for gains from reallocation. Using microdata from three African countries, they show that differences across production units are significantly reduced after accounting for various sources of heterogeneity across farms. Although residual differences remain, the potential income gains from a reallocation to the most productive units are unlikely to narrow the APG by much. They conclude that interpreting the observed productivity differences across countries, sectors, or even production units within sectors is not simple.

Another important source of measurement error is also a more basic accounting issue. In macrostatistics, it is assumed that all workers classified as agricultural represent a monolithic block of workers working full time in agriculture (Herrendorf and Schoellman 2015; McCullough 2017). New micro-level data question this assumption, showing that the actual time agricultural workers spend farming is significantly less than full time, with substantial time spent on secondary (nonfarm) activities. This concern is consistent with the insights from a separate strand of literature focused on understanding the functioning of rural labor markets and the allocation of time by rural households and individuals, the majority of whom are farmers. From this literature, it has been abundantly clear for quite some time that farmers, especially smallholders, rarely spend all their time solely on the farm or in agricultural activities. Agricultural labor use is seasonal and dictated by distinct crop calendars (de Janvry, Duquennois, and Sadoulet 2018). Labor is routinely supplied (by farmers and their family members) for nonfarm activities—both during slack times within an agricultural season and in lean periods between agricultural seasons (Rosenzweig 1980; Huffman 1980; Olfert 1992; Mishra and Goodwin 1997; Abdulai and Delgado 1999; Skoufias 1993, 1996; Haggblade, Hazell, and Reardon 2010).

These empirical realities raise two important questions: First, how do the national statistics account for multiple uses of labor? Second, how much labor is in fact spent on the farm, legitimately engaged in "agricultural labor," compared to the standard national accounts estimates? The elimination or substantial reduction of APG with better accounting for labor would suggest that even while ignoring the restrictive assumption on sectoral technology in the benchmark model, there would be limited scope for productivity gains from labor reallocation.

Although agriculture may not be as unproductive as might appear from the macrostatistics, the existence or magnitude of the APG does not address the issue of misallocation. For misallocation, a more conclusive test would be the existence of a significant AWG, which would more concretely reflect barriers to labor mobility. Given the potentially wide-ranging implications for policy—not only in agriculture but also in rural development, urbanization, and industrial policy (Gollin 2018)—closer examinations of both APG and AWG are warranted.

How Much Labor Is Supplied to Agriculture?

Recent studies have increasingly pointed to mismeasurement as a potential source of bias in the macroestimates of measured labor productivity because of how the NAS classify workers (as agricultural and nonagricultural) and the typical hours worked in each sector (Gollin, Lagakos, and Waugh 2014). A major shortcoming of national accounts is that they rarely provide details on the time that individuals allocate to different activities. NAS typically associate workers with the sector of their reported "main" occupation, with the assumption that the workers pursue that activity full time. Yet empirical analyses from developed and developing agricultural contexts have long noted that agricultural workers often do not work full time in agriculture. Thus even after the careful refinements in accounting for the sector of work made by Gollin, Lagakos, and Waugh (2014), potential biases likely remain, owing to mismeasurement of the actual time that individuals spend on specific activities (farming, nonfarm work, domestic work, and so on) (McCullough 2017).

Evidence from newly available microsurveys from distinct development settings (four countries in Africa, India in South Asia, and China in East Asia) provide consistent and robust evidence that the estimates of rural labor from national accounts are not reliable (see box 2.2 for a description of the data used). Data on labor supplied to different activities by individual household members, along with detailed data on wages, revenues, and costs, provide a better comparison of earnings across different activities. These data are more reliable for estimating the actual time spent on specific activities, in terms of days and, in some cases, hours.

A consistent finding across all six countries (large and small) is that macrostatistics overestimate labor use in agriculture. For the Sub-Saharan African countries McCullough (2017) examines labor supplied by household members to farm and nonfarm sectors using alternative measures of labor supply: total hours supplied to different activities by all working adults; a per person estimate, using the primary sector (the sector to which the individual supplies most hours) of each adult in the household; and a per person estimate using the primary sector of the household head. These estimates are then compared with the estimate from the national accounts data (and an alternative source, the Demographic Health Surveys). Figure 2.3 displays the results, with big differences across the different measures of labor supplied to agriculture.

Rural workers typically work in multiple activities and sectors. Ignoring this leads to an overestimation of labor use in agriculture, as in the case of national accounts. The national accounts estimate in figure 2.3 shows, as expected, the highest share of labor is allocated to agriculture. Consistent with this, the share of labor used in agriculture, based on the per person allocation to different sectors (whether considering only the household head or all adults), similarly shows higher labor use in agriculture. In contrast, the more accurate estimate using hours supplied shows significantly less labor supplied to agriculture.

The mismeasurement of labor used in agriculture is not a peculiarity of Sub-Saharan Africa, however. The data from China show an even more pronounced divergence between the national accounts and microdata labor supplied to agriculture.

High-Quality Microdata Sets Provide New Insights on Rural Labor

The findings summarized in this section come from three rich sources of microdata. One is the Living Standards Monitoring Surveys–Integrated Surveys on Agriculture (LSMS-ISA) data on four African countries (Ethiopia, Malawi, Tanzania, and Uganda), analyzed and described in depth by McCullough (2017). This box summarizes key findings from this study (no additional analysis is done). The second source is a large, nationally representative survey of rural households in China conducted by the Research Center for Rural Economy (RCRE) in Beijing. This survey is administered to about 20,000 households each year, on average; the data for this analysis are from 2003 to 2013. These surveys are administered once a year with data collected on an annual recall basis. As far as is known, these data have not been used for this type of analysis before. The third source are the Village Dynamics in South Asia (VDSA) surveys conducted by the International Crops Research Institute for the Semi-Arid Tropics (ICRISAT). Covering 30 villages in 8 diverse states of India, these surveys offer perhaps the most detailed data available on the economic activities households are engaged in. The data are from 2009 to 2014, collected on a monthly basis. The surveys provide details on the days and hours worked by individuals on different activities, providing much greater accuracy on the allocation of time across activities. More details on the China and India surveys are given in annex 2A.

Despite the high quality and detailed information provided by these surveys, it is important to note that microsurveys are not immune to measurement errors. The RCRE surveys are based on an annual recall, as is standard for most national surveys. Recall bias remains a potential source of mismeasurement in input use, especially labor (as memory of actual hours worked may be blurred by the end of a year or even a cropping season) (Arthi et al. 2018). To test this, the authors undertook a separate randomized survey of households in Tanzania and found a large reporting bias even in the end-of-season LSMS-ISA surveys, already an improvement compared to annual surveys. Labor input is found to be systematically and substantially over-reported (up to four times higher) in the end-of-season recall compared to weekly survey data. Thus, despite the quality of LSMS-ISA surveys, labor supply still likely reflects some measurement bias. In this regard, the VDSA data are better placed. The high frequency of data collection, on a monthly basis by resident enumerators, likely reduces potential biases associated with recall.

The nationally representative panel surveys (available for 2003–13) conducted by the Beijing-based Research Center for Rural Economy (RCRE) help shed light on this. As expected, virtually all households in the RCRE sample are rural in that they hold a rural *hukou*.[7] Despite this, significant trends are evident over the 11-year study period. The rural labor force has declined, in part reflecting the changing demographics in China, a trend evident even in the macrostatistics. The average household size has fallen, as has the household labor force, while the number of household members not in the labor force has risen—more sharply for women than for men. These changes are consistent with an aging rural workforce, with the younger and more educated

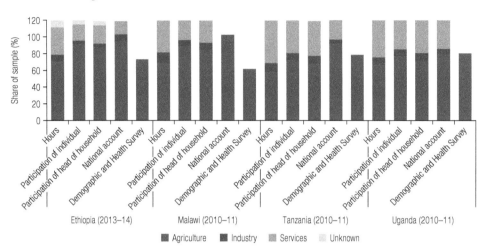

FIGURE 2.3   **Different Measures Yield Different Estimates of the Share of Labor in Agriculture and Other Sectors in Four African Countries**

Source: McCullough 2017.

Note: The "Hours" measure is from variables generated using LSMS-ISA data. The "Participation of individual" measure is based on the primary occupation (most reported hours) of individuals in the data set. The "Participation of head of household" measure is based on the primary occupation of the household head. The "National account" measure is from the World Development Indicators database.

workers increasingly holding nonfarm jobs outside the township—despite the *hukou* system. The average age of workers in agriculture surpassed 50 in 2013. Workers in nonfarm jobs within the township had a slightly lower average age of about 46, but workers in nonfarm jobs outside the township were distinctly younger, with an average age of about 36.

The data also provide details on the time allocated by each worker across different activities. Using reported time (in labor days) spent on farm and nonfarm activities (aggregated over all family members), on average only about one-third of households' total work time is spent on farming activities (figure 2.4). In other words, even rural *hukou* holders spend about two-thirds of their time on nonfarm activities.

What does this mean for aggregate labor supplied to agriculture? According to official statistics, 44 percent of China's total labor force in 2013 is classified as rural under the *hukou* system. Using the microestimate of the share of time spent on farm activities (one-third) by rural *hukou* holders and applying it to the national estimate of rural *hukou* holders implies that only 14.7 percent of the aggregate labor force is effectively engaged in agriculture. The remaining time of the rural *hukou* holders, or 29.3 percent equivalent of the national labor force, is spent pursuing nonfarm activities. Importantly, according to the RCRE data, most of this nonfarm engagement (61 percent of men's time and 57 percent of women's time) is on activities outside the township, a trend that is increasing for both male and female workers (figure 2.4).

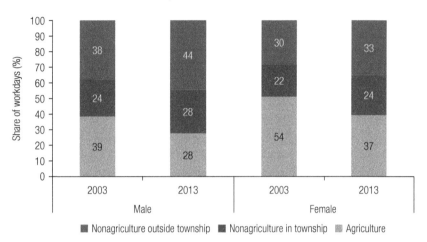

FIGURE 2.4 **Only about One-Third of Rural Households' Total Work Time Is Spent on Farming Activities in China, 2003–13**
Allocation of labor days to farm and nonfarm activities

Source: RCRE (Research Center for Rural Economy) surveys, 2003–13.

Macrostatistics, on the other hand, provide a significantly higher estimate of the labor force employed in agriculture. As noted, data from the National Bureau of Statistics do show a decline in the agricultural workforce, but their estimate of the labor force as employed in agriculture in 2013 is still notably high at 31.4 percent.[8] This is in sharp contrast to the estimate derived from microdata that suggests that less than half the macroestimate (or 14.7 percent), in full-time equivalents (FTEs), was actually engaged in agriculture in 2013. A natural corollary to this finding is that labor supplied to nonfarm activities is significantly higher than the macrostatistics might suggest, implying that the mismeasurement of labor supply affects not only estimates of average labor productivity in agriculture but also in other sectors.

Finally, the data from India provide further, and perhaps the most detailed, insights into the rural labor markets. The comprehensive Village Dynamics in South Asia (VDSA) surveys collect information on the myriad of economic activities that households and their individual members engage in (see annex 2A for more details on the VDSA surveys). These data allow alternative measures of labor supplied to different (agricultural and nonagricultural) activities to be estimated (see discussion that follows). An important advantage of the VDSA data over the others (the four African countries and China) is that they are collected and recorded on a monthly basis by enumerators resident in the village. This reduces the potential for recall bias associated with data collected on seasonal or yearly recall basis (Arthi et al. 2018).

The VDSA data allow three alternative measures of labor supplied to individual activities to be estimated. The first is based on self-declared "main occupation," as done in macrostatistics; this is referred to as the per person estimate. The second is based on the number of labor days spent on specific activities—or a per day estimate. The third is based on the number of hours of labor spent on each activity—the per hour estimate. Combining the data on the hours of labor used for different activities throughout the growing season with the detailed input and output production accounts collected for each parcel a household cultivates provides the most accurate account of labor use on and off the farm.[9]

The data clearly demonstrate that rural households follow multiple strategies to secure livelihoods. Households in the sample are engaged in as many as six different activities, with the majority engaged in three to four activities. In terms of time allocation across activities, days spent working on different activities in a typical month by an average adult rural worker are shown in figure 2B.1 in annex 2B. Assuming a normal work month of 25 days, the figure shows marked fluctuations over time, yet by and large the amount of work reported, including "domestic work," is higher than the average workload. The time spent on income-earning activities (assuming that domestic work is unpaid work so although it has a number of direct and indirect economic benefits, it does not generate income) appears to be about 67 percent of the time (approximately 15–17 days out of the 25 used to describe "full time").

The significant share of domestic work may suggest unemployment or underemployment in rural areas and could be interpreted as an indicator of labor market frictions preventing households from seeking employment. Note, however, that this is an average over all rural individuals. A more nuanced picture emerges by age group and gender. Focusing on working adults and distinguishing between male workers (who report an average of 23 days of work) and female workers (who report an average of 15 days of work), figure 2.5 shows how the month stacks up in terms of time spent by individuals classified by their main occupation.

Two main points relevant to the measurement of labor productivity emerge from figure 2.5 and the figures that follow. One is that the labor force engagement is sharply different for male and female workers. Except for salaried female workers, all other female workers appear to be significantly less engaged in economic activities. Male salaried and business workers also report working more than full time (reflecting some participation in other activities), while farm-based workers (agricultural and livestock workers) appear to be occupied slightly less (at about 92 percent of their labor endowment). Importantly, however, the amount of time spent farming, even by farmers, is significantly less, with a substantial part of their time engaged in nonfarming activities. Farm laborers on average are least engaged, at about 82 percent of the time.

The second important point is the seasonality of labor use in agriculture. Agriculture is a seasonal activity, and within each season, labor demand follows a distinct crop calendar (see de Janvry and Sadoulet forthcoming; de Janvry, Duquennois, and Sadoulet 2018) The observed slack in average worked time for farmers and farm labor in figure 2.5 hides the seasonal fluctuations in agricultural workers' labor supply (on and

FIGURE 2.5 **Distribution of Workdays by Farm and Nonfarm Activities in a Typical Month for an Average Adult Worker in India**

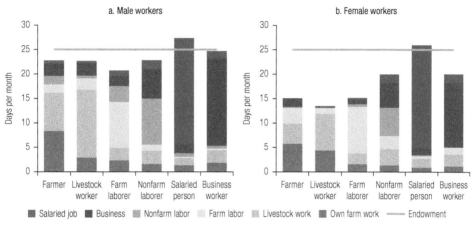

Source: VDSA (Village Dynamics in South Asia) surveys; ICRISAT (International Crops Research Institute for the Semi-Arid Tropics).
Note: The figure shows the labor use of an average rural adult worker (aged 15–65) in a month. A full-time work month is assumed to be 25 days.

off the farm). This temporal fluctuation is clearer in figure 2.6. While salaried workers are engaged at a constant level through the year (not shown in figure 2.6), agricultural work, especially work related to crop production, has a distinct seasonal pattern. Farm labor supplied outside of the household farm shows an identical pattern to labor use on the household farm. Interestingly, nonfarm labor and business work show countercyclical patterns with supply of labor to those activities rising when agricultural activities are less. In other words, enterprises appear to be an important source of alternative employment in the "lean" agricultural periods.

How Large Is the Agricultural Productivity Gap?

The implications of better accounting for labor use are significant. Across all case studies from Africa, China, and India, the different measures of labor provide a strikingly different assessment of the APG. This issue is systematically examined by comparing the APG estimated using three alternative measures: per worker, per day, and per hour of labor supplied. Labor productivity is defined as average earnings per unit of labor. Earnings from agricultural and business activities are defined as valued added, and earnings for labor and salaried work are defined as wage or salary earnings.[10]

To set the context, figure 2.7 shows labor productivity (valued added per worker) in industry and services as a ratio of the labor productivity in agriculture, as measured from the macrostatistics for the countries included in this analysis. Recall that figure 2.2 presented the same information for the regions of the world. The two figures tell a consistent story: macrostatistics show significant productivity differentials between

FIGURE 2.6 **The Seasonality of Farm Work Is an Important Factor in the Distribution of Workdays Each Month for Adult Rural Workers between Farm and Nonfarm Work**

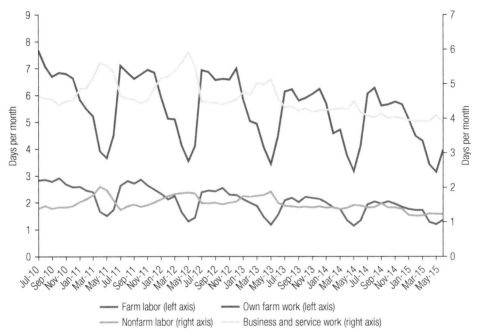

Source: VDSA (Village Dynamics in South Asia) surveys; ICRISAT (International Crops Research Institute for the Semi-Arid Tropics).

agriculture and other sectors. The APG varies by country in figure 2.7 and by region in figure 2.2, but in all cases, labor would appear to be much more productive outside of agriculture.

How Large Is the Agriculture Productivity Gap in Sub-Saharan Africa?

Not only is labor productivity in Sub-Saharan Africa measured to be low relative to other regions, but Sub-Saharan Africa has the highest cross-sectoral productivity gap, based on macrostatistics (figure 2.7). McCullough (2017) examines gaps in labor productivity between agriculture and other sectors using two measures: a per worker measure (a good proxy for the macroestimate of output per worker); and a per hour measure (output produced per hour spent in each sector). The key finding is that the large labor productivity gaps between sectors observed in the national accounts data, or a per person estimate, shrink significantly when labor productivity is measured using the actual time spent on each activity, or a per hour estimate (figure 2.8). The APG disappears for Ethiopia, whereas a gap remains for the other countries (Malawi, Tanzania, and Uganda).

These are important insights on labor productivity gaps but come with a caveat about the data. As mentioned, despite the quality and detail of LSMS-ISA surveys, these

FIGURE 2.7 **Across the Six Countries Analyzed, Macrostatistics Show That Labor Productivity Is Higher in Industry and Services Than in Agriculture**

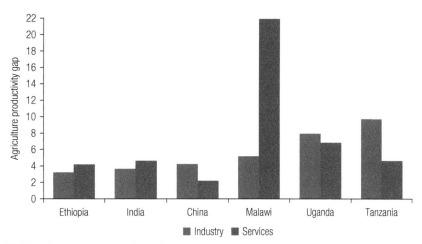

Source: World Development Indicators, World Bank, https://data.worldbank.org/products/wdi.

Note: Bars represent the average productivity gap (ratio of average labor productivity in industry or services to the average labor productivity in agriculture) from 2011 to 2015.

FIGURE 2.8 **Gaps in Labor Productivity Observed across Sectors Diminish When a Measure Based on Hours Worked, Rather Than the Primary Sector of Work, Is Used**

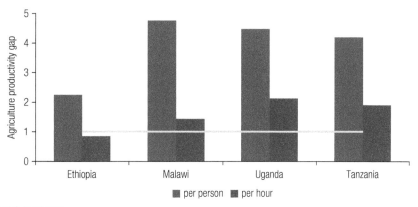

Source: McCullough 2017.

Note: Bars represent ratio of nonagriculture output per unit of labor to agriculture output per unit of labor, using two measures: per person employed (based on declared main occupation); and per hour worked. A ratio of 1, marked by the yellow line, indicates no gap in labor productivity between agriculture and other sectors.

labor productivity estimates may still reflect some measurement bias (associated with the end-of-season recall bias in labor supply).

How Unproductive Is Agricultural Labor in China?

Following three decades of stellar performance, averaging double-digit annual growth, as China transitions to a "new normal" with more moderate economic growth, a key question is whether China can sustain its past pattern of growth with labor transitioning from agriculture to other sectors. In other words, how much surplus labor remains in rural areas? And perhaps more importantly, what is the size of the gap between agricultural and nonagricultural labor productivity? The issue of the size of APG is dealt with here, and the issue of how efficiently labor markets function is discussed later in the chapter.

The findings on labor allocation across sectors in China, presented in the previous section, imply that labor productivity in agriculture is underestimated by a factor of two (recall that the estimate of effective labor supplied to agriculture from microdata is 14.7 percent, which is a little less than half the estimate from macrostatistics that 31.4 percent of the labor force is employed in agriculture). This means, as also noted, that the size of the nonagricultural workforce is underestimated. Simple arithmetic suggests that nonagricultural labor productivity is overestimated by about 24 percent. When these simple adjustments are taken into account, the labor productivity differential across sectors, or the APG, vanishes.

Going back to the microdata, figure 2.9 shows how more accurate accounting can affect estimates of agricultural labor productivity. As expected, a more accurate estimate of labor input (using value added per worker from crop cultivation as a proxy) shows significantly higher average productivity per worker compared to the estimate using the full time of individuals whose main occupation is declared to be agriculture—irrespective of the time they actually spend in agriculture (which is the assumption

FIGURE 2.9 Average Labor Productivity in China Is Significantly Higher Using Actual Labor Time Spent on Agriculture Instead of Assuming "Agricultural Workers" Spend All Their Work Time in Agriculture

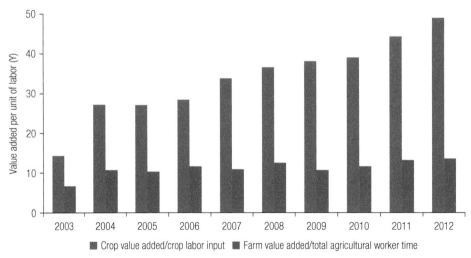

Source: RCRE (Research Center for Rural Economy) surveys, 2003–13.
Note: Y = Chinese yuan.

maintained in macrostatistics on sectoral labor). The estimated labor productivity per worker is significantly lower than labor productivity per day spent in crop production.

Why Do So Many Workers Remain in Agriculture in India?

A more elaborate and comprehensive assessment of the productivity gap across sectors that rural households are engaged in emerges from the VDSA (Village Dynamics in South Asia) surveys. Before proceeding to the APG, it is useful to set the context for why households engage in multiple activities. Using the declared primary or "main" occupation of each working adult, households are classified as farm, nonfarm, or mixed, depending on whether all members work only in agricultural, only nonagricultural, or in both types of activities.[11] However, individuals often participate in secondary activities, so to maintain a distinction between household typology and the source of income, the actual income received is aggregated across all members in two broad categories, agriculture and nonagriculture. The results (figure 2.10, panel a) show that average annual household incomes (that is, the sum of agricultural and nonagricultural incomes) are almost similar for pure farm and pure nonfarm households. Mixed households (those participating in both farm and nonfarm activities), however, have much higher earnings than specialized households, demonstrating the benefits of livelihood diversification.

FIGURE 2.10 Returns to Labor from Farm and Nonfarm Activities in India Vary by How Labor Is Measured, 2010–14

Average earnings from different sources by type of household

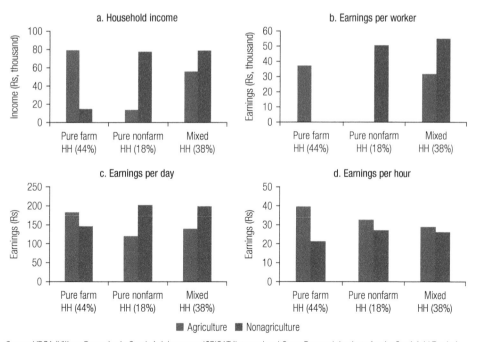

Source: VDSA (Village Dynamics in South Asia) surveys; ICRISAT (International Crops Research Institute for the Semi-Arid Tropics).
Note: Percentages in parentheses show share of sample in each category of household types. HH = household; Rs = Indian rupees.

When household income is normalized by the number of workers classified based on the sector of their primary occupation (panel b), earnings per nonfarm worker in a pure nonfarm household are on average 35 percent higher than earning per farm worker in a pure farm household. Even within mixed households, the earnings for non-farm workers are on average 73 percent higher than for farm workers. The APG is lower than indicated by macrostatistics, but there is still a significant gap in labor productivity between a farm worker and a nonfarm worker.

Taking into account the time actually spent on farming activities, in terms of days and hours, panel c shows the difference in earnings per day between farm and nonfarm activities (grossly defined) is much less than the difference in earnings per worker. Importantly, farmers who participate in both farm and nonfarm work earn more from their farm activities than from their nonfarm activities, which might explain their attraction to agriculture.

Finally, considering the actual hours spent on each activity, an even starker picture emerges (panel d). Returns to labor use in farming are now higher for all types of households engaged in farming, regardless of whether the household is classified as farm, nonfarm, or mixed based on the main occupation of household members. For farm households, the hourly earnings from agriculture are almost double the hourly earnings from nonagricultural activities. Importantly, workers in nonfarm households and mixed households also earn more per hour spent on agricultural work (but with a smaller differential) than from nonagricultural work, again, providing insights on the likely rationale for their continued involvement in agricultural activities.

The main conclusion that emerges is that farmers appear to be rational in staying in agriculture, because the returns to the labor they expend in agriculture are higher than returns they expect from nonfarm activities they may be able to pursue. In other words, nonagricultural work perhaps may be a "filler" for their downtime. The implication for policy and strategy is to reduce the seasonality in agriculture by increasing irrigation or through diversification into higher-valued crops and nonfarm activities.

The discussion so far has focused on broadly categorizing households as either "farm" or "nonfarm" based on the stated main occupations of household members. Yet, households and their individual members engage in multiple activities (even within the broad categories of farm and nonfarm). How does the profile of labor productivity, defined as earnings per person, change when individual (though still highly aggregated) activity categories are considered? To do this, jobs (activities individuals participate in) are allocated to six categories: farm work, livestock work, farm labor (on other than own farms), nonfarm labor, business and service activities, and salaried work. The same three definitions of labor—per worker (as used in macrostatistics), per day, and per hour of labor supplied to each activity—are applied to each activity. The results are displayed in figure 2.11. Figure 2.11, panel a, shows the earnings per worker. Except for labor, earnings from business/service activities and

FIGURE 2.11 **How Labor Is Measured Completely Changes the Relative Attractiveness of Agriculture Work in India, 2010–14**
Annual average labor earnings

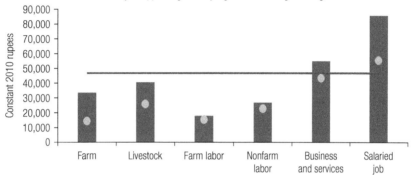

a. Per worker

On a per worker basis, earnings from business/service activities and salaried jobs appear significantly higher than earnings from agriculture.

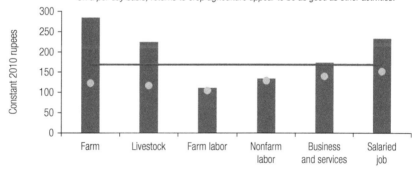

b. Per day

On a per day basis, returns to crop agriculture appear to be as good as other activities.

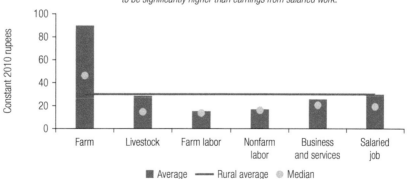

c. Per hour

On a per hour basis, earnings from agriculture in India appear to be significantly higher than earnings from salaried work.

■ Average ── Rural average ● Median

Source: VDSA (Village Dynamics in South Asia) surveys; ICRISAT (International Crops Research Institute for the Semi-Arid Tropics).

salaried jobs appear significantly higher than earnings from agricultural activities. The differences are robust, as indicated by the consistent pattern in median wages, shown as a green dot in the middle of each column. These results are consistent with macrostatistics in showing a significant divergence between agricultural (crops and livestock) and nonfarm activities.

The earnings profile changes significantly when earnings per day are considered (panel b). Returns to farm work (crop agriculture) now appear to be better, on average, than other activities, and returns to livestock are similar to salaried work (and more than business and services). The reason for this dramatic shift in the earnings profile is that agricultural work requires fewer days per year because it is seasonal, in contrast to the regular daily work of a salaried job.

Finally, the profile shifts even more dramatically when using hours of labor input by activity (panel c). Total labor hours used are lower in agriculture (recall that farmers on average spend a considerable amount of time in other activities). On a per hour basis, earnings from farm work appear to be significantly higher than earnings from salaried work—a complete reversal of the profile based on per worker earnings (panel a). Considering that labor on the farm is used for crops and livestock (the vast majority of smallholders practice integrated crop-livestock production), the returns to the effort (measured in hours) invested in these activities provide a rationale for why farmers may be reluctant to give up agriculture to seek seemingly "better" nonfarm jobs.

One remaining concern is the potential for measurement errors in household reporting other than for labor use (that is, potential end-of-season recall bias, which is reduced because VDSA surveys collect data on a monthly basis). These errors may introduce systematic biases by farm size, as some studies suggest (for potential biases related to land measurement, see Carletto et al. 2016; for potential biases in farmer-reported output, see Desiere and Jolliffe 2018, and Gourlay, Kilic, and Lobell 2017). The key question then is whether the results on the reversal of labor productivity gaps reflect other potential reporting biases, likely correlated with farm size. This does not appear to be the case with the VDSA sample. Annex 2C shows the estimates of labor productivity for each land class (landless, small, medium, and large farmers), using broadly defined agricultural and nonagricultural activities (for ease of presentation) (panels a–c). The comparison shows that although mismeasurement of labor productivity is correlated with farm size, it is not due to any apparent small-farmer reporting bias. For landless and small farmers, the labor productivity gap narrows or disappears when moving from per worker to per hour labor productivity, but for medium and large farmers the gap reverses—with agricultural labor productivity significantly higher on a per hour basis compared to the per worker measure.

Alternatively, considering any systematic differences in labor productivity by the level of education of the household, defined by the educational attainment of the household head, annex 2D shows that although labor productivity is higher for the more educated households, consistent with the idea of selection based on human capital, the shift from higher labor productivity in nonagricultural activities on a per worker basis to higher labor productivity in agricultural activities on a per hour basis is consistent across all levels of educational attainment (figure 2D.1). Importantly, average productivity per day is correlated with education level, with daily earnings higher for farm-based work than nonfarm work at all levels of education, providing further rationale for why individuals at different levels of education might persist with agriculture as an occupation.

Misallocation? Understanding the Agricultural Wage Gap

The discussion so far has focused on average labor productivity and the specific issue of measurement errors in the accounting for labor input in NAS. Correct accounting for labor either greatly diminishes (in African countries) or eliminates (in China and India) the APG. In itself, this is an important finding suggesting that perhaps agriculture may not be as unproductive (considering the amount of labor put into it) as might appear from NAS. But, as noted, the size of the APG does not speak to the issue of misallocation. To detect potential misallocation of labor, the focus needs to be on the gaps in the marginal productivity of labor in different sectors, which would be reflected in a wage gap.

So, what is the evidence on wage gaps? A large AWG would suggest labor market distortions, perhaps due to some wedge or friction in labor mobility. Identifying and addressing these wedges or frictions might release labor trapped in the low-productivity sector (presumably agriculture) to move to a more productive (and remunerative) sector, resulting in economy-wide productivity gains. As noted, the *hukou* system is often cited as such a barrier to labor mobility (Herrendorf and Schoellman 2018; Adamopoulus et al. 2017).

A simple comparison of average wages across sectors, however, is not helpful, because wages for different activities reflect different levels of skills or ability. As discussed, adjustments for human capital based on observed characteristics, for example education level, help explain some of the wage differentials but do not account for selection based on unobserved skills or ability (Hicks et al. 2017; Herrendorf and Schoellman 2018). Controlling for such effects requires, ideally, earnings data from individuals who participate in both agricultural and nonagricultural work. Using such data from Kenya and Indonesia, Hicks et al. (2017) find insignificant gains in earnings from individuals who switched from agricultural to nonagricultural jobs. Similar results are obtained by Herrendorf and Shoellman (2018), using panel data from the United States, showing that wage gains for "switchers" are relatively small, suggesting much smaller barriers to reallocation of labor than generally perceived based on macrostatistics.

Turning to the case studies discussed in this section, for the four African countries examined, McCullough (2017) does not analyze wages or the AWG. She finds instead an "employment gap," which accounts for the difference between the per worker and per hour average labor productivities. The existence of unemployed or underemployed labor may well reflect potential barriers to labor mobility, but this issue of potential misallocation remains unaddressed for these countries.

Analysis of the AWG is feasible from the data for China and India. For China, farm wage is estimated as the village average daily wage paid for hired farm labor. Nonfarm wage is measured as the actual daily wage for household members working in nonfarm activities, but only activities that individuals engage in outside the township are considered.[12] This comparator reflects the opportunity cost of household labor, appropriate to understand the farm and nonfarm labor allocation decisions. Worker selection is tested using observed individual characteristics (age, gender, education, nature of work, health status of individuals, and controlling for farm size, whether household has surplus labor within the household, and year fixed effects). Whether individuals participate in more than one activity at a time is not observed in the data, so unobserved ability, skills, or motivation are thus not controlled for (along the lines of Hicks et al. [2017]). Nevertheless, the findings based on controlling only for observable characteristics provide important new insights on the functioning of China's rural labor markets.

Without controlling for individual characteristics, the unadjusted or unconditional wage gap shows that the wage rate for labor supplied by rural households to nonfarm activities (considering only activities outside the township) is lower than the wage paid for labor that is hired-in to perform agricultural activities (figure 2.12). That is, the unadjusted AWG appears to be negative. This finding may appear counterintuitive, but it is consistent with a likely lower opportunity cost for an aging, relatively less educated, and possibly unhealthier workforce selecting into farm work. As such, raw comparisons of average farm and nonfarm wages (across all workers, ignoring age, sex, or health status) may not be a valid comparison. This bias holds, even if attention is restricted to adult male workers engaged in nonfarm work—also shown in figure 2.12 with a marginally smaller but still substantial gap. Wages paid to hired-in farm labor remain at a premium, and this premium has risen over time.

Testing the existence of the AWG controlling for individual characteristics provides a more robust test for misallocation of labor (or the existence of a rural labor surplus). And the econometric results confirm the widely held but casual observation that labor markets in China, including in rural areas, appear to be competitive, despite the frictions attributed to the current system of residency permits (*hukou*) and land rights. It is important to note that the personal characteristics of labor hired in for agricultural tasks are not known, whereas the characteristics of household members supplying nonfarm labor are observed. A reasonable assumption is that workers hired to provide agricultural labor are able-bodied, relatively skilled, and probably hired at times of

FIGURE 2.12 **Trends in Farm and Nonfarm Wages in China: Agricultural Wage Workers Earn a Premium Wage, Which Has Risen over Time**

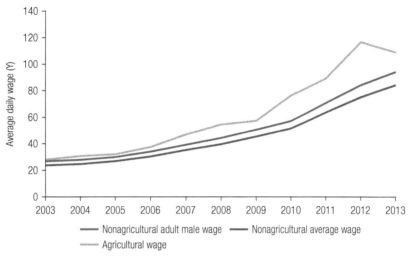

Source: RCRE (Research Center for Rural Economy) surveys, 2003–13.
Note: Y = Chinese yuan.

peak labor demand associated with the crop growth cycle. As such, the model tests the influence of the demographic and health characteristics of household members supplying nonfarm labor in explaining how far their wages deviate from the observed agricultural market wages.

The results from a wage differential model confirm that controlling for observed personal characteristics, adult male wages for farm or nonfarm work do not appear to be statistically different (see annex 2E). The difference fluctuates by year but in no systematic fashion. These results also suggest that the wage differential reflects the opportunity cost of labor remaining in rural areas, reflecting the traditional gender bias in wage rates, human capital, and health condition (physical ability).[13]

The analysis of data from India reveals a pattern like the one observed in China, namely, that farm wages appear to be higher than the wages for nonfarm work that household members are engaged in. Using wage rates from the village-level survey and comparing wages for hired agricultural labor with wages for nonfarm casual labor at the nearest market (instead of in the village itself), figure 2.13 shows that wages for farm work are higher than casual nonfarm wages throughout the year. The wage trend reveals seasonal fluctuation, with reverse-AWG highest during periods of land preparation (at or just before the monsoon rains start), but the difference persists throughout the year.

A similar pattern emerges from the wage rates derived from the household survey, for individuals participating in farm and nonfarm labor work. Restricting attention

FIGURE 2.13 **Wages for Farm Work Are Higher Than Casual Nonfarm Wages throughout the Year at the Village Level in India**

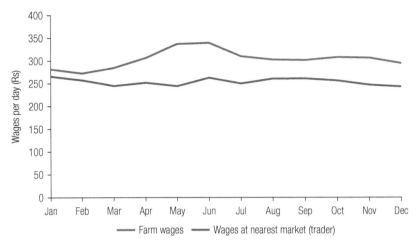

Source: VDSA (Village Dynamics in South Asia) surveys, 2009–14.
Note: Rs = Indian rupees.

FIGURE 2.14 **Wages Reported by Households Confirm the Reverse Wage Gap for Male Workers, but Not Female Workers**
Farm and nonfarm wages by gender, household level

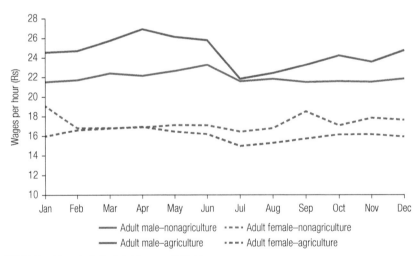

Source: VDSA (Village Dynamics in South Asia) surveys, 2009–14.
Note: Rs = Indian rupees.

to adult males and females, figure 2.14 shows a significant difference between the male and female labor markets. For males, farm wages are higher than nonfarm wages, as observed with data from the village-level survey (figure 2.13). For females, however, a positive AWG is observed for most months except the lean agricultural

TABLE 2.1 **Urban-Rural Daily Wage Premiums for Male and Female Workers and Cost of Living Differences in India**
Per capita per day

Nominal wages	Rural	Urban	Premium
Casual males	149.3	178.8	1.20
Casual females	103.3	108.8	1.05
Regular males	322.3	469.9	1.46
Regular females	201.6	366.2	1.82
Poverty line (2011/12)	27.2	33.3	1.22

Source: ILO 2018; Government of India 2014.

period from February to March. This pattern appears to be consistent with withdrawal of females from the labor force since 2004/05, a phenomenon observed in national sample surveys (Chatterjee, Murgai, and Rama 2015; Pande 2017). The positive AWG suggests frictions restricting women's participation in nonfarm activities, even though nonfarm wages are higher than farm wages. These frictions may be due to social norms (Pande 2017) or disutility associated with work outside the home or off the farm (Baysan et al. 2019). The reverse-AWG for males is consistent with rapid and faster growth in real agricultural wages than nonagricultural and urban wages, also since 2004/05, and the widely perceived "shortage" of labor for agricultural work.

What emerges from these findings is that local markets appear to be working for male labor, with surplus labor likely keeping local wages lower than the agricultural wages. In other words, compared to the options available, it appears rational to work in agriculture as a laborer rather than in the nonfarm sector. It must be reiterated that this represents the local labor market situation, and perhaps the accessible (likely rural) nonagricultural activities are not yet remunerative enough to pull labor completely out of agriculture.

Although these findings provide limited evidence of misallocation at the local level, a key question is whether the wage gap persists along the gradient from remote rural to urban areas. This remains an open question and an area for further research. Recent work by Chatterjee, Murgai, and Rama (2015) suggests that the rural-urban divide, in terms of jobs opportunities, is not as clear-cut as might be perceived. Additional evidence, providing a rationale for the lack of mass migration from rural to urban areas, is provided by the rural-urban average casual labor wages. Average wage rates derived from the 2011/12 National Sample Survey Office survey, taken from International Labour Organization (ILO 2018), are summarized in table 2.1. In nominal terms there is a premium attached to urban wages for males in both the casual and regular labor markets. For females, the premium for casual wages is negligible, but the premium for regular worker wages is substantial. These differences are in nominal terms, however. Adjustment for the differences in cost of living (COL) between rural and urban areas is needed to make them truly comparable. Using the national rural and urban poverty lines estimated by the (then) Planning Commission's "Expert Group to Review the Methodology and Measurement of Poverty" (Government of India 2014) as benchmarks for the COL (averages over all rural and urban areas), the COL premium is also given in table 2.1. What emerges is that regular workers (males but especially females) command a significant premium relative to the COL. But the wage differences for casual labor do not cover the basic cost-of-living differentials between urban and rural areas. That is, even from the nationally representative survey, and using national averages, there appears to be little evidence to support the case for any significant misallocation of labor. Attention needs to more squarely focus on facilitating the creation of better (more remunerative) jobs in the nonfarm sector to "pull" labor out of the farm sector, while investing in human capital and skills to help rural labor access better jobs.

Implications for Accelerating Productivity Growth and Structural Transformation

Microempirical evidence from three diverse regions of the world—four countries in East Africa, India in South Asia, and China in East Asia—consistently suggest that potentially large, systematic measurement errors underlie the gap in labor productivity between agriculture and other sectors that is observed in macrostatistics. Labor use in agriculture appears to be typically overestimated; hence labor productivity in agriculture is systematically underestimated. APG estimated from microdata is significantly lower in three of the African countries (Malawi, Tanzania, and Uganda), and nonexistent in China and India. The most granular data from India even suggest a reverse APG: that is, labor productivity per hour appears to be higher in agriculture than most other activities that rural household members participate in. These findings provide insights on why agricultural household members may want to stay in agriculture: for the effort that they put in, returns are as high or better than the alternatives they face.

Although the disappearance of APG in China, or the reverse APG in India, challenges the standard narrative based on macrostatistics about how unproductive agriculture might be, it does not address the issue of misallocation. Establishing misallocation requires comparing marginal productivities of labor, or wages, in functioning rural labor markets. And the evidence on wage gaps does not provide strong evidence on misallocation. In China, wages for work on and off the farm appear to have equalized, despite the *hukou* system, widely considered to be a wedge in labor markets and the basis of potential misallocation of labor. The findings on India are even more dramatic, with agricultural wages typically higher than nonfarm labor wages for agricultural households. These findings suggest local equilibria, indicating little evidence on barriers restricting the functioning of local labor markets. Whether there are other major wedges restricting spatial labor mobility in India—for example, along the rural-urban gradient—is not obvious but cannot be ruled out. This remains an agenda for further research.

These results have significant policy implications. One implication is that although there are likely policies and market failures with potential to create "frictions" in labor markets, the data from China and India suggest that local labor markets are quite competitive, and as optimizing economic agents, households appear to be maximizing their returns. The findings from Chinese data clearly confirm strong worker selection, in the sense of Hicks et al. (2017). That is, worker demographic characteristics (education, age, gender) and health status explain the observed differences in wages of farm and nonfarm workers. This finding of the equalization of wages, and by implication marginal productivities, is important for China, given the current labor market distortions (embodied in the *hukou* system), because it questions the potential productivity gains by removing the policy distortion. It puts the onus of productivity growth back on innovation and human capital deepening.

The data from India provide a more nuanced insight. With agricultural wages higher than local nonfarm labor wages for males, instead of wedges or frictions there appear to be insufficient nonfarm job opportunities to attract male labor out of agriculture. Female labor markets, however, do suggest frictions, perhaps social, that make nonfarm wage labor jobs unattractive to women—a finding consistent with the recent evidence on the withdrawal of women from the labor force.

Examining the constraints and opportunities to enhance productivity in the non-farm sector (both rural and urban) are beyond the scope of this chapter. A relevant question for further research remains how the seasonally underutilized rural labor (as highlighted in figure 2.6) can be best harnessed for more productive uses. Because this surplus labor is seasonal and part time, and the returns to the time spent in agricultural work are high, an important challenge for promoting faster structural transformation is providing gainful employment or better and more attractive jobs to rural residents closer to their farms to better meet the needs of seasonally underemployed or unemployed agricultural workers.

One option may be to reduce the seasonality of agriculture through temporal and spatial diversification, for example by raising cropping intensity with irrigation or encouraging cultivation of high-value crops, which are also typically more labor intensive. Another may be to encourage investment in rural nonfarm activities as well as to raise the productivity of rural nonfarm activities. There is evidence that rural nonfarm employment is countercyclical to the agricultural growing season—a trend that could be significantly scaled up through investments in nonfarm enterprises.

The findings also point toward a rethinking of development strategy, which has traditionally concentrated on large urban centers, to give greater emphasis on the development of small towns and secondary cities, as suggested by a growing body of literature (Christiaensen and Kanbur 2018; Gibson et al. 2017; Christiaensen et al. 2017). More vibrant small towns closer to the villages might offer greater opportunities for seasonal employment opportunities. In either case, the structure and role of the food system is going through an enormous transformation and offers significant potential for jobs and income opportunities that are often underappreciated as drivers of structural transformation (Gollin and Probst 2015; Townsend et al. 2017; World Bank 2007). Urbanization and rising incomes drive profound changes in consumer demand for food, as well as changes in the structure of the food industry, offering significant potential for better jobs along agri-food value chains, and in agroprocessing and rural industry.

Annex 2A. Microdata Sources for Measuring Labor Productivity in China and India

China

The data used for China are from a large annual household survey administered each year by the Research Center for the Rural Economy (RCRE) under the Ministry of Agriculture of China. This is a nationally representative survey that covers all provinces. The survey has been carried out annually since 1986 but was significantly redesigned in 2003. The data available for this analysis are from 2003 to 2013, covering all provinces with a sample size of about 20,000 each year. The survey is comprehensive in collecting data on all major agricultural activities at the farm/household level; detailed data on individual household members including on demographics (gender, age, education in terms of years of schooling, self-reported health condition, profession, family composition); details on individual members' employment and earnings, including income received from labor supplied to nonfarm activities, the time allocated (in days) to on-farm work, and time allocated to nonfarm work—recorded separately by the days spent on nonfarm work within the township and outside the township. Data on agricultural inputs include details on hired labor in terms of days and daily wage rates paid.

Daily wage earnings from farm and nonfarm activities are used as proxy measures for labor productivity. Since not all households hire labor, the estimated median wage paid at the village level each year is used to represent the market wage for agriculture labor. Nonfarm wage is estimated as the daily earnings for each individual household member, considering only the earnings from work performed in nonfarm jobs outside the township.

India

The source of data for India is the Village Dynamics in South Asia (VDSA) panel surveys conducted by the International Crops Research Institute for the Semi-Arid Tropics (ICRISAT). The VDSA project has collected data from 30 villages located in humid and semi-arid tropics (SAT) regions of India, with 18 villages located across 6 states in semi-arid tropical regions of India (Andhra Pradesh, Gujarat, Karnataka, Madhya Pradesh, Maharashtra, and Telangana), and another 12 villages located in three states in East India (Bihar, Jharkhand, and Odisha). These states provide a range of poor and least developed states in East and Central India to the more developed and advanced states in the South and West of India. The surveys are unique in that they were administered by enumerators resident in each village for the survey period from 2009 to 2014, with data collected on a monthly basis. Total number of sample households were 1,346 in 2010 and increased to 1,366 in 2014.

The VDSA surveys are designed as a purposive sample and are not statistically representative of either the states or the zones where the samples are collected. The survey is done with a specific structure that has been followed since the original panel surveys were launched as part of the ICRISAT Village-Level Studies program in 1975, to study systematic differences between four categories of households—the landless, and small, medium, and large farmers. The data are known for their quality and detail of data collected. Nevertheless, given that they are from a handful of villages with equal weights given to landless, small, medium, and large farmers, a legitimate concern is generalizability of the results. On this, a comparison with nationally representative secondary data sources such as the National Sample Surveys (NSS) on employment and unemployment and the farm situation survey indicates that that sample is not in any sense an outlier, but quite representative of the broader agroecological environment.

The VDSA panel surveys collected information on almost all aspects of economic activities that households and individual members are engaged in, including data on labor supplied by individuals for both agricultural and nonagricultural activities. The data include details on the number of days individuals report working on different activities, as well as the hours they spent on each activity. Net income from wage labor (both farm and nonfarm works), businesses and services, and salaried work are reported directly, along with time use of households' members in those activities. Net returns to farm and livestock activities are calculated based on the detailed input and output data collected for each agricultural activity. Labor returns from farm activities are estimated at the household level as actual labor time spent in the farm activities, aggregated from each plot and crop cultivated by the farm household in the sample. To avoid the complexity of measuring actual returns from the livestock activities, the estimated median wage for hired labor at the village level is used to estimate the labor returns from households' labor time used in livestock-rearing activities.

Annex 2B. Distribution of Workdays by Farm and Nonfarm Activities in a Typical Month for an Average Adult Worker in India

FIGURE 2B.1   Workdays Spent on Different Activities in a Typical Month for an Average Adult Rural Worker

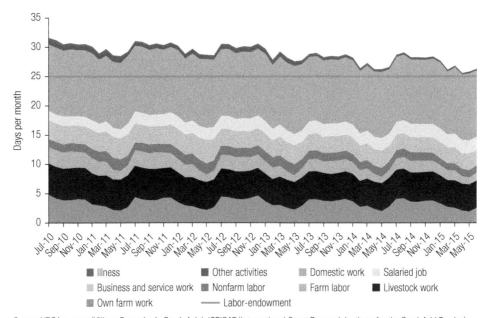

Source: VDSA surveys (Village Dynamics in South Asia); ICRISAT (International Crops Research Institute for the Semi-Arid Tropics).
Note: A full-time work month is assumed to be 25 days.

Annex 2C. Labor Productivity Differences by Farm Size

FIGURE 2C.1 **Average Earnings by Farm Size, India, 2010–15**

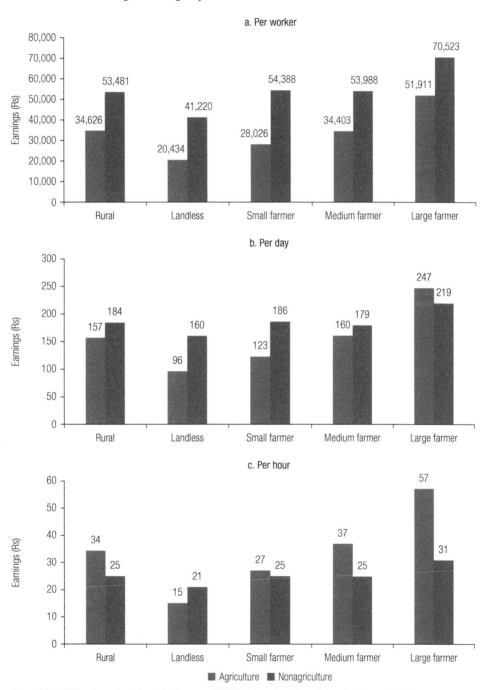

Source: VDSA (Village Dynamics in South Asia) surveys; ICRISAT (International Crops Research Institute for the Semi-Arid Tropics).
Note: Rs = Indian rupees (constant 2010).

Annex 2D. Labor Productivity Differences by Education Level

Data from India show that average productivity per day is correlated with education level, with daily earnings higher for farm-based work than nonfarm work at all levels of education.

FIGURE 2D.1 **Annual Earnings by Education Level, India, 2010–14**

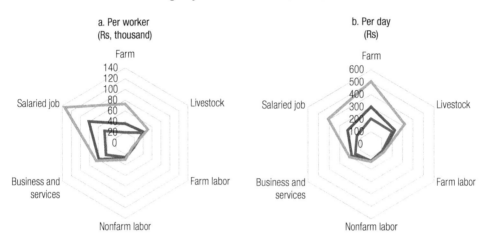

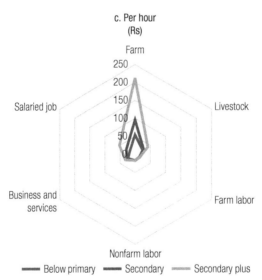

Source: VDSA (Village Dynamics in South Asia) surveys; ICRISAT (International Crops Research Institute for the Semi-Arid Tropics).
Note: Below primary refers to less than 5 years of formal schooling; secondary refers to formal schooling between 5 and 12 years; and secondary plus refers to formal schooling for more than 12 years. Rs = Indian rupees.

Annex 2E. Drivers of Wage Differentials between Farm and Nonfarm Work in China

TABLE 2E.1   **Regression Results**

Dependent variable log (nonfarm wage/farm wage)	Basic	Extended	For workers (15–65) Basic	For workers (15–65) Extended
Constant	0.29	0.26	0.29	0.27
Age-gender (ref. male adult)				
Female adult	−0.27***	−0.25***	−0.265***	−0.254***
Male youth	−0.06***	−0.06***	−0.06***	−0.062***
Female youth	−0.24***	−0.25***	−0.243***	−0.243***
Male old	−0.35***	−0.28***		
Female old	−0.59***	−0.53***		
Male child	−0.22**	−0.22**		
Log (schooling years)		0.01*		0.009*
Labor supply ratio (total worktime/total available labor days)		0.036**		0.036**
Profession (ref. operation agriculture labor)				
Operation nonagriculture labor		0.037*		0.038*
Hired labor		−0.045***		−0.044***
Other nonagriculture professions		−0.04**		−0.038**
Health category (ref. excellent)				
Good		−0.019		−0.021*
Moderate		−0.053*		−0.051*
Bad		−0.159**		−0.168**
Lost work capability		−0.133		−0.132
Log (farm size)		0.006		
Year dummies (ref. 2004)				
2005	0.002	0.002	0.001	−0.001
2006	−0.022	−0.026	−0.026	−0.027
2007	−0.141***	−0.134***	−0.144***	−0.139***
2008	−0.069***	−0.066***	−0.071***	−0.069***
2009	0.009	0.011	0.007	0.009
2010	−0.5**	−0.046*	−0.052*	−0.048*
2011	0.023	0.029	0.022	0.023
2012	−0.008	−0.005	−0.011	−0.007
2013	0.069***	0.069**	0.069**	0.069***
Observations	15,714	15,486	15,559	15,401
Adjusted R-squared	0.126	0.128	0.126	0.127

Source: RCRE (Research Center for Rural Economy) surveys, 2004–13.

Notes

1. This chapter is based on two background papers for this volume: Gautam and Ahmed (2019a); Rada and Fuglie (2019).

2. In economics, the "agency problem" arises when one person (the agent) is able to take actions that affect another person (the principal) and the two parties have different information sets and conflicting interests. In the case of labor markets, it is costly for employers (principals) to supervise employees (agents), and employees may not always act in the best interest of the employer (such as shirking or producing low-quality work).

3. For the five case studies and a synthesis paper, see Rada and Fuglie (2019).

4. See http://surveys.worldbank.org/lsms/programs/integrated-surveys-agriculture-ISA.

5. Wedges and frictions are often used interchangeably in the literature. These are distinguished here to maintain a difference, with wedges referring to barriers that are created by an existing policy, whereas frictions often reflect an underlying market failure calling for policy options to address them.

6. Hicks et al. (2017) also apply the same analysis for the gap across workers employed in the rural and urban areas.

7. *Hukou* refers to the residency permit granted to individuals under China's current registration system.

8. Notably, the estimate of labor in agriculture is significantly lower than the share of rural *hukou* holders (44 percent), recognizing labor mobility despite the *hukou* system.

9. One piece of missing data is the hourly labor input for livestock, for which only reported days are available. To derive labor productivity per hour, data from cost of labor are used, divided by the village wage rates for livestock activities (as available from a separate "village-level" survey module).

10. Earnings from agriculture, livestock, and business activities are derived as net returns to family labor (gross revenues less all purchased inputs, including the value of hired labor and imputed land rent). For labor and salaried work, it is effectively the daily or hourly wage (wages for labor and earnings divided by days or hours for salaried workers).

11. Rural workers are classified as farm or nonfarm workers based on their reported main occupations in agricultural and nonagricultural sectors, respectively. But, as noted, workers often pursue secondary activities in addition to their stated main occupational sector.

12. Labor supplied for nonfarm activities within the township is not used because this may include community work and time spent on other social obligations, including reciprocity, which may or may not reflect the true market wages.

13. The constant term in the regression tests for the adult male real wage differential, controlling for provincial and year fixed effects and individual characteristics. The results indicate that the constant is significant in only 3 of the 10 years for which data are available, and in only 4 out of the 31 provinces. The nonfarm-to-farm differential is negative in 2007 and 2008, positive in 2013, and not statistically different for the other years.

References

Abdulai, A. and C. Delgado. 1999. "Determinants of Nonfarm Earnings of Farm-Based Husbands and Wives in Northern Ghana." *American Journal of Agricultural Economics* 81: 117–30.

Adamopoulos, T., L. Brandt, J. Leight, and D. Restuccia. 2017. "Misallocation, Selection, and Productivity: A Quantitative Analysis with Panel Data from China." NBER Working Paper 23039, National Bureau of Economic Research, Cambridge, MA. doi: 10.3386/w23039.

Adamopoulos. T., and D. Restuccia. 2014. "The Size Distribution of Farms and International Productivity Differences." *American Economic Review* 104 (6): 1667–97. doi: 10.1257/aer.104.6.1667.

Ali, D. A., and K. Deininger. 2015. "Is There a Farm Size-Productivity Relationship in African Agriculture? Evidence from Rwanda." *Land Economics* 92: 317–43.

Arthi, V., K. Beegle, J. De Weerdt, and A. Palacios-Lopez. 2018. "Not Your Average Job: Measuring Farm Labor in Tanzania." *Journal of Development Economics* 130 (C): 160–72.

Barrett, C. 1996. "On Price Risk and the Inverse Farm Size-Productivity Relations." *Journal of Development Economics* 52: 193–215.

Barrett, C., M. Bellemare, and J. Hou. 2010. "Reconsidering Conventional Explanations of the Inverse Productivity-Size Relationship." *World Development* 38 (1): 8–97.

Baysan, C., M. H. Dar, K. Emerick, and E. Sadoulet. 2019. "The Agricultural Wage Gap Within Rural Villages." Working Paper, Tufts University.

Bazzi, S. 2017. "Wealth Heterogeneity and the Income Elasticity of Migration." *American Economic Journal: Applied Economics* 9 (2): 219–55.

Binswanger, H. P., K. Deininger, and G. Feder. 1995. "Power, Distortion, Revolt and Reform in Agricultural Land Relations." In *Handbook of Development Economics*, Volume 3, edited by J. Behrman and T. N. Srinivasan, 2659–772. Elsevier, B.V.

Bryan, G., S. Chowdhury, and A. M. Mobarak. 2014. "Underinvestment in a Profitable Technology: The Case of Seasonal Migration in Bangladesh." *Econometrica* 82 (5): 1671–1748.

Bryan, G., and M. Morten, 2017. "The Aggregate Productivity Effects of Internal Migration: Evidence from Indonesia." NBER Working Paper 23540, National Bureau of Economic Research, Cambridge, MA. http://www.nber.org/papers/w23540.

Carletto, C., S. Gourlay, S. Murray, and A. Zezza. 2016. "Land Area Measurement in Household Surveys: Empirical Evidence and Practical Guidance for Effective Data Collection." LSMS Guidebook Series. Washington DC, World Bank. https://siteresources.worldbank.org/INTLSMS /Resources/3358986-1423600559701/LandGuide_web_final_b.pdf.

Carletto, C., S. Gourlay, and P. Winters. 2015. "From Guestimates to GPStimates: Land Area Measurement and Implications for Agricultural Analysis." *Journal of African Economics* 25: 593–628.

Carter, M., and K. Wiebe. 1990. "Access to Capital and Its Impact on Agrarian Structure and Productivity in Kenya." *American Journal of Agricultural Economics* 72 (5): 1146–50.

Caselli, F. 2005. "Accounting for Cross-Country Income Differences." Chapter 9 in *Handbook of Economic Growth* Vol. 1, Part A 679–741. Elsevier B. V.

Caselli, F., and W. J. Coleman. 2005. "The U.S. Structural Transformation and Regional Convergence: A Reinterpretation." *Journal of Political Economy* 109 (3): 584–616. https://doi.org/10.1086 /321015.

Chatterjee, U., R. Murgai, and M. Rama. 2015. "Job Opportunities along the Rural-Urban Gradation and Female Labor-Force Participation." Poverty and Equity Global Practice Working Paper No. 4, World Bank, Washington, DC.

Christiaensen, L., J. De Weerdt, B. Ingelaere, and R. Kanbur. 2017. "Migrants, Towns, Poverty and Jobs: Insights from Tanzania." Policy Research Working Paper 8340, World Bank, Washington, DC.

Christiaensen, L., and R. Kanbur. 2018. "Secondary Towns, Jobs and Poverty Reduction." *World Development* 108: 219–220.

Collier, P., and S. Dercon. 2014. "African Agriculture in 50 Years: Smallholders in a Rapidly Changing World?" *World Development* 63: 92–101. doi: 10.1016/j.worlddev.2013.10.001.

Cordoba, J. C., and M. Ripoll. 2009. "Agriculture and Aggregation." *Economics Letters* 105 (1): 110–12.

de Janvry, A., C. Duquennois, and E. Sadoulet. 2018. "Labor Calendars and Rural Poverty: A Case Study for Malawi." Working Paper, University of California at Berkeley.

de Janvry, A., and E. Sadoulet. Forthcoming. "Transforming Developing Country Agriculture: Push and Pull Approaches." *World Development.*

Deininger, K., and D. Byerlee. 2012. "The Rise of Large Farms in Land Abundant Countries: Do They Have a Future?" *World Development* 40: 701–14.

Deininger, K., S. Jin, Y. Liu, and S. K. Singh. 2018. "Can Labor-Market Imperfections Explain Changes in the Inverse Farm Size-Productivity Relationship? Longitudinal Evidence from Rural India." *Land Economics* 94 (2): 239–58.

Deininger, K., S. Savastano, and F. Xia. 2017. "Smallholders' Land Access in Sub-Saharan Africa: A New Landscape?" *Food Policy* 67: 78–92.

Desiere, S., and D. Jolliffe. 2018. "Land Productivity and Farm Size: Is Measurement Error Driving the Inverse Relationship?" *Journal of Development Economics* 130: 84–98. doi: 10.1016/j. jdeveco.2017.10.002.

Eastwood, R., M. Lipton, and A. Newell. 2010. "Farm Size." In *Handbook of Agricultural Economics*, Volume 4, edited by P. L. Pingali and R. E. Evenson, 3323–97. Elsevier.

Eswaran, M., and A. Kotwal. 1986. "Access to Capital and Agrarian Production Organization." *Economic Journal* 96: 482–98.

Feder, G. 1985. "The Relation between Farm Size and Farm Productivity: The Role of Family Labour, Supervision and Credit Constraints." *Journal of Development Economics* 18 (2/3): 297–313.

Foster, A., and M. Rosenzweig. 2017. "Are There Too Many Farms in the World? Labor-Market Transaction Costs, Machine Capacities and Optimal Farm Size." NBER Working Paper 23909, National Bureau of Economic Research, Cambridge, MA.

Gautam, M., and M. Ahmed. 2019a. "Misallocation, Labor Productivity and Structural Transformation." Background paper for *Harvesting Prosperity: Technology and Productivity Growth in Agriculture*, World Bank, Washington, DC.

———. 2019b. "Too Small to Be Beautiful? The Farm Size and Productivity Relationship in Bangladesh." *Food Policy* 84 (April): 165–75.

Geertz, C. 1968. *Agricultural Involution: The Process of Ecological Change in Indonesia.* Berkeley, CA: University of California Press.

Gibson, J. G. Datt, R. Murgai, and M. Ravallion. 2017. "For India's Rural Poor, Growing Towns Matter More Than Growing Cities." *World Development* 98: 413–29.

Gollin, D. 2018. "Gaps, Wedges, Measurement Problems, and Strategies: Lessons from Recent Literature on Agricultural Productivity." Briefing Note for the Agriculture Global Practice, World Bank, Washington, DC.

Gollin, D., D. Lagakos, and M. Waugh. 2014. "The Agricultural Productivity Gap." *Quarterly Journal of Economics* 129 (2): 939–93. https://doi.org/10.1093/qje/qjt056.

Gollin, D., S. Parente, and R. Rogerson. 2007. "The Food Problem and the Evolution of International Income Levels." *Journal of Monetary Economics* 54: 1230–55.

Gollin, D., and L. Probst. 2015. "Food and Agriculture: Shifting Landscapes for Policy." *Oxford Review of Economic Policy* 31: 8–25.

Gollin, D., and C. Udry. 2019. "Heterogeneity, Measurement Error, and Misallocation: Evidence from African Agriculture." NBER Working Paper 25440, National Bureau of Economic Research, Cambridge, MA.

Gourlay, S., T. Kilic, and D. Lobell. 2017. "Could the Debate Be Over? Errors in Farmer Reported Production and Their Implications for the Inverse Scale-Productivity Relationship in Uganda." Policy Research Working Paper 8912, World Bank, Washington, DC. http://documents .worldbank.org/curated/en/242721505231101959/pdf/WPS8192.pdf.

Government of India. 2014. *Report of the Expert Group to Review the Methodology and Measurement of Poverty.* New Delhi: The Planning Commission.

Haggblade, S., P. Hazell, and T. Reardon. 2010. "The Rural Nonfarm Economy: Prospects for Growth and Poverty Reduction." *World Development* 38 (10): 1429–41. https://doi.org/10.1016/j.worlddev.2009.06.008.

Helfand, S., and E. Levine. 2004. "Farm Size and Determinants of Productive Efficiency in the Brazilian Center-West." *Agricultural Economics* 31: 241–49.

Heltberg, R. 1998. "Rural Market Imperfections and the Farm Size–Productivity Relationship: Evidence from Pakistan." *World Development* 26 (10): 1807–26. https://doi.org/10.1016/S0305-750X(98)00084-9.

Henderson, H., and A. G. Isaac. 2017. "Modern Value Chains and the Organization of Agrarian Production." *American Journal of Agricultural Economics* 99: 379–400. https://doi.org/10.1093/ajae/aaw092.

Herrendorf, B., and T. Schoellman. 2015. "Why Is Measured Productivity So Low in Agriculture?" *Review of Economic Dynamics* 18 (4): 1003–22. doi: 10.1016/j.red.2014.10.006.

———. 2018. "Wages, Human Capital and Barriers to Structural Transformation." *American Economic Journal: Macroeconomics* 10 (2): 1–23. https://doi.org/10.1257/mac.20160236.

Hicks, J. H., M. Kleemans, N. Y. Li, and E. Miguel. 2017. "Reevaluating Agricultural Productivity Gaps with Longitudinal Microdata." NBER Working Paper 23253, National Bureau of Economic Research, Cambridge, MA. doi: 10.3386/w23253.

Hsieh, C., and P. Klenow. 2009. "Misallocation and Manufacturing TFP in China and India." *Quarterly Journal of Economics* 124: 1403–48.

Huffman, W. E. 1980. "Farm and Off-Farm Work Decisions: The Role of Human Capital." *Review of Economics and Statistics* 62 (1): 14–23.

ILO (International Labour Organization). 2018. *India Wage Report: Wage Policies for Decent Work and Inclusive Growth*. Geneva: ILO.

Ingelaere, B. L. Christiaensen, J. De Weerdt and R. Kanbur. 2018. "Why Secondary Towns Can Be Important for Poverty Reduction—A Migrant Perspective." *World Development* 105: 273–82.

Jayne, T. S., J. Chamberlin, L. Traub, N. Sitko, M. Muyanga, F. K. Yeboah, W. Anseeuw, A. Chapoto, A. Wineman, C. Nkonde, and R. Kachule. 2016. "Africa's Changing Farm Size Distribution Patterns: The Rise of Medium-Scale Farms." *Agricultural Economics* 47: 197–214. https://doi.org/10.1111/agec.12308.

Julien, J., B. Bravo-Ureta, and N. Rada. 2019. "Assessing Farm Performance by Size in Malawi, Tanzania, and Uganda." *Food Policy* 84: 153–64.

Key, N., 2019. "Farm Size and Productivity Growth in the United States Corn Belt." *Food Policy* 84: 186–95.

Kislev, Y., and W. Peterson. 1982. "Prices, Technology, and Farm Size." *Journal of Political Economy* 93: 578–95.

———. 1996. "Economies of Scale in Agriculture: A Reexamination of the Evidence." In *The Economics of Agriculture: Papers in Honor of D. Gale Johnson*, edited by J. M. Antle and D. A. Sumner, 156–70. Chicago: University of Chicago Press.

Liu, Y., W. Violette, and C. Barrett. 2016. "Structural Transformation and Intertemporal Evolution of Real Wages, Machine Use, and Farm Size-Productivity Relationships in Vietnam." IFPRI Discussion Paper 01525, International Food Policy Research Institute, Washington, DC.

MacDonald, J. M., P. Korbe, and R. Hoppe. 2013. *Farm Size and the Organization of U.S. Crop Farming*. Economic Research Report 152, Economic Research Service, US Department of Agriculture, Washington, DC.

MacDonald, J. M., and W. McBride. 2009. "The Transformation of U.S. Livestock Agriculture: Scale, Efficiency, and Risks." Economic Information Bulletin 43, Economic Research Service, US Department of Agriculture, Washington, DC.

McCullough, E. B. 2017. "Labor Productivity and Employment Gaps in Sub-Saharan Africa." *Food Policy* 67: 133–52. https://doi.org/10.1016/j.foodpol.2016.09.013.

McMillan, M., and D. Headey. 2014. "Introduction—Understanding Structural Transformation in Africa." *World Development* 63: 1–10. https://doi.org/10.1016/j.worlddev.2014.02.007.

McMillan, M., and D. Rodrik. 2011. "Globalization, Structural Change and Productivity Growth." In *Making Globalization Socially Sustainable*, edited by M. Bacchetta and M. Jense, 49–84. International Labour Organization (ILO) and World Trade Organization (WTO).

Mishra, A. K., and B. K. Goodwin. 1997. "Farm Income Variability and the Supply of Off-Farm Labor." *American Journal of Agricultural Economics* 79: 880–87.

Munshi, K., and M. Rosenzweig. 2016. "Networks and Misallocation: Insurance, Migration, and the Rural-Urban Wage Gap." *American Economic Review* 106 (1): 46–98. http://dx.doi.org/10.1257/aer.20131365.

Muyanga, Milu, and T. S. Jayne. 2019. "Revisiting the Farm Size-Productivity Relationship Based on a Relatively Wide Range of Farm Sizes: Evidence from Kenya." *American Journal of Agricultural Economics* 101 (4): 1140–63. https://doi.org/10.1093/ajae/aaz003.

Olfert, M. 1992. "Nonfarm Employment as a Response to Underemployment in Agriculture." *Canadian Journal of Agricultural Economics* 40: 443–58.

Otsuka, K., Y. Liu, and F. Yamauchi. 2016. "Growing Advantage of Large Farms in Asia and Its Implications for Global Food Security." *Global Food Security* 11: 5–10. https://doi.org/10.1016/j.gfs.2016.03.001.

Pande, R. 2017. "Getting India's Women into the Workforce: Time for a Smart Approach." International Growth Centre, London School of Economics and Political Science. https://www.ideasforindia.in/topics/social-identity/getting-indias-women-into-the-workforce-time-for-a-smart-approach.html.

Peterson, W., and Y. Kislev. 1986. "The Cotton Harvester in Retrospect: Labor Displacement or Replacement?" *Journal of Economic History* 46: 199–216.

Rada, N., and K. Fuglie. 2019. "New Perspectives on Farm Size and Productivity." Background paper for *Harvesting Prosperity: Technology and Productivity Growth in Agriculture*, World Bank, Washington, DC. Also published in *Food Policy* 84 (April): 147–52.

Rada, N., S. Helfand, and M. Magalhães. 2019. "Agricultural Productivity Growth in Brazil: Large and Small Farms Excel." *Food Policy* 84: 176–85.

Rada, N., C. Wang, and L. Qin. 2015. "Subsidy or Market Reform? Rethinking China's Farm Consolidation Strategy." *Food Policy* 57: 93–103.

RCRE (Research Center for Rural Economy). Household Panel Surveys conducted by the Research Center for Rural Economy, Beijing.

Restuccia, D., and R. Rogerson. 2008. "Policy Distortions and Aggregate Productivity with Heterogeneous Establishments." *Review of Economic Dynamics* 11: 707–20.

Restuccia, D., and R. Santaeulalia-Llopis. 2017. "Land Misallocation and Productivity." NBER Working Paper 23128, National Bureau of Economic Research, Cambridge, MA. doi: 10.3386/w23128.

Restuccia, D., D. T. Yang, and X. Zhu. 2008. "Agriculture and Aggregate Productivity: A Quantitative Cross-Country Analysis." *Journal of Monetary Economics* 55 (2): 234–50.

Rogerson. R. 2017. "Structural Transformation and Productivity Growth: Cause or Effect?" Princeton University. Unpublished.

Rosenzweig, M. 1980. "Neoclassical Theory and the Optimizing Peasant: An Econometric Analysis of Market Family Labor Supply in a Developing Country." *Quarterly Journal of Economics* 94: 31–55.

Schimmelpfennig, D. 2016. *Farm Profits and Adoption of Precision Agriculture*. Economic Research Report 217, Economic Research Service, US Department of Agriculture, Washington, DC.

Schultz, T. W. 1964. *Transforming Traditional Agriculture*. New Haven, CT: Yale University Press.

Sen, A., 1962. "An Aspect of Indian Agriculture." *Economic Weekly*, Annual Number 14, 243–66.

Sheng, Y., and W. Chancellor. 2019. "Exploring the Relationship Between Farm Size and Productivity: Evidence from the Australian Grain Industry." *Food Policy* 84: 196–204.

Sheng, Y., S. Zhao, K. Nossal, and D. Zhang. 2014. "Productivity and Farm Size in Australian Agriculture: Reinvestigating the Returns to Scale." *Australian Journal of Agricultural and Resource Economics* 59: 16–38.

Skoufias, E. 1993. "Labor Market Opportunities and Intrafamily Time Allocation in Rural Households in South Asia." *Journal of Development Economics* 40: 277–310.

———. 1996. "Intertemporal Substitution in Labor Supply: Micro Evidence from Rural India." *Journal of Development Economics* 51: 217–37.

Townsend, R., R. M. Benfica, A. Prasann, M. Lee, and P. Shah. 2017. *Future of Food: Shaping the Food System to Deliver Jobs.* Washington, DC: World Bank. http://documents.worldbank.org/curated/en/406511492528621198/Future-of-food-shaping-the-food-system-to-deliver-jobs.

VDSA (Village Dynamics in South Asia). Household Panel Surveys Conducted by the International Crops Research Institute for the Semi-Arid Tropics (ICRISAT), Hyderabad, India. http://vdsa.icrisat.ac.in/vdsa-index.htm.

Vollrath, D. 2007. "Land Distribution and International Agricultural Productivity." *American Journal of Agricultural Economics* 89: 202–16.

———. 2009. "How Important Are Dual Economy Effects for Aggregate Productivity?" *Journal of Development Economics* 88: 325–34.

———. 2014. "The Efficiency of Human Capital Allocations in Developing Countries." *Journal of Development Economics* 108 (2014): 106–18.

Wang, X., F. Yamauchi, K. Otsuka, and J. Huang. 2016. "Wage Growth, Landholding, and Mechanization in Chinese Agriculture." *World Development* 86: 30–45. https://doi.org/10.1016/j.worlddev.2016.05.002.

World Bank. 2007. *World Development Report 2008: Agriculture for Development.* Washington, DC: World Bank.

———. 2018. World Development Indicators, World Bank, Washington, DC (accessed January 10, 2018), http://databank.worldbank.org/data/reports.aspx?source=world-development-indicators#.

Yamauchi, F. 2016. "Rising Real Wages, Mechanization, and Growing Advantage of Large Farms: Evidence from Indonesia." *Food Policy* 58: 62–69. https://doi.org/10.1016/j.foodpol.2015.11.004.

Young, A. 2013. "Inequality, the Urban-Rural Gap, and Migration." *Quarterly Journal of Economics* 128 (4): 1727–85.

3. Investing in Innovation

Agriculture Innovation Policy in a Changing Global Context

Agriculture is heavily dependent on productivity for growth, as described in chapter 1. Whereas about one-third of world economic growth comes from increases in total factor productivity (TFP) (Jorgenson, Fukao, and Timmer 2016), in agriculture, TFP accounts for about three-quarters of output growth at the global level and virtually all growth in industrialized countries (see chapter 1). This reliance on productivity reflects agriculture's dependence on inherently limited natural resources like land and water. It is these resource constraints that give rise to concerns that population may overreach the world's capacity to produce food sustainably and affordably.

The fact that agricultural productivity has been able to grow sufficiently to meet rising demand is no accident. It reflects to a large degree a deliberate choice to commit resources to agricultural research and development (R&D). In what are today's advanced industrialized nations, the establishment of public agricultural research institutions in the latter part of the nineteenth century helped set in motion a process of technological and structural transformation of their agricultural systems (Ruttan 1982). That process continues today and has been extended to include most of the world. Nearly all countries now have national agricultural research institutions of one form or another. In addition, international agricultural research partnerships like CGIAR[1] have been established (Alston, Dehmer, and Pardey 2006), and the private sector has increased its role in generating new technology for agriculture (Fuglie et al. 2011).

Because positive externalities from R&D lead to an undervaluation of innovation in the marketplace, governments have a critical role in creating the knowledge capital required for economic growth.[2] Positive externalities from knowledge capital have had a central role in economic growth theories going back to Arrow (1962). As articulated by Romer (1990), once new knowledge is created, it is available everywhere to all forever, except as constrained by insufficient human capital to make use of it and by legal or other measures to protect the intellectual property of inventors. This should be good news for developing countries—in principle, they could just borrow freely what the advanced countries have already invented.

But taking advantage of advanced country knowledge in agriculture is likely to be much more challenging than the general knowledge capital envisioned by Romer. For one, because agricultural technology is sensitive to environmental conditions, much more attention must be given to local adaptation. Second, as environments change (through the coevolution of pests and diseases, the degradation of water and land resources, and climate change), new threats to agricultural productivity emerge and new technologies need to be developed as existing technologies become obsolete. The need to pursue continued research just to maintain agricultural productivity has been dubbed "the curse of the Red Queen" (Olmstead and Rhode 2002).[3] In advanced agricultural systems "maintenance research" may constitute around 40 percent of total R&D (Sparger et al. 2013). A third factor, not unique to but probably accentuated in agriculture, is that because producers tend to be highly dispersed, heterogeneous, and predominantly smallholders, agricultural technologies are taken up relatively slowly. These characteristics of agriculture suggest that (1) there is need for local R&D capacity for technology adaptation; (2) there will be a relatively long lag between R&D spending and when that spending results in significant improvements to aggregate farm productivity; (3) productivity gains will be achieved only when new technologies are widely disseminated among producers, which requires a favorable enabling environment for technology adoption; and (4) these productivity gains will dissipate unless R&D capital is renewed (Huffman and Evenson 2006; Alston et al. 2010). Moreover, market failures plague the supply and uptake of agricultural innovations because of the knowledge spillovers from R&D, asymmetric information among producers unfamiliar with new technologies, and missing markets for risk and capital. Such failures provide a rationale for a strong public role in stimulating technical change in agriculture, especially through investment in agricultural R&D and other supportive policies.

However, science and innovation policies for agriculture are not just about spending adequately on R&D. To be effective, these policies need to adjust and reform in the face of twenty-first century global developments in agricultural science and technology as well as the changing nature of food and agricultural markets.

One global development has been the move toward freer international trade in food and agricultural products. As a result, agricultural trading patterns and domestic production will become more closely aligned with comparative advantage. An implication for policy makers is that comparative advantage should guide agricultural R&D investments more than in the past. Under freer trade, national food security can be achieved without requiring self-sufficiency in food staples, and more attention can be given to higher-value commodities and more diverse food and nonfood products.

A second major development is structural change in agricultural and food marketing systems, including the rise of supermarkets and vertically coordinated market chains. These changes are being driven by demands from the rising middle class for food product diversity, quality, and safety, and by economies of scale in food processing and marketing. Structural changes in food systems in turn are changing the types of technologies needed—at the farm and along agri-food value chains.[4] For example, private food quality standards and supply chain management decisions made by food companies are affecting the types of commodities demanded and how they are grown, stored, transported, and processed. Food marketing and processing companies are becoming important players in creating and disseminating new technologies to farmers in order to meet these standards. Although the growing presence of agribusiness in marketing chains does not overcome the pervasive market failures in agricultural innovation systems, these structural developments open up new opportunities for public-private partnerships. Chapter 5 describes the changes occurring in global food and agricultural marketing systems and how this is affecting technological innovation and dissemination along market value chains.

A third change in the global context is the emergence of important new sources of advanced agricultural science and technology. Historically, universities and government laboratories in developed countries have been a primary source of major scientific and technological developments in agriculture. Although these advanced research institutes continue to be important, the global landscape in agricultural sciences is becoming more diverse. In particular, national research systems in some large emerging economies, notably Brazil, India, and China, have expanded their capacities in agricultural sciences, and are likely to become increasingly important sources of technology spillovers for global agriculture.

Fourth is the emergence of the private agricultural input supply sector as a provider and disseminator of new technologies. Agribusiness firms specializing in crop seed and biotechnology, agrochemicals, veterinary medicines, and farm machinery are investing considerable resources in R&D. Several of these firms have established discovery laboratories and international research networks to develop and disseminate proprietary innovations in agriculture for global markets. This offers developing countries the possibility of harnessing the private sector to increase the flow of international technology transfer and expand the overall national R&D effort.

For developing-country research systems to be able to access these new global technology sources for use in their local adaptive research, they need to not only develop effective relationships and networks with these sources, but also enact and enforce laws and regulations governing intellectual property rights, the movement of genetic material, health and safety, and new technology registration and approval. These issues are taken up in detail later in this chapter.

Finally, the rapidly expanding access to new digital information and communication technologies (ICT) around the world offers new modalities for knowledge development and dissemination. The impressive (though not yet complete) penetration of Internet and mobile phone networks even to remote rural areas of low-income countries presents new opportunities for disseminating technical information and educational materials for farmers and farm service providers. Although digital technologies substantially reduce the cost of information, the successful application to improve farm practices and promote technology adoption in agriculture obviously depends on the quality and local relevance of the messaging. Chapter 4 discusses how ICT and other technology delivery innovations may help speed up the adoption of agricultural technologies by smallholder farmers in developing countries.

The rest of this chapter lays out specific ways policy makers can provide incentives to stimulate the pace of agricultural innovation. Throughout, the focus is on how developing countries can both increase the investment in agricultural research and the quality and effectiveness of that investment. In pursuing these two goals, the discussion stresses the importance of the twin agendas of improving the enabling environment and of raising the human and innovative capabilities that populate it.

The next section focuses on public investment in agricultural R&D and reviews evidence of its impact on productivity. It shows that the pattern of this R&D spending has been highly uneven across developing countries, and that productivity growth achieved by these countries has been highly correlated with past spending on agricultural R&D. Furthermore, the social rate of return to these research investments has been high, suggesting that most countries significantly underinvest in agricultural research. Especially among many of the world's poorest countries, low funding and limited capacities continue to plague their agricultural R&D systems.

The third section describes specific measures that countries can take to improve funding and performance of public agricultural research systems, including design issues that affect incentives within these public institutions. The fourth section focuses on the growing role of the private sector in agricultural innovation, and how policies can provide incentives to stimulate increased R&D investment and technology transfer by the business sector. It presents a systemic view of the interactions and necessary conditions for a well-functioning agricultural innovation system.

Agriculture R&D Spending Worldwide: Increasing but Uneven

Although new discoveries and innovations can arise from many sources—not only in research laboratories and experiment stations—spending on dedicated R&D activities has been shown to be a key indicator of creation of "knowledge capital" that generates sustained economic growth (Evenson and Westphal 1995). For public agricultural R&D, spending by developing countries tripled (in constant 2011 purchasing power parity [PPP] dollars) from $7,686 million to $22,406 million between 1981 and 2011 (table 3.1). Spending rose faster in developing countries than developed countries, with the developing-country share of the total rising from about 38 percent in 1981 to 53 percent by 2011.

The pattern of agricultural R&D investment remains highly uneven across the world, however. Relative to the size of the agricultural sector (as a share of agricultural gross domestic product [GDP], per hectare of cropland, and per agricultural worker), there is a considerable gap across global regions. In 2011, developed-country

TABLE 3.1 **Spending on Public Agricultural R&D by Developing Countries Tripled between 1981 and 2011, but Agricultural R&D Investment Remains Uneven across Regions**

Region	Agricultural R&D expenditure		Agricultural research intensity		
			R&D/ GDP	R&D/ cropland	R&D/ agricultural labor
	1981	2011	(%)	Trend	($/hectare)	($/worker)
	(2011 PPP$, million)		(%)	Trend	($/hectare)	($/worker)
Public agricultural R&D						
Latin America and the Caribbean	2,820	4,689	1.06	↑	24.98	106.71
Brazil	1,397	2,484	1.65	↑	31.09	173.70
West Asia and North Africa	978	2,253	0.49	↑	26.45	79.55
East Asia and South Asia	2,709	13,572	0.46	↑	27.11	22.28
China	970	7,768	0.73	↑	46.94	39.56
Southeast Asia	859	2,005	0.34	↓	17.64	16.87
South Asia	880	3,798	0.30	↑	17.15	12.93
Sub-Saharan Africa	1,179	1,893	0.38	↓	9.25	10.11
Developing-country total public R&D	7,686	22,406	0.52	↑	22.91	25.79
Developed-country total public R&D	11,522	18,426	3.25	↓	52.22	1,311.15
Transition-country total public R&D	1,246	1,533	0.44	↑	6.18	53.78
World public agricultural R&D	20,454	42,365	0.81	↓	26.83	46.49
Developing-country share of public R&D	38%	53%				
Private agricultural R&D	6,374	12,939	0.25	↑	8.19	14.20
CGIAR R&D	158	707	0.01	↑	0.45	0.78
Total world agricultural R&D	*26,981*	*56,011*	*1.07*	*↑*	*35.47*	*61.47*

Sources: Research and development (R&D) spending for developing countries and CGIAR is from ASTI (2018); public R&D spending for developed countries is from Heisey and Fuglie (2018); and private agricultural R&D spending is from Fuglie (2016). Agricultural GDP, cropland area, and agricultural labor are for 2011 and from World Development Indicators (World Bank 2018). Trend in R&D/GDP is over 2001–13.

Note: CGIAR = CGIAR Consortium of International Agricultural Research Centers (see note 1); GDP = gross domestic product; PPP = purchasing power parity; R&D = research and development.

investment in agricultural R&D was equivalent to 3.25 percent of agricultural GDP, $52 per hectare of cropland, and $1,300 per farm worker. For developing countries, these measures of research intensity were 0.52 percent of agricultural GDP, $23 per hectare of cropland, and $26 per farm worker (table 3.1). Among developing countries, Brazil and China invested relatively high amounts in agricultural R&D, while Sub-Saharan Africa and South Asia had the lowest spending relative to agricultural GDP, farmland, and the size of the agricultural work force. Moreover, in Sub-Saharan Africa, since at least 2001, agricultural research spending has been growing more slowly than the growth of the agricultural output, so that its research intensity is declining.

The expenditures on public agricultural R&D reported in table 3.1 refer to funding support for several types of research organizations. Although the most prominent are usually government-run research centers, a significant share of public research funding is directed toward universities, and a portion may also be provided to the private or nongovernment sectors. Agricultural research at universities is an integral part of advanced degree training and human capacity development. In the 1960s, many developing countries in Asia launched long-term initiatives to strengthen agricultural higher education. India currently allocates more than one-third of its total public agricultural R&D spending to universities (Lele and Goldsmith 1989; Pal and Byerlee 2006). Countries in Sub-Saharan Africa, on the other hand, route less than 10 percent of public agricultural R&D funding through universities (Pardey and Beintema 2001). The quality of graduate training programs at African agricultural universities has been undergoing a serious decline, and this decline is crippling the ability of these institutions to train African scientists and create effective agricultural research capacity in this region (Eicher 2004; Osuri, Nampala, and Ekwamu 2016).

Besides government-supported R&D, table 3.1 also shows global estimates of agricultural R&D by private companies and the CGIAR Consortium of International Agricultural Research Centers. Worldwide, spending on agricultural R&D by private agribusiness grew from $6.4 billion to $12.9 billion between 1981 and 2011 (constant 2011 PPP$).[5] Although the bulk of this private R&D spending was by companies located in high-income countries, a significant share of their R&D effort is likely directed to meet the rising demand for improved farm inputs in developing countries. In 2014, about 28 percent of farm input sales by companies spending at least $100 million/year on agricultural R&D were in developing countries (Fuglie 2016). If this R&D spending was apportioned toward their markets served, it would imply that these companies allocated about $3.3 billion in agricultural R&D for developing countries. The fourth section of this chapter contains more detailed information on trends in private agricultural R&D investment—by both multinational and domestic firms, in specific developing countries.

The final category of institutions investing in agricultural R&D in table 3.1 is by the CGIAR Consortium of International Agricultural Research Centers (see note 1). CGIAR supports research on agricultural technology, natural resources management, and policies affecting food and agriculture in developing countries. A significant share of CGIAR research is directed toward crop improvement, especially of major food staples. In 2011, total spending by CGIAR research centers was $707 million, or about 3 percent of the total public agricultural R&D spending in developing countries.[6]

R&D Investment and Agricultural TFP Growth

The evidence linking R&D capacity and investment to productivity growth in agriculture is compelling, whether assessed for specific commodities, at the sector level for a country, or through international comparisons. Studies comparing the long-term performance of national agricultural sectors consistently find that countries that invested more in agricultural R&D achieved higher agricultural productivity growth

(Evenson and Kislev 1975; Craig, Pardey, and Roseboom 1997; Thirtle, Lin, and Piesse 2003; Evenson and Fuglie 2010). Brazil and China, for example, had the highest R&D spending per hectare of cropland among the developing regions shown in table 3.1 and achieved among the world's highest rates of agricultural TFP growth. Sub-Saharan Africa, on the other hand, invested substantially less in agricultural R&D relative to the size of its agricultural sector and had the slowest rate of agricultural TFP growth among major global regions (Fuglie and Rada 2013).

Table 3.2 summarizes results from 27 studies that econometrically estimate the impact of R&D on agricultural growth in developing countries. One of the challenges

TABLE 3.2 Numerous Studies Confirm a Very Strong Relationship between R&D Investment and Agricultural Total Factor Productivity

Study	Geographic coverage	Period	Data	R&D elasticities[a]			
				Total—all sources	National public	CGIAR	Private or international
Craig, Pardey, and Roseboom (1997)	World	1965–1990	88-country panel	0.10	0.10	n.a.	n.a.
Wiebe et al. (2000)	World	1961–1997	88-country panel	0.16	0.16	n.a.	n.a.
Johnson and Evenson (2000)	DC	1960–1989	90-country panel	0.13	0.03	n.a.	0.10
Fulginiti and Perrin (1993)	DC	1961–1984	18-country panel	0.07	0.07	n.a.	n.a.
Craig, Pardey, and Roseboom (1997)	DC	1965–1990	67-country panel	0.09	0.09	n.a.	n.a.
Thirtle, Lin, and Piesse (2003)	DC	1985, 1990, 1995	48-country panel	0.44	0.44	n.a.	n.a.
Fan and Pardey (1998)	Asia	1972–1993	12-country panel	0.17	0.17	n.a.	n.a.
Thirtle, Lin, and Piesse (2003)	Asia	1985, 1990, 1996	11-country panel	0.34	0.34	n.a.	n.a.
Evenson (2003)	Asia	1970–2000	10 food crops	n.a.	n.a.	0.15	n.a.
Evenson and Quizon (1991)	Philippines	1948–1984	9-region panel	0.31	0.31	n.a.	n.a.
Rada and Fuglie (2012)	Indonesia	1985–2005	22-province panel	0.36	0.27	0.09	n.a.
Suphannachart and Warr (2012)	Thailand	1971–2006	National	0.20	0.17	0.04	n.a.
Jin et al. (2002)	China	1981–1995	16-province panel	0.37	0.33	0.04	n.a.
Fan (2000)	China	1975–1997	25-province panel	0.25	0.25	n.a.	n.a.
Fan, Zhang, and Zhang (2002)	China	1970–1997	29-province panel	0.09	0.09	n.a.	n.a.
Pray and Ahmed (1991)	Bangladesh	1947–1981	National	0.12	0.12	0.004	n.a.
Rahman and Salim (2013)	Bangladesh	1948–2008	National	0.13	0.13	n.a.	n.a.
Fan, Hazel, and Thorat (2000)	India	1970–1993	17-state panel	0.30	0.30	n.a.	n.a.

(Table continues on the following page.)

TABLE 3.2 **Numerous Studies Confirm a Very Strong Relationship between R&D Investment and Agricultural Total Factor Productivity** *(continued)*

Study	Geographic coverage	Period	Data	R&D elasticities[a]			
				Total—all sources	National public	CGIAR	Private or international
Evenson, Pray, and Rosegrant (1999)	India	1956–1987	271-district panel	0.17	0.05	0.11	0.01
Rada and Schimmelpfennig (2015)	India	1980–2008	16-state panel	0.28	0.17	0.11	n.a.
Thirtle, Lin, and Piesse (2003)	LAC	1985,1990	15-country panel	0.20	0.20	n.a.	n.a.
Evenson (2003)	LAC	1970–2000	10 food crops	n.a.	n.a.	0.05	n.a.
Fernandez-Cornejo and Shumway (1997)	Mexico	1960–1990	National	0.64	0.13	n.a.	0.50
Rada and Buccola (2012)	Brazil	1985, 1996, 2006	558-district panel	0.03	0.03	n.a.	n.a.
Bervejillo, Alston, and Tumber (2012)	Uruguay	1981–2000	National	0.68	0.57	n.a.	0.12
Thirtle, Hadley, and Townsend (1995)	Africa	1971–1986	22-country panel	0.02	0.02	n.a.	n.a.
Thirtle, Lin, and Piesse (2003)	Africa	1985,1990	22-country panel	0.36	0.36	n.a.	n.a.
Lusigi and Thirtle (1997)	Africa	1961–1991	47-country panel	0.05	0.02	0.03	n.a.
Evenson (2003)	WANA	1970–2000	10 food crops	n.a.	n.a.	0.07	n.a.
Fan et al. (2006)	Egypt	1980–2000	3-region panel	0.25	0.25	n.a.	n.a.
Frisvold and Ingram (1995)	SSA	1973–1985	28-country panel	0.08	0.08	n.a.	n.a.
Block (2014)	SSA	1981–2000	27-country panel	0.20	0.20	n.a.	n.a.
Alene (2010)	SSA	1986–2004	15-country panel	0.20	0.20	n.a.	n.a.
Fuglie and Rada (2013)	SSA	1977–2005	32-country panel	0.08	0.04	0.04	n.a.
Evenson (2003)	SSA	1970–2000	10 food crops	n.a.	n.a.	0.03	n.a.

Source: Fuglie 2018.

Note: CGIAR = CGIAR Consortium of International Agricultural Research Centers (see note 1); DC = developing countries; LAC = Latin America and the Caribbean; n.a. = not applicable; SSA = Sub-Saharan Africa; TFP = total factor productivity; WANA = West Asia and North Africa.

a. The R&D elasticity measures the percentage change in TFP given a 1 percent change in the R&D stock, whereby R&D stock is an accumulation of past R&D spending. All studies considered R&D contributions from national agricultural research systems, and some also took into account R&D contributions from CGIAR, the private sector, or other countries. The "total-all sources" R&D elasticity is the combined effect of innovations from all of these sources.

of assessing the impact of R&D is that the accumulation of R&D capital is a relatively slow process that may take several years to result in measurable effects on productivity. To improve robustness, studies have used long time series with panels of countries or panels of regions within countries. The use of panel data allows for comparison of long-term growth trends among countries or regions that have had different amounts of R&D investment. It also allows these models to test whether R&D spillovers from other regions, the private sector, or CGIAR International Agricultural Research Centers may have also contributed to productivity growth.

The elasticities reported in table 3.2 give the percent change in TFP due to a 1 percent change in R&D capital from these various sources, whereby R&D capital is an accumulation of past investment in R&D, taking into account gestation time for research to result in adopted technology. These elasticities indicate important features about the relative performance of R&D systems across global regions:

- Public investment in agricultural R&D has been closely associated with TFP growth in all developing regions—Asia, Latin America, and Africa.
- R&D-led growth, however, is least developed for Africa. Elasticities of public R&D in Africa average about 0.15, whereas in other regions they average between 0.2 and 0.4. Differences in total elasticities are even more pronounced, due in part to the absence of a significant role for private R&D in Africa.
- Even though CGIAR is a relatively small component of the global agricultural R&D infrastructure and focuses heavily on staple food crops, it has had a noticeable impact on aggregate agricultural TFP growth, particular in Asia and Africa.
- The private sector has been an important source of agricultural technology and TFP growth in Latin America and India.
- For all the studies listed in table 3.2, the elasticity of total R&D is less than 1.0. This implies that R&D spending grows faster than TFP. It also implies that R&D intensity (total R&D spending as a share of GDP) will tend to increase over time. However, as countries develop and with appropriate incentives, the private sector can assume a larger share of total R&D spending.

Returns to Agricultural Research

The most recent studies of returns to R&D confirm the recurrent findings of very high returns overall and in industry and agriculture specifically. Among manufacturing firms in the United States, Bloom, Schankerman, and van Reenen (2013) find a social rate of return to R&D of 45 percent. Doraszelski and Jaumandreu (2013) find similar returns for Spain. Further, recent studies examining Schumpeter's (1934) argument that follower countries, by virtue of being able to use R&D to adopt existing technologies rather than invent them, have shown that returns to R&D rise with a country's distance from the productivity frontier and become very high (Griffith, Redding, and van Reenen 2004; Goñi and Maloney 2017). A social rate of return of around 45 percent implies that the optimal investment is about double current spending levels. But firms underinvest in R&D because private returns are substantially lower than social returns, due to R&D spillovers to other firms and other sectors.

The existing evidence suggests this is not only true for R&D investment in "high-tech" sectors: returns in agriculture are similarly high. The elasticities reported in table 3.2. provide direct evidence that returns to agricultural research spending are of the same order of magnitude as in industry (see box 3.1 for an explanation relating values of R&D

BOX 3.1

R&D Capital, R&D Elasticities, and the Rate of Return to Research

Econometric models that have tried to quantify the relationship between productivity and invest-ment in research typically estimate a model of the following form:

$$\ln(TFP_{it}) = \alpha + \beta \ln(S_{it}) + \gamma X_{it} + \varepsilon_{it} \qquad (1)$$

where, in country or region i at time t, TFP_{it} is an index of total factor productivity; S_{it} is the accumulated stock of research capital from past research investments; X_{it} is a vector of other factors that might affect TFP; and ε_{it} is a random error term to account for things like weather and mismeasurement. The model provides estimates for the α, β, and γ parameters, whereby β is the elasticity of research, or the percent change in TFP given a 1 percent change in research stock. In other words, research produces new technology that, when adopted by farmers, raises their average productivity. Since a change in *TFP* is equivalent to a change in output (relative to some base period), holding inputs constant, the research elasticity β also indicates how technical change affects output net of any increase in inputs that might complement the adoption of a new technology.

Since research is expected to affect the trend growth rate in productivity, the studies listed in table 3.2 in the text have used long time spans of several decades to estimate the relationship in equation 1. Moreover, by using panels of countries or regions, many studies have been able to compare trend productivity growth among regions that have had very different levels of spending on agricultural research. The consistent and robust finding is that *the pattern of past investments in agricultural research explains much of the current growth (and lack of growth) in agricultural TFP around the world*. It lends credence to the importance of this public investment for sustaining and accelerating growth in the farm sector.

The elasticity estimates produced by models like equation 1 also provide evidence on the economic returns to research. Since research and development (R&D) is a long-lived investment, today's spending on R&D raises productivity for several years into the future, until technological obsolescence sets in. Returns to research—the value of future increases in output relative to dollars invested in research—can be derived directly from the elasticities. Abstracting for a moment from the lag structure of R&D, assume that today's investment in R&D generates a permanent increase in TFP (or, equivalently, R&D increases value added—that is, higher output holding inputs or costs fixed). Suppose that R&D spending is equivalent to 1 percent of gross domestic product (GDP) and that the estimated value of the R&D elasticity β is 0.3. Then one year's investment in R&D generates a stream of benefits worth 0.3 percent of GDP each year into the future, giving a social rate of return of 30 percent. In other words, the rate of return to research is β times 100 percent.

Although this "back of the envelope" estimate is a handy way to see the returns to research, a more rigorous analysis of the economics of research spending needs to consider a number of other issues. One is the lag structure of research—how long it takes R&D spending to result in usable technologies that are adopted by farmers, and how long before R&D capital eventually depreci-ates. Another issue is to account for social costs beyond R&D spending that are often necessary to achieve rapid and widespread diffusion of new technologies, such as public extension. Many studies include aggregate research and extension spending or include extension as an additional variable in an econometric model like the one shown in equation 1. A third issue is to account for

(Box continues on the following page.)

R&D Capital, R&D Elasticities, and the Rate of Return to Research *(continued)*

the effects of policies that distort prices and costs. Such policies may affect marginal (social) value of productivity gains in a sector.

Applied studies have used many approaches to determine the lag structure between research investment and productivity growth. Some studies have estimated the relationship directly using time series methods (such as using lagged values of research spending to explain current TFP). Studies have also incorporated a diffusion period—following an initial lag of L years for research to mature into a useable innovation—during which the advance begins to slowly increase aggregate productivity of a farm sector until it is fully disseminated and impact peaks. The productivity effect subsequently declines due to technological obsolescence. These models may allow for 10 or 20 years between research spending and its full impact on productivity. Models may also allow for increases in aggregate productivity to reduce output prices, thus reducing the marginal value of future increases in productivity or output. For a thorough discussion of methods for assessing economic returns to agricultural research, see Alston, Norton, and Pardey (1995).

elasticities to estimates of social returns to research). In addition to these sector-level studies, hundreds of studies have conducted cost-benefit analysis of specific agriculture research projects, comparing R&D spending with the value of benefits from the higher farm productivity achieved from adoption of technologies developed by the R&D. Table 3.3 summarizes findings from a meta-analysis of 292 studies that estimated returns to agricultural research spending in specific countries and commodities (Alston et al. 2000). The median value of the internal rate of return (IRR) to agricultural research in developing countries estimated by these studies was 43 percent.[7] Among commodity groups, the median IRR to research was higher for field crops (43.6 percent) and livestock (53.0 percent) than for tree crops, forestry, and natural resource management (13.6 percent or higher), but even these areas earned median returns generally acceptable for public finance. These exceptional returns from a public investment reflect the fact that the value of productivity improvements in agriculture has been orders of magnitude higher than what governments typically invest in research. Even with long gestation periods, the present value of those benefits is high relative to what has been spent on research. Such high returns suggest persistent underinvestment in research as a welfare-enhancing objective for public policy (Alston et al. 2000).

Revitalizing Public Research

Strengthening the Capacity and Performance of Public Research Systems

In addition to expanding the scientific frontier, public institutions continue to provide much of the new technologies adopted by farmers, especially in developing countries.

TABLE 3.3 **Nearly 300 Studies Have Shown That Returns to Agricultural Research Spending in Specific Countries and Commodities Are Exceptionally High, on Average**

Geographic or commodity area	Median internal rate of return (%)	Number of estimates
Developed countries	46.0	990
Developing countries	43.3	683
Asia-Pacific	49.5	222
Latin America and the Caribbean	42.9	262
West Asia and North Africa	36.0	11
Sub-Saharan Africa	34.3	188
CGIAR and other international agricultural research	40.0	62
All agriculture	44.0	342
Annual crops	43.6	916
Tree crops	33.3	108
Livestock	53.0	233
Natural resource management	16.5	78
Forestry	13.6	60

Source: Alston et al. (2000), based on a meta-analysis of 292 studies on returns to agricultural research conducted since 1953; some studies reported multiple estimates.

Note: CGIAR = CGIAR Consortium of International Agricultural Research Centers (see note 1).

Whereas private research is focused on specific crops and on improving specific inputs—like hybrid seed, agrochemicals, and machinery that can be sold to farmers—public research addresses a much broader range of scientific and technical issues, commodities, and resource constraints. Examples of applied research in which the public sector continues to play a leading role are breeding improved varieties of self-pollinating and orphan crops; farm practices that enhance soil and water conservation; integrated pest and disease management for crops and livestock; integrated crop-livestock production systems; and food safety. Many methods of crop and livestock pest and disease management rely on technologies that require public R&D together with collective implementation to prevent these pests from being reintroduced once under control. Examples of such collective action include successful biological control of the cassava mealybug and eradication of rinderpest disease in cattle in Africa. Although such efforts rely heavily on government support, specific R&D components may be contracted out to private firms, such as development of animal vaccines. Public capacity in agricultural science and technology is also needed to support government regulatory actions permitting the use of new technologies, establishing and enforcing sanitary and phytosanitary standards, and assuring safe food products. The fact that social returns are much higher than private returns to R&D indicate the strong "public good" nature of research benefits, and provide direct evidence of persistent societal underinvestment in R&D.

Despite its high potential payoff, government spending on agricultural research in many developing countries has languished. Since 1980 more than half of the growth in public agricultural R&D spending by developing countries has occurred in just three countries: Brazil, India, and China (the BIC countries) (Pardey et al. 2016). In constant 2009 PPP$, between 1980 and 2011, public agricultural R&D spending in BIC countries grew by a factor of four, from $2.1 billion to $8.2 billion, while for all other developing countries combined, spending roughly doubled from $4.9 billion to $9.8 billion. For Sub-Saharan Africa, spending increased from $1.5 billion to $2.4 billion over this period (more slowly than the rate of growth in agricultural GDP). For most developing countries, spending on agricultural R&D remains very low relative to the size of their agricultural sectors, at far less than 1 percent of GDP (see table 3.1). Some of the same issues that make R&D unattractive to private firms—such as the long time horizon for investments to pay off—can also discourage political support for R&D. But it is not just underinvestment that plagues many of these R&D systems. Problems with institutional design have resulted in unstable funding from year to year; low levels of staff education, retention, and performance; few operational funds available after salaries and fixed costs are met; limited means of performance evaluation; and the special challenges faced by small countries in establishing a critical mass of research capacity.

To address these issues, many countries (both developed and developing) have experimented with various reforms to their public agricultural research systems. These experiences have relevant lessons for countries wishing to strengthen their own systems, recognizing that what works best for any particular country will depend on specific national circumstances. The discussion that follows describes a number of innovations in the financing and performance of public agricultural research systems that have met with some degree of success.

Reforming Public Agricultural Research Institutes

Successful research institutions foster a climate of innovation, in which creativity and collaboration are encouraged and performance is recognized and rewarded. International best practice suggests several factors have contributed to high-performing public research institutes:

Establish Institutional Autonomy

Many public research institutes are located within ministries of agriculture and are subject to government-wide budgetary and human resource rules and regulations. These rules are typically designed to assure hierarchical control of policies or programs and their implementation, but often interfere with the incentives necessary to encourage high performance in research programs.

In 1973 Brazil embarked on a major reform of its federal agricultural research system. It combined its agricultural research institutes under a new public corporation, known as EMBRAPA (Empresa Brasileira de Pesquisa Agropecuária, Brazilian

Agricultural Research Corporation).[8] As an independent public corporation, EMBRAPA had greater flexibility in its management, operations, and human resource policies compared with other government agencies. It also enabled EMBRAPA to diversify funding sources and establish its own policies for engaging in public-private partnerships. As funding for EMBRAPA was increased, it was able to build its human resource capacity, offer salaries competitive with the private sector, and expand collaborative research with universities, the private sector, and foreign partners.

Other countries have adopted a similar organizational model for their public agricultural research system, but not always with the same degree of success as EMBRAPA. The performance of any research organization will be vulnerable to external factors, such as macroeconomic instability or civil conflict. In 1993, Colombia attempted to emulate the Brazilian model by grouping its government agricultural research institutes into CORPOICA (Corporación Colombiana de Investigación Agropecuaria), a public corporation for agricultural research. However, CORPOICA's funding support remained relatively low (at less than 0.5 percent of agricultural GDP, compared with 2 percent of GDP for Brazil's EMBRAPA) and its operations were significantly constrained by civil conflict within the country (Stads et al. 2016). Since 2011, however, financial support for CORPOICA has been substantially increased, and in 2016 a national peace accord was reached, ending the country's long civil war. These factors have significantly improved the prospects for agricultural research and innovation in Colombia. Other countries that have taken a similar approach as Brazil and Colombia by giving greater autonomy to all or part of its public agricultural research system include Chile, Côte d'Ivoire, Indonesia, and Malaysia.

Provide Incentives to Scientists

Research institutes need to provide incentives for aggressive pursuit of high-quality knowledge that is of direct relevance to the local context. As in any research institute, the attraction and motivation of staff are perhaps the central challenges. To provide incentives to scientists, research institutes need to structure their human resource policies to reward performance. Some institutions provide bonuses and promotions to staff whose research has led to demonstrable outputs and impact. Plant breeders, for example, might be remunerated on the basis of area planted to varieties they developed. Another important source of staff remuneration is to provide opportunities for further education, training, and career advancement for staff who consistently perform at a high level. Institutes should avoid pressures to expand staff numbers if it means diluting resources for research and staff development (that is, if expenditure per scientist declines).

One of the key factors behind the success of Brazil's EMBRAPA was the priority it gave to the human resource development of its staff. EMBRAPA provided them with attractive career paths that rewarded performance, and achieved staff retention by offering salary and benefit packages competitive with the private sector. In its early years EMBRAPA was investing as much as 20 percent of its budget in training and staff development, including support for degree programs (Martha, Contini, and Alves 2012). Because of its status as a public corporation, it could offer greater flexibility in its human resource policies than a government agency, in which staff rank and salary are often more closely tied to length of service than performance. In contrast, many public research institutes in developing countries have faced significant challenges in maintaining or upgrading staff quality. In Sub-Saharan Africa, low staff retention, high absenteeism, and salary structures that do not reward performance or are competitive with the private sector are depleting human resources at many public agricultural research institutes (Beintema and Stads 2017).

Ensure Stable and Diversified Financing

Public agricultural research institutions have historically depended on general government revenues for funding, usually as institutional block grants for staff salaries, facility maintenance, and research programs. Some national research institutions in low- and lower-middle-income countries have also relied heavily on donor support from bilateral or multilateral aid programs. Many institutions have suffered from low and unstable funding. To increase total funding and also to reduce budget volatility, public research institutions have experimented with diversifying their sources of financial support.

One potential source of supplementary funding for research is through producer levies. Levies are assessments made on the value of sales or exports of commodities. Revenues from levies may be channeled through producer organizations and used to fund a range of cooperative activities, including research, extension, and market promotion. Governments may give statutory authority to producer associations to impose mandatory levies on all its members when a majority of members are in favor. Levies are mostly used for commodities that are grown commercially and for export, and that are marketed through a limited number of outlets, such as processing mills or ports (which reduces the transaction cost of collecting the levy).

A number of countries have made extensive use of producer levies to support public agricultural research. In Colombia, producer associations have enacted mandatory levies on sales of coffee, sugarcane, oil palm, rice, cotton, and cocoa. Some of these associations have established their own research stations, and others have contracted research through CORPOICA, the main public research institute (Estrada, Holmann, and Posada 2002). In 2013, nearly 40 percent of the total spending on agricultural R&D in Colombia was funded through producer levies (Stads et al. 2016). In Côte d'Ivoire, producer organizations raise research funds through membership fees. In 2014, these organizations financed about 45 percent of the research conducted by Côte d'Ivoire's National Agricultural Research Center (ASTI 2017). Several countries in Sub-Saharan Africa have also used levies to support agricultural research for export commodities, particularly for cocoa, coffee, tea, sugar, and tobacco (Pray, Byerlee, and Nagarajan 2016).

To encourage producers to fund agricultural research, the Australian government matches producer levies dollar for dollar, up to 0.5 percent of gross crop value. The matching provision significantly strengthens the incentive for producers to assess levies for research. When enacted in the 1980s, several commodity groups imposed levies to obtain the maximum government match (Alston et al. 1999). In contrast, producer organizations in the United States, which also have statutory authority to assess levies on commodity sales but with no government match, provide only limited support for research, preferring to allocate most of the levies they do raise for market promotion (Heisey and Fuglie 2018).

Another potential source of research funding is by charging fees for technology products and services. Although government agencies may be prohibited by law from profiting from their own activities, under the public corporation model there is often more flexibility for the research institute to recoup at least some of their costs through user fees. Some product revenues can be raised simply through sales of surplus commodities produced on experiment stations, or licensing fees can be charged for new technologies, such as for foundation seed of improved crop varieties. Generally, however, earnings from technology licensing have not been an important source of revenue for public agricultural research systems, even in high-income countries like the United States (Knudson, Lower, and Jones 2000). Since an important goal of public research is to accelerate productivity growth through rapid adoption of new technologies, these institutions are reluctant to charge high fees that may discourage use. Moreover, public institutions often work in partnership with private companies on commercializing new technology, and seek to avoid activities that would duplicate (and therefore crowd out) commercial endeavors.

Some public research institutes have tried to raise financial support by investing some of their assets into business ventures unrelated to research, such as for hotels or office parks (Huang et al. 2002). This can result in diversion of resources away from research. It also creates considerable liabilities for the institutes should these ventures fail.

Align Programs with Clients through Public-Private Partnerships

A perennial challenge of public research programs is aligning R&D efforts to the needs of its farmer, agribusiness, and consumer clients. One way of improving alignment with local farmer needs and to facilitate dissemination of agricultural innovations to farmers is through partnerships with producer groups and agribusinesses. Funding of public research through producer associations, as described earlier, ensures that producers have a direct stake (and say) in R&D program orientation. Joint R&D ventures, in which public institutes and private companies share in the development costs, also help ensure alignment of research with client needs.

Public-private joint ventures have been widely used in the seed industry. Although the public sector usually assumes the major role in crop breeding, the tasks of seed multiplication and marketing often involve private seed companies. Once a new variety has been developed and approved for release, the public research institute makes available a limited amount of foundation seed to seed companies and other seed multipliers. These private partners then multiply the seed, under government oversight, to assure quality and purity, and sell this "certified seed" to producers. Farmers in turn may save some of their harvest as seed for their following crop or sell or share it with other farmers. The specific roles of the public and private partners in seed development, multiplication, and marketing vary by crop, depending on the characteristics of the crop and seed market. For crops like maize that are grown using hybrid seed (which cannot be saved by farmers because the progeny does not maintain the characteristics of the parent seed), private companies often invest in both breeding and seed multiplication. Public-private partnerships are typical for most field crops grown from self-pollinating seed. However, for some crops, the public sector may need to take a dominant role in both breeding and seed multiplication. Seed markets are often poorly developed for clonally propagated crops like roots, tubers, bananas, and other tree crops, due to slow multiplication rates and greater technical challenges in maintaining disease-free planting material. In some cases, the public sector may need to subsidize private companies to multiply and disseminate seed, for example, when the market for improved seed is small but the crops are being promoted to advance a public goal such as nutrition security, such as highly nutritious or locally important indigenous crops.[9]

Another example of public-private joint ventures in food and agriculture R&D is the use of Cooperative Research and Development Agreements (CRADA) by the US Department of Agriculture (USDA). A CRADA typically involves a government laboratory collaborating with a single company to develop a specific technology for commercialization (Day-Rubenstein and Fuglie 2000). For example, the first CRADA entered into by the USDA resulted in a new method of vaccinating poultry *in ovo* (in the egg), now used worldwide to protect poultry against a number of infectious diseases. In a CRADA, both parties commit in-house resources to R&D (matched funding ensures alignment with client needs), and the private sector partner may provide the government laboratory with some research funds. Government laboratories may provide personnel, equipment, and laboratory privileges (but not funds), to the private partner. Patents resulting from a CRADA may be jointly owned, and the private partner has first rights to negotiate an exclusive license for patents resulting from the CRADA. Some research data also may not be publicly disclosed for a certain period of time. Having a private partner can not only economize on public costs but also ensure rapid commercial adoption of the technology. A potential drawback of public-private joint ventures is if public R&D favors particular firms or stymies market competition.

Foster Regional and International Links

Although agricultural technologies need to be tailored to location-specific conditions, much of the pool of knowledge and genetic resources that scientists draw upon to make these adaptions is supplied by universities and research institutes in developed countries or centers participating in the CGIAR, which are sometimes referred to as agricultural research institutes, or ARIs. Basic and applied research at ARIs continues to make major methodological advances in the scientific tools used in agricultural research. Over the past couple of decades, for example, major advances have been made in the science of crop and animal breeding. The use of the haploid method in maize breeding has reduced the time needed to develop improved parent lines from ten to two generations. Using genetic markers in animal breeding now enables scientists to predict the milk producing potential of dairy calves as soon as they are born (as opposed to waiting four to five years for the animals to mature and produce). The merging of molecular biological and information technologies has dramatically improved the rate of genetic progress possible through breeding. The recent emergence of low-cost gene editing tools has opened up new avenues for making targeted genetic improvements. ARIs are also sources of broad and accessible collections of crop genetic resources, such as those maintained by the CGIAR centers and the USDA's Agricultural Research Service.

Many developing countries cannot hope to create the necessary scale in their agricultural science institutions to replicate the basic science activities and resources of the ARIs. Hence linking their institutes and farmers to this global knowledge is critical. To make use of these scientific advances and resources, agricultural scientists in developing countries need to form networks and collaborative relationships with scientists in ARIs. This needs to be built into their budgets and human resource policies, for example by enabling staff to attend international conferences, take study leaves abroad, and engage in collaborative research with scientists from ARIs.

Such links take advantage of the significant economies of scale in scientific activities that produce global public goods, like crop genetic conservation, characterization, and prebreeding (moving genetic traits from wild relatives to crop breeding parent lines). By linking their national research programs with the CGIAR centers and other ARIs, developing countries can gain access to these scientific developments, avoid duplicative efforts, and focus their own limited R&D resources on local adaptation. One study found that in global wheat improvement, for example, due to economies of scale in its global research program, the International Maize and Wheat Improvement Center (CIMMYT) produced such superior traits in the parent lines it developed that they accounted for more than two-thirds of new varieties released in developing countries. Many developing countries could afford to have fewer wheat breeders and focus their wheat research on adapting this material to local conditions (Maredia and Eicher 1995). In fact, through such partnerships even small countries can earn high returns from public R&D. In Sub-Saharan Africa, even though larger countries tended to have higher rates of return to public agricultural research, returns in small countries were still sufficiently high to justify additional spending on public agricultural R&D (Fuglie and Rada 2016).[10]

Over the past couple of decades, countries like Brazil, India, and China have significantly strengthened their national agricultural research systems and are becoming important sources of advances in agricultural science and technology. Annual spending on public agricultural research by China now exceeds that of the United States (Clancy, Fuglie, and Heisey 2016). These countries are likely to be an increasingly important source of advances in innovation in coming decades. Forging collaborative research alliances with ARIs in these countries will facilitate access to and transfer of this knowledge to agricultural research systems in less developed countries.

For smaller countries without the ability to create a research organization on the scale of a developed or BIC country, one approach has been to form regional research organizations with neighboring countries. For example, English-speaking Caribbean nations formed a regional agricultural research organization, CARDI (the Caribbean Agricultural Research and Development Institute), and sugar plantations in the region established the West Indies Sugar Cane Breeding and Evaluation Network. In West and Central Africa, with World Bank support, countries have collectively identified regional "centers of excellence" to lead R&D on particular commodities for the whole region. However, postcolonial experience with West African regional research organizations showed that it is difficult to sustain collective financing for regional research centers, and such organizations typically rely heavily on donor funding (Ruttan 1986). Regional organizations may also be less likely to adjust to changing comparative advantage. In the Caribbean, support for CARDI has languished in countries that have seen their comparative advantage shift away from agriculture and toward tourism and banking (Roseboom, Cremers, and Lauckner 2001).

Strengthening Agricultural Universities

An additional characteristic of a viable agricultural research system is integral involvement of higher education and training in research. This is essential if developing countries are to remove the scientific human resource constraints that limit their capacity to move to productivity-based agricultural growth. Graduate-level education in agricultural sciences is most effective when it occurs in association with a significant research program. Thus, universities play a fundamental role in agricultural research systems. Agricultural universities are home to some of the most highly skilled scientists, who have the essential task of training the researchers and technicians that staff research and development organizations in both the public and private sectors. Governments in Asia and Latin America have allocated one-third or more of public R&D funding for agriculture through universities, but in Sub-Saharan Africa the university share is less than 10 percent. The quality of graduate education in agricultural sciences has been in noticeable decline in many African countries.

Providing Incentives for Private Innovation

The twenty-first century environment for agricultural innovation requires that science policies not only create strong public research institutions but also give explicit attention to incentives facing the private sector.[11] Worldwide, private agribusiness is playing a growing role in agricultural innovation systems. Large and small companies are developing and introducing improved inputs and practices along the entire agricultural-food (agri-food) supply chain. This part of the chapter focuses specifically on the innovative behavior of companies that improve and manufacture agricultural inputs, like seeds, chemicals, animal health products, and machinery, for use by farmers to grow agricultural commodities. The two subsections that follow describe the nature, extent, and economic motivations behind the R&D investments by these firms. The third subsection discusses policies that encourage or constrain these firms to improve the quality and diversity of their products and manufacturing processes.

The Expanding Role of Private Research and Innovation

Investment in agricultural research by private companies has increased significantly in recent decades (Pray and Fuglie 2015; Fuglie 2016). By 2011, agricultural R&D by private firms worldwide amounted to about 23 percent of total global spending on farm-oriented R&D (see table 3.1). Although much of this spending is by large multinational corporations (MNCs) based in high-income countries, there are also thousands of small and medium-size companies, many based in developing countries, which engage in innovative activity to supply improved inputs to farmers and food products to consumers. In addition, some companies from developing countries have emerged to become competitive developers and exporters of improved farm inputs to other countries. These developing-country MNCs, as well as the more established MNCs from developed countries, have acquired significant internal R&D capacities and have established global research and manufacturing networks that enable them to compete and engage in technology transfer in international markets.

The full extent of private agricultural R&D is often hard to observe. Several manufacturing sectors—including biotechnology, chemical, machinery, and pharmaceutical—conduct R&D for agriculture. Often, firms within these manufacturing sectors establish a division that focuses on spinning off agricultural applications from its manufacturing R&D program. In other cases, industrial firms spin off these divisions to create firms dedicated to manufacturing inputs for agriculture. Getting an understanding of private investment in agricultural R&D often requires using specialized surveys that target such firms across a range of manufacturing sectors. This information presented next draws upon studies that have conducted such surveys in a number of developing countries. These include small, low-income countries in Sub-Saharan Africa and South Asia and the large emerging economies of Brazil, India, and China. The estimates of R&D include spending by both domestic and foreign firms within a country, as well as by for-profit state-owned enterprises (SOEs).[12]

According to these surveys, by the late 2000s, the private sector accounted for about one-quarter of total agricultural R&D spending in China, India, and Bangladesh (table 3.4). In Brazil, private agricultural R&D rose dramatically from $49 million in 1996 to $393 million in 2012–13 (in constant 2011 PPP$) to account for about 15 percent of total agricultural research in that country (da Silviera, da Silva, and Pray 2014). The increases in private R&D spending helped raise the agricultural research intensity (the ratio of R&D to GDP) in these countries. By the late 2000s, the agricultural research intensities of South Africa and Brazil were over 2 percent, a level typical of many high-income countries (Heisey and Fuglie 2018). For low-income countries in Africa, private R&D is increasing but is still relatively low. For the four African countries with available data and included in table 3.4 (Kenya, Senegal, Tanzania, and Zambia), in 2008–09 investment by private companies in agricultural R&D was only about one-tenth the level of public agricultural R&D spending.

Table 3.5 shows the composition of private agricultural R&D across different manufacturing sectors. By the first decade of the twenty-first century, the private sector had grown to play a major role in developing and disseminating to farmers improved seeds, methods for crop protection (pesticides), fertilizers, farm machinery, animal health products, and food manufacturing processes and products. Particularly impressive has been the growth of private R&D in crop seed and biotechnology in India. After India

TABLE 3.4   The Private Sector's Role in Agricultural R&D Is Increasing around the World

Country	1995/96[a]			Circa 2010		
	Total agriculture R&D spending (million $)	Private sector share (%)	Total agriculture R&D/agriculture GDP (%)	Total agriculture R&D spending (million $)	Private sector share (%)	Total agriculture R&D/agriculture GDP (%)
Brazil, 1996–2013	1,673	2.9	2.0	2,719	14.4	2.3
India, 1995–2009	449	13.5	0.3	1,140	24.8	0.4
China, 2001–10	1,647	7.6	0.4	5,730	25.3	0.9
Bangladesh, 2008	—	—	—	80	26.1	0.4
South Africa, 2008	—	—	—	272	19.2	2.4
Kenya, Senegal, Tanzania, and Zambia, 2008	—	—	—	159	8.0	1.0
United States, 1995–2010	6,993	38.5	5.4	9,643	50.1	6.2

Sources: For developing countries, public agricultural R&D spending is from ASTI (2018); private agricultural R&D spending is from Pray et al. (2018); and agricultural GDP and exchange rates are from the World Bank (2018). Data for the United States come from USDA-ERS (2019).

Note: National currencies converted to US$ using market exchange rates. Private agriculture R&D includes R&D by agricultural input supply companies and excludes food-sector R&D. GDP = gross domestic product; R&D = research and development; $ = US dollar; — = not available.

a. 2001 for China.

TABLE 3.5 **Private Food and Agricultural R&D Is Spread across Multiple Industries in Brazil, India, and China**

Country	Year of survey	Crop seed and biotechnology (million $)	Crop pesticides (million $)	Fertilizers (million $)	Farm machinery (million $)	Animal health and nutrition (million $)	Food manufacturing and plantations (million $)
Brazil	2012–13	274.9	47.1	0	44.2	3.9	22.6
India	1984–85	1.5	10.1	7.6	4.2	1.0	2.5
	1995–96	5.5	19.1	7.5	7.3	7.0	14.4
	2008–09	99.5	41.6	8.9	45.5	29.7	57.2
	2015–16	111.4	82.2	26.6	119.4	—	—
China	2001	—	21.0	22.2	9.9	—	82.6
	2007	—	80.7	143.3	73.2	—	381.0
	2010	171.5	120.4	305.2	82.7	—	770.6

Source: Pray et al. 2018.

Note: Data are in millions of constant 2011 US dollars, using market exchange rates. — = not available.

began to liberalize its seed market in the 1980s, private R&D on crop breeding and biotechnology increased rapidly (Pray and Ramaswami 2001), rising from almost nothing in 1980 to more than $100 million by 2015. Part of this is directed toward crops that have been genetically modified for crop protection traits, especially insect resistance. But it also includes increased investment in conventional breeding, especially for field crops grown from hybrid seed like maize, cotton, sorghum, and millet, as well as many vegetable crops.

The growth in private agricultural R&D across multiple industrial sectors suggests that firms have found it profitable to invest in agriculture. The fact that many of these innovations have been widely adopted indicates that farmers have also derived significant economic benefits from them. And, if the increase in supply due to such productivity gains is large enough to lower market prices or improve product quality, then consumers have benefitted from this private R&D as well. Although there have been numerous assessments of the social value of public research, relatively few studies have attempted to assess social benefits (that is, benefits of technology beyond the profits of the firms that develop them) of private R&D in developing countries. In one study, Evenson, Pray, and Rosegrant (1999) examined the effects of public and private R&D on the growth of TFP in Indian agriculture over 1956–86. Even though private R&D was relatively low during these years, they find that it accounted for about 11 percent of the total agricultural TFP growth over this period. A more recent study by Bervejillo, Alston, and Tumber (2012) find that in Uruguay, private R&D increased the number of improved crop varieties available to farmers and that this had a significant impact on the country's agricultural TFP growth over 1985–2010.

Other analysis has focused on quantifying the economic impacts of specific technologies in which the private sector played a leading R&D role, such as the development of genetically modified (GM) crops. In a meta-analysis of 147 studies on the impact of GM crops worldwide, Klümper and Qaim (2014) find that across these studies the average impact of GM crop adoption was to reduce pesticide use, increase crop yields, and increase farm profits. Their review finds that impacts in developing countries were larger than impacts in developed countries. Besides GM crops, other technologies in which the private sector has played a leading R&D role in developing countries include hybrid maize and rice, poultry genetics and husbandry, farm machinery, crop pesticides, and veterinary medicines. Reviewing evidence on the impacts of private R&D in developing countries Pray, Fuglie, and Johnson (2007) and Pray and Fuglie (2015) identify several cases in which private R&D resulted in significant economic benefits to smallholder farmers.

With a supportive policy environment, private-sector innovation can help farmers respond nimbly to new technological and market opportunities. For example, in many developing countries the rising middle class is demanding more animal protein in their diets. To intensify production of animal-based food products, farmers need access to improved animal breeds, better animal health products, as well as husbandry practices that provide for humane treatment of animals and safe handling of animal products. For two recent case studies of instances when private-led innovation has enabled smallholder farmers to respond to rising consumer demand for animal proteins, see box 3.2.

What Drives Private Investment in Agricultural R&D?

To understand why private R&D in agriculture has grown and how this might be influenced by policy, it is useful to start with a simple conceptual model. Profit-maximizing firms, in theory, will invest in R&D up to the point at which the marginal cost of research and commercialization of the new technology just equals the firm's expected marginal revenue from it, appropriately adjusted for risk and for the lag between the time that costs are accrued and the revenue realized. Much of the costs of research and commercialization represent upfront, fixed costs to the firm. Even after a new product is developed, bringing it to market may involve obtaining regulatory approvals and attracting farmers or customers to use or adopt it. Returns to these upfront costs are recouped by charging a premium over marginal costs on product sales. Or, in the case of process innovations, they must enable the firm to manufacture its products at lower unit costs than prevailing market prices, thus increasing profits. Four main factors influence the returns to private research: (1) the size of the market for a new product; (2) the degree of appropriability of the product's benefits (that is, the ability to charge price premiums above marginal costs); (3) the researchable opportunities for improving technologies given the current state of science; and (4) the costs of R&D inputs, such as wage rates for scientists and technicians (Dasgupta and Stiglitz 1980).

The Expansion of Animal Protein Industries in Nigeria and Bangladesh

A generally supportive enabling environment and limited direct interventions in markets by the government may be all that the private sector needs to grow. This may explain the rapid growth of poultry in Nigeria and farm-raised fish in Bangladesh. In both instances, employment and productivity increased with limited involvement by the government except for providing favorable investment conditions, including placing few restrictions on imports of technology.

Poultry in Nigeria

In Nigeria, egg output tripled between 1980 and 2012, while chicken meat production more than doubled from 1980 to 2008. The poultry sector transitioned from small backyard operations to confinement operations run primarily by large and medium enterprises. Nigeria is an important recent example of the global trend in which a country imports poultry technology originally developed in the United States and Europe to modernize its domestic poultry industry. The technology—consisting of poultry hybrid breeds, feed concentrates, veterinary services, new management techniques, and equipment—has rapidly increased poultry production and productivity in Latin America and Asia and is now moving into Africa (Narrod, Pray, and Tiongco 2008). The parent stock of the new poultry breeds used in Nigeria come from the United States and Europe. Sixty percent of the day-old chicks are supplied by Ajanla Farms, a Nigerian company owned by the feed and food conglomerate CHI Foods (Ajanla Farms, undated). The Ajanla broiler breeds come from Aviagen (based in the United States), and the layer breeds come from Hendrix Genetics (based in Europe). Veterinary pharmaceuticals and equipment for poultry production come from abroad. Feed additives are also imported and then mixed with local feed grains to produce poultry feed concentrates. Since 1980, feed production has increased some 600 percent, led by local firms, notably Premier Feed Mills, Livestock Feeds, CHI Foods, and Zartech Ltd (Liverpool-Tasie et al. 2017). All these firms are food industry conglomerates with substantial foreign shareholdings.

The key policies were few or no restrictions on foreign direct investment (FDI) and poultry technology imports, as well as substantial tax incentives for agribusiness investments. Government support in the form of veterinary services was also important. Use of antibiotics in feed is also permitted.

Aquaculture in Bangladesh

Between 1984 and 2014, aquaculture production in Bangladesh grew more than 9 percent a year, on average, rising from 0.12 million tons to nearly 2 million tons (Hernandez et al. 2018). This growth was driven largely by internal demand as Bangladesh's population and per capita income grew. Unlike Nigeria's poultry industry, which obtained proprietary breeds from foreign multinationals, the fish breeds that drove the aquaculture revolution in Bangladesh were not proprietary, though some were imported. Over time, local carp have been gradually replaced by tilapia and perch species brought in from Southeast Asia. These species grow rapidly at higher stocking densities using commercial feed. The animal feed industry, which originally focused on poultry and shrimp, developed or imported feed combinations for farm-raised fish, including feed that floated so that less was wasted at the bottom of ponds. The big players are CP from Thailand, New Hope from China, and Godrej from India. With this technology available, small and medium farms invested in larger and improved ponds. The area of aquaculture production went from 360,896 hectares in 2001 to 575,493 hectares in 2014, and output per hectare of

(Box continues on the following page.)

The Expansion of Animal Protein Industries in Nigeria and Bangladesh (continued)

pond rose from 1.0 tons to 2.2 tons (calculated from Hernandez et al. 2018). The upstream supply chain developed as small and medium-size enterprises invested in nurseries, feed businesses, and input supply channels to reach farmers. Downstream from the farmers, improvements to the marketing chain that brought the fish to urban markets were also developed by Bangladeshi entrepreneurs.

The role of the government was important but limited. The Bangladesh Fisheries Research Institute experimented with new imported fish species and government organizations provided training to farmers on how to establish and manage nurseries. The pro-business policies of the government were probably equally important, encouraging investments by foreign companies in the feed business and allowing tilapia species to be brought in by private firms from Southeast Asia. The most recent phase of technology development—producing high-value local fish varieties using modern methods—seems to be led by Bangladeshi fish farmers and marketers.

Market Size

Large and growing markets clearly provide more opportunities for firms to profit from research. Developing countries have seen a rapid increase in the farm demand for modern agricultural inputs, and this growth in demand has been a primary factor in the rise in private R&D spending for agriculture. This growth in demand for modern inputs in turn has been driven by the need to find substitutes for increasingly scarce resources like land and labor and to meet growing consumer demand for food and fiber as populations increase, as well as changing consumer tastes for higher quality and more diverse food products as per capita income rises. For example, in India farm purchases of quality seed, fertilizer, and tractors have risen steadily over the past 40 years (table 3.6). As domestic capacity to supply these inputs increased, Indian companies also gained competitiveness in international markets. Exports of tractors and pesticide manufactured in India grew because India is a low-cost producer of these products. China has followed a similar path to that of India. Internal demand has been the major driver of growth and export demand has become important in some industries, like pesticides and farm machinery. Demand for inputs in Brazil has been driven by internal increases in food demand but even more by the international demand for agricultural commodities produced in Brazil, especially soybeans, maize, meat, citrus, sugar, and coffee.

But even in large markets, the willingness of companies to investment in R&D will be influenced by policies on foreign direct investment (FDI), technology imports, and enforcement of intellectual property rights (IPRs) like patents and trademarks. These policies may vary widely across countries. For example, China places

TABLE 3.6 **The Use of Agricultural Inputs Has Risen Steadily in India for More Than Four Decades**

Agricultural inputs	1971	1981	1991	2001	2011	2015
Seed (quality seed distribution) (1,000t)	52	450	575	918	2,773	3,031
Fertilizer consumption (NPK) (1,000t)	2,000	5,300	12,000	18,000	28,300	25,600
Pesticide consumption (1,000t)	25.8	47.0	72.1	43.6	55.5	57.4
Tractors (1,000 units sold)	520	750	1,400	2,500	5,500	6,300

Source: Ministry of Agriculture, Government of India; updated from Pray and Nagarajan (2014).

Note: By convention, the NPK aggregate is obtained by using weights of N, P_2O_5, and K_2O equivalents in the various fertilizers used. t = tons.

conditions on FDI to encourage technology transfer and is protective of innovations by local companies. In contrast, Brazil is more open to FDI in its agricultural input industries, aiming to provide the best technologies to its farmers whether the technologies are produced domestically or imported. For smaller countries, the formation of common markets with low tariffs and harmonized regulations can increase the effective market size for companies and encourage them to invest in R&D for that market.

Appropriability

Intellectual property rights like patents provide a temporary monopoly to an inventor over the use of an invention. This monopoly power allows the inventor to charge fees for commercial uses of the invention in order to recoup sunk costs of research and development. Although the temporary monopoly creates welfare losses (new technology is more expensive while under patent), IPRs can contribute significantly to economic growth if they stimulate more investment in R&D.

To be successful, innovations must offer advantages to users. Improved inputs that raise farm productivity and profitability increase farmers' willingness to pay for them. Similarly, consumers are willing to pay more for food products that offer higher quality, convenience, and taste. To recoup the sunk costs of product research and development, firms need to set prices above their marginal costs. The degree to which firms can capture, or appropriate, some of the greater willingness to pay for their innovations is affected by the level of competition in these markets. IPRs such as patents, plant breeders' rights (PBRs), and trademarks provide legal means for firms to limit the ability of competing firms to supply copycat products. Some types of innovations such as improved seed varieties and other biological technologies are particularly easy to copy, and without strong IPRs firms have difficulty appropriating (capturing) returns. An exception is the case of crops produced from hybrid seed. With hybrid seed, farmers need to repurchase seed each season from the seed supplier because saved seed deteriorates significantly in terms of yield and quality. The breeder of hybrid seed can protect intellectual property by restricting access to the parent lines used to multiply the seed. However, due to technical factors, it is not economical to grow all crops using hybrid seed. Further, hybrid seed is generally more expensive to produce than nonhybrid seed, so it must offer a substantial yield advantage to make it profitable to use. Hybrid seed is most widely used to grow maize, sorghum, cotton, some vegetable crops, and to a limited degree rice and wheat.

Opportunities for Technology Development and the Cost of R&D Inputs

Scientific breakthroughs that expand opportunities for commercial applications help provide incentives for the private sector to invest in applied R&D because they increase the likelihood that an R&D investment will result in an economically significant innovation. Scientific advances in biotechnology and informatics, for example, have stimulated the private sector to invest in the development of genetically modified crops and precision agricultural practices.

Scientific advances in biotechnology have been particularly notable to stimulating the development of the crop seed and biotechnology industry in Brazil and India. Private R&D in these industries has grown rapidly since the 1990s (see table 3.5). Biotechnology played a key role in stimulating more research in the seed industry, especially for cotton (Pray and Nagarajan 2013). Productivity advances made possible by improved cotton genetics resulted in India moving from being a net importer to a major exporter of raw cotton. Farmer demand for GM and hybrid cotton seed turned the cotton seed market into the largest and most profitable component of the Indian seed sector. MNCs like Monsanto and DuPont-Pioneer made major investments in agricultural biotechnology laboratories in India, linking them into their global research networks. Likewise, in Brazil, GM soybeans, maize, and cotton became profitable crops for Monsanto, DuPont-Pioneer, Bayer, and other seed/biotechnology companies. In China, however, the private sector response to opportunities in agricultural biotechnology has been more muted. The potential profits from biotechnology have induced a few local companies to invest in biotech research. Foreign MNCs like Syngenta, Monsanto, and DuPont-Pioneer also invested in applied biotechnology research in China, but because of government restrictions they located their basic biotechnology research elsewhere (in India, for example). As these restrictions persisted over time, these companies appeared to have reduced their biotechnology research investment in China.

Policies to Encourage Private Research and Technology Transfer

Several policy tools are available to policy makers to encourage private R&D in agriculture. Some of the major policy levers and their attributes are listed in table 3.7. One broad lever is policies that influence market size for innovations. Industrial policy sets rules governing business participation in specific industries and influences the level of competition in various sectors. Countries have used industrial policy together with market liberalization to increase (foreign and domestic) competition in agricultural input markets, including eliminating monopolies held by SOEs. Industrial policies also include subsidy, tax, and trade policies. Private input markets

TABLE 3.7 **Various Policies Can Support Private Agricultural R&D, Innovation, and Technology Transfer**

Government policy and investment area	Plantation/processing	Input industries	Levy-based research
Business climate and industrial policy	• Allow private investment by local and foreign firms, and reduce size of parastatals • Enact antimonopoly policies to ensure competition and regulate natural monopolies	• Allow private investment by local and foreign firms, and reduce size of parastatals • Enact antimonopoly policies to ensure competition and regulate natural monopolies	• Allow private investment by local and foreign firms, and reduce size of parastatals • Support policies that allow collaboration on research
Policies that influence market size for innovations	• Reduce agricultural export and import barriers, as well as other measures that tax agriculture • Privatize parastatals, state-owned enterprises	• Reduce agricultural export and import barriers, as well as other measures that tax agriculture • Reduce technical barriers on trade and harmonize regulations • Support public extension services to encourage adoption of new technology	• Reduce agricultural export and import barriers, as well as other measures that tax agriculture • Facilitate collective action on R&D at the regional level
Intellectual property rights	• Introduce a fairly strong intellectual property regime to support the acquisition of technology from abroad	• Improve the enforcement of patents and PBRs	
Technology regulations and quality control	• Establish government laboratories to ensure product quality	• Pursue science-based regulations on new products • Improve control of counterfeit and dangerous inputs	• Establish government laboratories to ensure product quality
Policies to create new technological opportunities and reduce the cost of private research	• Encourage public-private R&D partnerships and contract research • Invest in PhD training and research universities	• Support the provision of advanced breeding lines and germplasm by national agricultural research systems to private seed firms • Invest in PhD training and research universities • Subsidize venture capital funds for financing R&D facilities	• Encourage public-private R&D partnerships • Invest in PhD training and research universities • Provide government funds to match commodity levies

Source: Based on Pray, Byerlee, and Nagarajan (2016).

Note: PBRs = plant breeders' rights; R&D = research and development.

could be encouraged by reducing input subsidies that are confined to existing products and that thus are not available for new products or that channel input sales through government tenders rather than markets. Another dimension of industrial policy is trade policy. Tariff and nontariff barriers to trade in seed, breeding stock, and other agricultural inputs can discourage research and technology transfer, especially in countries with relatively small domestic markets.

Strengthening IPRs and reforming regulatory systems governing the introduction of new technology are additional policy tools that influence the level and direction of private R&D (table 3.7). IPRs enable firms to appropriate some of the gains from new technologies they develop, which is essential if companies are to earn a positive return on their R&D investments (Pray and Nagarajan 2014). The absence of regulatory protocols for GM seed has been a major deterrent to their wider use in developing countries. Although regulations are necessary to ensure health and safety of new products, onerous or duplicative regulations impose costs on firms that may limit their willingness to invest in R&D. Regulatory reforms can have a large impact on the pace at which improved technologies are introduced. Effective regulations and trademark protection help assure farmers that the seed or pesticides they buy do in fact have the characteristics advertised on their packaging. Such regulations can also reduce exposure to dangerous pesticides and other chemicals by restricting their use. In addition, establishing regulatory protocols allowing the use of safe GM crops could induce more research by seed and biotechnology companies.

A final set of policies to encourage private R&D in table 3.7 is support for research at public institutes and universities. Policy makers may think of private research as being a substitute for public research, but it is better to view these R&D activities as complementary. Advanced degree training at universities increases the pool of scientific personnel and resources and expands the set of technological opportunities available for commercialization. These public investments lower the cost of private innovation, thus stimulating more R&D by the private sector. However, public research may also "crowd out" private research if it duplicates activities that could profitably be undertaken by private firms.

An example of a case in which policy reforms helped stimulate innovation is Asia's agricultural machinery industry. The 1980s and 1990s saw rapid expansion in the availability and use of low-cost, small-scale irrigation pump sets in Asia. As Green Revolution technologies made irrigation more profitable, farm demand for pump sets increased. Reforms in China allowed for-profit firms to manufacture and export pump sets, and trade policy reforms in South and Southeast Asia reduced import restrictions on farm machinery. Hundreds of small and medium-size firms emerged in China to meet the growing market demand for small, low-cost pump sets among smallholder farmers in Asia. The clustering of these firms in certain locations facilitated the spread of design innovations and standards across firms (Huang, Rozelle, and Hu 2007). More recently, rising rural wages in many Asian countries have led to greater demand for tractors and many specialized types of agricultural machinery. Policies can have important but complex influences on how private industry is able to respond to new market demands (see box 3.3).

The discussion that follows describes a number of specific policy actions that influence incentives for private R&D, based on a review of developing-country experiences. This evidence provides insights on how science and innovation policies in developing countries can be used to increase private R&D investment in agriculture.

Liberalize Markets

One of the key policy reforms that has served as an incentive for private R&D in developing countries has been the elimination of government monopolies in agricultural input markets. Allowing private companies to compete in these markets is a prerequisite for private agricultural research and innovation. However, studies have shown that privatization alone may not lead to greater private research unless other conditions are in place.

BOX 3.3

Policies and Innovation in China's Agricultural Machinery Industry

China's agricultural machinery industry has experienced impressive growth in recent decades, although concerns have been raised as to whether it can maintain a high level of innovation as the farm tasks needing to be mechanized become more complex. Up to now, the industry has been dominated by small and medium enterprises, many of which do little formal R&D. Restrictions (recently liberalized) on foreign direct investment (FDI) have discouraged foreign multinational corporations (MNCs) from entering the market.

The extent to which government policies have influenced innovation and productivity in China's agricultural machinery industry was investigated in a recent study by Deng (2018). Using firm-level data from 2005–07 and a methodology pioneered by Crépon, Duguet, and Mairessec (1998), the study examined whether restrictions on FDI, agricultural machinery research and development (R&D) by public research institutes, and direct subsidies to machinery manufacturers and farmers for purchasing machinery might have affected R&D and innovation by these firms. To measure innovation, the study used the number of patents. To measure productivity, the study estimated unit profitability (revenue minus manufacturing costs per machine).

The study found that larger firms invested more in R&D as a percentage of sales (research intensity) than smaller firms, at least up to a point. Among very large firms, diseconomies of scale seemingly started to lower research intensity, innovation, and productivity of these firms. Generally, private firms were more innovative and productive than state-owned enterprises (SOEs).

Relaxing FDI rules to allow more foreign participation in the agricultural machinery industry had mixed effects. Foreign firms on average were more productive than domestic private firms and SOEs. However, allowing 100 percent foreign ownership actually reduced R&D intensity, presumably because importation of technology reduced incentives (or the need) for local innovations.

Public R&D appeared to have limited measurable influence on private research and innovation. Although having more public institutes doing research on agricultural machinery in a province was positively correlated with the number of private firms in that province doing R&D, the level of public R&D spending on agricultural mechanization did not lead to measurably higher innovation or productivity by these firms.

Direct government subsidies (often in the form of low-interest loans) to machinery manufacturers did appear to induce more R&D spending by these firms. These subsidies also were positively associated with the level of innovations and productivity of the firms. This result is different from the studies of Howell (2017), who finds that across all industries subsidies increased innovation but reduced productivity. However, subsidies to farmers to buy tractors were not positively associated with private R&D or innovation.

In many countries, SOEs continue to provide goods and services to farmers in competition with private firms, although policies toward SOEs vary widely across countries. The largest agricultural input markets—in Brazil, India, and China—have all undergone gradual liberalization since the 1980s, with declining market shares by SOEs in most sectors (figure 3.1). The Brazilian government never played a large role in supplying inputs except for fertilizer, and that SOE was privatized in the 1990s. FDI has been permitted in the farm machinery and pesticide industries since the late 1960s and in the seed industry since 1988.[13] In the 1980s and 1990s, Brazil also allowed imports of farm inputs to gradually increase (Santana and Nascimento 2012). By 2012, the state had almost completely exited all farm input and food processing sectors.

In India, until the 1980s the production and distribution of seed, pesticide formulation, and agricultural implements was limited to SOEs, small manufacturers, and cooperatives. Imports of most inputs except fertilizer were banned or faced high tariffs. In the late 1980s, the Indian government started allowing large domestic and foreign privately owned firms to participate in the seed market. It also allowed vegetable seed to be imported. Further reforms occurred in the 1990s, when foreign companies were allowed to have majority ownership in agribusinesses. Meanwhile, government support for state-owned pesticide, farm machinery, and seed enterprises was reduced, and some of these enterprises were privatized. By 2015, the market share of SOEs in seed was less than 10 percent, and SOEs had completely exited the markets for pesticides and farm machinery (figure 3.1). Fertilizer is one sector in which SOEs continue to command a large market share in India—about 45 percent in 2015 (Pray and Nagarajan 2014).

In China, the government provided all agricultural inputs until the early 1980s, when commercial enterprises were first allowed to enter the livestock, fisheries, crop, and food industries and farm input supply sectors. Markets were introduced gradually and differed from industry to industry and province to province. Pesticide and farm machinery industries were liberalized first. The seed industry was one of the last that private firms were allowed to enter. In 2000, the Chinese government passed the first seed law to define legal roles for the private sector.

A number of countries could likely stimulate growth in private R&D by further liberalizing and privatizing agricultural input and processing industries. The Kenya Agricultural and Livestock Research Organization (KALRO) still has a monopoly on the production of foundation seed of public maize varieties, and the Kenya Seed Company (KSC) remains a government corporation. The presence of SOEs and government-controlled cooperatives in seed markets has discouraged private firms from investing in hybrid seed development (Pray and Nagarajan 2014). However, liberalization of seed markets in African countries has not always been sufficient to stimulate private R&D. Other factors, such as regulatory hurdles in getting new products approved, can also present formidable barriers to private companies. For a discussion of the mixed results from liberalization in Africa's maize seed markets, see annex 3A.

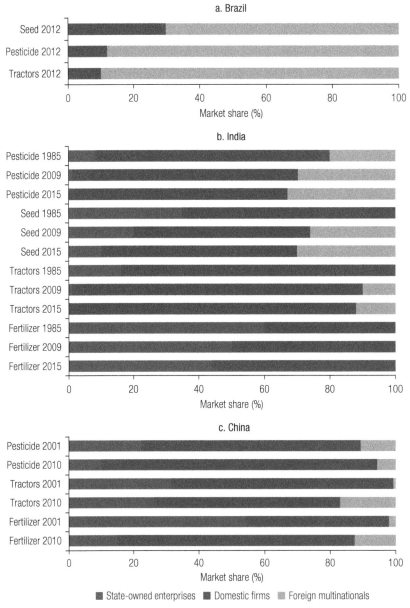

FIGURE 3.1 Liberalization of Agricultural Input Markets Is Proceeeding in Different Ways in Brazil, India, and China

Source: Pray et al. 2018.

Although many countries have reduced or eliminated the role of SOEs in agricultural inputs, China continues to see a role for these companies. Several SOEs that are controlled by the central government are being strengthened to make them into "national champions" that can compete with foreign multinationals. Tools the government has used to encourage them to grow include allowing mergers and acquisitions, favorable access to credit from government banks, and access to private capital by listing shares on stock markets (Cai 2017). In the food and agricultural sector, after years of declining market shares, giant SOEs have emerged. In 2011, the SOE ChemChina bought the Israeli generic pesticide company Makhteshim Agan (renamed ADAMA), and in 2017 it acquired the Swiss company Syngenta, the world's largest pesticide company and also an important player in the seed and agricultural biotechnology industry. Another chemical SOE, SinoChem, merged with the two major government pesticide research programs. Both these companies have billions of dollars in annual sales of agricultural inputs.

Another dimension of industrial policy is competitiveness, or antitrust policies. A large body of literature, starting with Schumpeter (1934), shows that firm size is positively related to research intensity up to a point, but then starts to decline if the firm gets so large as to stifle market competition. So far, however, there is little evidence that rising concentration in global agricultural input markets has reduced R&D spending (Fuglie et al. 2011). In the Indian seed industry, market liberalization, including allowing participation by foreign MNCs, increased competition and R&D spending in this sector (Pray and Nagarajan 2010). Generally, antitrust measures have rarely been used in developing countries as a means to influence agricultural R&D and innovation. In India, a recent court ruling that Monsanto and MAHYCO had a monopoly on GM traits led to controls on input prices and royalties, but this resulted in reduced R&D spending by these firms (Pray and Nagarajan 2010).

Protect Intellectual Property

IPRs and more generally the ability to appropriate returns from research provide incentives for firms to invest in R&D. Ascension to membership in the World Trade Organization (WTO) requires countries to adhere to the Agreement on Trade-Related Aspects of Intellectual Property Rights (TRIPS), which establishes minimum standards for IPRs, including plant breeders' rights (PBRs) over new crop varieties. Even apart from TRIPS requirements, some countries have enacted reforms to their IPR policies to strengthen incentives for private innovation in agricultural industries. For example, amendments to India's patent laws in 2005 permitted product patents for agricultural chemicals, biotechnology innovations, and veterinary medicines for the first time since 1972. In an econometric model of Indian agricultural input firms, Pray and Nagarajan (2014) find that the ability to patent had a positive impact on private research in those industries.

Evidence is also emerging that adopting TRIPS has increased private R&D in agriculture. China changed its patent laws in 1993 to include agricultural chemicals, and introduced further reforms in 2001 to be in compliance with TRIPS. Both these measures stimulated innovation in China's agricultural chemical industry, mostly in pesticide manufacturing processes (Shi and Pray 2012). IPR reforms in Brazil were essential to the significant expansion of private breeding on soybeans (Silva, Braga, and Garcia 2018) and wheat (Flister and Galushko 2016), two crops grown using self-pollinated seed. In the absence of enforcement mechanisms, farmers will save seed of self-pollinated crops, reducing companies' incentives to do research. The IPR reforms established royalty systems to collect fees on saved seed. The World Bank Group examined this important development in a 2006 report, *Intellectual Property Rights: Designing Regimes to Support Plant Breeding in Developing Countries*.

Although the evidence of IPR's positive impact on private R&D from middle-income countries is robust, results from low-income countries are mixed. Stronger IPRs alone may be insufficient if market size is small or regulatory regimes too onerous. For a review of how plant breeders' rights in different countries of Sub-Saharan Africa have affected private plant breeding, see annex 3B.

Reform Regulations of New Technologies

The commercialization of new technologies for agriculture often involves lengthy and costly regulatory protocols that require substantial data to be collected and submitted to government regulators on a product's safety and performance. Even when the same or very similar product has been approved and is widely used in other countries, national regulations may require that these testing requirements be repeated. Regulatory frameworks that require duplicative environmental, health, and efficacy testing for new technologies that have already passed these requirements in other countries with similar growing conditions are an example of policies that can create redundant costs and discourage technology transfer (Gisselquist, Nash, and Pray 2002).

Virtually all governments share some common practices in regulating new agricultural technologies. For example, governments require truth in labeling, provide lists of allowed pesticide products based on risk and efficacy data, and supervise the importation of plants and animals to prevent the inadvertent introduction of foreign pests and diseases (see table 3.8). Such regulations are necessary to protect public health and the environment and avoid fraudulent practices. However, regulations may also be used as nontariff trade barriers to protect domestic industries. Duplicative and lengthy regulatory practices can impose large costs on the private sector, discourage technology transfer from other countries, and keep innovative products out of the hands of farmers and consumers.

Reform of regulatory policies can help reduce the costs they impose, and thus make private investment in research and technology transfer more attractive. Gisselquist, Nash, and Pray (2002) document a number of instances when regulatory reforms have led to significant improvements in farm productivity in developing countries. For example, reforms to seed regulations that allowed for seed imports and voluntary variety registration led to the rapid introduction and spread of improved maize varieties in Bangladesh, Turkey, and Zimbabwe and increased crop yields. Relaxation of regulations in Bangladesh that restricted the availability of irrigation water pumps and power tillers led to a much wider variety of machinery products available to farmers and had a significant increase in access to groundwater irrigation among smallholders.

TABLE 3.8 Common Regulatory Practices Regarding Agricultural Production Inputs

Input	Regulatory practice	Implications for technology transfer
Conventional seeds	Two systems are common in the world: 1. Voluntary variety registration. Companies may sell seeds that government has not tested and listed, although governments may test and recommend varieties. 2. Compulsory variety registration for specific crops. Governments do not allow sale of seed except for varieties that have passed performance tests; some governments accept varieties tested and listed in other countries.	Voluntary registration facilitates private introduction of new cultivars. Voluntary registration also allows sale of seed for unregistered traditional varieties, and public varieties from other countries.
Seeds with genetically modified (GM) traits	For each crop variety with one or more genetically modified traits, governments list allowed products for use in food, feed, and direct cultivation, all of which require environmental and health risk tests. Permitting use as food or feed allows GM crops to be imported but not planted. Permits for cultivation may also require performance testing if this is also required for conventional seed. Some countries accept data from risk tests done in other countries; other countries have banned cultivation of GM seed or require labeling of food products containing GM products. Many countries have yet to establish clear regulatory guidelines and procedures for GM seed.	Options to facilitate technology transfer include developing clear regulatory guidelines and accepting risk data from other countries.
Pesticides	Virtually all governments list allowed products based on risk and performance; some countries accept risk data from other countries and most require in-country performance tests. The United States registers biopesticides without performance tests.	Options to facilitate technology transfer include accepting efficacy data from other countries and waiving efficacy data for biopesticides and low-risk products.
Livestock medicines	Most countries allow products based on risk and efficacy; many countries accept data from tests done in other countries.	
Fertilizers and animal feed	Some countries list allowed products based on expert decision about optimum nutrient compositions; other counties allow dealers to sell any composition but insist on truth in labeling.	Allowing markets to determine composition facilitates private technology transfer.
Agricultural machinery	Some countries list allowed makes and models based on official performance tests; other countries allow sales of new makes and models without tests.	

Source: Adapted from Gisselquist, Nash, and Pray (2002).

Many countries have been slow to implement regulations governing the use of genetically modified (GM) seed. Government attitudes toward GM seed in African countries in particular have been influenced by alarmist rhetoric, often originated in developed countries, Paarlberg (2008) notes. While GM seed has been widely adopted in North and South America, and in many Asian countries and South Africa, use and availability of GM seed in the rest of Sub-Saharan Africa is still very limited. This has reduced the access of African farmers to important crops traits like resistance to pests, disease, and drought, according to Paarlberg (2008).

One approach some countries have adopted to reduce regulatory costs is regional harmonization. In this approach, a group of countries agree to recognize the outcomes of regulatory reviews in other countries and permit cross-border trade in the approved technology products. The case of herbicides in West Africa provides an example of such an approach.

By accepting lists of approved products from other countries in their region, the need for duplicative testing is reduced and more products can be made available to farmers. This has led to increased use of herbicides and improved weed control in many West African countries (see annex 3C on regional harmonization of herbicide regulations in Africa).

Lower the Cost of R&D

Given that even private R&D is likely to generate economic benefits beyond what can be appropriated by inventors (that is, its social returns are higher than its private returns), many countries use subsidies to encourage private R&D. Subsidies can take the form of direct R&D grants to firms, special tax allowances for R&D spending or on sales of technology products, and other types of financial assistance to firms. Such subsidies need to be designed to encourage additional private R&D and not just substitute for research that would have been undertaken anyway. For example, many R&D grant programs require a private company to fund at least half the total cost of an R&D project.

Although there has been substantial research on the effects of R&D subsidies to industrial firms in high-income countries (for a review, see David, Hall, and Toole 2000), evidence on the effect of R&D subsidies on private agricultural innovation in developing countries is very limited. Brazil, India, and China have all used tax policies to subsidize agricultural R&D, and China has also made extensive use of direct R&D grants to small and medium-size agribusiness firms. A survey of over 1,300 Chinese food and agricultural business firms showed that about 10 percent of the total R&D spending by these firms came through government subsidies (Hu et al. 2011). After control for the size and type of firm, Hu et al. (2011) find that R&D subsidies significantly increase firms' own investment in R&D—each $1 of subsidy was associated with an additional $0.3 in firms' internal R&D spending. In a study of R&D and innovation in China's farm machinery industry, Deng (2018) also finds that direct government R&D grants increased the rate of innovation by private firms. Deng (2018) finds no evidence, however, that government subsidies to farmers for purchasing new farm machinery led to any increase in the rate of innovation by machinery manufacturers (see box 3.3).

One of the principal constraints faced by private firms to increasing R&D activity is the scarcity of highly trained research and technical personnel and other R&D services. Public investment in research at universities and government institutes not only increases the supply of R&D personnel but also creates new ideas for potential commercialization. By reducing the private R&D cost of commercialization, public R&D can make private R&D more profitable and therefore crowd in more private R&D investment. However, if public research institutes and universities provide technologies to farmers at marginal cost (that is, without price premiums to recover sunk costs of R&D) that directly compete with privately developed technologies, then public R&D could crowd out private R&D.

Several recent studies have attempted to characterize the nature of agricultural R&D and the interactions between the public and private sectors—especially whether they are complements or substitutes. Complementarity takes place when public R&D investments stimulate additional private R&D investments. It happens most readily when public and private research organizations conduct different types of research. For instance, if public researchers emphasize basic or fundamental science, the results may improve technological opportunities for private firms conducting applied research. Substitution, or crowding out, takes place when public R&D supports activities that would otherwise have been carried out by the private sector. It is more likely when public and private researchers work in the same topical areas (such as hybrid maize breeding) and conduct research that is of the same nature and with similar objectives. The evidence on whether public agricultural R&D crowds in or crowds out private R&D has been mixed, varying by country. Hu et al. (2011) find evidence that applied agricultural research by public institutions in China crowded out private research. Similarly, Alfranca and Huffman (2003) find substitution effects between public and private agricultural R&D in European countries. For the United States, however, Fuglie and Toole (2014) review a number of studies that have consistently found public and private agricultural R&D to be complements. Apparently, articulation between public and private research bodies has been sufficient to avoid duplication and crowding out (in fact, public R&D has resulted in significant crowding in of private R&D, according to these studies). As private capacities in agricultural research evolve, public institutions need to adjust their priorities to avoid direct competition with private firms.

Concluding Remarks

Building an effective innovation system capable of generating and disseminating innovations for agriculture has been an essential ingredient for countries wishing to accelerate and sustain productivity growth in this sector. And, given the unique features of agriculture—the diverse set of commodities produced, the prevalence and geographic dispersion of smallholder producers, and the local nature of technology—governments have a large role to play in this innovation system, both as investors in knowledge creation and to aid in technology dissemination and utilization. This requires a combination of targeted public investments as well as policy reforms that serve as incentives for public institutions and private companies to create knowledge relevant to the needs of users along the agri-food value chain.

One key role for government is direct spending on agricultural R&D. Although nearly all countries now have public institutions dedicated to agricultural research, most governments continue to significantly underinvest in agricultural research. The high average return that has been earned from public spending on agricultural R&D reflects this underinvestment—significant opportunities for growth are being missed because public resources are being allocated to other areas offering lower returns.

Moreover, because spillovers from agricultural R&D are so pervasive (and thus benefits widely shared in an economy), the social return is much higher than the private return to R&D. Thus, especially for low-income countries, most agricultural research will need to be financed by the public sector. With appropriate incentive policies, the private sector can be expected to take on an increasing share of the technology generation effort for agriculture. But even in high-income countries, public spending still accounts for about half of the overall investment in agricultural R&D.

Countries in Sub-Saharan Africa in particular continue to invest relatively little in agricultural research, and this region continues to suffer from low levels of agricultural productivity and slow rates of productivity growth. Declining capacities in African agricultural universities are especially worrisome. Low-quality agricultural universities, particularly at the graduate level, where research capabilities are developed, are constraining long-term capacity development in human resources and knowledge creation in this region.

In addition to adequate funding, building an effective public research system requires a set of supportive policies that incentivizes scientists, directs activity to the needs of clients, and is connected to scientific developments in the rest of the world. Specific measures that have been found to improve performance and impact of public research include

- *Institutional autonomy*. Provide flexibility in human resource policies and funding strategies.
- *Performance-based incentives*. Reward staff performance and upgrade staff quality.
- *Stable and diversified funding*. Supplement robust public support with nongovernment sources.
- *Program alignment*. Ensure that research responds to needs and interests of farmers, agribusinesses, consumers, and government stakeholders.
- *Links to international science networks*. This is especially important for small countries to counter the lack of economies of scale in research systems.

Worldwide, the private sector is playing an increasingly important role in developing and disseminating new technologies all along the agri-food value chain. Encouraging the private sector to invest in research and technology transfer is another key component of a national innovation strategy. In a competitive marketplace, private innovation can be especially adroit in responding to rapidly changing consumer and market demands for new, more diverse, safer, and more nutritious foods. Specific measures governments can take to encourage private sector innovation include the following:

- *Liberalize food and agricultural input markets*. Allow private companies, foreign and domestic, to invest in and sell improved technologies to farmers and new food products to consumers, and ensure that these markets are competitive.

- *Protect intellectual property*. Enable private innovators to earn adequate returns to their sunk costs in research and product development.
- *Reduce burdensome regulation*. Focus science-based regulations on product safety and efficacy, harmonize regulatory protocols to avoid redundant product testing, and allow technology imports.
- *Lower the cost of R&D*. Use public and university R&D to expand the supply of R&D resources and knowledge.

The next chapter focuses on policies that help foster technology dissemination to farmers. It pays particular attention to reforming agricultural extension services, exploiting new opportunities for knowledge transfer using information and communication strategies, and providing farmers with new tools for managing risk and accessing financial services. This theme is continued in chapter 5, which describes transformations taking place in agri-food value chains, how this is creating new opportunities and challenges for linking smallholder producers to technology and markets, and how policies can help foster and strengthen these links.

Annex 3A. Market Liberalization in Africa's Maize Seed Industry

Government monopolies by state-owned enterprises (SOEs) act as barriers to entry by private companies. Beginning in the 1980s, many countries in Africa began to dismantle SOEs and allow private companies to participate in agricultural and commodity markets, with the hope that this would increase innovation and productivity in the farm sector. For agricultural seed, several countries enacted reforms to encourage greater private sector participation in breeding, multiplying, and disseminating improved crop varieties to farmers. The largest commercial seed market in Africa is for hybrid maize seed. Several domestic and international companies have become active in this market. Because hybrid seed does not reproduce with the same yield vigor, farmers typically repurchase hybrid seed each season from the companies that control the parent lines used to produce the seed. Because of the greater potential for repeat seed sales, private companies have assumed a larger role in breeding hybrid seed for African farmers. Experiences so far, though, have varied markedly across countries:

- Zambia is an example where maize seed market liberalization led to an increase in maize productivity. In the mid-1990s, as part of structural adjustment policies, the Zambian government liberalized its seed market, allowing private firms (domestic and international) to undertake R&D and sell proprietary maize seed to farmers. The government also improved procedures to release varieties, strengthened seed quality control regulations, and established liberal seed trade policies allowing imports and exports of seed. As a result, the numbers of maize varieties available to farmers greatly increased (to more than 210 varieties by 2015), with about 16 new varieties released each year. Between 1995 and 2015, maize yields in Zambia increased from about 1.5 t/ha (tons per hectare) to over 2.5 t/ha (figure 3A.1), and the export of maize seed grew to more than 36 tons.

- Ethiopia represents a case where even a partial liberalization of the seed sector can have dramatic effects on productivity. Although the Ethiopian government retains considerable control over the seed industry, it has allowed some foreign seed companies to introduce proprietary varieties and also conduct maize breeding in the country. The US-based Pioneer Hybrid Seeds has released several improved hybrids that have gained market share and contributed to yield improvement in the country. Over 2000–16, national average maize yields increased from around 1.7 t/ha to over 3.7 t/ha (figure 3A.1).

- In Ghana, reforms resulted in a new seed law, but the impact on productivity has been marginal so far. Although the reforms were supposed to have liberalized the seed market, these provisions have yet to be effectively implemented. According to Tripp and Ragasa (2015), seed growers who previously worked under contract with the old state seed company, in collaboration with Ministry of Agriculture staff who regulate the seed industry, have largely replaced the parastatal monopoly with a semiprivate monopoly. As late as 2009, hardly any private maize seed companies were conducting breeding in Ghana and there had been few releases of new maize hybrids. Maize yields have stayed below 2 t/ha.

- Kenya has probably gone further than any other African country in liberalizing and deregulating its seed markets, but so far without noticeable impacts on farm productivity. Policy reforms began in the early 1990s, when the monopoly on maize seed held by the parastatal Kenya Seed Company was ended and the market opened to private firms. To encourage private research and the importation

FIGURE 3A.1 Seed Market Reforms Had Different Effects on Maize Yields in Ethiopia, Ghana, Kenya, and Zambia

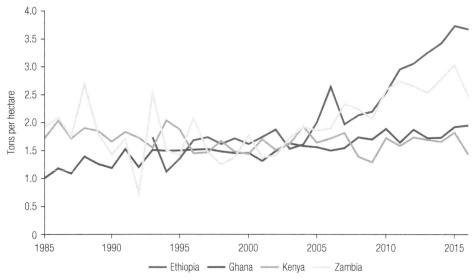

Source: FAOSTAT (FAO 2018).

Harvesting Prosperity

of proprietary technology, Kenya introduced plant breeders' rights (PBR) and measures to enforce them. The first proprietary varieties were released in 1997, and in 1999 Kenya became the second country in Sub-Saharan Africa after South Africa to join the International Union for the Protection of New Varieties of Plants (UPOV). Several private seed companies entered the Kenya maize seed market and the number of new varieties released increased significantly. By 2014, Kenya had issued PBRs for 1,457 new crop varieties (UPOV 2018). For maize, of the 354 improved maize varieties released between 1964 and 2015, 333 had been introduced after 1999 (Nagarajan, Naseem, and Pray 2019). However, market share of the new proprietary varieties has remained low, and maize yields have remained stagnant at about 1.5 t/ha (figure 3A.1). Kenya Seed Company, which mainly sells older hybrids, continues to dominate the market—partly because many of the new releases cost more but offer only a limited yield advantage over farmers' current varieties under prevailing farm practices, according to Nagarajan, Naseem, and Pray (2019).

- In Zimbabwe, before policy reform in 1990, smallholder farmers had access to only a dozen maize hybrids provided by a government monopoly. After the seed market was liberalized, four private firms began to market a total of 30 hybrids, giving farmers a wider choice of superior hybrids. By 1996 the introduction of these new maize hybrids resulted in a 3 percent increase in national maize production (Gisselquist, Nash, and Pray 2002). However, deteriorating macroeconomic conditions in the country led to a subsequent decline in maize yields.

Annex 3B. Do Plant Breeders' Rights Stimulate Investment in Crop Improvement?

Most developing countries are members of the World Trade Organization, which requires member countries to have in place systems that recognize intellectual property rights over new inventions, including plant breeders' rights (PBRs) over new crop varieties. Advocates for PBRs argue that they will stimulate private investment in crop breeding, allow greater imports of foreign-sourced technology, and facilitate a more competitive market, all of which will eventually lead to more improved crop varieties available to farmers and higher productivity growth in crops.

A new study by Campi (2017) examined the effect of PBRs on the rate of growth in cereal yields across a panel of high-, middle-, and low-income countries over a 40-year period. Campi (2017) hypothesized that in the absence of PBRs yield growth would be stronger for crops grown using hybrid seed (such as maize) compared with crops that are self-pollinated (such as wheat) because farms cannot save hybrid seed for subsequent plantings without a significant deterioration in terms of yield and quality. However, with strong PBRs that require farmers to pay royalties on saved seed, incentives for commercial breeding are enhanced and therefore yield growth rates should not differ as much between the types of crops. Results were positive for high-income countries but mixed for developing countries. The implication of Campi's (2017) work is that stronger IPRs may not automatically lead to higher innovation and productivity, but as she observes, "The relation between IPRs and yields is probably mediated and affected by several factors related to the idiosyncratic features of each single country in terms of innovation capabilities, as well as to their distinctive economic, political, and social characteristics" (Campi 2017, 27).

The cases of PBRs in Kenya and South Africa indicate the challenges and limitations in providing incentives for private investment in innovations to increase agricultural productivity in Africa. In Kenya, PBRs did appear to stimulate the development of new maize varieties, but there was no measurable effect on rate of growth in national average crop yield (Nagarajan, Naseem, and Pray 2019). The continued dominance of the state-owned Kenya Seed Company, which still provides 70 percent of the country's maize seed (often at subsidized prices), may have reduced the incentives of private firms to invest in research and capture market share with superior hybrids. In South Africa, the impact of PBRs on private wheat breeding has also been mixed. Although South Africa enacted PBRs as early as 1977, most wheat research in South Africa was funded by the Wheat Control Board and performed by the government's Agricultural Research Council–Small Grains Institute (ARC-SGI). Pannar was the only private company that had an independent wheat breeding, seed production, and marketing system. Another seed company, Sensako, mainly engaged in multiplication and marketing of ARC-SGI varieties. In 1996, however, funding for ARC-SGI wheat research was substantially reduced. The combination of PBRs, ARC's decline, and Sensako's strong wheat seed sales encouraged Sensako to develop its own wheat breeding research. A favorable policy toward foreign direct investment (FDI) encouraged Monsanto to buy Sensako in 1999 and expand Sensako's wheat breeding further. As figure 3B.1 shows, Sensako wheat varieties came to occupy over 90 percent of the area planted to wheat, largely at the cost of ARC varieties. At the same time, Sensako was selling much less wheat seed than expected because South African PBRs allowed farmers to plant saved seed free of royalty payments. As a result, in 2008 Monsanto sold off Sensako to local South African investors (*Farmer's Weekly* 2008).

A similar dilemma has affected the South African market for genetically modified (GM) soybean seed. Although 95 percent of country's soybean area is planted with GM soybeans, 80 percent is planted with saved seed, limiting revenues by seed companies. In 2017, the seed producers and suppliers of the GM traits worked with the key players in the soybean value chain to set up a new company to collect royalties on soybeans through an end-point royalty system like that in Brazil (ISAAA 2017, 48). Through an end-point royalty system, farmers declare their variety at point of crop sale, and a small fee is assessed and returned to the seed company with PBR on that variety. It is too early to tell how well this system will work. It may, however, be the only system through which royalties on self-pollinated crops such as wheat and soybeans can be collected.

One Company Came to Dominate Market Shares of Wheat Varieties Cultivated in South Africa

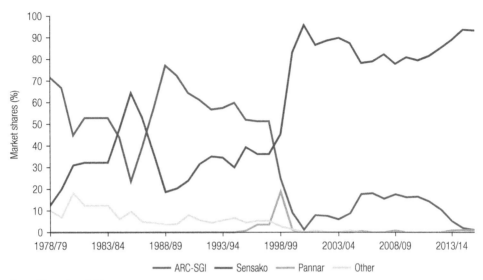

Source: Nhemachena 2018.

Note: The market share of wheat seed sold is based on area estimates of varieties grown in national production. ARC-SGI = Agricultural Research Council–Small Grains Institute.

Annex 3C. Herbicide Demand and Regional Harmonization of Regulations in Africa

The provision of herbicides in Africa presents a valuable case study on the private sector's role in supplying modern inputs that respond to farmers' needs—in this instance, farmers' need to cope with weed problems and labor shortages. This case provides a number of policy lessons. First, subsidies are not needed for rapid dissemination of profitable technologies like the herbicides in Africa. Second, health and environmental regulations can be structured so that they are not barriers to the spread of new agricultural technology. However, stronger efforts are needed to ensure that farmers are able to use the new technologies safely and effectively.

Herbicide use expanded rapidly in Africa after 2000, due to rising wages for labor employed in weeding and declining prices for and greater availability of off-patent pesticides. Many new companies entered African pesticide markets offering cheaper, generic versions of off-patent pesticides. For example, the price of glyphosate, the world's most widely used herbicide, fell dramatically after its patent expired in 2000. The source of herbicide imports shifted from pesticide companies based in Europe and the United States to Chinese and Indian manufacturers that sold generic versions of the product. For example, Chinese companies had 9 percent of the Ethiopian herbicide market in 2005 and 47 percent by 2015. The share by Indian companies rose from 0 to 15 percent over the same period (Tamru et al. 2017). Between 2000 and 2014, imports of herbicides into the West African nation of Mali increased more than 20-fold while herbicide prices declined by about half (Haggblade et al. 2017).

The spread of herbicide use appears to have not been due to government intervention. Unlike fertilizer and seed, pesticide is rarely subsidized by African governments. Private firms took over the supply of pesticides (including herbicides) in most African countries after many of the parastatals that had monopolies on imports and supply of farm inputs were dismantled in the 1990s. Even in countries such as Ethiopia, where the government plays a major role in supplying seed and fertilizer, most farmers purchase pesticides from private companies (table 3C.1). Imports of herbicides by Ethiopia grew rapidly after 2000. By 2015 herbicides were applied to one-quarter of the entire area planted to grains and to some 37 percent of the country's high-potential areas. In the growing of teff (a local grain staple), herbicide use increased labor productivity by between 9 and 18 percent (Tamru et al. 2017).

To reduce the cost of obtaining regulatory approval for new pesticides, West African countries have worked to harmonize their regulatory protocols. Following devastating droughts and a series of large-scale pest infestations in the 1970s, Sahelian countries decided to harmonize their pesticide regulations so they could better coordinate a regional response to pest attacks. In 1992, all nine Sahelian countries established a common regional regulator, the Comité Sahelien des Pesticides (CSP), to harmonize pesticide regulation and use among member countries. Any pesticide reviewed and approved by the CSP can be legally sold in any member country, providing a one-stop-shop for companies wishing to introduce new pesticides in the region (Diarra and Haggblade 2017). By 2015, 426 pesticide products had been registered for sale in CSP member countries. In the 2010s, coastal nations of West Africa also sought to join this arrangement and establish a regionwide regulatory body through the Economic Community of West African States (ECOWAS). Progress has been slow, however, given

TABLE 3C.1   Sources of Pesticide, Fertilizer, and Improved Seed Sold to Farmers in Ethiopia in 2011
Percent market share by source

Source	Herbicides	Insecticides	Fungicides	Chemical fertilizer DAP	Chemical fertilizer Urea	Improved seed
Government-related	27.0	31.4	43.3	83.3	84.8	87.6
Private	67.7	64.0	51.1	13.9	11.9	6.2
Other farmers	3.8	2.7	2.7	1.1	1.0	2.3
Development and church organizations	0.3	0.7	1.6	1.4	1.9	2.4
Others	1.1	1.2	1.4	0.3	0.4	1.4
Total	100.0	100.0	100.0	100.0	100.0	100.0

Source: Tamru et al. 2017.

Note: DAP = diammonium phosphate.

substantial differences among these countries in existing regulatory procedures (Diarra and Haggblade 2017).

The current regulations in place, whether regional or national, have not been able to stop the sales of unregistered pesticides or ensure safe use practices. Studies of pesticide markets find that 60 percent of herbicides in Mali and 27 percent in Ghana were unregistered (Diarra and Haggblade 2017). A study using plot-level data from 22,000 farm households in Ethiopia, Nigeria, Tanzania, and Uganda finds that although plots with pesticide treatments had higher values of output, farmers using pesticides (more than 10 percent of the sample) reported higher health expenditures and more days of lost work due to sickness (Sheahan, Barrett, and Goldvale 2017). These results suggest that more effective regulation is required to improve use of safe and reliable pesticides in Sub-Saharan Africa.

Notes

1. CGIAR (formerly the Consultative Group on International Agricultural Research) is composed of the CGIAR Consortium of International Agricultural Research Centers (currently consisting of 14 centers); the CGIAR Fund, which coordinates financing of the centers by national, multilateral, and private donors; and an Independent Science for Development Council that provides expert advice on strategic direction.

2. Governments create knowledge capital through direct investment in education and research and by establishing intellectual property rights, which create partial excludability conditions to incentivize private inventors.

3. As the Red Queen said to Alice in Lewis Carroll's *Through the Looking Glass* (1871), "Now, here, you see, it takes all the running you can do, to keep in the same place."

4. The agri-food value chain refers to all public and private enterprises that add value to farm and food products, including agricultural input developers, manufacturers and distributors, agricultural commodity producers (farmers, fishermen, and foresters), the food processing, marketing, storage, wholesaling and retailing industry, and government, business, and nonprofit research, as well as advisory, finance, and regulatory bodies.

5. These estimates of private agricultural R&D include only R&D directed toward improving farm inputs like seeds, agrochemicals, and farm machinery, and does not include a much larger R&D investment in food manufacturing and food product development.

6. Besides the CGIAR, a number of developed countries have other mechanisms to engage universities or support specialized research institutions to focus on developing-country agriculture. Probably the most significant of these is the French-based Agricultural Research Center for International Development (CIRAD), which had annual expenditures of €204 million in 2011. Other initiatives, such as support by the US Agency for International Development (USAID) for US university "innovation labs," the Australian Center for International Agricultural Research, the Japan International Research Center for Agricultural Science, and philanthropic organizations like the Bill and Melinda Gates Foundation collectively fund around $200 million–$250 million per year at developed-country institutions for developing-country agriculture, according to annual reports of these institutions.

7. A simplified interpretation of an IRR of 43 percent is that a one-time investment in a research project of $100 generates an annual stream of benefits of $43/year over the lifetime of the project, typically 30–50 years until the technology depreciates or becomes obsolete. Taking into account lag times between costs and benefits and using standard discount rates, the IRRs reported in table 3.3 give benefit-cost ratios in the neighborhood of 10:1 or higher.

8. EMBRAPA has been heralded as an agricultural and institutional success story, helping to transform Brazil from a recipient of food aid to a major agricultural exporter. For a concise history of EMBRAPA and its institutional innovations and achievements, see Martha, Contini, and Alves (2012). For a recent assessment of factors contributing to EMBRAPA's success, see Correa and Schmidt (2014).

9. For an excellent discussion of public-private roles in seed development for different types of crop and country circumstances, see the "Early Generation Seed Study" by Monitor Deloitte (2015) that was supported by the US Agency for International Development (USAID) and the Bill and Melinda Gates Foundation.

10. Fuglie and Rada (2016) estimated that over 1977–2005, the internal rate of return to agricultural research by large African countries averaged 40 percent, in mid-size countries 29 percent, and in small countries 17 percent. Although this gives an indication of clear economies of size in research programs, even the returns earned by small countries are sufficiently high to justify increased public investment. In this study, small countries were defined as those producing less than $1 billion in gross agricultural output in 2005 international dollars, according to the United Nations Food and Agriculture Organization (FAO).

11. This section of the chapter draws on Pray et al. (2018).

12. The inclusion of SOEs as elements of the private sector is justified if these firms sell their products at market or near-market prices. China, for example, considers SOEs and private firms to be "commercial" enterprises. Most SOEs are under pressure to generate sufficient revenue to meet their costs and contribute to government coffers, but they are also required to meet certain goals of their governments. So this chapter follows the conventions adopted by the Chinese government and others, such as the World Bank (2014).

13. Personal communication in 2012 with Dr. Eliseu Alves, former Director General, EMBRAPA, Brasilia.

References

Ajanla Farms. Undated. "Poultry." http://ajanlafarm.com/product-range/poultry/.

Alene, A. 2010. "Productivity Growth and the Effects of R&D in African Agriculture." *Agricultural Economics* 41 (3-4): 223–38.

Alfranca, O., and W. E. Huffman. 2003. "Private R&D Investments in Agriculture: The Role of Incentives and Institutions." *Economic Development and Cultural Change* 52 (1): 1–21.

Alston, J. M., M. Andersen, J. James, and P. G Pardey. 2010. *Persistence Pays: US Agricultural Productivity Growth and the Benefits from Public R&D Spending.* New York: Springer.

Alston, J. M., C. Chan-Kang, M. Marra, P. G. Pardey, and T. Wyatt. 2000. "A Meta-Analysis of Rates of Returns to Agricultural R&D." International Food Policy Research Institute (IFPRI), Washington, DC.

Alston, J. M., S. Dehmer, and P. G. Pardey. 2006. "International Initiatives in Agricultural R&D: The Changing Fortunes of the CGIAR." In *Agricultural R&D in the Developing World: Too Little, Too Late?* edited by P. G. Pardey, J. M. Alston, and R. Piggott, 313–60. Washington, DC: International Food Policy Research Institute (IFPRI).

Alston, J. M., M. S. Harris, J. D. Mullen, and P. G. Pardey. 1999. "Agricultural R&D Policy in Australia." In *Paying for Agricultural Productivity*, edited by J. Alston, P. Pardey, and V. Smith, 118–71. Baltimore: The Johns Hopkins University Press.

Alston, J. M., G. W. Norton, and P. G. Pardey. 1995. *Science under Scarcity: Principles and Practice for Agricultural Research Evaluation and Priority Setting.* Ithaca, NY: Cornell University Press.

Arrow, K. 1962. "The Economic Implications of Learning by Doing." *Review of Economic Studies* 29(39):155-173.

ASTI (Agricultural Science and Technology Indicators). 2017. "Agricultural R&D Indicators Factsheet: Côte D'Ivoire." ASTI, International Food Policy Research Institute (IFPRI), Washington, DC.

————. 2018. Agricultural Science and Technology Indicators (ASTI). International Food Policy Research Institute (IFPRI), Washington, DC (accessed December 2018). www.asti.ifpri.org.

Beintema, N., and G.-J. Stads. 2017. *A Comprehensive Overview of Investments and Human Resource Capacity in African Agricultural Research. Agricultural Science and Technology Indicators.* Washington, DC: International Food Policy Research Institute.

Bervejillo, J. E., J. M. Alston, and K. P. Tumber. 2012. "The Benefits from Public Agricultural Research in Uruguay." *Australian Journal of Agricultural and Resource Economics* 56 (4): 475–97.

Block, S. 2014. "The Post-independence Decline and Rise of Crop Productivity in Sub-Saharan Africa: Measurement and Explanations." *Oxford Economic Papers* 66: 373–96.

Bloom, N., M. Schankerman, and J. van Reenen. 2013. "Identifying Technology Spillovers and Product Market Rivalry." *Econometrica* 81 (4): 1347–93.

Cai, J. 2017. "Forget Privatisation, Xi Has Other Big Plans for Bloated State Firms." *South China Morning Post*, September 6, 2017. https://www.scmp.com/news/china/economy/article/2109943/how-china-making-its-state-firm-dinosaurs-bigger-and-richer.

Campi, M. 2017. "The Effect of Intellectual Property Rights on Agricultural Productivity." *Agricultural Economics* 48 (3): 327–39.

Clancy, M., K. Fuglie, and P. Heisey. 2016. "U.S. Agricultural R&D in an Era of Falling Public Funding." *Amber Waves* 14 (November). Economic Research Service, US Department of Agriculture, Washington, DC.

Correa, P., and C. Schmidt. 2014. "Public Research Organizations and Agricultural Development in Brazil: How Did Embrapa Get It Right?" Economic Premise Number 145, World Bank, Washington, DC.

Craig, B., P. G. Pardey, and J. Roseboom. 1997. "International Productivity Patterns: Accounting for Input Quality, Infrastructure and Research." *American Journal of Agricultural Economics* 79: 1064–76.

Crépon, B., E. Duguet, and J. Mairessec. 1998. "Research, Innovation, and Productivity: An Econometric Analysis at the Firm Level." *Economics of Innovation and New Technology* 7 (2): 115–58.

da Silviera, J., J. da Silva, and C. E. Pray. 2014. "Private Agribusiness Research in Brazil." University of Campinas, Campinas, Brazil.

Dasgupta, P., and J. Stiglitz. 1980. "Industrial Structure and the Nature of Innovative Activity." *Economic Journal* 90 (358): 266–93.

David, P. P. Hall, and A. Toole. 2000. "Is Public R&D a Complement or Substitute for Private R&D? A Review of the Econometric Evidence." *Research Policy* 29 (4-5): 497–529.

Day-Rubenstein, K., and K. Fuglie. 2000. "The CRADA Model for Public–Private Collaboration in Agricultural Research." In *Public-Private Collaboration in Agricultural Research: New Institutional Arrangements and Economic Implications*, edited by K. Fuglie and D. Schimmelpfennig, 155–74. Ames, Iowa: Iowa State University Press.

Deng, T. 2018. "Policy, R&D, Innovation and Productivity in China: A Case Study of the Agricultural Machinery Industry." M.Sc thesis, Department of Agricultural, Food and Resource Economics, Rutgers University, New Brunswick, NJ.

Diarra, A., and S. Haggblade. 2017. "Regulatory Challenges in West Africa: Instituting Regional Pesticide Regulations during a Period of Rapid Market Growth." Policy Research Brief No. 52, Feed the Future Innovation Lab for Food Security, Michigan State University, East Lansing, MI.

Doraszelski, U., and J. Jaumandreu. 2013. "R&D and Productivity: Estimating Endogenous Productivity." *Review of Economic Studies* 80: 1338–83.

Eicher, C. 2004. "Rebuilding Africa's Scientific Capacity in Food and Agriculture." Background Paper No. 4 commissioned by the InterAcademy Council Study Panel on Science and Technology Strategies for Improving Agricultural Productivity and Food Security in Africa.

Estrada, R. D., F. Holmann, and R. Posada. 2002. "Farmer and Industry Funding of Agricultural Research in Colombia." In *Agricultural Research Policy in an Era of Privatization*, edited by

D. Byerlee and R. G. Echeverria, 67–80. Wallingford, UK: CABI (Centre for Agriculture and Bioscience International) Publishing.

Evenson, R. E. 2003. "Production Impacts of Crop Genetic Improvement." In *Crop Variety Improvement and Its Effect on Productivity: The Impact of International Agricultural Research,* edited by R. E. Evenson and D. Gollin, 447–72. Wallingford, UK: CAB International.

Evenson, R. E., and K. Fuglie. 2010. "Technology Capital: The Price of Admission to the Growth Club." *Journal of Productivity Analysis* 33: 173–90.

Evenson, R. E., and Y. Kislev. 1975. *Agricultural Research and Productivity.* New Haven, CT: Yale University Press.

Evenson, R. E., C. E. Pray, and M. W. Rosegrant. 1999. "Agricultural Research and Productivity Growth in India." Research Report 109, International Food Policy Research Institute (IFPRI), Washington, DC.

Evenson, R. E., and J. Quizon. 1991. "Technology, Infrastructure, Output Supply, and Factor Demand in Philippine Agriculture." In *Research and Productivity in Asian Agriculture*, edited by R. E. Evenson and C. E. Pray, 195–205. Ithaca, NY: Cornell University Press.

Evenson, R. E., and L. Westphal. 1995. "Technological Change and Technology Strategy." In *Handbook of Development Economics*, Volume 3, Part A, edited by H. Chenery and T. N. Srinivasan, 2209–99. Amsterdam: Elsevier.

Fan, S. 2000. "Research Investment and the Economic Returns to Chinese Agricultural Research." *Journal of Productivity Analysis* 14 (2): 163–82.

Fan, S., P. Al-Riffai, M. El-Said, B. Yun, and A. Kamaly. 2006. "A Multi-level Analysis of Public Spending, Growth and Poverty Reduction in Egypt." DSGD Discussion Paper No. 41, International Food Policy Research Institute, Washington, DC.

Fan, S., P. Hazel, and S. Thorat. 2000. "Government Spending, Growth and Poverty in Rural India." *American Journal of Agricultural Economics* 82 (4): 1038–51.

Fan, S., and P. Pardey. 1998. "Government Spending on Asian Agriculture: Trends and Production Consequence." In *Agricultural Public Finance Policy in Asia*. Tokyo: Asian Productivity Organization (APO).

Fan, S., L. Zhang, and X. Zhang. 2002. *Growth, Inequality and Poverty in Rural China: The Role of Public Investments.* Research Report 125, International Food Policy Research Institute (IFPRI), Washington, DC.

FAO (Food and Agriculture Organization of the United Nations). 2018. FAOSTAT (database). http://www.faostat.fao.org.

Farmer's Weekly. 2008. "Seed Saving Forces Monsanto to Sell Wheat Operations." *Farmer's Weekly*, July 11, https://www.farmersweekly.co.za/archive/seed-saving-forces-monsanto-to-sell-wheat-operations/.

Fernandez-Cornejo, J., and C. Shumway. 1997. "Research and Productivity in Mexican Agriculture." *American Journal of Agricultural Economics* 79 (3): 738–53.

Flister, L., and V. Galushko. 2016. "The Impact of Wheat Market Liberalization on the Seed Industry's Innovative Capacity: An Assessment of Brazil's Experience." *Agricultural and Food Economics* 4 (1): 11. https://doi.org/10.1186/s40100-016-0055-8.

Frisvold, G., and K. Ingram. 1995. "Sources of Agricultural Growth and Stagnation in Sub-Saharan Africa." *Agricultural Economics* 13 (1): 51–61.

Fuglie, K. 2016. "The Growing Role of the Private Sector in Agricultural Research and Development World-Wide." *Global Food Security* 10 (September): 29–38.

———. 2018. "R&D Capital, R&D Spillovers, and Productivity Growth in World Agriculture." *Applied Economic Perspectives & Policy* 40(3): 421–44.

Fuglie, K., P. Heisey, J. King, C. E. Pray, K. Day-Rubenstein, D. Schimmelpfennig, S. L. Wang, and R. Karmarkar-Deshmukh. 2011. *Research Investments and Market Structure in the Food Processing, Agricultural Input, and Biofuel Industries Worldwide.* Economic Research Report 130. Washington, DC: US Department of Agriculture Economic Research Service (USDA-ERS).

Fuglie, K., and N. Rada. 2013. *Resources, Policies, and Agricultural Productivity in Sub-Saharan Africa.* Economic Research Report 45. Washington, DC: US Department of Agriculture Economic Research Service (USDA-ERS). https://ageconsearch.umn.edu/bitstream/145368/2/err145.pdf.

———. 2016. "Economies of Size in National Agricultural Research Systems." In *Agricultural Research in Africa: Investing in Future Harvests,* edited by J. Lynam, N. Beintema, J. Roseboom, and O. Badiane, 59–82. Washington, DC: International Food Policy Research Institute (IFPRI).

Fuglie, K., and A. Toole. 2014. "The Evolving Institutional Structure of Public and Private Agricultural Research." *American Journal of Agricultural Economics* 96 (3): 862–83.

Fulginiti, L., and R. Perrin. 1993. "Prices and Productivity in Agriculture." *Review of Economics and Statistics* 75 (3): 471–82.

Gisselquist, D., J. Nash, and C. E. Pray. 2002. "Deregulating the Transfer of Agricultural Technology: Lessons from Bangladesh, India, Turkey, and Zimbabwe." *World Bank Research Observer* 17 (2): 237–65.

Goñi, E., and W. F. Maloney. 2017. "Why Don't Poor Countries Do R&D? Varying Rates of Factor Returns across the Development Process." *European Economic Review* 94 (May): 126–47.

Griffith, R., S. Redding, and J. van Reenen. 2004. "Mapping the Two Faces of R&D: Productivity Growth in a Panel of OECD Industries." *Review of Economics and Statistics* 86 (4): 883–95.

Haggblade, S., M. Smale, A. Kergna, V. Theriault, and A. Assima. 2017. "Causes and Consequences of Increasing Herbicide Use in Mali." *European Journal of Development Research* 29 (3): 648–74.

Heisey, P. W., and K. Fuglie. 2018. "Agricultural R&D in High-Income Countries: Old and New Roles in a New Funding Environment." *Global Food Security* 17 (June): 92–102.

Hernandez, R., B. Belton, T. Reardon, C. Hu, X. Zhang, and A. Ahmed. 2018. "The 'Quiet Revolution' in the Aquaculture Value Chain in Bangladesh." *Aquaculture* 493 (1): 456–68.

Howell, A. 2017. "Picking 'Winners' in China: Do Subsidies Matter for Indigenous Innovation and Firm Productivity?" *China Economic Review* 44 (July): 154–65.

Hu, R. F., Q. Liang, C. E. Pray, J. K. Huang, and Y. H. Jin. 2011. "Privatization, Public R&D Policy, and Private R&D Investment in China's Agriculture." *Journal of Agricultural and Resource Economics* 36 (2): 416–32.

Huang, J., R. Hu, C. E. Pray, and S. Rozelle. 2002. "Reforming China's Agricultural Research System." In *Agricultural Research Policy in an Era of Privatization,* edited by D. Byerlee and R. G. Echeverria, 245–64. Wallingford, UK: CABI (Centre for Agriculture and Bioscience International) Publishing.

Huang, Q. Q., S. Rozelle, and D. Hu. 2007. "Pump-Set Clusters in China: Explaining the Organization of the Industry That Revolutionized Asian Agriculture." *Asia-Pacific Development Journal* 14 (December): 75–105.

Huffman, W., and R. Evenson. 2006. *Science for Agriculture: A Long-Term Perspective.* Ames, IA: Blackwell.

ISAAA (International Service for the Acquisition of Agri-biotech Applications). 2017. "Global Status of Commercialized Biotech/GM Crops in 2017: Biotech Crop Adoption Surges as Economic Benefits Accumulate in 22 Years." Brief 53, International Service for the Acquisition of Agri-biotech Applications, Ithaca, NY.

Jin, S., J. Huang, R. Hu, and S. Rozelle. 2002. "The Creation and Spread of Technology and Total Factor Productivity in China's Agriculture." *American Journal of Agricultural Economics* 84 (4): 916–30.

Johnson, D., and R. Evenson. 2000. "How Far Away Is Africa? Technological Spill-overs to Agriculture and Productivity." *American Journal of Agricultural Economics* 82:743–49.

Jorgenson, D., K. Fukao, and M. Timmer, eds. 2016. *The World Economy: Growth or Stagnation?* Cambridge, UK: Cambridge University Press.

Klümper, W., and M. Qaim. 2014. "A Meta-Analysis of the Impacts of Genetically Modified Crops." *PLoS ONE* 9 (11): e111629.

Knudson, M., R. Lower, and R. Jones. 2000. "State Agricultural Experiment Stations and Intellectual Property Rights." In *Public-Private Collaboration in Agricultural Research: New Institutional Arrangements and Economic Implication*, edited by K. Fuglie and D. Schimmelpfennig, 155–74. Ames. IA: Iowa State University Press.

Lele, U., and A. Goldsmith. 1989. "Development of National Agricultural Research Capability: India's Experience with the Rockefeller Foundation and Its Significance for Africa." *Economic Development and Cultural Change* 37 (2): 305–44.

Liverpool-Tasie, L., B. Omonona, A. Sanou, W. Ogunleye, S. Padilla, and T. Reardon. 2017. "Growth and Transformation of Food Systems in Africa: Evidence from the Poultry Value Chain in Nigeria." *Nigerian Journal of Agricultural Economics* 7 (1): 1–15.

Lusigi, A., and C. Thirtle. 1997. "Total Factor Productivity and the Effects of R&D in African Agriculture." *Journal of International Development* 9 (4): 529–38.

Maredia, M. K., and C. K. Eicher. 1995. "The Economics of Wheat Research in Developing Countries: The One Hundred Million Dollar Puzzle." *World Development* 23 (3): 401–12.

Martha, Jr., G. B., E. Contini, and E. Alves. 2012. "Embrapa: Its Origins and Changes." In *The Regional Impact of National Policies*, edited by W. Baed. Elgar Publishers.

Monitor Deloitte. 2015. "Early Generation Seed Study." Report prepared for the Bill and Melinda Gates Foundation and USAID in collaboration with Monitor Deloitte (April). https://docs.gatesfoundation.org/documents/BMGF%20and%20USAID%20EGS%20Study%20Full%20Deck.pdf.

Nagarajan, L., A. Naseem, and C. E. Pray. 2019. "Contribution of Policy Change on Maize Varietal Development and Yields in Kenya." *Journal of Agribusiness in Developing and Emerging Economies* 9 (1): 4–21. https://doi.org/10.1108/JADEE-01-2018-0013.

Narrod, C., C. E. Pray, and M. Tiongco. 2008. "Technology Transfer, Policies, and the Role of the Private Sector in the Global Poultry Revolution." IFPRI Discussion Paper 841, International Food Policy Research Institute, Washington, DC.

Nhemachena, C. R. 2018. "Biological Innovation in South African Agriculture: Economics of Wheat Varietal Change, 1950–2012." Ph.D. thesis, University of Pretoria, Pretoria, South Africa.

Olmstead, A., and P. Rhode. 2002. "The Red Queen and the Hard Reds: Productivity Growth in American Wheat, 1800–1940." *Journal of Economic History* 62 (4, December): 929–66.

Osuri, M., P. Nampala, and A. Ekwamu. 2016. "African Faculties of Agriculture within an Expanding University Sector." In *Agricultural Research in Africa: Investment in Future Harvests*, edited by J. Lynam, N. Beintema, J. Roseboom, and O. Badiane, 229–52. Washington, DC: International Food Policy Research Institute.

Paarlberg, R. 2008. *Starved for Science: How Biotechnology is Being Kept Out of Africa*. Cambridge, MA: Harvard University Press.

Pal, S., and D. Byerlee. 2006. "India: The Funding and Organization of Agricultural R&D." In *Agricultural R&D in the Developing World: Too Little, Too Late?* edited by P. G. Pardey, J. M. Alston, and R. Piggott, 155–94. Washington, DC: International Food Policy Research Institute (IFPRI).

Pardey, P. G., C. Chan-Kang, S.P. Dehmer, and J.M. Beddow. 2016. "Agricultural R&D Is on the Move." *Nature* 537 (7620): 301–03.

Pardey, P. G., and N. Beintema. 2001. *Slow Magic: Agricultural R&D a Century after Mendel*. Washington, DC: International Food Policy Research Institute.

Pray, C., and Z. Ahmed. 1991. "Research and Agricultural Productivity in Bangladesh." In *Research and Productivity in Asian Agriculture*, edited by R. Evenson and C. Pray, 114–32. Ithaca: Cornell University Press.

Pray, C. E., D. Byerlee, and L. Nagarajan. 2016. "Private-Sector Investment in African Research." In *Agricultural Research in Africa: Investing in Future Harvests,* edited by J. K. Lynam, N. Beintema, J. Roseboom, and O. Badiane, 171–200. Washington, DC: International Food Policy Research Institute.

Pray, C. E., and K. Fuglie. 2015. "Agricultural Research by the Private Sector." *Annual Review of Resource Economics* 7 (1): 399–424. https://doi.org/10.1146/annurev-resource-100814-125115.

Pray, C. E., K. Fuglie, and D. K. N. Johnson. 2007. "Private Agricultural Research." In *Handbook of Agricultural Economics,* Volume 3, edited by R. Evenson and P. Pingali, 2605–40. Amsterdam: Elsevier.

Pray, C. E., and L. Nagarajan. 2010. "Price Controls and Biotechnology Innovation: Are State Government Policies Reducing Research and Innovation by the Ag Biotech Industry in India?" *AgBioforum* 13 (4): 297–307.

———. 2013. "Role of Biotechnology in Stimulating Agribusiness R&D Investment in India." *AgBioforum* 16 (2): 104–11.

———. 2014. "The Transformation of Indian Agricultural Input Industries: Has It Increased Agricultural R&D?" *Agricultural Economics* (45), 145–56. https://doi.org/10.1111/agec.12138.

Pray, C. E., L. Nagarajan, A. Naseem, and J. R. Anderson. 2018. "Policies to Encourage Private Agribusiness to Contribute to Innovation and Agricultural Productivity in Developing Countries." Background paper for *Harvesting Prosperity: Technology and Productivity Growth in Agriculture,* World Bank, Washington, DC.

Pray, C. E., and B. Ramaswami. 2001. "Liberalization's Impact on the Indian Seed Industry: Competition, Research, and Impact on Farmers." *International Food and Agribusiness Management Review* 2 (3–4): 407–20.

Rada, N., and S. Buccola. 2012. "Agricultural Policy and Productivity: Evidence from Brazilian Censuses." *Agricultural Economics* 43 (4): 355–67. https://doi.org/10.1111/j.1574-0862.2012.00588.x.

Rada, N., and K. Fuglie. 2012. "Shifting Sources of Agricultural Growth in Indonesia." In *Productivity Growth in Agriculture: An International Perspective*, edited by K. Fuglie, S. Wang, and E. Ball, 199–214. Wallingford, UK: CABI (Centre for Agriculture and Bioscience International) Publishing.

Rada, N., and D. Schimmelpfennig. 2015. *Propellers of Agricultural Productivity in India.* Economic Research Report 203. Washington, DC: US Department of Agriculture Economic Research Service (USDA-ERS). https://www.ers.usda.gov/webdocs/publications/45507/55655_err-203_summary.pdf?v=0.

Rahman, S., and R. Salim. 2013. "Six Decades of Total Factor Productivity Change and Sources of Growth in Bangladesh Agriculture (1948–2008)." *Journal of Agricultural Economics* 64 (2): 275–94. https://www.ers.usda.gov/webdocs/publications/44992/28920_err137.pdf?v=0.

Romer, P. 1990. "Endogenous Technological Change." *Journal of Political Economy* 98 (5): S71–S102.

Roseboom, J., M. Cremers, and B. Lauckner. 2001. *Agricultural R&D in the Caribbean: An Institutional and Statistical Profile.* ISNAR Research Report Number 19. The Hague, Netherlands: International Service for National Agricultural Research.

Ruttan, V. W. 1982. *Agricultural Research Policy.* Minneapolis, MN: University of Minnesota Press.

———. 1986. "Toward a Global Agricultural Research System: A Personal View." *Research Policy* 15 (6): 307–27.

Santana, C. A. M., and J. R. Nascimento. 2012. "Public Policies and Agricultural Investment in Brazil." Food and Agriculture Organization of the United Nations (FAO), Rome.

Schumpeter, J. A. 1934. *The Theory of Economic Development.* Cambridge, MA: Harvard University Press.

Sheahan, M., C. B. Barrett, and C. Goldvale. 2017. "Human Health and Pesticide Use in Sub-Saharan Africa." *Agricultural Economics* 48 (S1): 27–41. https://doi.org/10.1111/agec.12384.

Shi, G. M., and C. E. Pray. 2012. "Modeling Agricultural Innovation in a Rapidly Developing Country: The Case of Chinese Pesticide Industry." *Agricultural Economics* 43 (4): 379–90. https://doi.org/10.1111/j.1574-0862.2012.00590.x.

Silva, F. F., M. J. Braga, and J. C. Garcia. 2018. "Link between R&D Intensity and Market Concentration: Analysis of Brazilian Corn and Soybean Seed Markets." *Italian Review of Agricultural Economics* 73 (2): 105–24.

Sparger, J. A., G. W. Norton, P. W. Heisey, and J. Alwang. 2013. "Is the Share of Agricultural Maintenance Research Rising in the United States?" *Food Policy* 38 (2013): 126–35.

Stads, G.-J., S. Perez, A. Londono, and N. Beintema. 2016. "Colombia Agricultural R&D Indicators Factsheet." Agricultural Science and Technology Indicators. International Food Policy Research Institute, Washington, DC.

Suphannachart, W., and P. Warr. 2012. "Total Factor Productivity in Thai Agriculture: Measurement and Determinants." In *Productivity Growth in Agriculture: An International Perspective,* edited by K. Fuglie, S. Wang, and E. Ball, 215–36. Wallingford, UK: CABI (Centre for Agriculture and Bioscience International) Publishing.

Tamru, S., B. Minten, D. Alemu, and F. Bachewe. 2017. "The Rapid Expansion of Herbicide Use in Smallholder Agriculture in Ethiopia: Patterns, Drivers, and Implications." *European Journal of Development Research* 29 (3): 628–47. https://doi.org/10.1057/s41287-017-0076-5.

Thirtle, C., D. Hadley, and R. Townsend. 1995. "Policy-Induced Innovation in Sub-Saharan African Agriculture: A Multilateral Malmquist Productivity Index Approach." *Development Policy Review* 13 (4): 323–48.

Thirtle, C., L. Lin, and J. Piesse. 2003. "The Impact of Research-Led Agricultural Productivity Growth on Poverty Reduction in Africa, Asia and Latin America." *World Development* 31 (12): 1959–75.

Tripp, R., and C. Ragasa. 2015. "Hybrid Maize Seed Supply in Ghana." GSSP Working Paper 40, International Food Policy Research Institute (IFPRI), Washington, DC. http://ebrary.ifpri.org/cdm/ref/collection/p15738coll2/id/129746.

USDA-ERS (US Department of Agriculture Economic Research Service). 2019. Agricultural Research Funding in the Public and Private Sectors. Online database. Washington, DC (accessed July 2019), https://www.ers.usda.gov/data-products/agricultural-research-funding-in-the-public-and-private-sectors/.

UPOV (International Union for the Protection of New Varieties of Plants). 2018. PLUTO: Plant Variety Database. International Union for the Protection of New Varieties of Plants. http://www.upov.int/pluto/en/.

Wiebe, K., M. Soule, C. Narrod, and V. Breneman. 2000. "Resource Quality and Agricultural Productivity: A Multi-country Comparison." Conference Paper, American Agricultural Economics Association, Tampa, FL.

World Bank. 2006. *Intellectual Property Rights: Designing Regimes to Support Plant Breeding in Developing Countries.* Washington, DC: World Bank. http://documents.worldbank.org/curated/en/528331468328595898/Intellectual-property-rights-designing-regimes-to-support-plant-breeding-in-developing-countries.

———. 2014. *Corporate Governance of State-Owned Enterprises: A Toolkit.* Washington, DC: World Bank.

———. 2018. World Development Indicators. Database. https://datacatalog.worldbank.org/dataset/world-development-indicators.

4. Improving the Enabling Environment for Technology Adoption

Removing Constraints and Adopting Policies to Promote Diffusion of Technology

The previous chapters established the central role played by technological innovation in raising the productivity of small farms and documented the substantially high returns that can be earned from investments in research and development (R&D) to develop technologies appropriate for local contexts. But a long-standing puzzle remains why even when technologies appear to be farm ready, they may diffuse slowly if at all among a farm population (Ruttan 1977; Feder and Umali 1993; Udry 2019). Simply subsidizing or sponsoring R&D will be effectively "pushing on a string" if farmers are unable or unwilling to adopt these innovations. This chapter discusses elements of the enabling environment required for rapid and efficient technological diffusion. A key component is to allow market incentives to reward high-performing farmers. But the chapter also describes how market failures can constrain technology adoption and how they might be corrected through appropriately designed policy interventions.

Historically, policies in many developing countries have discriminated against agriculture, effectively taxing farmers to provide subsidies to urban dwellers or nonagricultural sectors (Kreuger, Schiff, and Valdés 1988; Anderson 2016). Such policies lower returns to agricultural investment, discourage technology adoption, and lead to inefficient use of economic resources. At the same time, due to the unique characteristics of agriculture—farms are highly heterogeneous and geographically dispersed, production is seasonal and subject to severe weather shocks, and property rights over land and other assets are often insecure—markets suffer from asymmetric information and high transactions costs, and may fail to provide critical services needed for rapid and efficient technology adoption. From a farmer's perspective, these factors can make technology appear unprofitable and too risky. Overcoming barriers to technology adoption may require government policies that

- Produce profitable technologies for farmers to adopt (see chapter 3)
- Remove policy biases against agriculture that suppress farm prices
- Close educational gaps between genders and between rural and urban populations
- Improve farmer access to information and learning

- Help farmers manage and hedge risk
- Strengthen financial services
- Provide secure land tenure
- Build rural marketing infrastructure

With appropriately designed policies, market failures constraining technology adoption may be corrected. However, what characterizes "appropriate policy design" has been elusive. Many development projects that have sought to provide credit, information, orderly supply of complementary inputs, infrastructure, and so on have fallen short of expectations. This chapter reviews lessons learned from economic research on policy design to overcome constraints to technology adoption. This discussion continues in chapter 5, which describes how new developments in agri-food value chains can be harnessed to address some of these market failures and enable smallholder farms to raise their productivity and product quality.

The Technology Adoption Puzzle

The Green Revolution of the 1960s and 1970s saw the spread of new crop varieties, fertilizers, and other agricultural technologies to smallholder farmers in developing countries, particularly in Asia and Latin America. However, across and within regions, large differences in technology adoption and input use are evident (table 4.1). The first generation of Green Revolution crop varieties was limited to cereal grains grown in irrigated areas. Subsequent agricultural R&D has extended improved technologies to more environments and more crops, although significant adoption gaps remain. By the 2010s, modern varieties of rice and maize had been adopted on more than 90 percent of the crop area in Asia but half or less their crop area in Africa. Irrigation, fertilizer, and tractor use in Africa also remain very low, at only a fraction of the utilization rates seen in other developing regions. These differences in adoption of modern agricultural technologies have exacerbated productivity and yield gaps around the world.

Understanding farmers' behavior regarding adoption of new agricultural technologies and how policies might accelerate diffusion has been the subject of hundreds of studies since at least the early days of the Green Revolution. Differences in factor prices is one reason: in countries where land is scarce but labor is abundant, farmers are keen to intensify land use, and tend to adopt improved seed-fertilizer-irrigation technologies to raise yields. In countries where wages are rising and land is relatively abundant, farmers adopt tractors and other kinds of farm machinery to substitute for farm labor. This helps explain why, for example, fertilizer and irrigation use is relatively high in Asia, whereas tractor use is high in Latin America (see table 4.1). Early adopters of new technology tend to be larger farms with secure land tenure, access to credit and extension services, and ability or willingness to take risks (Feder, Just, and Zilberman 1985). But studies have found that for scale-neutral technologies likes improved seed and

TABLE 4.1　Use of Modern Agricultural Inputs Varies across Developing Countries

Modern input	Year	East Asia	South Asia	Latin America	Middle East and North Africa	Sub-Saharan Africa
Modern crop variety		Area in modern varieties/crop harvested area (%)				
Wheat	1960	0.0	0.0	0.0	0.0	0.0
	1980	27.5	78.2	61.3	33.8	4.1
	2000	89.1	94.5	93.2	69.1	47.4
	2010/14[a]	100.0	95.6	—	—	62.5
Rice	1960	0.0	0.0	0.0	0.0	0.0
	1980	40.9	36.3	46.2	2.2	3.1
	2000	80.5	71.0	32.3	10.4	31.0
	2010/14[a]	91.0	99.7	—	—	38.0
Maize	1960	0.0	0.0	0.0	—	0.0
	1980	61.7	34.4	11.2	—	0.4
	2000	89.6	53.5	56.5	—	16.8
	2010/14[a]	96.3	86.5	—	—	52.8
Irrigation		Share of crop area equipped for irrigation (%)				
	1960	21.1	18.8	8.1	16.0	2.4
	1980	31.0	27.2	10.2	33.4	3.1
	2000	32.1	39.3	11.9	30.1	3.5
	2015	34.6	45.7	12.7	34.6	3.4
Fertilizer		Kg of fertilizers/hectare of cropland				
	1960	8.2	2.8	6.3	10.6	1.4
	1980	102.3	31.3	42.9	54.1	6.4
	2000	189.6	96.0	75.5	80.7	6.5
	2015	258.1	150.6	72.0	105.1	10.6
Tractors		Tractors/1,000 farm workers				
	1960	0.2	0.2	4.9	11.0	0.7
	1980	1.9	2.2	26.6	25.9	1.1
	2000	2.3	10.2	50.7	38.0	1.0
	2015	11.1	21.9	66.0	47.6	1.0

Sources: Cropland, irrigated area, fertilizer, and tractor use (FAO 2019); adoption of modern crop varieties for 1960–2000 (Evenson and Gollin 2003); variety adoption area for Sub-Saharan Africa in 2010 (Walker et al. 2015) and for Asia in 2014 (Maredia et al. 2016).
Note: Modern crop varieties are defined as improved varieties released since 1970. kg = kilogram; — = not available.
a. 2010/14 = variety adoption area in 2010 for Sub-Saharan Africa and 2014 for Asia.

fertilizers, differences in farm characteristics only temporarily slow adoption in areas where they are profitable to use (Feder and Umali 1993). However, when technology adoption hits a ceiling—with many farmers choosing not to adopt—it is often the case they simply do not find it profitable or consider it too risky. Low farm-gate prices for commodities due to high marketing costs and policies which heavily tax agriculture can make technology adoption unprofitable.

Low or stagnant adoption of improved seed varieties has been particularly prevalent in less favorable environments, such as rainfed farming systems in Africa (Jansen, Walker, and Barker 1990; Suri 2011; Fuglie and Marder 2015). As late as 2010, modern varieties of food crops had been adopted on only about one-third of the cropland in Sub-Saharan Africa (Walker et al. 2015). There was also large variation in adoption rates of improved varieties across crops and countries in Africa (table 4.2). This may simply reflect low profitability of the new varieties in many of these cropping systems, or it

TABLE 4.2 **Adoption of Modern Crop Varieties Is Highly Uneven across Sub-Saharan Africa, circa 2006–10**

Crop	Total crop area (1,000 ha)	Modern crop variety adoption (%)	Country	Number of crops surveyed	Area of crops surveyed (1,000 ha)	Modern crop variety adoption (%)
Soybean	1,185	89.7	Zimbabwe	4	1,628	91.9
Maize (WCA)[a]	9,972	65.7	Cameroon	6	1,154	67.9
Wheat	1,454	62.5	Zambia	6	1,505	66.8
Pigeon pea	366	49.9	Kenya	8	2,413	62.6
Maize (ESA)[a]	14,696	44.0	Ghana	6	2,081	52.6
Cassava	11,036	39.7	Benin	6	1,388	50.5
Rice	6,787	38.0	Côte d'Ivoire	6	1,982	50.3
Potato	616	34.4	Malawi	8	2,705	47.2
Barley	971	32.7	Senegal	6	2,862	43.7
Yam	4,673	30.2	Sudan	4	6,736	41.0
Groundnut	6,357	29.2	Nigeria	9	27,023	40.6
Beans	2,497	29.0	Madagascar	1	1,400	35.2
Sorghum	17,966	27.4	Mali	6	4,265	34.9
Cowpea	11,472	27.2	Congo, Dem. Rep.	6	4,209	33.9
Pearl millet	14,090	18.1	Ethiopia	9	5,604	33.9
Chickpea	250	15.0	Guinea	5	1,657	31.8
Faba bean	615	14.0	Uganda	11	4,305	31.5
Lentils	95	10.4	Tanzania	10	7,022	31.1
Sweet potato	1,478	6.9	Angola	2	2,393	17.4
Banana	916	6.2	Niger	4	14,850	14.0
Field pea	230	1.5	Mozambique	5	3,143	12.9
			Burkina Faso	6	4,637	11.8
Total[b]	107,722	35.3			104,962	34.9

Source: Walker et al. 2015.

Note: Modern crop varieties defined as improved varieties released since 1970. ha = hectares.

a. Maize (WCA) = maize in West and Central Africa; Maize (ESA) = maize in East and Southern Africa.

b. Total by crops is larger than total by country because it includes data from additional countries not listed in the table.

could reflect deficiencies in the enabling environment that empower farmers to access new technology and profit from adoption. In cases in which there are large farm-to-farm differences in productivity within an area or within similar cropping systems, it could indicate that particular elements of the enabling environment are preventing some farms from making technical and managerial improvements to their farms. What elements are most constraining adoption is likely to be context- and area-specific. The remainder of this chapter discusses findings from recent research on constraints to technology adoption and specific policies governments might take to help farmers access and successfully adopt new technology and practices. One emerging conclusion from this research is that farmers often face multiple constraints to adoption, and especially in rainfed agriculture considerations of risk loom large. It may not be enough to "fix" just one aspect of the enabling environment, and multidimensional and holistic approaches may be necessary to accelerate technology diffusion in agriculture.

Removing Policy Bias against Agriculture

Farmers adopt new technologies to improve their welfare. Whether a new technology's benefits (in the form of higher net returns, more stable income, or other attributes valued by a farm household) justify the costs of adoption—including the fixed costs of learning how to use a new technology and costs of associated inputs—will be heavily influenced by the prices faced by farmers. Policy interventions in markets and trade have a large influence on prices farmers receive for their agricultural products as well as the prices they pay for purchased inputs and nonagricultural goods—that is, the agricultural terms of trade. Policies that are biased against agriculture can lower agricultural terms of trade and thus reduce incentives to invest in and adopt new technologies.

Two measures of policy bias in agricultural markets are the nominal rate of assistance (NRA) and the relative rate of assistance (RRA) to agriculture. The agricultural NRA compares actual gross farm income (at national prices, which includes the effects of policies) and what gross farm income would be if border prices prevailed (that is, without market interventions by government). A negative value of the NRA implies that policies effectively tax agriculture by lowering prices farmers receive for their products or making them pay more for inputs, and a positive value implies that governments are subsidizing agriculture (either through commodity price supports, input subsidies, or undervalued exchange rates). But governments may also subsidize or protect nonagricultural sectors, which can raise the prices farm households pay for nonfarm goods and services. The RRA compares assistance to agriculture with assistance to nonagricultural sectors, and thus provides a more comprehensive measure of the overall policy bias for or against agriculture. Negative values of NRA and RRA imply an antiagricultural policy bias.

As figure 4.1 shows, until the 1980s NRAs were negative for most developing regions, meaning that policies were effectively taxing agriculture. Policy reforms have gradually

FIGURE 4.1 **Evidence That Policies Are Discriminating against Farmers and Lowering the Agricultural Terms of Trade Can Be Found in Negative Nominal and Relative Rates of Assistance**

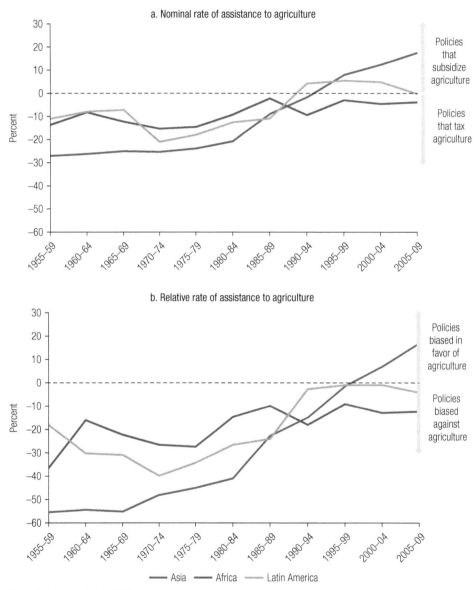

a. Nominal rate of assistance to agriculture

b. Relative rate of assistance to agriculture

— Asia — Africa — Latin America

Source: Anderson and Nelgen 2013.

reduced this bias over time, and by the 1990s, Asia had moved to providing significant net subsidies to its agricultural sector. But taxation of agriculture has often been accompanied by subsidies or protection for nonagricultural sectors, reflected in larger negative values for the RRA (Anderson and Nelgen 2013). Before the 1990s, policy bias against agriculture was very high in Asia, Africa, and Latin America, and remained significant in Africa as late as 2005–09. Although more recent comprehensive data on NRA and RRA are not available, statistics on closely related measures, like the nominal rate of protection and the producer support estimate (PSE), show that in many developing countries policy biases against agriculture remain a significant problem.[1]

Do these policies make a difference to agriculture? Econometric evidence from a number of countries has shown that better policies and institutions that strengthen farmer incentives, combined with investments in rural public goods, can have enormous impacts on agricultural productivity and growth. One of the most powerful examples comes from China, which adopted a series of institutional and policy reforms in the late 1970s and 1980s that stimulated a vast improvement in the country's agriculture (Fan 1991; Lin 1992). These reforms centered on allowing farm households to make their own decisions about (and earn rewards from) the use of family and farm resources, and freeing up market prices to signal incentives on what to grow and how to produce it. Supporting this view is a set of recent set of studies by Rada and colleagues, who find that investments in agricultural R&D and policy reforms that reduced policy bias against agriculture (measured by changes in the NRA to agriculture) stimulated growth in agricultural total factor productivity (TFP) in India, Indonesia, and Sub-Saharan Africa.[2] These findings are also consistent with those of Goyal and Nash (2017), who show that spending on rural infrastructure, agricultural R&D, and technology dissemination have had large poverty alleviation effects in Asia. For Latin America, Lopez and Galinato (2007) find that agricultural and rural economic growth increased after reforms were enacted that shifted public investment away from providing private goods and services to specific groups of producers and toward increased provision of public goods. During 1984–2001, 51 percent of all spending by Latin American governments in rural areas was for subsidies to private goods. But Lopez and Galinato (2007) estimate that a reallocation of 10 percentage points of public expenditures to public goods would increase per capita agricultural income by about 2.3 percent without increasing total spending. Improvements in the policies affecting trade, regulations, and public spending enhance the incentives for producers and crowd in private investment.

Closing Education Gaps

Providing more formal education to farmers and rural families provides two essential functions in the agricultural transformation process. First, it helps farmers adopt and use new agricultural technology more effectively. Second, it prepares many farm and rural households with necessary skills to eventually exit agriculture and join the nonfarm sector.

One consistent finding from technology adoption studies is that more educated farmers adopt new technologies earlier and get more profit out of them (Schultz 1975; Foster and Rosenzweig 2010). Because education facilitates the acquisition and processing of new information, the effects of education on farm productivity and income are higher in environments undergoing technological and structural transformation (Lockheed, Jamison, and Lau 1980). For example, in pre–Green Revolution India, after controlling for farm size and other factors, peasants with primary education earned about 10 percent more from farming than illiterate peasants, but in post–Green Revolution years this productivity gap grew to 40 percent, Foster and Rosenzweig (1995) find. An important finding from this study is that the higher private returns to schooling brought about by technical change caused Indian farm households to invest more in their children's schooling. In a review of 20 studies from 13 countries, Lockheed, Jamison, and Lau (1980) estimate that in a traditional environment with little or no technical change, an additional year of schooling added only 1.3 percent to farm income, whereas in a modernizing environment, returns rose to 9.5 percent per year of schooling. To make effective use of the new technology required agricultural workers to acquire more formal education.

In the last several decades, average schooling levels of the labor force have increased significantly across the developing world (figure 4.2). By 2010, each adult worker in South Asia and Sub-Saharan Africa had on average five years of formal schooling, about the amount that one in Latin America and East Asia had in 1980. However, a significant gender gap has persisted in many of these countries. The lag in education of female workers is especially important for agriculture since women form a major part of the workforce and often manage their own farms.

FIGURE 4.2 **In Many Developing Countries, Gender Gaps Persist in Labor Force Schooling Levels**

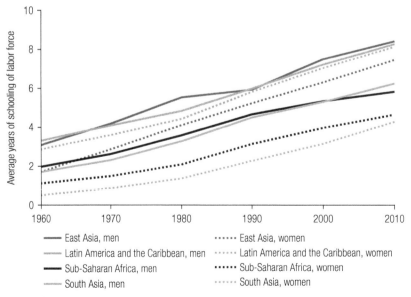

Source: Barrow and Lee 2013.

In addition to the gender gap, a second type of education gap in developing countries is the difference in schooling levels between farm and nonfarm labor. Drawing on data from 124 developing and developed countries, Gollin, Lagakos, and Waugh (2014) find that the average schooling level of a farm worker was almost three years less than the average schooling of a nonfarm worker, a gap that was most pronounced in low-income countries (figure 4.3). Although this gap partly reflects higher skill requirements of many nonfarm jobs and the fact that investment in schooling by farm families is often used to facilitate migration out of agriculture, it also reflects an urban bias in the provision of education (and other public) services. Not only do rural students stay fewer years in school, but their schooling quality is also lower: average test scores of rural students are consistently lower than urban student test scores at similar grade levels (Patrinos and Angrist 2018).

Whereas early adoption of modern crop varieties and synthetic fertilizers that characterized much of the Green Revolution did not generally require more than basic literacy skills, new agricultural technologies are likely to be increasingly management- and skill-intensive (Gollin, Morris, and Byerlee 2005). Post–Green Revolution technologies place greater emphasis on improving the efficiency of resource use, upgrading product quality, financial and risk management, and marketing and negotiating skills. Acquiring facility with numbers, competency in information and communication technology (ICT), and other skills needed in this environment will require continually upgrading the formal schooling levels of the farm workforce.

As countries develop and incomes rise, it is almost inevitable that many farm and rural family members will migrate to nonfarm jobs and cities. A dynamic agricultural

FIGURE 4.3   Agricultural Workers Get Less Schooling Than Nonagricultural Workers

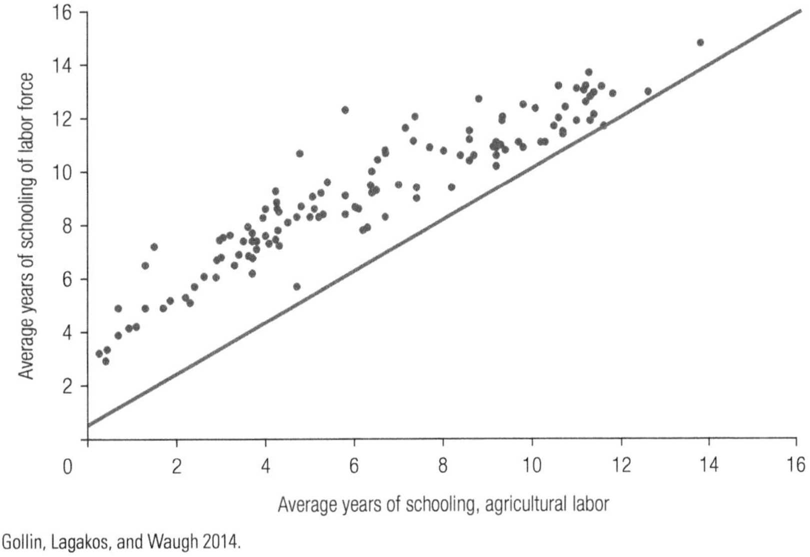

Source: Gollin, Lagakos, and Waugh 2014.

sector undergoing rapid technological change may also be disruptive for many farm households, especially those not able to rapidly acquire new technology and stay competitive in the sector. Education helps prepare farm and rural households to face social and economic disruptions that economic development may bring about. It makes them more able and prepared for jobs in other sectors. Closing the rural-urban education gap will help these family members compete for employment opportunities in the broader economy.

Securing Land Tenure Rights for Smallholders

Land tenure security refers to the right to remain on one's land and make use of and profit from it. In many parts of the world farmers do not hold formal title to their land and may be subject to eviction or loss of rights to use land (and water). They may also lack means to transfer land rights to other parties. Enhancing tenure security can contribute to agricultural productivity and efficiency by (1) raising incentives for making land improvements that boost crop yields; (2) improving access to formal credit through use of land as collateral; (3) increasing the opportunity for efficiency-enhancing land transfers to more productive producers; and (4) improving overall governance, including reducing the likelihood of conflicts over land (Deininger 2003).

Lack of tenure security can be a major constraint to making investments in land improvements necessary for sustainable productivity growth. Ditching, terracing, land leveling, green manuring, tree planting, fencing, and other practices that enhance land quality often have high upfront costs. Benefits, however, accrue only gradually. If land transactions are possible, the benefits from land improvements also get capitalized into the sale or rental value of land. It may make sense for farmers to make such investments only if they are assured of future user rights to the land and/or they can earn the capitalized value of the land improvements by having the right to rent out or sell it. Deininger and Jin (2006) find that in highland Ethiopia, where land degradation from soil erosion is a serious concern, tenure security coupled with transfer rights unambiguously increased farmer investment in land terraces, a practice that reduced soil erosion and raised crop yield and land value.

The most pressing tenure security reforms in rural areas include clarifying rights of land users, recognizing and expanding rights for women to use and transfer property, managing potentially conflicting claims of property users (such as between pastoralists and farmers), and creating more effective dispute resolution mechanisms. An important dimension for policy in such an environment is to enable newly forming households to gain access to land. In many parts of Africa, traditional tenure systems in which local inhabitants have user rights to communally owned land are giving way to formal titling systems (Jayne et al. 2016). Land policies that facilitate the emergence of land rental arrangements can provide a means through which poor households can gain access to such land (Deininger, Savastano, and Xia 2017; Eastwood, Lipton, and Newell 2010).

Besides rental markets, New Wave Land Reform (NWLR) is a mechanism that emphasizes consensual, decentralized, and market-assisted means to transfer land ownership from large to small farms. Such consensual agreements often require subsidies to provide compensation for land transfers, funded either by taxpayers or donors willing to share the costs of land redistribution (Deininger 1999; Pedersen 2016).

Providing Information Services

The State of Agricultural Extension around the World

Most countries provide agricultural extension or advisory services in rural areas to overcome information asymmetries about new agricultural technologies and market opportunities. Worldwide, governments employ about 1 million agricultural extension agents, or on average about 1 agent per 500 farms. However, the distribution of extension services is highly uneven across countries, with a few countries accounting for the lion's share of this global capacity (table. 4.3). China accounts for about 60 percent of the world's total number of extension agents, and in Sub-Saharan Africa, Ethiopia alone accounts for about half the region's total extension capacity. Despite these sizeable investments, evidence on the impact of public agricultural extension systems on farm productivity is mixed, sometimes achieving high returns (Evenson 2001), but with many systems plagued by design failures (Anderson and Feder 2007).

The impact of public investments in agricultural extension will be strongly influenced by the capacity of a country's knowledge generation system (especially its public agricultural research institutions). No matter how well an extension system is organized and managed, its success will be dependent on an innovation system that is

TABLE 4.3   Agricultural Extension Workers Are Highly Concentrated in a Few Countries

Geographic area or country	Number of public extension agents	Farmers per extension agent
Sub-Saharan Africa	86,190	524
Ethiopia	45,812	235
Latin America and the Caribbean	36,576	436
Brazil	24,000	216
East Asia and Pacific	885,092	478
China	617,706	325
West Asia and North Africa	43,728	360
Turkey	14,644	210
Developing countries	1,051,586	475
World	1,087,690	479

Source: Number of extension agents is from Swanson and Davis (2014); number of farms is from FAO (2014).
Note: Data are from 2009–13 and cover 83 countries that contain about 90 percent of the world's farms.

producing a steady stream of well-adapted and profitable new technologies and practices for farmers to adopt. No extension service can be expected to generate high returns if it does not have innovations to extend. In the 1970s, the training and visit (T&V) extension model was promoted in over 50 developing countries to address what was perceived to be weak links between research and extension, but performed poorly, especially in Sub-Saharan Africa (Anderson, Feder, and Ganguly 2006). The T&V model was based on improving research-extension training and included frequent visits by extension agents to "contact farmers," who were then expected to disseminate learning to the general farm population. When many T&V projects fell short of achieving measurable impacts, political support waned. One complaint from farmers was that the system was too "top down" and was not flexible enough to address the widely varying needs of farmers (Hussain, Byerlee, and Heisey 1994). Another problem was that contact farmers did not receive adequate incentives to pass on training received to other farmers (Gautam 2000). But in other cases, especially in areas undergoing significant technology change, the T&V system helped farmers improve crop management and increase profitability (Feder, Lau, and Slade 1987). As with formal schooling, the value of external knowledge will be high in economies undergoing rapid technological and structural changes, but in static systems, traditional knowledge will be of greater relevance (Schultz 1975).

In the 1990s emphasis in agricultural extension shifted to more participatory learning methods like farmer field schools (FFS). FFS are viewed as a way of diffusing knowledge-intensive technologies by helping farmers develop their analytical skills, and were first widely deployed to extend integrated pest management in Southeast Asian rice systems. The FFS approach is relatively costly per participant, and thus like the T&V system depends on participants sharing their knowledge with other farmers to achieve broader impacts. Although FFS has been shown to significantly improve farmer knowledge on complex subjects, it has suffered from scaling issues and a lack of knowledge diffusion beyond immediate participants (Waddington et al. 2012).

Recent efforts in extension design have given more explicit attention to how social learning occurs and how incentives among participants can be improved (de Janvry, Macours, and Sadoulet 2017). Learning for technology adoption in agriculture is a complex process. Farmers often use multiple points of contact in acquiring information to make their adoption decisions. Choice of contact farmers should depend on the barriers to be overcome for securing diffusion through social networks. Using mass media to inform social networks about new technologies can create demand for information and induce farmers to seek out contact farmers for further learning. Farmer-led demonstration trials with field days open to the community can encourage relevant information sharing among social networks. Providing small financial or in-kind payments to contact farmers based on the number of farmers who successfully adopt a technology can encourage greater farmer-to-farmer contact and dissemination of quality information (BenYishay and Mobarak 2014). In the successful effort to eradicate cattle plague (Rinderpest) worldwide, for example, such incentives played an important role mobilizing community-based animal health workers to vaccinate cattle. In Ethiopia, community health workers working in remote areas achieved herd immunity rates matching or surpassing levels achieved by national veterinary services in more accessible locations (Roeder, Mariner, and Kock 2013).

When value chains are well developed, a more diverse set of agents (agribusiness partners, agrodealers, for-profit consultants, and nongovernmental organizations (NGOs) can play an important role in information dissemination. These agents may have their own motives (boosting sales of specific products, for example), and third-party certification, rating, and performance audits become necessary to establish credibility and trust. In such situations, the role of public extension moves from being a core service provider to that of a regulator, coordinator, and provider of targeted services (such as to marginal groups) to complement what the private sector does.

Reforming Agricultural Advisory Services

Some of the key challenges facing agricultural advisory services include linking extension more closely with research and other sources of knowledge generation, being responsive to diverse needs of farmers, and assuring fiscal sustainability of programs. Many countries have decentralized responsibility for extension services to local governments in an effort to make them more demand-driven and accountable to local communities. Agricultural advisory services have also experimented with alternative models for program delivery (such as the training and visit system and farmer field schools), service provision (such as contracting delivery to private service providers), and financing (including fee-for-service and producer levies for extension services). An analytical framework in which governance structures for extension services can be assessed in terms of their ability to minimize or reduce the transactions costs of meeting system goals and objectives can be found in a discussion paper by the International Food Policy Research Institution by Birner et al. (2006).

Reform experiences point to a number of steps governments can take to strengthen agricultural advisory services. Recent research survey articles (Birner et al. 2006; Feder, Birner, and Anderson 2011) highlight key elements of successful reforms.

- Encourage pluralistic delivery systems. Although the public sector will continue to play a leadership role in funding, managing, and coordinating agricultural advisory services, multiple actors can be effective service providers. Private companies and NGOs may possess specialized skills and local capacities that can be contracted to provide high-quality advisory services. But to address the information asymmetry problem, private- and NGO-led extension often needs to be subsidized and provided with technical support.
- Reform governance structures. Public extension agencies need to be accountable and responsive to needs of farmers and other clients. Several

countries have decentralized responsibility for extension program delivery to local governments and increased the voice of farmer and commodity organizations in setting program priorities and planning. Producer organizations can also be involved in cofinancing advisory services, such as through commodity levies.

- Invest in new skills and capacities. As market value chains respond to the growing complexity of consumer demands for safe, convenient, and diverse food products, this creates the need for new types of advisory services. Farmers will need more timely information about market opportunities and detailed technical knowledge about how to meet higher product quality standards. With greater diversity of potential service providers, public extension agents will need increased networking and coordination skills to make sure this knowledge and information are accessible to diverse groups of farmers, including smallholders and women (see chapter 5).

- Maintain strong links between research, extension, and farmers. In an efficient innovation system, information and understanding must flow efficiently among researchers, extension providers, and farmers. A challenge posed by the decentralization of extension services is that looser coordination may result between research and extension. Explicit attention needs to be given to maintaining strong links and coordination among these groups. Extension systems often employ highly trained subject specialists to provide an accessible link between field agents and research institutes.

Digital Technology Offers the Potential to Provide Tailored Extension Services at Lower Cost

A promising new development in agricultural extension is the opportunity to reduce the costs of knowledge and information provision by using modern information and communication technologies (ICT) (World Bank 2016). Over the past decade, mobile phone subscriptions have become ubiquitous in most countries of the world, and access to Internet services is spreading rapidly. By 2017, nearly half the world's population used the Internet (figure 4.4). Although Internet penetration was considerably less in South Asia and Sub-Saharan Africa as of 2017, they appear to lag only about five years behind other developing regions. These digital technologies are already having impacts on market efficiency and farm productivity in developing countries (Deichmann, Goyal, and Mishra 2016).

The advent of low-cost digital technologies offers radically new alternatives to enable extension services and farmers to exchange tailored, frequent, and timely information at a reduced cost, particularly in remote areas. This implies a greater penetration of knowledge precisely in areas with the most poverty. Furthermore, digital technologies permit information to be tailored precisely to the specific context (Deichmann, Goyal, and Mishra 2016; Davis and Sulaiman 2014).

FIGURE 4.4 **Access to Information and Communication Technologies Is Rapidly Gaining in Developing Countries**

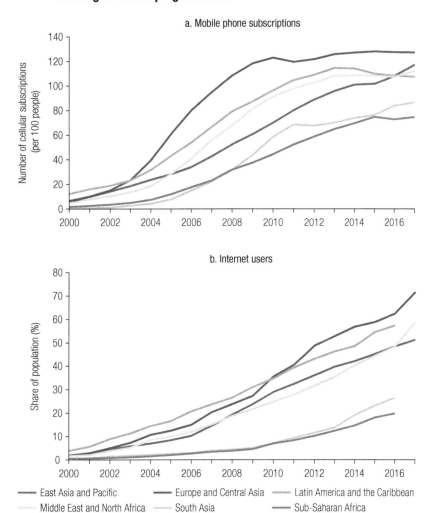

a. Mobile phone subscriptions

b. Internet users

| — East Asia and Pacific | — Europe and Central Asia | — Latin America and the Caribbean |
| — Middle East and North Africa | — South Asia | — Sub-Saharan Africa |

Source: World Bank, World Development Indicators.

Note: Data for East Asia and Pacific and Europe and Central Asia excludes high-income countries.

Digital-based or electronic extension systems have typically included a wide range of tools, software, platforms, and devices with diverse sources of information. The simplest forms of e-extension are call lines/hotlines and radio/television programs, often using a Questions-and-Answers approach. In places where modern digital technologies are not yet widespread, these simpler tools remain effective, even though they allow for limited customization or interactivity. For example, a principal outreach strategy of Ethiopia's Agricultural Transformation Agency that now reaches 13 million smallholders relies on radio communication (EATA 2015). At the other end of the scale are highly advanced extension systems combining mobile tools linked to online platforms that are operated via smartphones or tablets. The e-extension system can be in the form of an online repository or information bank, with specific information on best practices for different crops suited to varying agroclimatic conditions, along with a database of input retailers and input prices. Similarly, e-extension can be in the form of participatory training videos disseminated via farmer groups and cooperatives. For instance, they can be used to send real-time updates and pictures of damaged crops to identify the cause and provide advice on treatment. In rural areas, the added value of e-extension is that extension officers can reach out to many more farmers than solely through field visits, especially in situations when the extension officer-to-farmer ratio is very high, as is common in many Sub-Saharan African countries. They can use mobile phones for about one-quarter the price of traveling to visit a farmer, Aker (2011) estimates (figure 4.5).

In addition to making extension services more efficient, the improved outreach leveraged by such technologies increases inclusion and equity among the farmers. Although e-extension cannot entirely replace field advisory visits, demonstration plots, and field days, it can still have a positive impact on farming and growth. In rural India, for instance, information provided via mobile phones to farmers increased their knowledge of available options for inputs such as seeds and fertilizers as well as choices of different crops, Cole and Fernando (2012) show. This led to changes in their investment decisions and eventually to planting more profitable crops. The study demonstrates that the low-cost information ($0.60 per month) was able to influence farmer behavior. Similarly, the Digital Green project, which started in India and has spread to

FIGURE 4.5   In Niger, the Marginal (per Search) Cost of Obtaining Agricultural Information Varies Greatly by Communication Method

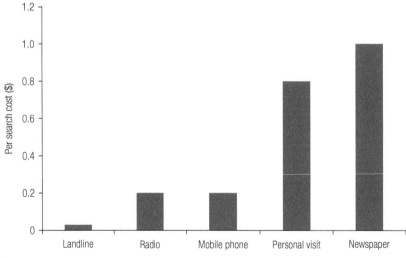

Source: Aker 2011.

Note: In Niger, newspapers are relatively expensive because they are primarily concentrated in urban areas, are expensive, and are inaccessible to the illiterate population (Aker 2011). $ = constant 2005 US dollars.

other countries including Ethiopia, uses a participatory process to let farmers get access to agricultural advice by connecting farmers with experts through a local social network. By minimizing the distance between instructors and learners, the initiative increased adoption of some agricultural practices seven-fold over classical extension approaches (Gandhi et al. 2009). In the same way, a Chilean farming cooperative (Coopeumo) has used text messages to help small-scale farmers increase productivity, especially by providing targeted planting advice and weather updates that are particularly useful to farmers at critical points such as sowing and harvest (World Bank 2011).

Field studies from a wide range of countries have documented how e-extension can dramatically lower costs of providing information to farmers. For instance, in cooperation with agricultural research and extension services, organizations such as Digital Green, the Grameen Foundation, Reuters Market Light, and Technoserve have been able to deliver timely, relevant, and actionable information and advice to farmers in South Asia, Latin America, and Sub-Saharan Africa at a dramatically lower cost than traditional services (Nakasone, Torero, and Minten 2014). Rather than always having to travel to visit a farmer, extension agents use a combination of voice, text, videos, and Internet to reduce transaction costs and increase the frequency of interaction with farmers. Similarly, governments, in partnership with mobile operators, use phones to coordinate distribution of improved seeds and subsidized fertilizers in remote areas through e-vouchers, as in Nigeria's large-scale e-wallet initiative. Technology firms such as Climate Corp, based in Silicon Valley, are pioneering the provision of agrometeorological services for early warning of weather and climate risks. A number of innovations aim for real-time and accurate weather monitoring using remote sensing and technologies enabled with geographic information systems (GIS) for climate-resilient agriculture.

Although formal evaluations of these interventions are few to date, evidence is emerging of their potential. In India, an interactive voice response system (at the time called Avaaj Otalo) provided timely information on weather and inputs as well as specific answers to farmers' questions about agronomic practices. A randomized evaluation of the Avaaj Otalo hotline found that farmers switched to more effective inputs, dedicated more land to cash crops, and saw increased yields (Cole and Fernando 2016). The Avaaj Otalo hotline particularly helped farmers switch to less visually appealing but more effective pest management practices. The impacts were greater for the group that received reminders at specific times aligned with growing season activities. In a randomized trial in Kenya, one-way text messages provided agricultural advice and reminders to contract farmers throughout the sugarcane planting, growing, and harvesting cycles. Combined with a complaint hotline, the text messages led to increased fertilizer use and reduced the nondelivery of inputs (Casaburi et al. 2014, preliminary results).

ICT also opens the door to more sophisticated precision farming systems that are more commonly applied at technologically advanced farms and plantations. The underlying logic is to combine various remote sensing data and satellite imagery for a given farm parcel (such as sensors for soil conditions, groundwater level, and rainwater precipitation detectors combined with irrigation optimization systems) to provide precise, real-time crop management advice. As this can be done remotely, it saves significant time and labor when compared to manual sampling. The use of calibrated technology makes the system less prone to error when assessing appropriate growth conditions (Hamrita and Hoffacker 2005). The benefit of the system is the resource optimization that can be done with the help of the information acquired. For example, the system can detect where there are nutrient deficiencies in the soil and thus additional fertilizers can be distributed to the areas where there is the most acute need. Irrigation or pesticide needs can similarly be detected and precisely applied. Digital tools can be applied to irrigation systems such as pumps that can be automated and controlled via mobile phones, such as the Nano Ganesh system in Pune, India, where farmers are able to save water, energy, and time by remotely controlling their irrigation pumps (Tulsian and Saini 2014). Precision farming requires investments in these systems, but once the systems are installed, they contribute directly to time, resource, and cost savings and efficiency improvements. Precision farming systems have also been shown to support environmental sustainability because the natural resources are being continuously monitored, and actions are taken accordingly, before nutrition depletion or drought takes place.

Exploiting these new technologies requires the basic infrastructure—cable backbone plus wireless connectivity—as well as appropriate regulatory conditions. However, it is absolutely critical to emphasize that ICT infrastructure cannot be a substitute for content. It cannot be a substitute for excellence in agricultural research, active connectivity with external centers, and well-trained extension specialists who, although working in a different modality, still have the understanding of how to approach farmers and understand their needs. ICT offers the opportunity to greatly increase the flow of information among research, extension, and farmers, enhancing the role of extension agents as intermediaries and communicators.

Helping Farmers Manage Risk

Exposure to Risk Features Heavily in Farmers' Decisions

Uncertain and variable income are salient features of agriculture. Two major sources of risk are production risks, whereby yield fluctuates in reaction to weather, pests, and diseases, and market risks due to the variability of prices of outputs, inputs, and credit. But in addition to these, farmers also face risks regarding resource availability (timeliness of supply of seeds, labor, or irrigation water); health (due to accidents, sickness, or death); and theft of or damage to their assets. How to smoothen consumption and protect capital in the face of these uncertainties weighs heavily on how farmers manage their resources. Risk-reducing strategies include crop diversification, intercropping, farm fragmentation, and diversification into nonfarm sources of income. Although these may help stabilize household incomes, they may require farmers to forgo more profitable alternatives. When major crop or animal losses do occur, farmers rely on a number of risk-coping mechanisms, such as use of credit, temporary migration to nonfarm jobs, redirecting household expenditures (for example, from school fees to food purchases), sales of assets or own food stocks, mutual aid or kin-support systems, or reducing food consumption. Risk-coping mechanisms can be quite costly and perpetuate a "poverty trap," in which households are unable to accumulate sufficient physical or human capital assets that enable them to rise out of chronic poverty (Carter and Barrett 2006). Importantly, risk-coping mechanisms often cannot deal effectively with the covariance of risks among farm households in a local area. When everyone loses their crop due to a drought and tries to find other work or sell assets at the same time, it can drive down wages and asset prices (Binswanger and Rosenzweig 1986; Binswanger and McIntire 1987; Hazell 1992).

Formal agricultural banking and insurance services offer potentially important benefits to farmers by helping them manage risk. Access to banking services enables a farmer to reallocate income from the past and future to the present through savings and borrowing. With crop insurance, farmers know they would be compensated if yields are catastrophically low for reasons beyond their control, and thus would be more likely to allocate resources in profit-maximizing ways. For example, a farmer will grow more of the most profitable crops even if they are riskier and will be more likely to adopt improved but unfamiliar technologies. The net effect could be an increase in value added from the agricultural sector, an increase in farm incomes, and a reduction in rural poverty.

In practice, however, private banking and insurance institutions have faced major challenges in providing services to smallholder farmers. To protect their own capital, commercial banks adjust interest rates to reflect risk premiums and insist on collateral, such as transferable land titles. Collateral not only helps insure loans but reduces the incentive for willful default. Because smallholder farmers often lack such collateral, they are perceived by banks as being high risk. But rather than charge high interest rates— which through adverse selection may cause only the farmers least likely to repay to apply for such loans, banks may exclude smallholder farmers altogether. This leads to a situation in which many farmers may be credit constrained—that is, they are willing to borrow and repay at market interest rates but are unable to obtain such loans. Similarly, private insurance markets are far from complete. Even where available, they are limited to coverage of insurable risks[3] and to situations when insurance can be provided at a cost that is lower than the benefits it provides (Hazell 1992). Insurable risk in agriculture is usually limited to production risks associated with a catastrophic weather event like a severe drought, flood, or hail. But a wide range of production risks, such as preventable damage from pests and diseases, as well as most resource risks, are not strictly insurable. It is also difficult to viably insure smallholder farmers because of high administrative costs of verifying claims on individual farm plots.

Research has found that in many farming areas risk and uncertainty are major impediments to adoption and use of modern inputs and technology. One study found that in India, limited options to manage risk led farmers to self-insure by accumulating marketable assets such as livestock instead of more profitable but less marketable assets like irrigation pumps (Rosenzweig and Wolpin 1993). In Ethiopia, farmers significantly underapply fertilizers (and forgo profits) to avoid downside risks should harvests fail (Dercon and Christiaensen 2011). Farmers in a drought-prone region of Tanzania chose to grow safer but lower return crops, forgoing up to 20 percent of their income as an implicit insurance premium (Dercon 1996), as did farmers in Mali, who limited their use of available credit and grew less of the most profitable crop, cotton, because it was riskier than alternatives (Elabed et al. 2013). Thus, risk reduction is obtained at a cost to efficiency.

If reliable and low-cost means can be found to insure farmers against severe short-falls in agricultural income, then such insurance could unlock access to credit (by reducing the risk of loan default) and make farmers more willing to adopt profitable crops and technologies even if they are perceived to be more risky. A key question for policy is whether, given the highly covariate nature of many agricultural risks, public interventions into farm credit and insurance markets can provide a more efficient alternative than traditional mechanisms of risk management.

Can Weather Index Insurance Products Mitigate Agricultural Risk?

One insurance mechanism that has attracted considerable attention is weather index insurance. Weather index insurance provides payouts to farmers in a specific area based on levels of a readily observable variable, like rainfall, that is highly correlated with crop yield. Such insurance instruments have much lower administrative costs because they do not require individual farm losses to be verified. Index insurance also avoids problems associated with moral hazard (whereby insured farmers pay less attention to their crops) and adverse selection (whereby farmers who face greater risk are more likely to buy insurance) because the index is independent of a particular farmer's yield or behavior. Because weather index insurance typically only insures against crop or livestock losses due to drought, it is likely to be most viable in situations when such measurable weather events make up a significant share of the total risk faced by famers.

Weather index insurance products have been extended to millions of farmers in dozens of developing countries (Carter et al. 2017; Jensen and Barrett 2017). The use of weather index insurance products has been shown to increase farmers' willingness to invest more in agricultural inputs and adopt more profitable activities (see Karlan et al. 2014 for maize in Ghana; Elabed and Carter 2013 for cotton in Mali; and Mobarak and Rosenzweig 2014 for crops generally in India). Weather index insurance has also helped Kenyan pastoralists cope better with severe drought (Janzen and Carter 2019). But despite these sizeable benefits, in virtually all cases these insurance products included heavy public subsidies on insurance premiums (Jensen and Barrett 2017). Without such subsidies, demand for weather index insurance from farmers has remained very low.

As stand-alone products, weather index insurance for smallholder farmers has not yet become commercially viable or able to attract private insurance providers (Skees, Hazell, and Miranda forthcoming).

A major, if not the major, constraint limiting the demand for weather index insurance products is basis risk (Miranda and Farrin 2012; Carter et al. 2017). Basis risk is the remaining uninsured risk a farmer faces after having obtained insurance. It is the difference between measured insurance risk and events and losses actually experienced by the insured. The less-than-perfect correlation between the predicted yield from the weather index and actual yield experienced on individual farm plots means some farmers who incur losses do not get compensated, and some who do not have losses nonetheless receive payouts. Basis risk can arise from two sources: the insurance contact may cover only one source of yield shock (that is, from drought, but not from pests, floods, or heat), and the area wide weather index may not be perfectly correlated with how weather affected yield on a particular farm. Basis risk is different for each individual farmer each season. High basis risk implies that the insurance contract is not insuring against most actual farm losses. The result is that the index insurance product may be more like a lottery ticket than an actual insurance policy, offering purchasers negative expected returns with negligible correlation between indemnity payouts and actual losses suffered (Jensen and Barrett 2017).

Other reasons for low farm demand include lack of trust in the insurance provider and low financial literacy among smallholder farmers (Carter et al. 2017). Pilot projects with weather index insurance often encounter potential clients who have no prior experience with an index product or the insurance provider. Although indexing removes one dimension of trust by not requiring assessment of damages by the insurer for payments to be made (a well-known source of conflict with indemnity insurance), it does require the client to believe that indemnities will actually be paid under the terms of the contract and have legal recourse in case of contractual nonperformance. Experimental studies have found that improved understanding of an insurance product and trust in the insurer are important factors affecting demand (Cai, de Janvry, and Sadoulet 2015; Jensen, Barrett, and Mude 2016; Patt, Suarez, and Hess 2010).

On the supply side, undeveloped regulatory frameworks and the high cost of reinsurance[4] raise the cost and lower the quality of weather index insurance. Legal and regulatory environments need to establish minimum quality standards for insurance products and capital-to-liability holding requirements for insurers and assure that clear mechanisms are available for settling disputes. High mark-ups charged by insurers and reinsurers may reflect uncertainties about the probabilities of large payouts, which require considerable historical data to determine and may be shifting over time due to climate change (Jensen and Barrett 2017).

Better ways of constructing weather indexes and innovations in insurance product design could improve uptake of index insurance by smallholder farmers. Advances in satellite-based remote sensing and improvements in agronomic crop models linking climate variables to biomass accumulation in crops provide more granular crop and pasture yield predictions that can reduce basis risk (Carter et al. 2017). Elabed et al. (2013) designed and tested a multiscale weather index contract whereby an indemnity payment is triggered when both a regional and village-level weather index falls below an established threshold. The first trigger is to prevent moral hazard, and the second trigger is designed to reduce basis risk. In an experiment with Malian cotton growers, they found that demand for the multistage contract could be as much as 40 percent higher than demand for a conventional single-trigger weather index insurance contract, although field validation of these findings is ongoing. In another innovation, some insurance products combine weather indexes with a local yield audit that is carried out if a sufficient number of farmers request it. Although conducting yield audits raises costs, a pilot insurance product in Tanzania that combined a weather index with audits significantly reduced basis risk (Flatnes and Carter 2016).

Given the current state of knowledge, large public subsidies for crop or livestock insurance are unlikely to be a high-return investment or provide the necessary kind of assurance to overcome risk barriers to technology adoption. However, innovations in contract design and improvements in weather index measures that reduce basis risk could raise the prospects for risk-mitigating insurance. One promising use of weather index insurance is as a complement to cooperatives and other institutions that practice mutual insurance. In these arrangements, an insurance contract is made with the group, and the group allocates payouts among its members based on observed losses. Field experiments using informal village support groups in Ethiopia have shown promising results (Dercon et al. 2014). Another potential use of subsidized insurance is as a social safety net. Crop insurance programs offered by the government of China and the CADENA program in Mexico are examples of multiperil insurance programs targeted toward catastrophic production risks faced by smallholder farmers and ranchers. These programs typically subsidize 70 percent to 90 percent of the insurance premiums and use weather indexes and/or area-yield measures to trigger payouts. Although such programs are costly, they can reduce the need for disaster assistance and make smallholders more willing to adopt more profitable but potentially riskier innovations.

Risk-Reducing Technologies as a Complement to Insurance

Uncertainties about how new technologies perform and higher costs of investment in technology-related inputs pose significant barriers to technology adoption. However, technologies can also be designed to reduce production risks. For example, crop varieties bred to resist pests and diseases or tolerate droughts and floods can reduce losses from environmental events and help stabilize farm production and income. Crop breeders have achieved some of their biggest successes by developing new varieties that offer resistance to locally important insect pests and fungal and viral diseases. Breeders have also achieved important successes against abiotic stresses like drought by developing short-duration varieties. In regions of the developing world where modern crop varieties had been widely adopted, national average crop yields showed greater stability, Gollin (2006) finds. The coefficient of variation of national wheat yields in Asia and Latin America, for example, fell by more than half between 1970 and 2000. In Africa, significant progress has been made in developing maize varieties that are better able to withstand moderate drought (Edmeades 2013). In South Asia, rice varieties that tolerate flooding have been adopted by farmers (see box 4.1). In both the cases, the improved varieties appear to yield as well as farmer's existing varieties under normal weather conditions but do markedly better when subject to moderate environmental stresses. However, under extreme weather events, even the varieties bred to tolerate these abiotic stresses are likely to fail. An insurance or safety net program may still be needed to cover risks of catastrophic events.

In addition to technologies that affect yield risk on individual farms, at the regional or national level the scientific and technical capacity to monitor and control the spread of pests and diseases, especially in animals, can go a long way toward reducing risks to farm income and assets as well as protecting national food security. National agricultural research institutes play a critical role in supporting government regulatory agencies in responding to threats posed by the introduction of exotic pests, diseases, and other invasive species. Such efforts may also require international collaboration. In Africa, the successful programs to contain locust plagues, introduce biological control of the cassava mealybug, and eradicate rinderpest disease in cattle are examples of internationally coordinated efforts that have paid off handsomely in reducing risks to agriculture. However, because such threats involve significant externalities, they depend on government-led action. Developing effective responses to ongoing threats posed by animal and crop pests requires investment in national scientific and technical capacities in agriculture.

In summary, index insurance is work in progress, with notable improvements being made in design, data, training, and marketing. However, in general, risk reduction in agriculture requires a portfolio approach that combines savings, emergency credit, insurance, social assistance, and technology development.[5] Relying on index insurance alone is unlikely to release constraints to low technology adoption.

Improving Access to Financial Services

The seasonality of agriculture makes borrowing and saving essential features of farm household decision making. At the beginning of each crop season, farmers must commit considerable resources for seed, fertilizers, labor, machinery services, and other inputs to get a crop established. The income from the crop will not be realized until several months later, with the value of harvest subject to production and market risk. However, many smallholder farmers in developing countries do not have access to formal financial services, either to obtain credit or to serve as a safe and reliable means for saving.

BOX 4.1

Farmer Adoption of Flood-Tolerant Rice in Odisha, India

A new rice variety developed by the International Rice Research Institute, Swarna-Sub1, has been shown to tolerate prolonged submergence under water. This could have major benefits for smallholder rice growers in South Asia, where a substantial share of the rice crop is vulnerable to flooding. In a two-year randomized control experiment in farmers' fields, Dar et al. (2013) found that the new variety outyielded existing varieties in fields where floods submerged the crop for up to 14 days, with no yield penalty in fields without flooding (figure B4.1.1). The greatest share of the Swarna-Sub1 yield gains went to scheduled-caste farmers, whose land was disproportionally in flood-prone areas.

FIGURE B4.1.1 **The Yield Advantage of Swarna-Sub 1 Increases for Up to Two Weeks of Continuous Flooding**

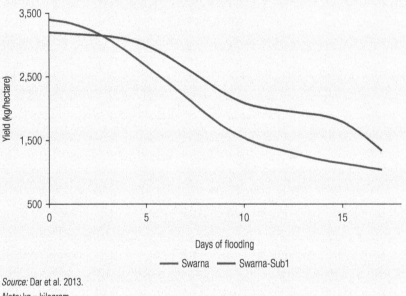

Source: Dar et al. 2013.
Note: kg = kilogram.

The substantial reduction in downside risk led farmers to invest more in their crop production, increasing their use of a labor-intensive planting method, fertilizer, and credit. As a result, rice yields were 10 percent higher even in a nonflood year (Emerick et al. 2016). On average, the new variety increased farmers' gross revenue by Rs 2,970 per hectare, with 37 percent of the additional revenue reinvested in the crop. Although the new variety did not eliminate yield losses from flooding, the improvement was enough of a risk reduction to crowd in other technical improvements and crop investments.

Why Smallholder Farmers Do Not Use Formal Credit

The failure of formal credit institutions like commercial banks to serve agriculture stems from high transactions costs and the difficulty of securing loan repayment. If potential customers (many of them smallholders) lack credit histories or collateral in the form of a durable and transferable asset (like formal land ownership), banks may not be willing to lend at any price. These conditions can lead to market failure—in which farmers' investment decisions are credit-constrained. When farmers do use credit, they often rely on informal moneylenders who charge high rates of interest. Although such practices are common in Asia, in Sub-Saharan Africa few smallholder farmers use either formal or informal credit, instead financing the purchase farm inputs from their own income or by borrowing from family and relatives (Adjognon, Liverpool-Tasie, and Reardon 2017).

Use of microfinance (small loans for short periods that use group guarantees or promises of future credit in place of requiring collateral to provide an incentive for repayment) have generally not worked well in agriculture. Microfinance is not well suited to the long production cycles and low profit margins that characterize much agricultural activity. Group-liability microfinance models will not function well when members of the group face the same risks in common. If everyone's harvest is devastated by the same local flood or pest, then group members may be unable to insure other members who cannot pay back a loan.

The appropriate design of inclusive financial services starts with the recognition that farm and rural households are highly diverse and face different needs for credit and insurance. Very low-income, semisubsistence farmers typically have diversified sources of income and need general financial products to meet broader household financial needs beyond farming. They may lack access to micro loans, social safety nets to meet disaster risk, and life and health insurance, as well as savings accounts (which would enable them to accumulate resources not only to purchase agricultural inputs but also to cover school fees and health expenses). For more commercially oriented smallholder farmers, more specialized financial products that address risks and agricultural-related expenses may be needed. Producers who participate in tight agricultural value chains (such as contact farming) are more likely to obtain credit from food and agricultural marketing and processing enterprises than from the formal banking sector.

Economic experiments carried out with smallholder farmers on the use of credit find that farmers often turn down credit even when it is available because they are risk averse (Karlan et al. 2014). There is mounting evidence, especially from rainfed crop production systems, that uninsured risk is a primary constraint to agricultural investment and adoption of promising new technologies. In a randomized trial with farmers in northern Ghana, Karlan et al. (2014) find that provision of cash grants only led to increased agricultural investment among farmers who were also offered crop insurance. In an experiment in Mozambique, Carter, Laajaj, and Yang (2016) find that when offered fertilizer subsidies, farmers increased fertilizer use, but when the subsidies were paired with savings interventions, the subsidy impact disappeared. Instead, households used the subsidy to accumulate bank savings. In other words, households appear to face savings constraints that make it expensive for them to preserve money over time so they can cope with fluctuations in farm income. The risk-reducing effect of accumulated savings was a preferable option than the higher but more volatile farm income associated with increased fertilizer use (Carter, Laajaj, and Yang 2016).

Limited options to mobilize savings is one reason why many households find themselves in poverty traps (Barrett and Carter 2013). Market frictions, including high transaction costs, lack of trust in financial institutions, and regulatory barriers, hinder the supply of formal savings accounts for poor households in developing countries. But despite these barriers, evidence suggests that the poor have substantial (latent) demand for savings. Even when formal savings products are unavailable or unaffordable, poor households still attempt to save, although their options are often limited to forms that generate zero or low returns (like holding cash) or have low liquidity (Karlan, Ratan, and Zinman 2014). Several recent studies have pointed to significant impacts on savings behavior from efforts to make low-cost savings accounts available to low-income households in developing countries. Savings-facilitation interventions have been shown in randomized studies to improve household expenditure levels and composition, labor supply, asset accumulation, and the ability to cope with shocks (see Karlan, Ratan, and Zinman 2014 for a review).

Because ICT tools can significantly lower transaction costs of doing business, innovations like "digital finance" hold promise of extending greater financial services at lower cost to smallholder farmers. Several countries have seen an explosion of "mobile money," a financial innovation that allows individuals to transfer money using SMS technology (text messaging using cell phones) over long distances at very little cost. One study conducted in Kenya finds that access to mobile money services allowed these households to weather income shocks significantly better than households without these services (Jack and Suri 2014). A number of efforts are under way to extend digital financial services in developing countries, but so far there have been few rigorous evaluations of their impact on savings and borrowing behavior in smallholder agriculture.

Tailoring Financial Products to Smallholders' Needs

Economic experiments with smallholder farmer credit suggest a number of ways that financial products can be tailored to meet the particular needs of this client group. Findings synthesized by the Agricultural Technology Adoption Initiative (ATAI undated) suggest that access to financial services by smallholder farmers can be enhanced by helping them build credit histories, offering flexible collateral arrangements, and accommodating seasonality into loan repayment schedules.

- *Establish credit histories.* Lack of information about a loan applicant's creditworthiness is often a barrier to obtaining commercial bank loans. Credit histories are also very important for the development of e-lending and the possibility of scoring clients. In an experiment carried out with a microfinance lender in Guatemala, the use of a credit bureau to track repayment history and establish creditworthiness of individual borrowers improved the lender's ability to screen loan applicants and led to significantly higher repayment rates and larger loan sizes (de Janvry, McIntosh, and Sadoulet 2010). Finance institutions that can track history of loan repayments can significantly improve repayment rates.

- *Offer flexible collateral arrangements.* Land is the classic collateral used by farmers to obtain formal loans. But lacking formal property rights to their land or being unwilling to risk losing it through loan default often prevents farmers from obtaining bank loans. Offering more flexible collateral arrangements may help farmers overcome this barrier. For example, some technical innovations involve significant capital investments, such as purchase of machinery or structures, which are beyond the reach of farmers to purchase on their own. One option is to use the value of the asset as loan collateral, whereby failure to make scheduled loan payments risks repossession of the asset by the lender. In an experiment with dairy farmers in Kenya, farmers were given such an option in obtaining loans to purchase milk tanks. Farmers who were able to collateralize nearly all of the loan on the tank (requiring little down payment) were more willing to purchase a tank and had almost the same repayment rates as farmers who were required to make a larger down payment or obtain a guarantor for the loan (Jack et al. 2019).

- *Account for seasonality in loan repayment schedules.* Loans farmers obtain at planting (for seed, fertilizer, and other inputs) often need to be repaid at harvest, when crop prices are lowest. This can prevent farmers from storing their crops and benefitting from price arbitrage over time. Burke, Berquist, and Miguel (2019) estimate that by storing their maize crop after harvest, Kenyan farmers could on average earn the equivalent of an additional one to two months of wages, even after accounting for storage costs and losses. Randomized experiments with harvest-time loans had high uptake rates, increased farm income, and helped smooth seasonal consumption of these households. With more of the harvest placed in storage, seasonal price fluctuations were also reduced, benefitting consumers (Burke, Berquist, and Miguel 2019).

In summary, credit is not always a constraint to the adoption of profitable technologies or technologies that reduce risk. But financial inclusion for smallholders still requires major efforts in design, customization, availability, flexibility (credit lines), and service cost reduction to meet the diverse needs of this target group.

Linking Farmers to Markets

Rural infrastructure includes roads, electrification, irrigation, rail, and (air)ports, as well as public transport, warehousing, cold chain facilities, designated trading areas, and ICT. Improvements to infrastructure can raise prices received by producers, lower the costs they pay for purchased goods and services, and provide a strong incentive to expand trade.

Improving rural infrastructure can contribute to both intensive growth (raising yield on existing agricultural land) and extensive growth (expanding production to new land). In regions with low rural population density, the impact of improved roads may be largely due to extensive growth, whereas in more densely populated areas opportunities for land expansion may be more limited. In Sub-Saharan Africa, the travel time to the nearest urban market is a major determinant of crop production. Travel time, in turn, is strongly affected by the quality and density of rural roads. For regions with travel time to markets of under four hours, Dorosh et al. (2012) find that total crop production approached 50 percent of the region's maximum agronomic potential, but fell off sharply with longer travel times (figure 4.6). For farms eight hours or more from markets, total crop production fell to less than 10 percent of potential production. Although farms near urban markets were producing considerable surpluses for sale, most farms far from markets produced only for subsistence. However, roads alone may not be sufficient to stimulate crop production in sparsely populated regions unless labor is attracted to these areas and land under cultivation expands.

For farmers, the costs of just reaching the nearest road can be a major consideration. In Ethiopia, one study finds that the transportation and transactions cost of procuring

FIGURE 4.6 **High Travel Costs Constrain Crop Production in Sub-Saharan Africa**

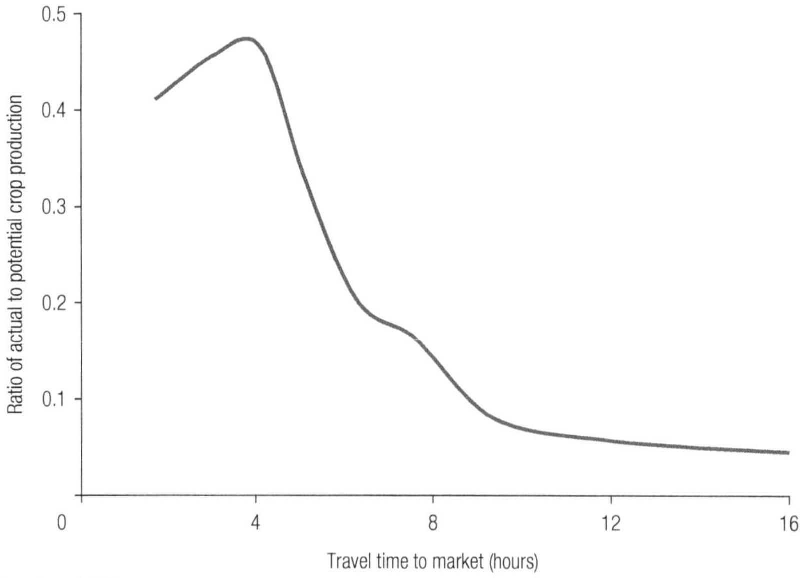

Source: Dorosh et al. 2012.

fertilizer 10 kilometers to a farm from the rural distribution center can equal the cost of trucking the fertilizer 1,000 kilometers from the port to the distribution center (Minten, Koru, and Stifel 2013). These high costs (repeated again for moving surplus grain from the farm to the market) can make agricultural intensification unprofitable. The same study finds that as transport costs increased, farmers used significantly less fertilizer and improved seed per hectare of cropland (figure 4.7). With two-thirds of Africa's population living more than 2 kilometers from the nearest road (Rural Access Index, World Bank), improving infrastructure to reduce farm-to-market costs may be critical to incentivizing adoption of new technology and raising farm productivity.

The case of Ethiopia, one of the world's lowest-income countries, illustrates how government policy can have a significant impact on improving market access, promoting technology adoption, and accelerating agricultural growth. Ethiopia's population is mostly rural and includes millions of smallholder farm households relying on rainfed cropland and pastures for their livelihood. In the late 1990s the Ethiopian government committed to a policy of Agricultural Development–Led Industrialization and significantly increased its spending on rural infrastructure and agriculture. Over the subsequent decade and a half, its agricultural sector achieved one of the fastest growth rates in Africa, with output more than doubling between 2001 and 2015. Moreover, this growth has occurred primarily in the smallholder sector. Policies especially important to Ethiopia's success have included (1) liberalizing agricultural markets, (2) investing in agricultural research and extension, (3) building rural transportation infrastructure, (4) establishing an effective social safety net, and (5) providing macroeconomic stability (Dorosh and Rashid 2012). These policies have encouraged farmers to adopt new crops and improved crop varieties, increase their use of fertilizers and other modern inputs, and invest in land improvement (see box 4.2).

FIGURE 4.7 High Transport Costs Reduce the Use of Modern Agricultural Inputs in Ethiopia

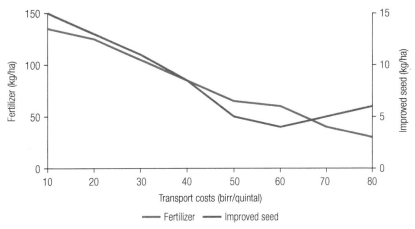

Source: Minten, Koru, and Stifel 2013.

Note: birr/quintal = birr (currency unit)/100 kilograms; kg/ha = kilograms per hectare.

Ethiopia: An Emerging African Success Story in Agricultural-Led Development

In the latter part of the twentieth century, periodic droughts, political upheaval, and civil conflict further impoverished Ethiopia, already one of the world's lowest-income countries, cumulating in a devastating famine that claimed at least 400,000 lives in 1984–85 (de Waal 1997). But over the past decade and a half, Ethiopian agriculture has achieved one of the fastest growth rates in Africa, with output more than doubling between 2001 and 2015 (see figure B4.2.1). Moreover, a substantial share of that increase was achieved through productivity gains. Agricultural total factor productivity (TFP) grew at an annual rate of 1.9 percent between 2001 and 2015, accounting for about one-third of the growth in gross agricultural output, the USDA-ERS estimates. Underlying this growth acceleration has been a strong policy commitment to agriculture.

FIGURE B4.2.1 Ethiopian Agricultural Growth Soared between 2001 and 2015

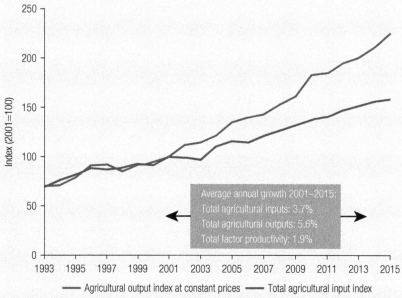

Average annual growth 2001–2015:
Total agricultural inputs: 3.7%
Total agricultural outputs: 5.6%
Total factor productivity: 1.9%

—— Agricultural output index at constant prices —— Total agricultural input index

Source: USDA-ERS.

TABLE B4.2.1 Impacts of Agricultural and Economic Growth in Ethiopia

Indicator	2001	2015
Cereal yield (tons/hectare)	1.12	2.56
Agricultural GDP/worker (2010 US$)	$333	$538
Agricultural employment (million)	22.6	32.3
Poverty rate (share of population earning <$1.90/day)	61.2% (1999)	27.3%

Source: World Bank, World Development Indicators.
Note: GDP = gross domestic product.

(Box continues on the following page.)

Ethiopia: An Emerging African Success Story in Agricultural-Led Development (*continued*)

The result of more rapid agricultural and economic growth has greatly improved the liveli-hoods of millions. Even as Ethiopia's population and labor force grew, employment and earnings from agriculture increased (see table B4.2.1). By 2015, the share of the Ethiopian population sub-sisting on less than $1.90/day had fallen to 27.3 percent, from 61.2 percent in 1999.

The costs of Ethiopia's agriculture-led development strategy have been substantial. Total spend-ing on agriculture by the Ethiopian government between 2001 and 2015 was $5.45 billion, nearly 10 percent of total government expenditures (FAO 2019). Over these years, foreign donors com-mitted $4.10 billion to Ethiopia for agriculture, agro-industry, and rural development, and another $7.04 billion in food and nutrition assistance (FAO 2019). But these commitments have paid off. Between 2001 and 2015. The cumulative value of the growth in agricultural gross domestic product (GDP) was $58.2 billion, with roughly half of that coming from higher value added TFP. Growth multi-pliers to the rest of the economy likely increased this impact a further 29 percent (Daio et al. 2007).

Note: All figures are in constant 2010 US$.

For agricultural exports, travel times to ports may be as or even more important a bar-rier to trade as taxes and tariffs. Drawing on data from 146 countries on the time it takes to move goods from producers to a ship destined for export, Djankov, Freund, and Pham (2010) find that each additional day a shipment is delayed reduces trade by about 1 percent. They also show that in the case of perishable products, such as fruits and vegetables, the effects of time delays are even more severe, in some cases making it impossible for some countries to export such products. For example, the authors find that in Sub-Saharan Africa it takes 48 days, on average, to ship a container, whereas most fresh fruits and vege-tables will perish within five weeks after harvest, even when chilled. Improved marketing infrastructure not only lowers transportation costs but also reduces food losses and waste.

Improved physical infrastructure may not be the only policy action needed to reduce marketing costs. If the markets for transportation and trade services are not competitive, if shippers are subject to arbitrary fees or high risk of theft, or if volumes shipped are small, marketing costs may remain inordinately high. Some of the main road transport corridors in Africa, for example, exhibit signs of noncompetitive behavior in the pricing of transportation services (Teravaninthorn and Raballand 2008). In such cases additional government action may be required—such as breaking up trucking monopolies or improving security along roadways—to bring down marketing costs and boost producer incentives for agricultural growth. Marketing margins are also high along secondary routes to rural market towns and villages. But the source of these high margins is contro-versial. In an experimental study among maize traders in rural Kenya, traders appeared to exhibit oligopsony power and local collusion that restricted trade and drove up margins (Bergquist 2017). However, in a review of 26 studies on crop marketing in Africa, Dill and Dambro (2017) conclude that the evidence broadly supports the notion that these mar-kets are competitive: trading profits are highly variable, trade entry and exit rates are high, and price comovement between markets suggests relatively efficient levels of competitive arbitrage.

Just as policies that tax or discriminate against agriculture reduce the agricultural terms of trade, high marketing costs and inefficient marketing systems also reduce the profitability of technology adoption and productivity growth in agriculture. In many instances, poor physical infrastructure, such as lack of well-maintained roads, makes use of modern inputs in agriculture prohibitively expensive. But physical infrastructure will not be enough if other factors stand in the way of efficient markets, such as uncompetitive supply of transportation and other marketing services.

Concluding Remarks

What does the evidence from smallholder agriculture reveal about the technology adoption puzzle? One fundamental lesson is that new technologies must be profitable before farmers will adopt them. Removing policy biases that lower returns to agricultural activities will encourage farmers to invest in new technologies and raise their productivity. Examples of policies that have discriminated against agriculture include government interventions that push commodity prices below market levels, limit trade, overvalue exchange rates, put high tariffs on imported agricultural inputs and export commodities, and offer protection for nonagricultural sectors. The high cost of marketing and transportation services also impose large costs on the agricultural sector and limit incentives for technology adoption. Public investment in rural feeder roads and policies to assure competitively priced marketing services can significantly reduce marketing margins and raise returns to technology adoption. Low farm-level profitability is a major reason behind the technology adoption puzzle.

A second fundamental lesson is that payoffs from public efforts to accelerate technical change in agriculture will be much higher when countries have in place agricultural R&D institutions that are producing profitable new innovations for farmers to adopt. Within traditional agricultural production systems, farmers are already likely to be fairly efficient in their use of resources, but when new, unfamiliar technologies become available and begin to spread, inefficiencies among farms are likely to grow. Public support for extension and training can accelerate technology adoption and improve efficiency in crop selection, farm and marketing management, and resource allocation. But R&D institutions need to be capable of adapting technologies to local conditions and addressing farmers' practical needs.

A third lesson is that in many agricultural environments, uninsured risk discourages farmers from adopting technologies and purchasing inputs that can raise productivity. The increase in average income from such investments is insufficient to compensate these households for the greater risks such investments impose. One option to address this constraint is to offer weather index insurance products, which have much lower administrative costs than traditional crop insurance. But so far demand for such insurance products has been low, even when heavily subsidized. More attention needs to be given to the design of effective insurance options for farmers, including provision of stronger social safety nets. Complementary to providing insurance against income losses is developing technologies that have greater tolerance for environmental stresses like drought and pests. Public animal health systems that can quickly respond to and control the spread of infectious diseases can also lower risks faced by smallholder farmers and pastoralists.

Improving financial services, especially by offering low-cost and reliable means for low-income households to accrue savings, can help smallholder farmers stabilize household expenditures and lessen their aversion to risk taking. Utilizing ICT to create new instruments like digital finance and mobile money can dramatically lower the cost of financial transactions. These innovations offer new opportunities to extend financial services that better serve smallholder agriculture. Securing land tenure rights for farmers, especially for women and other disadvantaged groups, can improve their access to formal credit. Tenure security also strengthens the incentive to invest in land improvement and conserve natural resources.

The growing complexity of agricultural production and marketing systems requires steadily upgrading farmers' human capital through improved education and extension services. In many countries, agricultural extension has been underfunded and poorly designed and structured. New opportunities and models have emerged that diversify provision of agricultural advisory services beyond the public extension agent. But except for some specific high–value added market chains, farm advisory services, even if provided by the private sector, will likely require a public subsidy. Innovations in e-extension using ICT to deliver messages to farmers offer opportunities for advisory services to reach more clients at significantly lower cost per farmer. But again, because of the public good nature of information, even e-extension is unlikely to be adequately supplied strictly by providing it on a fee-for-service basis. Increased public investment in quality advisory services is likely to be necessary for rapid uptake of new technologies by smallholder farmers.

Finally, investing in people will increase prospects for inclusive agricultural and economic growth. As agricultural productivity grows and the demand for nonfarm goods and services increases, more farm labor will exit agriculture and move to other sectors and urban areas. Improving the quality and availability of rural education and health care will facilitate this structural transformation. But significant gaps in access to quality schooling—between rural and urban populations and between boys and girls—persist in many countries and need to be closed.

Although the list of policy priorities for the enabling environment may seem long, individual countries and communities can focus on addressing the most constraining factors first. Moreover, many countries already commit considerable resources to low-return activities, like subsidizing private goods or favoring particular firms or industries. Shifting public resources to high-return investments in public goods like well-designed R&D, extension, and infrastructure and removing impediments to competitive markets can be extremely effective in crowding in private investment and stimulating sustained growth in agricultural productivity.

Notes

1. Detailed and recent estimates of the nominal rate of protection can be found in the *Agincentives* database (http://www.ag-incentives.org/). The Organisation for Economic Co-operation and Development (OECD) maintains a database of producer support estimates that covers most developed and many emerging economies (http://www.oecd.org/unitedstates/producerandconsumer-supportestimatesdatabase.htm).

2. For India, see Rada and Schimmelpfennig (2015); for Indonesia, see Rada and Fuglie (2012); and for Sub-Saharan Africa, see Fuglie and Rada (2013).

3. Insurable risks have three characteristics. First, the likelihood of the event must be readily quantifiable. Second, the damage it causes must be easy to attribute and value. And third, neither the occurrence of the event nor the damage it causes should be affected by the insured's behavior (that is, moral hazard is absent). Typhoon damage is an example of an insurable risk—it is easy to monitor, damage is often total, and the farmer cannot affect its occurrence or the damage it causes. Crop damage from pests, on the other hand, is usually an uninsurable risk. Its likelihood of occurrence and damage caused are hard to quantify, and the farmer can, through negligent practices, increase both the likelihood of occurrence and the damage it causes (Hazell 1992).

4. Reinsurance is the guarantee of insurance contracts by a third party. Insurance providers reinsure their contracts in secondary markets in order to diversify their portfolios and assure their ability to pay indemnities. The cost of reinsuring weather index crop insurance in international markets has been relatively high, which may be due in part to uncertainty about the likelihood of large payouts from these contracts (Jensen and Barrett 2017).

5. For a very readable and practicable account of how through anticipatory planning and coordination governments can lessen the impact of natural disasters, see Clarke and Dercon (2016).

References

Adjognon, S., L. S. Liverpool-Tasie, and T. Reardon. 2017. "Agricultural Input Credit in Sub-Saharan Africa: Telling Myth from Facts." *Food Policy* 67 (February): 93–107.

Aker, J. 2011. "Dial 'A' for Agriculture: Using ICTs for Agricultural Extension in Developing Countries." *Agricultural Economics* 42 (6): 631-47.

Anderson, J. R., and G. Feder. 2007. "Agricultural Extension." In *Handbook of Agricultural Economics*, Vol. 3, edited by R. Evenson and P. Pingali, 2343–78. Elsevier.

Anderson, J. R., G. Feder, and S. Ganguly. 2006. "The Rise and Fall of Training and Visit Extension: An Asian Mini-drama with an African Epilogue." Policy Research Working Paper 3928, World Bank, Washington, DC.

Anderson, K. 2016. *Agricultural Trade, Policy Reforms, and Global Food Security*. London and New York: Palgrave Macmillan.

Anderson, K., and S. Nelgen. 2013. "Updated National and Global Estimates of Distortions to Agricultural Incentives, 1955 to 2011, Regional Aggregates." World Bank, Washington, DC.

ATAI (Agricultural Technology Adoption Initiative). Undated. "Credit and Savings to Support Smallholder Farmers in South Asia and Sub-Saharan Africa." Policy Brief, Agricultural Technology Adoption Initiative, Center for Effective Global Action and the Abdul Latif Jameel Poverty Action Lab. www.atai-research.org.

Barrett, C., and M. Carter. 2013. "The Economics of Poverty Traps and Persistent Poverty: Empirical and Policy Implications." *Journal of Development Studies* 49(7): 976-90.

Barrow, R. J., and J. W. Lee. 2013. "A New Data Set of Educational Attainment in the World, 1950–2010." *Journal of Development Economics* 104: 184–98.

BenYishay, A., and A. M. Mobarak. 2014. "Social Learning and Incentives for Experimentation and Communication." *Review of Economic Studies* 86 (3): 976–1009. https://doi.org/10.1093/restud/rdy039.

Bergquist, L. F. 2017. "Pass-Through, Competition, and Entry in Agricultural Markets: Experimental Evidence from Kenya." Working Paper, Becker Friedman Institute, University of Chicago.

Binswanger, H. P., and J. McIntire. 1987. "Behavioral and Material Determinants of Production Relations in Land-Abundant Tropical Agriculture." *Economic Development and Cultural Change* 36 (10): 73–00.

Binswanger, H. P., and M. R. Rosenzweig. 1986. "Behavioral and Material Determinants of Production Relations in Agriculture." *Journal of Development Studies* 22 (3): 503–39.

Birner, R., K. Davis, J. Pender, E. Nkonya, P. Anandajayasekeram, J. Ekboir, A. Mbabu, D. Spielman, D. Horna, S. Benin, and M. Cohen. 2006. "From 'Best Practice' to 'Best Fit': A Framework for Analyzing Pluralistic Agricultural Advisory Services Worldwide." Discussion Paper, International Food Policy Research Institute, Washington, DC.

Burke, M., L. F. Bergquist, and E. Miguel. 2019. "Selling Low and Buying High: An Arbitrage Puzzle in Kenyan Villages." *Quarterly Journal of Economics* 134 (2): 785–842.

Cai, J., A. de Janvry, and E. Sadoulet. 2015. "Social Networks and the Decision to Insure." *American Economic Journal: Applied Economics* 7 (2): 81–108.

Carter, M., and C. Barrett. 2006. "The Economics of Poverty Traps and Persistent Poverty: An Asset-Based Approach." *Journal of Development Studies* 42 (2): 178–99.

Carter, M., A. de Janvry, E. Sadoulet, and A. Sarris. 2017. "Index Insurance for Developing Country Agriculture: A Reassessment." *Annual Review of Resource Economics* 9: 421–38.

Carter, M., R. Laajaj, and D. Yang. 2016. "Subsidies, Savings and Sustainable Technology Adoption: Field Experimental Evidence from Mozambique." Working Paper, University of California, Davis, July 6.

Casaburi, L., M. Kremer, S. Mullainathan, and R. Ramrattan. 2014. "Harnessing ICT to Increase Agricultural Production: Evidence from Kenya." Working Paper, Harvard Business School, Harvard University, preliminary results.

Clarke, D., and S. Dercon. 2016. *Dull Disasters? How Planning Ahead Will Make a Difference.* Oxford, UK: Oxford University Press.

Cole, S., and A. Fernando. 2012. "The Value of Advice: Evidence from Mobile Phone-based Agricultural Extension." Working Paper 13–047, Harvard Business School, Harvard University, November.

Cole, S., and A. Fernando. 2016. "The Value of Advice: Evidence from the Adoption of Agricultural Practices." Working Paper, Harvard Business School, Harvard University, February.

Daio, X., B. Fekadu, S. Haggblade, A.Taffesse, K. Wamisho, and B. Yu. 2007. "Agricultural Growth Linkages in Ethiopia: Estimates Using Fixed and Flexible Price Models" IFPRI Discussion Paper No. 695, International Food Policy Research Institute, Washington, DC.

Dar, M., A. de Janry, K. Emerick, D. Raitzer, and E. Sadoulet. 2013. "Flood-Tolerant Rice Reduces Yield Variability and Raises Expected Yield, Differentially Benefitting Socially Disadvantaged Groups." *Scientific Reports* 3: 3315.

Davis, K., and R. Sulaiman. 2014. "The New Extensionist: Roles and Capacities to Strengthen Extension and Advisory Services." *Journal of International Agricultural and Extension Education* 21 (3): 341–55.

de Janvry, A., K. Macours, and E. Sadoulet. 2017. *Learning for Adopting: Technology Adoption in Developing Country Agriculture.* Clermont-Ferrand, France: Ferdi.

de Janvry, A., C. McIntosh, and E. Sadoulet. 2010. "The Supply and Demand-Side Impacts of Credit Market Information." *Journal of Development Economics* 93(2): 173-188.

Deichmann, W., A. Goyal, and D. Mishra. 2016. "Will Digital Technologies Transform Agriculture in Developing Countries?" *Agricultural Economics* 47 (Supplement): 21–33.

Deininger, K. 1999. "Making Negotiated Land Reform Work: Initial Experience from Colombia, Brazil and South Africa." *World Development* 27: 651–72.

———. 2003. *Land Policies for Growth and Poverty Reduction.* World Bank Policy Research Report. Washington, DC: World Bank.

Deininger, K., and S. Jin. 2006. "Tenure Security and Land-Related Investment: Evidence from Ethiopia." *European Economic Review* 50: 1245–77.

Deininger, K., S. Savastano, and F. Xia. 2017. "Smallholders' Land Access in Sub-Saharan Africa: A New Landscape?" *Food Policy* 67: 78-92.

Dercon, S. 1996. "Risk, Crop Choice, and Savings: Evidence from Tanzania." *Economic Development and Cultural Change* 44: 485–513.

Dercon, S., and L. Christiaensen. 2011. "Consumption Risk, Technology Adoption and Poverty Traps: Evidence from Ethiopia." *Journal of Development Economics* 96 (2): 159–73. https://doi.org/10.1016/j.jdeveco.2010.08.003.

Dercon, S., R. Hill, D. Clarke, I. Outes-Leon, and A. Taffesse. 2014. "Offering Rainfall Insurance to Informal Insurance Groups: Evidence from a Field Experiment in Ethiopia." *Journal of Development Economics* 106: 132–43.

De Waal, A. 1997. *Famine Crimes: Politics and the Disaster Relief Industry in Africa.* Bloomington, IN: Indiana University Press.

Dill, B., and C. Dambro. 2017. "How Competitive Are Food Crop Markets in Sub-Saharan Africa?" *American Journal of Agricultural Economics* 99 (5): 1344–61.

Djankov, S., C. Freund, and C. S. Pham. 2010. "Trading on Time." *Review of Economics and Statistics* 92 (1): 166–73.

Dorosh, P., and S. Rashid, eds. 2012. *Food and Agriculture in Ethiopia: Progress and Policy Challenges.* Philadelphia: University of Pennsylvania Press.

Dorosh, P., H. G. Wang, L. You, and E. Schmidt. 2012. "Road Connectivity, Population, and Crop Production in Sub-Saharan Africa." *Agricultural Economics* 43 (1): 89–2013.

Eastwood, R., M. Lipton, and A. Newell. 2010. "Farm Size." In *Handbook of Agricultural Economics,* Vol. 4, edited by P. Pingali and R. E. Evenson, 3323–97. Amsterdam: Elsevier.

EATA (Ethiopian Agricultural Transformation Agency). 2015. *Annual Report.* Ethiopian Agricultural Transformation Agency, Addis Ababa. www.ata.gov.et.

Edmeades, G. 2013. *Progress in Achieving and Delivering Drought Tolerance in Maize—An Update.* Ithaca, NY: ISAAA (International Service for the Acquisition of Agri-biotech Applications).

Elabed, G., M. F. Bellemare, M. Carter, and C. Guirkinger. 2013. "Managing Basis Risk with Multiscale Index Insurance." *Agricultural Economics* 44: 419–31.

Elabed, G., and M. Carter. 2013. "Basis Risk and Compound-Risk Aversion: Evidence from a WTP Experiment in Mali." Paper presented at the Annual Conference of the Agricultural and Applied Economics Association, August 4–6, Washington, DC.

Emerick, K., A. de Janvry, E. Sadoulet, and M. Dar. 2016. "Technological Innovations, Downside Risk, and the Modernization of Agriculture." *American Economic Review* 106: 1537–61.

Evenson, R. E. 2001. "Economic Impacts of Agricultural Research and Extension." In *Handbook of Agricultural Economics,* Vol. 1A, edited by B.L. Gardner and G. Rausser, 573–628. Amsterdam: Elsevier.

Evenson, R. E., and D. Gollin, eds. 2003. *Crop Variety Improvement and Its Effect on Productivity: The Impact of International Agricultural Research.* Wallingford, UK: CAB International.

Fan, S. 1991. "Effects of Technological Change and Institutional Reform on Production Growth in Chinese Agriculture." *American Journal of Agricultural Economics* 73: 266–75.

FAO (Food and Agricultural Organization of the United Nations). 2014. *The State of Food and Agriculture: Innovation in Family Farming*. Rome: FAO.

———. 2019. FAOSTAT. FAO, Rome (accessed April). http://www.fao.org/faostat/en/#data.

Feder, G., R. Birner, and J. R. Anderson. 2011. "The Private Sector's Role in Agricultural Extension Systems: Potential and Limitations." *Journal of Agribusiness in Developing and Emerging Economies* 1 (1): 31–54.

Feder, G., R. E. Just, and D. Zilberman. 1985. "Adoption of Agricultural Innovations in Developing Countries: A Survey." *Economic Development and Cultural Change* 33 (2): 255–98.

Feder, G., I. Lau, and R. Slade. 1987. "Does Agricultural Extension Pay? The Training and Visit System in Northwest India." *American Journal of Agricultural Economics* 69 (3): 688–86.

Feder, G., and D. Umali. 1993. "The Adoption of Agricultural Innovation: A Review." *Technological Forecasting and Social Change* 43 (3-4): 215–39.

Flatnes, J., and M. R. Carter. 2016. "Fail-Safe Index Insurance without the Cost: A Satellite Based Conditional Audit Approach." Working Paper, Department of Agricultural and Resource Economics, University of California, Davis.

Foster, A., and M. R. Rosenzweig. 1995. "Learning by Doing and Learning from Others: Human Capital and Technical Change in Agriculture." *Journal of Political Economy* 103 (6): 1176–1209.

———. 2010. "Microeconomics of Technology Adoption." *Annual Review of Economics* 2 (1): 395–424.

Fuglie, K., and J. Marder. 2015. "The Diffusion and Impact of Improved Food Crop Varieties in Sub-Saharan Africa." In *Crop Improvement, Adoption and Impact of Improved Varieties in Food Crops*, edited by T. S. Walker and J. Alwang, 338–69. Wallingford, UK: CABI.

Fuglie, K., and N. Rada. 2013. *Resources, Policy, and Agricultural Productivity in Sub-Saharan Africa*. Economic Research Report 145, Economic Research Service, US Department of Agriculture, Washington, DC.

Gandhi, R., R. Veeraraghavan, K. Toyama, and V. Ramprasad. 2009. "Digital Green: Participatory Video and Mediated Instruction for Agricultural Extension." *Information Technology for International Development* 5 (1): 1–15.

Gautam, M. 2000. *Agricultural Extension: The Kenya Experience: An Impact Evaluation*. World Bank: Washington, DC.

Gollin, D. 2006. "Changes in Yield Stability: Wheat and Maize in Developing Countries." Paper presented at the International Association of Agricultural Economics Conference, Gold Coast, Australia, August 12–18.

Gollin, D., D. Lagakos, and M. E. Waugh. 2014. "Agricultural Productivity Differences across Countries." *American Economic Review* 104 (5): 165–70.

Gollin, D., M. Morris, and D. Byerlee. 2005. "Technology Adoption in Intensive Post-Green Revolution Systems." *American Journal of Agricultural Economics* 87 (5): 1310-16.

Goyal, A., and J. Nash. 2017. *Reaping Richer Returns: Public Spending Priorities for African Agricultural Productivity Growth*. Africa Development Forum series. Washington, DC: World Bank. doi: 10.1596/978-1-4648-0937-8.

Hamrita, T., and E. Hoffacker. 2005. "Development of a 'Smart' Wireless Soil Monitoring Sensor Prototype Using RFID Technology." *Applied Engineering in Agriculture* 21 (1): 139–43.

Hazell, P. B. R. 1992. "The Appropriate Role of Agricultural Insurance in Developing Countries." *Journal of International Development* 4 (6): 567–81.

Hussain, S., D. Byerlee, and P. Heisey. 1994. "Impacts of the Training and Visit Extension System of Farmers' Knowledge and Adoption of Technology: Evidence from Pakistan." *Agricultural Economics* 10 (1): 39–47.

Jack, W. M. Kremer, J. de Laat, and T. Suri. 2019. "Borrowing Requirements, Credit Access, and Adverse Selection; Evidence from Kenya." Working Paper 22686, National Bureau of Economic Research, Cambridge, MA.

Jack, W., and T. Suri. 2014. "Risk Sharing and Transactions Costs: Evidence from Kenya's Mobile Money Revolution." *American Economic Review* 104 (1): 183–223.

Jansen, H., T. S. Walker, and R. Barker. 1990. "Adoption Ceilings and Modern Coarse Cereal Cultivars in India." *American Journal of Agricultural Economics* 72 (3): 653–66.

Janzen, S., and M. Carter. 2019. "After the Drought: The Impact of Microinsurance on Consumption Smoothing and Asset Protection." *American Journal of Agricultural Economics* 101 (3): 651–71.

Jayne, T. S., J. Chamberlin, L. Traub, N. Sitko, M. Muyanga, F. K. Yeboah, W. Anseeuw, A. Chapoto, A. Wineman, C. Nkonde, and R. Kachule. 2016. "Africa's Changing Farm Size Distribution Patterns: The Rise of Medium-Scale Farms." *Agricultural Economics* 47: 197–214. https://doi.org/10.1111/agec.12308.

Jensen, N., and C. Barrett. 2017. "Agricultural Index Insurance for Development." *Applied Economic Perspectives and Policy* 39 (2): 199–219.

Jensen, N., C. Barrett, and A. Mude. 2016. "Index Insurance Quality and Basis Risk: Evidence from Northern Kenya." *American Journal of Agricultural Economics* 98 (5): 1450–69.

Karlan, D., R. D. Osei, I. Osei-Akoto, and C. Udry. 2014. "Agricultural Decisions after Relaxing Credit and Risk Constraints." *The Quarterly Journal of Economics* 129 (2): 597–652. https://doi.org/10.1093/qje/qju002.

Karlan, D., A. Ratan, and J. Zinman. 2014. "Savings by and for the Poor: A Research Review and Agenda." *Review of Income and Wealth* 60 (1): 36–78.

Krueger, A., M. Schiff, and A. Valdés. 1988. "Agricultural Incentives in Developing Countries: Measuring the Effect of Sectoral and Economy-wide Policies." *World Bank Economic Review* 2 (3): 255–72.

Lin, J. Y. 1992. "Rural Reforms and Agricultural Growth in China." *American Economic Review* 82 (1): 34–51.

Lockheed, M., D. Jamison, and L. Lau. 1980. "Farmer Education and Farmer Efficiency: A Survey," *Economic Development and Cultural Change* 29 (1): 37–76.

Lopez, R., and G. Galinato. 2007. "Should Governments Stop Subsidies to Private Goods? Evidence from Rural Latin America." *Journal of Public Economics* 91 (5-6): 1071–94.

Maredia et al. 2016. "Varietal Release and Adoption Data for South, Southeast, and East Asia." SIAC Project (2013–2016). Rome: Independent Science and Partnership Council. Retrieved from https://www.asti.cgiar.org/siac.

Minten, B., B. Koru, and D. Stifel. 2013. "The Last Miles(s) in Modern Input Distribution: Pricing, Profitability, and Adoption." *Agricultural Economics* 44 (6): 629–46.

Miranda, M. J., and K. Farrin. 2012. "Index Insurance for Developing Countries." *Applied Economic Perspectives and Policy* 34 (3): 391–427.

Mobarak, A. M., and M. Rosenzweig. 2014. "Risk, Insurance and Wages in General Equilibrium." NBER Working Paper 19811, National Bureau of Economic Research, Cambridge, MA. doi: 10.3386/w19811.

Nakasone, E., M. Torero, and B. Minten. 2014. "The Power of Information: The ICT Revolution in Agricultural Development." *Annual Review of Resource Economics* 6 (1): 533–50.

Patrinos, H., and N. Angrist. 2018. "Global Dataset on Education Quality: A Review and Update (2000–2017)." Policy Research Working Paper 8592, World Bank, Washington, DC.

Patt, A. P. Suarez, and U. Hess. 2010. "How Do Small-holder Farmers Understand Insurance, and How Much Do They Want It? Evidence from Africa." *Global Environmental Change* 20 (1): 153–61.

Pedersen, R. 2016. "Access to Land Reconsidered: The Land Grab, Polycentric Governance and Tanzania's New Wave Land Reform." *Geoforum* 72: 104–13.

Rada, N., and K. Fuglie. 2012. "Shifting Sources of Agricultural Growth in Indonesia." In *Productivity Growth in Agriculture: An International Perspective*, edited by K. Fuglie, S. Wang, and E. Ball, 199–214. Wallingford, UK: CABI.

Rada, N., and D. Schimmelpfennig. 2015. *Propellers of Agricultural Productivity in India.* Economic Research Report 203. Economic Research Service, US Dept. of Agriculture, Washington, DC. https://www.ers.usda.gov/webdocs/publications/45507/55655_err-203 _summary.pdf?v=0.

Roeder, P. J. Mariner, and R. Kock. 2013. "Rinderpest: The Veterinary Perspective on Eradication." *Philosophical Transactions of the Royal Society B* 368 (1623): 20120139.

Rosenzweig, M. R., and K. Wolpin. 1993. "Credit Market Constraints, Consumption Smoothing, and Accumulation of durable Production Assets in Low-Income Countries: Investments in Bullocks in India." *Journal of Political Economy* 101 (20): 223–44.

Ruttan, V. W. 1977. "The Green Revolution: Seven Generalizations." Agricultural Development Council (ADC) Staff Paper, reprinted with permission from *International Development Review* XIX (4): 16–23. http://citeseerx.ist.psu.edu/viewdoc/download?doi=10.1.1.474.9944&rep=rep1 &type=pdf.

Schultz, T. W. 1975. "The Value of the Ability to Deal with Disequilibria." *Journal of Economic Literature* 13: 827–46.

Skees, J., P. B. R. Hazell, and M. Miranda. Forthcoming. "New Approaches to Public/Private Crop Yield Insurance." Washington, DC: World Bank.

Suri, T. 2011. "Selection and Comparative Advantage in Technology Adoption." *Econometrica* 79 (1): 159–209.

Swanson, B. E., and K. Davis. 2014. "Status of Agricultural Extension and Rural Advisory Services Worldwide." Global Forum for Rural Advisory Services, Rome.

Teravaninthorn, S. and G. Raballand. 2008. *Transport Prices and Costs in Africa: A Review of the Main International Corridors*. World Bank, Washington, DC.

Tulsian, M., and N. Saini. 2014. "Market-Driven Innovations in Rural Marketing in India." *International Journal of Scientific and Engineering Research* 5 (5): 1439–45.

Udry, C. 2019. "Information, Market Access and Risk: Addressing the Constraints to Agricultural Transformation in Northern Ghana." Working Paper, Northwestern University.

Waddington, H., B. Snilstveit, J. G. Hombrados, M. Vojtkova, J. Anderson, and H. White. 2012. "Farmer Field Schools for Improving Farming Practices and Farmer Outcomes in Low- and Middle-Income Countries: A Systematic Review." *Campbell Systematic Reviews* 10 (6). https://campbellcollaboration.org/media/k2/attachments/Waddington_FFS_Review.pdf.

Walker, T. S., A. Alene, J. Ndjuenga, R. Labarta, Y. Yigezu, A. Diagne, R. Andrade, R. Muthoni Andriatsitohaina, H. De Groote, C. Mausch, C. Yirga, F. Simtowe, E. Katungi, W. Jogo, M. Jaleta, S. Pandey, and D. Kumara Charyulu. 2015. "Variety Adoption, Outcomes and Impact." In *Crop Improvement, Adoption, and Impact of Improved Varieties in Food Crops in Sub-Saharan Africa*, edited by T. S. Walker and J. Alwang, 388–405. Wallingford, UK: CABI.

World Bank. Rural Access Index. https://datacatalog.worldbank.org/dataset/rural-access-index-rai.

World Bank. 2011. *ICT in Agriculture: Connecting Smallholders to Knowledge, Networks, and Institutions*. Report Number 64605. Washington, DC: World Bank.

———. 2016. *World Development Report 2016: Digital Dividends*. Washington, DC: World Bank.

5. The Challenge of Agricultural Productivity Policy and the Promise of Modern Value Chains

The Agricultural Productivity and Innovation System

Previous chapters discussed how increasing agricultural productivity requires first, ensuring that markets function well in reallocating land, labor, and inputs to producers; second, supporting institutions and arrangements that generate new technologies appropriate to local conditions, and making sure these technologies are diffused to farmers; and third, resolving additional constraints in information, market access, finance, and risk that impede technology adoption by farmers. Working to resolve these individually can be difficult and resolving failures in multiple complementary markets at the same time requires levels of government capabilities that are often elusive in follower countries. This chapter pulls together in a schematic way the discussion of the past chapters and then discusses how the emergence of modern value chains and interconnected stages linking farm to market offers farmers an opportunity to access higher-value markets, and provides governments one tool for managing the multidimensional reform effort that is required.

Figure 5.1 maps out the agricultural productivity and innovation system in a way that seeks to systematically present the factors discussed earlier. Although the book has focused primarily on the farm, the same basic principles apply to related industries. The outcome variable is total factor productivity, broadly construed as in chapter 1, including increased efficiency in input use (land, seeds, fertilizer), quality improvements, and the adoption of new, higher-value crops. In turn, these improvements can occur by reallocating factors of production from less productive to more productive farms/firms, by upgrading existing enterprises, or by the entry of new higher-productivity actors. In addition to the usual accumulation of human capital

This chapter draws from a 2019 background paper for this study, "Value Chains and Agricultural Productivity," by Johan Swinnen and Rob Kuijpers. It also draws on material from Cirera and Maloney (2017), *The Innovation Paradox: Developing Country Capabilities and the Unrealized Promise of Technological Catch-Up*, the first volume in the World Bank Productivity Project.

(the first brown arrow in the center of figure 5.1) and physical capital, other inputs, and land (the second brown arrow), the two processes of reallocation and upgrading are driven by innovation—broadly speaking—and the utilization of new ideas and technologies. This dynamic can be thought of as the accumulation of knowledge, treating knowledge as a factor of production as any other. Thus, knowledge is depicted in a third brown arrow in figure 5.1. Viewed this way, the agricultural productivity and innovation system is fundamentally about the accumulation and allocation of factors of production.

The figure highlights, first, that the critical players in the system are those farms and firms that are value chain leaders and that their decisions about accumulating capital, labor, or knowledge need to be jointly considered. Innovation is not, somehow, free floating; it is part of the same calculus and subject to the same incentives and barriers to accumulation as other factors of production.

Second, the figure broadly distinguishes demand for factors of production from the supply of those factors to highlight that without demand from farms and firms, supply-side policies to generate or disseminate relevant knowledge run the risk of pushing on a string. Clearly, the division between the two sets of variables is not so sharp, particularly in the knowledge area. The bidirectional arrow crudely capture the feedback relationship between farms/firms and knowledge institutions.

FIGURE 5.1   The Agricultural Productivity and Innovation System

Government oversight and resolution of market failures

SUPPLY	Accumulation/allocation barriers	DEMAND

H Human capital
K Land, physical capital, and inputs
A Knowledge capital

SUPPLY
- Educational and training system
- Available land, imported or domestically produced inputs
- Research and extension system
  – Extension services
  – Quality and standards programs
  – Domestic research institutes (public and private)
  – International innovation system, including international research institutes and multinational firms

Barriers to accumulation/reallocation
- Land and labor market rigidities
- Information barriers
- Lack of finance and mechanisms to diffuse risk
- Business/regulatory climate
- Contracting environment, land rights
- Infrastructure
- Innovation and self-discovery externalities, intellectual property rights

The farm/Lead firm in the value chain
- Incentives to accumulate factors of production
  – Macro context/volatility
  – Competitive structure
  – Access to markets, trade regime, and international networks
  – FDI regulations
- Farmer capabilities
  – Core competencies (management)
  – Higher-order technology capabilities

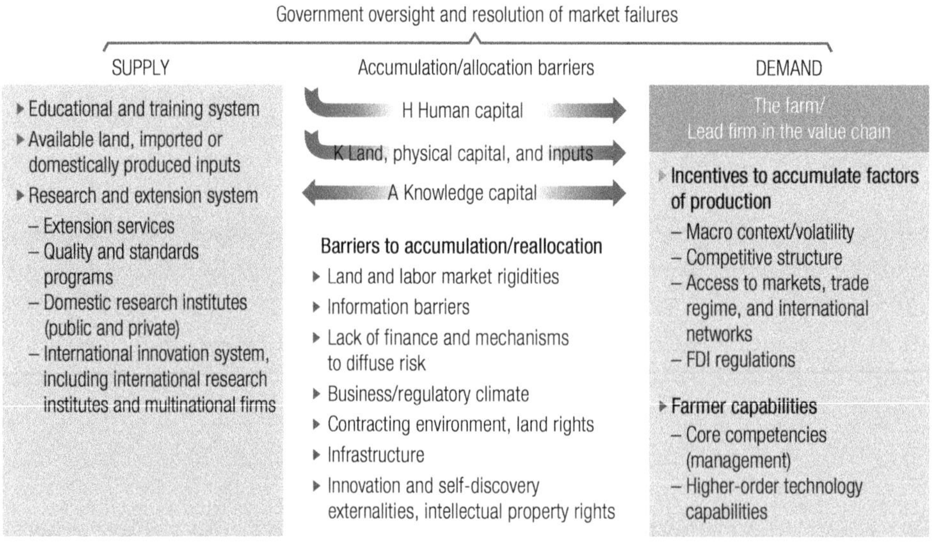

Source: World Bank, based on Cirera and Maloney (2017).
Note: FDI = foreign direct investment.

Demand

Incentives to Accumulate Factors of Production

The first group of variables on the demand side comprises the overall set of incentives to invest in and accumulate factors of production. This includes the macro context: in particular, the volatility of sales, the competitive structure, and the trade and investment regime that determine whether leader firms will seek to enter the market and grow and whether farmers will invest in new technologies. Issues of market access discussed in chapter 4 play a particularly important role, both domestically and externally. In addition, this component includes demand-related initiatives such as the development or connection to digital platforms that reduce search, matching, and informational transaction costs, as well as the establishment of domestic or international commercial networks, such as the value chains discussed in this chapter.

Farmer Capabilities

The second set of variables captures farm capabilities discussed in chapter 4: basic educational skills and managerial competencies, as well as training gained through extension services that enable a farmer to recognize an opportunity and act to take advantage of it. There are clear interactions between the sets of variables. The ability to participate in a large international market increases the likely benefits of upgrading and innovating, and better capabilities permit farmers to take advantage of these markets.

Supply

Education and Training System

On the supply side, sources of human capital include the entire set of institutions ranging from primary school to technical institutes to universities that provide basic skills to farmers, or advanced training to extension workers and scientists.

Available Land, Imported or Domestically Produced Inputs

On the physical capital side are land, domestic industries, access to imported capital and intermediate goods, and the contributions of value chain leaders.

Research and Extension System

This set of knowledge inputs includes the institutions that support farms, including the kinds of productivity and quality extension services found around the world, and services to disseminate new technologies or best practices. The science, technology, and quality systems discussed in chapter 3 specifically facilitate technological transfer, adapt existing knowledge, or generate new knowledge for the use of farmers. Investments in national food safety systems can play an important role in closing the gap between domestic/traditional and international/modern production standards. In addition to being important for public health, well-functioning national food safety systems also reduce compliance costs and attract investments in the agri-food value chain (Townsend et al. 2018). Actions to improve the food safety system encompass changes in regulations, building organizational capacity for inspection and enforcement, setting up laboratories, and investing in education and training.

Finally, the international innovation system generates most new knowledge; therefore, as discussed, alliances with foreign research services become key for technological transfer. Because many of these institutions lie outside the private market (government research institutes, universities, and so on)— particularly where crops and conditions are unfavorable to private sector provision of research— the question about what mechanisms and incentives link them to one another and, in this case, to farms, is prominent in the national innovation system literature. However, as stressed in both chapter 3 and this chapter, private providers of knowledge are increasingly important. Hence the productivity system needs to encourage their entry, including by providing favorable intellectual property rights, an efficient trade regime that permits easy import and exit, and generally supportive business environment.

Barriers to Accumulation/Reallocation

The center panel of figure 5.1 captures barriers to land and labor reallocation (discussed in chapter 2), as well as the lack of finance and mechanisms to diffuse risk, entry and exit barriers, and poor regulatory measures (discussed in chapter 4). Clearly, issues specific to innovation are important. For instance, there may be an absence of seed capital that would enable new modern firms to start up. With the arrival of new digital technologies that can radically decrease the costs of sharing information to distant farms, the digital transformation initiative for Africa backed by the World Bank and the African Union, for instance, could in theory reduce the costs of extension diagnostics and training. Finally, there are all the standard information-related market failures discussed earlier: those related to the appropriation of knowledge that have given rise to research and development (R&D) subsidies and tax incentives, and to intellectual property rights systems. Together with the incentives to accumulate, this space can be thought of as the enabling or operating environment that the various players in the agricultural space need to work.

As discussed in chapter 4, a failure in any part of the system can radically reduce the potential returns to R&D and other knowledge transfer policies. If a government allocates budgetary resources for R&D, but has few qualified agronomists, or incentives are poor in the research institutes, or scientists work in isolation with few connections to frontier outside think tanks, the quality of the generated knowledge will be poor. If extension services are weak, even high-quality knowledge will have little impact on the productive sector. On the demand side, if price distortions are severe, or markets closed, then the incentive to employ new knowledge will be small. If farmers have low levels of education and limited overall capabilities, they cannot recognize or exploit new opportunities. Even if the knowledge is relevant, and the farmers capable and motivated, if they have limited access to credit or face other barriers to accumulation of needed factors of production, they cannot enter markets or take up new technologies and innovations, upgrade, or expand. A failure in any one of these "markets" can mean that the returns to R&D promised in chapter 3 will be far lower than they potentially could be.

The Productivity Policy Dilemma in Agriculture and the Modern Value Chain

Obviously, figure 5.1 and the related discussion merely sketch the interactions that theory and empirical evidence suggest are potentially important to increasing productivity. However, the challenge facing an individual country is to identify where the most binding distortions or constraints lie and then remedy them. The fact that progress may have to be made on several fronts at once presents what previous volumes have termed "the productivity policy dilemma": moving back from the technological frontier, governments face more market failures and distortions at the same time that their capabilities in remedying them become weaker. A comprehensive discussion of improving governance is beyond the scope of this book. However, this section highlights some key dynamics of the problem and elements of solution, and then focuses on the promise of value chains as one possible approach.

The Need for Comprehensive Interventions with Limited Government Capabilities

The integrated rural development programs of the 1970s and 1980s sought to bring together agricultural credit, extension, technical assistance, supply of inputs, and marketing assistance in a coordinated fashion, precisely to resolve multiple market failures at once. In practice, however, it became difficult to coordinate the various agencies due to problems ranging from simple administrative incompetence to adverse political economy dynamics. In an early pilot in Cáqueza, Colombia, the technology assistance and input components substantially increased yields, but the market integration component—in particular, roads—was neglected, leading to a dramatic fall in local prices that offset the productivity gains. In the first phase of the Rural Development Investment Program (RDIP),[1] governments in some departments found it more politically compelling to give the separate components to distinct villages, thereby invalidating the initial concept, and high-level bureaucratic competition threatened to fragment it at the national level. In other cases, government capacity was just not available to execute the program.[2] By contrast, the Green Revolution in India was driven on a very large scale with reasonably tight coordination among ministries, thus eliminating the fragmentation issue, and enjoyed success in some regions with high capabilities, such as the Punjab, although less so elsewhere. However, to some degree this massive effort has become excessively institutionalized, not permitting the entry of private sector agents that might accomplish the tasks more nimbly and efficiently.

On the one hand, this discussion merely strengthens long-standing calls to raise the quality of governance in terms of diagnostics, design, execution, and evaluation of policies (see Cirera and Maloney [2017] for a review of the recent literature on these matters). However, this is a long-term strategy. In the short to medium term, the following may be applicable:

1. *Identify the binding constraints to progress in a region.* The point of chapter 4 is to present what recent literature suggests are binding constraints. Interestingly, finance does not emerge dramatically from their studies, whereas risk mitigation measures do. Clearly, what is relevant are the binding constraints in a region. This also highlights the need for better-quality data to identify areas of greatest need and diagnostics of market failures. As noted in chapter 3, despite the documented importance of research and development to the prosperity of the rural sector, credible data on R&D expenditures are scarce across the developing world, both in total amount and by destination.

2. *Reduce the dimensionality of the problem.* The perfect is often the enemy of the good. For example, the second phase of Colombia's Rural Development Investment Program shifted its focus to bringing a smaller number of productive components to regions that already had decent infrastructure and human capital and hence had a better chance of success. The program scaled back part of its targeting to the poorest regions. Realistically, in some settings at some times, complicated programs simply may not be feasible and other alternatives to raising well-being need to be considered. One approach is to acknowledge that different issues impinge at different levels of development. In previous volumes, the capabilities escalator was used to capture the idea that in the innovation process, for some countries, intellectual property rights and venture capital may be the most important constraint that needs attention, and for others, the most basic of managerial capabilities need to be the focus. For agriculture, de Janvry and Sadoulet (forthcoming) similarly argue that there are different stages of transformation of agriculture ranging from basic asset building through structural transformation that moves workers to the city (see box 5.1). For the very poor, the goal may be to reach minimum capital endowments (see Eswaran and Kotwal 1986; Barrett and Carter 2012; and Banerjee et al. 2015).

3. *Experiment, evaluate, and learn.* Effective solutions will often need to be tailored to a local context. This will require experimentation with design

The Agriculture for Development Sequence

To identify the specific market failure of missing input needed at difference stages of agricultural transformation, de Janvry and Sadoulet (forthcoming) have proposed the "Agriculture for Development Sequence." For the smallholder farmer at the earliest stages, the issues are accumulation of assets in the form of land, capital, health, and basic skills, for example, that would enable them to engage more actively in markets or participate in value chains. Subsequent stages would introduce new seeds and fertilizers for staple crops. In the agricultural transformation phase, the objective is to spread labor and land calendars over the year through multiple cropping (diversification). This requires irrigation to cultivate crops in the dry season, movement into higher-value crops, and the development of value chains for these crops. The rural transformation phase seeks to develop nonagricultural incomes in the rural sector. This requires the growth of a rural nonfarm economy, better functioning of land and labor markets, and mechanization of farming. During a final stage of structural transfromation, rural-urban migration occurs and the focus on urban industrialization intensifies.

TABLE B5.1.1 The Stages and Processes of the Agriculture for Development Sequence

Stages of tranformation	Processes
Asset building	Access to land and human capital for the landless and subsistence family farmers
Green Revolution	Adoption/diffusion of high-yield seeds and fertilizers for staple crops
Agricultural transformation	Diversification toward high-value cops
Rural transformation	Mechanization and land concentration Development of land and labor markets Growth of a rural nonfarm economy
Structural transformation	Rural-urban migration Urban-based industrialization and services

Source: de Janvry and Sadoulet forthcoming.

and implementation. Rapid evaluation of varying degrees of sophistication can permit timely course corrections and prevent entrenchment of weak policies. In addition, public expenditure reviews of the agricultural "innovation system" that track the flow of government resources through agencies and programs provide a point of entry into a systematic evaluation of government support programs. Again, having good data is the sine qua non of credible evaluation.

4. *Employ market incentives if feasible and look to the private sector to complement activities and investments when possible.* In cases in which government action is required to redress a failure, such as areas with a significant public goods dimension like agricultural research and extension, allowing researchers a share in the intellectual property they generate may help energize moribund

departments and help recruit new talent. As discussed in previous chapters, permitting prices to correctly allocate factors of production such as fertilizers is likely to improve efficiency and reduce the likelihood of capture by interest groups. In general, the private sector has a more intense incentive to implement necessary interventions in an efficient manner than government may. Part of the reason that the private sector is already not solving problems may be because of a lack of perceived return. Here again, government needs to identify the most binding barriers to private sector entry.

Clearly, the lighter, more circumscribed role of government becomes less tenable as the process moves down the transformative ladder. Ideally, government capabilities would improve to make more sophisticated interventions feasible. However, the next sections explore one increasingly important modality for leveraging the private sector to resolve many of the issues discussed here across the whole process—the modern value chain. The rise of value chains over the past few decades offers one potentially invaluable tool precisely for making progress on many of these issues in a coordinated fashion: providing new technologies in terms of modern inputs (improved seed, fertilizer, irrigation, mechanization), while opening the way to better access to markets, particularly high-value markets, credit, and risk mitigation. In contrast with traditional value chains, modern value chains are characterized by more stringent standards (in the form of product and process requirements) and by the use of modern technologies and innovations in the value chain to comply with those standards.

The emphasis here is complementary to that of de Janvry and Sadoulet (forthcoming). They posit two contrasting approaches to overcoming market and government failures that obstruct modernization. The first they term the "push" strategy. It consists of securing the existence and profitability of innovations, ensuring their local availability, and overcoming each of the four major constraints to demand and adoption through either better technology or through institutional innovations. The second "pull" strategy consists in creating incentives to modernization by building value chains for the particular product and overcoming the market failures.

The approach here differs in two ways. First, it stresses that the pull element must always be central if farmers are to be motivated to innovate. In fact, it is the push strategy, by removing barriers to access to markets and information, that creates demand, rather than increasing demand by pulling farmers into a value chain. The second, and larger difference, may be in refining the understanding of the "technology" of resolving the multiple market failures. Each is perhaps more suitable to and should be prioritized in different contexts. In the pull scenario, it is orchestrated more by the private sector market chains, and in the push scenario, it is more government driven.

Given the magnitude of these developments, it is important to understand value chain transformation and its implications for agricultural productivity as part of a larger process of structural transformation—and in turn, the implications for productivity policy. However, attracting and cultivating such modern value chains still require government reform efforts in terms of basic business climate, property rights, and traditional and digital infrastructure. The discussion that follows explores that question. It begins by examining how value chain transformation is thought to affect agricultural productivity. Next, it describes different value chain models that have emerged in practice and illustrates each model with examples. The discussion then turns to a review of the empirical literature on the productivity and poverty impacts of value chain transformation. The chapter concludes by drawing key lessons and discussing the implications for policy and development programs.

The Emergence of High-Value Markets

Value chain formation offers a way of approaching this problem. On the one hand, it can give farmers access to (higher-value) markets, which can enhance farmers' revenue. On the other, high potential profitability also justifies working through the problems of contracting and holdup endemic to interlinked contracts and provides a private sector solution to providing access to technologies (including farmer management capabilities), finance, and risk mitigation mechanisms. That said, starting value chains in countries with little infrastructure and low–value added crops is difficult and especially so when incentives to upgrade are absent.

Hence, in both cases, governments need to ensure that the overall enabling environment is one that encourages both the upgrading of individual farmers as well as the attraction of value chain leaders who can establish chains that can remedy many of the challenges discussed earlier. Hence, in discussing policy options, we need to focus on government efforts to remedy markets of direct relevance to farmers as well as to support them indirectly through value chains. This involves both upgrading the enabling environment depicted in figure 5.1 and increasing the capabilities of the farmers who work within it, either through education and training, or by importing those capabilities through foreign direct investment (FDI).

Agri-food value chains globally, and especially in emerging and developing countries, have transformed rapidly in the past few decades. There are several drivers behind this rapid transformation, some domestic, others global. Two of the key drivers are strong economic growth and urbanization in emerging and developing countries. Income growth has triggered an increase in demand for higher-quality products, and the rise in urbanization that accompanies economic development has increased demand for retail and processed products in urban areas. The third set of drivers are economic liberalization policies, which have stimulated investments in food chains and retail. The increase in investments by modern retailers and processors in developing and emerging countries has often been discussed under the heading of the "supermarket revolution" (Reardon et al. 2003; Barrett et al. 2017).

Although the vast majority of value chains in emerging and developing countries are domestic (Reardon, Timmer, and Minten 2012), international factors have also played an important role in the growth of modern value chains, particularly through foreign investments and trade. Over the past 20 years, liberalization policies have made it easier for FDI to flow into emerging and developing countries. The cumulative inflow of FDI in the agricultural and food sectors of Africa, Asia, and Latin America since 1990 is shown in figure 5.2. The total annual FDI into the agri-food sectors of these regions combined grew from $790 million in 1993 to about $8.3 billion by 2010. Asia and Latin America are clear front-runners in this globalization process, with Africa substantially lagging behind. Total FDI flowing into the African agri-food sectors was only about $360 million in 2010. Whereas most foreign investment in Asia and Latin America flows to the food, beverages, and tobacco sector (in other words, to agribusiness), almost all FDI in Africa goes to agriculture, forestry, and fishing.

Trade is a powerful international driver of modern value chains in developing and emerging countries (through so-called global value chains). Growth in trade has been strongest in higher-value products, which include fruits, vegetables, seafood, fish, meat,

FIGURE 5.2 **Although Foreign Direct Investment in the Agriculture and Food Sectors Has Increased Sharply in Asia and Latin America since 1993, It Has Lagged in Africa**

Cumulative investment in combined agriculture, forestry, and fishing sectors

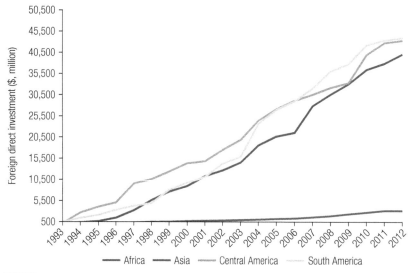

Source: FAOSTAT.

Note: $ = constant 2005 US dollars.

Harvesting Prosperity

and dairy products. The shift toward high-value exports has been most dramatic in developing regions (Maertens and Swinnen 2015). In Asia and in Latin America, for example, high-value products increased from around 20 percent of agricultural exports in the 1980s to around 40 percent in more recent years. Africa is similarly shifting toward high-value exports, although more slowly. Horticultural exports from Africa, Latin America, and Asia, for instance, have also increased greatly since the mid-1990s (figure 5.3).

Foreign investment (often at the level of the processor or retailer) and international trade can increase the demand for agricultural produce and, as such, the entire value chain (World Bank forthcoming). Through FDI and international trade, "rich-country standards" increasingly are transferred to producers in developing countries. The observed spread in standards encompasses both public and private standards and regulates diverse aspects of the product and production process, such as food quality, safety, and ethical and environmental measures (Henson and Reardon 2005; Jaffee and Henson 2004).[3] Figure 5.4 illustrates the rapid increase in public standards by showing the number of notifications of new sanitary and phytosanitary measures to the World Trade Organization (WTO), which have increased exponentially in the last 20 years. More than 50 percent of notifications have come from developing countries since 2007. As Cusolito and Maloney (2018) stressed, to the degree that this higher quality commands higher prices, measured total factor productivity (TFP) rises, as do farm incomes.

FIGURE 5.3 Horticulture Exports from Less-Developed Countries Have Soared since 1995

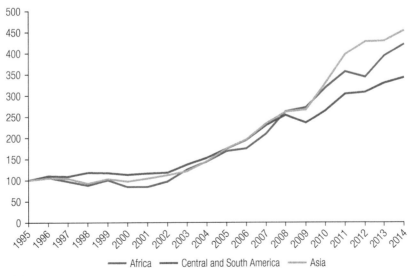

Source: FAOSTAT.

Note: The y-axis presents an index representing growth of horticultural exports.

FIGURE 5.4 **The Proliferation of Food Standards Is Illustrated by the Large Increase in Sanitary and Phytosanitary Notifications to the World Trade Organization**

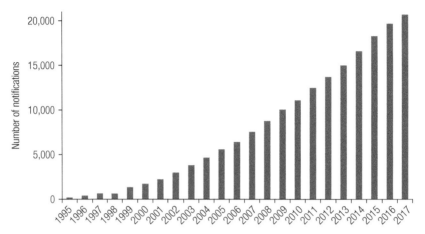

Source: Elaborations based on data provided by the yearly "Note from the Committee on Sanitary and Phytosanitary Measures" of the World Trade Organization.

In combination, these developments have changed the way that agricultural value chains are organized, bringing increased levels of vertical coordination, upgrading the supply base, and increasing the dominance of large multinational food companies. These changes have important ramifications for farmers—especially for small-scale and poor farmers seeking to satisfy the demands of modern companies—and for the structure of value chains. At the same time, research shows that value chain investments can enhance smallholders' access to high-value markets and resolve many of the barriers to productivity and income increase.

Value Chains and Agricultural Productivity: Some Conceptual Issues

Value chains can offer farmers access to markets (including higher-value markets) and increase agricultural productivity through a variety of channels. The most straightforward impact of value chains is through higher yields or higher quality. These improvements stem from process requirements inherent in modern value chains to adopt better technology or management techniques that increase the return on investment. The result is higher productivity or higher or more stable prices for farmers. An increase in farm revenue may also improve farmers' access to finance to make investments to enhance productivity. Institutional innovations introduced by lead firms within the value chain can also make it easier for producers to obtain productivity-enhancing technology.

The Productive Alliance (PA) approach, for example, has been instrumental in strengthening the links between producers, buyers, and the public sector within agriculture value chains. The approach provides holistic solutions to address market imperfections that inhibit the socioeconomic progress of smallholder producers. The design of the Productive Alliance approach encourages the development of two types of productive alliances: a horizontal alliance among the producers; and, most importantly, a vertical alliance between the producers and the buyers. Major motivations identified by both producers and buyers for joining a vertical alliance have been increased stability in prices and assured sales, as well as improvements in product quality and hence revenues. In addition, producers also value the opportunity to obtain technical assistance, improve their negotiating power, and receive payment promptly from the buyers (World Bank Group 2016).

Modern value chains often require institutional innovations to induce the specific farm-level investments that will permit the production of high-value raw material and ultimately final products. "Value chain innovations" should be understood as new ways to organize value chains or as different forms of vertical coordination, often—but not necessarily—involving credit and/or technology transfer (the provision of farm inputs, such as seed, chemicals, equipment, or feed, as well as information and technical/managerial training and assistance). These circumstances further imply that the structure and institutional organization of the value chain will be endogenous with respect to various factors that affect farm-level productivity, including local market imperfections and the absence of technology markets.

Technology Market Imperfections and Productivity

Consider a simple value chain governed by spot markets, as depicted in figure 5.5. With perfect markets, decisions to invest in technology are made independently at each stage of the chain. Demand and supply for a product with certain qualities determines the price level and thus the incentive to invest in the technology necessary to meet the quality criteria. For example, an increase in consumer demand for higher-quality food will translate into a demand for high-quality farm output and an incentive on the part of the farmer to upgrade technology—and thus lead to technology investments, if profitable.

Proceeding in parallel to the value chain is a flow of finance—but in the opposite direction. Access to finance at each stage of this chain is crucial because the burdens of production costs and technology investments are carried in full by the individual actors. Moreover, the costs of investments in technology are incurred at the start of the production cycle, whereas payment occurs at the end, making access to capital essential to bridge this gap. Next to the flow of finance in figure 5.5 is a flow of information that farmers need to adjust their production practices and technology when there is a change in demand, government regulations, or consumer preferences. Clearly, each of these decisions also implies risk to the farmer.

FIGURE 5.5 **Food Value Chain with Perfect Markets**

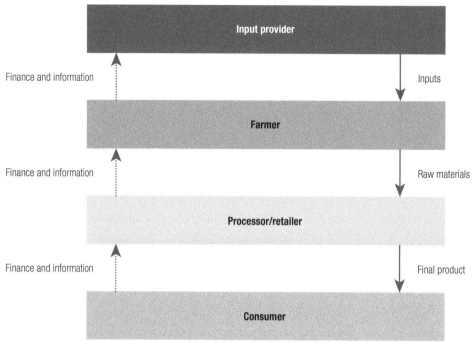

Source: World Bank.

However, in reality, the availability and/or transmission of information is often incomplete, particularly that related to meeting consumer and retail standards. Credit market failures remain problematic and the farmer faces uncertainty about the payoff to adopting technology. Uncertainty may arise from apprehensions about the quality of the technology, but it may also stem from concerns that holdups will occur with buyers at the time of delivery (Gow and Swinnen 2001; Klein, Crawford, and Alchian 1978), in the form of late payments, renegotiation of prices at product delivery, or the absence of transparent and reliable quality evaluation procedures, which could cause produce to be rejected mistakenly. Much empirical evidence indicates that holdups are a widespread problem in agri-food value chains in developing and transition countries (see, for example, Barrett et al. 2012; Cungu et al. 2008; Saenger, Torero, and Qaim 2014).

Institutional Solutions to Overcome Market Imperfections

The failure to adopt a technology affects not only the farmer but all other agents in the chain. For instance, processors may not get the raw material they need for producing consumer products, and consumers may not get the products they desire. All these agents have an incentive to resolve the farmers' adoption problems. For example, processors or input providers often have better access to the technology than the farmer and may find moving away from the spot-market model to other exchange systems will facilitate their adoption by the farmer. The previous section on the emergence of high-value markets presents several models and examples of such institutional innovations. One commonly observed model is "interlinked contracting" between farmer and processor, better known as contract farming. The processor provides the farmer access to the technology as part of a supply contract with payment conditions. Interlinked contracts to provide inputs such as fertilizer and seed have been analyzed in the traditional development literature (for example, by Bardhan 1989; Bell and Srinivasan 1989), but in modern value chains much more sophisticated forms of technology and information transfer occur. And interlinked contracting is far from being the only model of institutional innovation in value chains; in reality many different forms of value chain innovations with successful technology and information transfer are observed.

Contract Enforcement and Sustainability of Value Chain Arrangements

Value chain arrangements, however, depend critically on the confidence of all parties in the enforcement of contracts—which is often not the case. Breach of contract can take many forms. First, the farmer could decide to divert the technology to be provided under the contract by selling it or using it for different purposes. Second, the farmer could default on the contract by selling the product to an alternative buyer after applying the transferred technology. Such "side-selling" can be profitable, given that the alternative buyer does not have to account for the cost of the technology provided. Finally, a buyer could renegotiate the contract upon delivery by the farmer if the product produced with the advanced technology is worth more to the buyer than to any other buyer. In this type of holdup, the buyer, instead of paying the agreed contract price, can pay the farmer the value offered by the farmer's best alternative buyer at that point.

In the absence of public enforcement institutions, value chain actors can recur to "private enforcement mechanisms"—for instance, by ensuring enforcement by a third party or by including safeguards in the contracts to make them "self-enforcing." Safeguards can be formal, such as a realignment of incentives (by paying a price premium, for example; see Swinnen and Vandeplas 2011), or informal, such as reputation or goodwill (Dyer and Singh 1998; Goyal 2010).

Value in the Chain and the Nature of the Technology and Commodity

Value and Characteristics of the Product
Safeguards and third-party enforcement are costly solutions, however. They involve monitoring contract compliance and other (coordination) costs. These solutions are more likely to be feasible when the transfer creates sufficient value, part of which can be used to finance the enforcement mechanisms (Swinnen and Vandeplas 2011). For that reason, value chain innovations—such as complex forms of vertical coordination—are more likely to emerge in high-value commodity chains, and, in particular, for highly

FIGURE 5.6
Value Chain Innovations Are Likely to Occur When Both the Value of the Product and the Extent of Market Imperfections Are High

		Market imperfections	
		High	Low
Value of the product	High	Value chain innovation	No
	Low	No	No

Source: World Bank.

perishable products such as fruits, vegetables, fish, and milk, which require close coordination in the timing, quantity, and location of the transaction to minimize wastage and guarantee freshness.

These high-value chains can be domestic chains in emerging and transition countries, targeting a growing urban middle- and upper-income class, or they can be export chains in developing countries, targeting high-income consumers abroad. Figure 5.6 summarizes the relationship between value and market imperfections. In cases in which there are few market imperfections, there may be no need for value chains. In cases in which the value of the product is not sufficiently high, monitoring may not be necessary. It is precisely the emergence of high–value added products in the midst of perennial market failures that has led to the appearance of these value chain innovations.

Specificity of Technology

The value of the technology beyond the specific relationship between provider and farmer also influences the nature of contracts and their sensitivity to enforcement mechanisms (Swinnen et al. 2015; Klein, Crawford, and Alchian 1978; Williamson 1985). If the technology is completely specific to the transaction (for example, the technology is needed to comply with company-specific private standards, such as a traceability system), it might have no value outside the contract; if the technology is not specific and thus is valued by others (as in the case of fertilizer, for example), then the temptation to divert may be higher and hence the transfer of that technology is more risky.

Durability of Technology

Technology embedded in short-term inputs (such as fertilizer, seed, and feed additives) generally is used up in the production process. Other technologies come in the form of assets that can have a long-term influence on the production process, such as the transfer of knowledge or machinery. Short-term technologies typically are more closely linked to the contracting period. In contrast, long-term technology may have effects beyond the contract period. These different time horizons influence the feasibility of enforcing a technology transfer contract. The rewards to the farmer for diverting technology are larger for technology with long-term benefits, whereas reputational costs are expected to be smaller, making contract breach more likely and therefore technology transfers less likely. Long-term technologies typically require more "complex" institutional innovations (such as investment loans), which will, in turn, require more value in the chain to make contract enforcement possible. Figure 5.6 illustrates how the emergence of different types of vertical coordination depend on the value in the chain.

To summarize, conceptually the role of these value chain innovations varies strongly by the extent (and type) of market imperfections, competition in the destination market, and the type of technology being transferred. Value chain innovations are more relevant in a context of higher market imperfections. In a context of low market imperfections, value chain innovations that involve technology transfer or credit provision are not necessary to meet buyer and consumer requirements. For example, some argue that the relative absence of vertical coordination in China's agriculture is the result of relatively well-functioning spot and factor markets (Rozelle and Swinnen 2004). The section on models of value chains and organizations discusses how these factors, including the nature of the commodities, have affected agricultural productivity following major policy reforms in Asia, Africa, and Europe.

The Prevalence of Value Chain Innovations

The examples discussed so far and recent empirical work document that contracting and alternative forms of vertical coordination are becoming increasingly important forms of value chain governance, especially in higher-end market segments (see, for example, Bellemare and Bloem 2018; Kuijpers and Swinnen 2016; Ton et al. 2018). That said, there is considerable uncertainty and apparently conflicting evidence on how widespread these modern, vertically coordinated value chains may be, and on the size of the market share they command.

Several studies have reported on the strong rise in vertical coordination in Eastern Europe and Central Asian value chains after reforms in the 1990s and 2000s. Swinnen (2005) shows that at the end of the 1990s, 80 percent of corporate farms in the Czech Republic, the Slovak Republic, and Hungary sold crops on contract. White and Gorton (2005), using a survey of agri-food processors in five Commonwealth of Independent States countries (Armenia, Georgia, Moldova, the Russian Federation, and Ukraine), find that slightly more than one-third of food companies used contracts with suppliers in 1997 but almost three-quarters were doing so by 2003.

Although there is clear evidence that contracting of this kind has also developed in poorer countries of Asia and Africa, and studies document that in some cases thousands of farmers are involved in contract schemes—the horticulture export sector in

Madagascar (Minten, Randrianarison, and Swinnen 2009) and maize sector in Ghana (Ragasa, Lambrecht, and Kufoalor 2018) are two instances—other broad survey studies find little evidence of contract farming. For example, based on detailed surveys among rural households in Uganda, Ethiopia, northern Ghana, and Vietnam, Minot and Sawyer (2016) report that between 2.2 percent and 5.0 percent of the households surveyed had a contract with a buyer.

Such surveys are nevertheless likely to underestimate the importance, and especially the potential, of vertical coordination and value chain innovations for productivity growth in these countries. First, a significant share of poor farmers are not commercially oriented. Some 32 percent of farmers in Tanzania, 20 percent in Uganda, and 10 percent in Malawi sell no produce at all, and (more importantly) only 15 percent–30 percent of the total harvest is sold (17.6 percent in Malawi, 26.3 percent in Uganda, and 27.5 percent in Tanzania), Carletto, Corral, and Guelfi (2017) find. Second, the farmers included in the vertically coordinated value chains are likely to produce a disproportionately large share of the overall output because their farms typically are larger.

That said, the empirical literature is generally in agreement that value chain innovations have emerged mostly in medium to high-end markets, such as export markets, domestic supermarkets, or the processing sector. Evidence confirms that value chains for staple crops for domestic consumption are rare. The exceptions occur when high prices combine with severe technology market imperfections. One example of such conditions is the maize sector in Ghana in the past decade, which might explain the extensive participation in contract farming in that sector, described by Ragasa, Lambrecht, and Kufoalor (2018). Maize prices in Ghana were high in the decade after 2006, and contract farming was the only means for Ghanaian smallholders to acquire seed of highly productive maize varieties produced by the Pannar Seed company (estimated to be 15 percent–60 percent more productive and 18 percent–90 percent more profitable than the traditional variety, Obatanpa). Interestingly, the increased presence of development projects distributing free inputs or cheap credit has contributed to lower entry and higher exit from contract farming, Ragasa, Lambrecht, and Kufoalor (2018) suggest. These circumstances show that once technology market imperfections are solved (even if only temporarily as a result of a development project), contract farming becomes less attractive.

Value chain innovations to support long-term technology investments by farmers (such as cooling equipment for dairy value chains) is exclusively observed as part of triangular value chain structures. In these triangular arrangements, discussed in detail in the next section, processors collaborate with financial institutions (to offer investment loans to farmers, with the processor acting as guarantor) or form a company (a special-purpose vehicle) to share the risk entailed in reducing the technology constraints in value chains.

Models of Value Chain Innovations and Organization

Five main models of value chain innovations exist to overcome technology constraints at the farm level, Swinnen and Kuijpers (2017) argue: (1) interlinked contracting between the farmer and the buyer of produce; (2) interlinked contracting between the farmer and the technology company; (3) triangular (guarantee) structures; (4) special-purpose vehicles; and (5) vertical integration.[4] These models are described next and illustrated with examples from emerging and developing countries. For empirical reviews of contract farming and alternative forms of value chain governance, see Bellemare and Bloem (2018); Kuijpers and Swinnen (2016); Minot and Sawyer (2016); and Ton et al. (2018).

Farmer-Processor/Retailer Contracting

The most common value chain model is vertical coordination by downstream buyers with farmers. This coordination can vary from loose trading relations that buyers form with preferred suppliers to marketing contracts whereby agreements are made on the transaction, or production contracts that entail tighter coordination. The contract typically specifies an obligation to comply with buyer standards and a transfer of inputs (or credit, to make quality upgrading possible), linked to a purchasing agreement. Payment for these services is generally accounted for at the time a product is delivered. The inputs that are provided can be simple, such as specific seeds, fertilizers, or animal feeds. Much more complex forms of technology transfer also occur, especially if product quality becomes more important and long-term investments are required. More advanced forms of contract farming can include the provision of long-term technological improvements through extension services; technical and managerial assistance; quality control; specialized transport and storage services; investment loans; and investment assistance programs.

Farm-Input Company Contracting and Leasing

Input companies can also initiate innovations aimed at making high-standard value chains feasible and sustainable. Like food processing companies, input companies also find that financially constrained farmers cannot afford to purchase the appropriate inputs or technology. To assist farmers in purchasing the inputs (and to ensure payments), input suppliers have engaged in a variety of forms of contracting. Institutional innovations have focused on reducing farmers' financial constraints by introducing credit schemes, helping farmers sell their products to improve their cash flow and liquidity, and offering leasing arrangements. Leasing is a specific kind of financial contracting whereby the lessee (the farm) uses the equipment, which is still owned by the lessor (the input company), in exchange for paying a periodic fee. In essence, leasing is an in-kind loan, whereby the equipment forms the collateral (because the lessor keeps ownership). Leasing is often used by suppliers of lumpy technological solutions, such as expensive technology that is purchased only once in a great while, like machinery, to "sell" technology to farmers that have no access to credit or cannot come up with the necessary collateral for loans.

Triangular Structures and Special-Purpose Vehicles

Processors or retailers may be reluctant to provide loans to farmers for investments to upgrade quality because of the large amounts involved and corresponding risk of delayed payment or default. Instead, they may seek to involve a third-party financial institution. Such collaborations are referred to as "triangular structures". The processor or input provider typically offers a guarantee to the financial institution if it provides a loan to a farmer who has a contract with the company. The guarantee is essentially a promise by the buyer or input supply company that it will assume the debt obligation of the supplier in case of default. The underwriting is for specific loans for quality upgrading, related to the contract, and restricted to contracting farmers. Triangular structures require a smaller financial commitment from the processor or retailer given that the financing (loans) is now covered (at least partially) by the financial institution. The guarantee is also likely to reduce the interest rate for the farmer because the guarantee lowers the risk for the financial institution. The third party in a triangular structure can also be an input provider. In that case, the buyer provides a payment guarantee directly to the company that sells the inputs. The logic is very similar to the case with the financial institution.

During the transition period in Eastern Europe, such contracting structures were used regularly—for example, by sugar processors in the Slovak Republic (Gow, Streeter, and Swinnen 2000); retailers in Croatia to facilitate investments by fruit and vegetable suppliers in greenhouses and irrigation (Reardon et al. 2003); and dairy processors in several Eastern European countries (Dries et al. 2009). These examples have been well documented because their effects were quite dramatic in stimulating farm-level investments and productivity growth. More recently, such triangular structures have been observed in Africa. In Ghana, for example, the processor/exporter Profound Integration has implemented guarantees to buy fresh pineapples from six farmer cooperatives, and input dealers have agreed to supply those cooperatives with the necessary inputs on credit. Profound Integration directly covers the costs of the inputs by deducting them from the payment to the cooperative (Kolavalli, Mensah-Bonsu, and Zaman 2015).

A particular form of triangular value chain structures, the so-called "special-purpose vehicle," is a stand-alone company jointly owned by, for example, a processor, an input provider, and a bank. Typically, the special-purpose vehicle will then contract with the farms. The contract can include provisions on output, inputs, and credit. As triangular structures, institutions such as special-purpose vehicles allow the risk to be shared among various agents, and hence they stimulate investments by companies that otherwise might be deterred by the risk. An example is the collaboration between the Russian dairy processor Wimm Bill Dann and the Swedish dairy equipment seller De Laval. The processor and equipment seller created a special-purpose vehicle—a jointly owned Milk Rivers "project"—which leased combine harvesters and milking and cooling equipment to farmers (Swinnen 2005). Some triangular structures have also been developed with farmer participation (Gow and Swinnen 2001).

Vertical Integration

Some companies go so far as to take over the farming activities by "vertically integrating" the supply of raw materials into the company. Companies have several motivations to do so. One is the high transaction costs of market exchanges or the high risks of holdups in contracting (Klein, Crawford, and Alchian 1978; Williamson 1985). The proliferation of quality and sustainability standards, especially those imposed by private companies, may increase these transaction costs, particularly when monitoring is costly (for example, when there are restrictions on the use of pesticides or child labor). These costs of input transfer and monitoring are amplified when the capability of farmers is low and when standards are complex, as is often the case for private standards (Gereffi, Humphrey, and Sturgeon 2005).

Several studies show how the rise of standards in high-end value chains, and the associated requirement for farmers to invest in upgrading quality, have led to vertically integrated production systems. In the Senegalese horticulture subsector, for instance, the combination of available land and a tightening of public and private standards (such as HACCP and GLOBALG.A.P.)[5] induced exporters to move from contracting smallholders to integrated estate production (Maertens and Swinnen 2009; Maertens, Colen, and Swinnen 2011). Similar shifts to vertical integration and large estate sourcing have been observed in other parts of Africa, including Ghana (Suzuki, Jarvis, and Sexton 2011); Kenya (Dolan and Humphrey 2000); and Zimbabwe (Henson, Masakure, and Boselie 2005).

In almost all those cases, however, the shift toward vertical integration has only been partial, as processing companies maintained a mixture of sourcing channels. There are several motivations for this strategy. First, it might simply be difficult to acquire land, due to practical constraints (such as high population and farm density in fertile areas) or legal constraints (such as bans on foreign ownership of land). Second, social pressures—from surrounding communities or international civil society, for instance—can mean that large reputational costs are associated with perceived "land grabbing." Third, maintaining multiple and diverse types of suppliers is part of a risk management strategy (Swinnen 2007). Pineapple exporters in Ghana combine own-estate production with smallholder sourcing to anticipate unexpected fluctuations in demand, Suzuki, Jarvis, and Sexton (2011) explain. Similarly, for many years, Jesa Farm Dairy

Limited in Uganda has been sourcing half of its processing capacity (80,000 liters per day) from its own dairy farm to control quality and ensure supply. The rest is sourced mainly from contracted dairy farmers to whom the company offers price premiums. Vertical integration can also be initiated at the farm level. The Uganda Crane Creameries Cooperative Union, the apex body for over 100 primary dairy cooperatives in southwestern Uganda, is establishing a processing plant in Mbarara. The equity investment is paid from member contributions.[6]

The Impact of Value Chain Transformations on Productivity

Value chain transformations can affect agricultural productivity and rural poverty in several ways. Again, as discussed in chapter 1, increasing value added per worker can occur through efficiency gains, but also through upgrading of quality that may give a premium over the cost of production. This may occur by upgrading the quality of an existing crop, such as has happened in the wine industry in Latin America, transforming it to a differentiated product for which producers can charge higher margins. Somewhat surprisingly, empirical evidence on how value chains influence farm productivity is relatively limited. In general, participation in value chains increases and reduces the variance of prices,[7] which increases real revenue per farmer, and in turn serves as an incentive to adopt better, more productive technology or management techniques (Swinnen 2016). For example, Costa Rican coffee farmers who participate in the specialty coffee segment (producing gourmet, organic, shade-grown, or fair trade coffee) receive an average price that is $0.09/lb higher compared to the price received on conventional markets, Wollni and Zeller (2007) find.

Similarly, Kenyan vegetable producers who are both exporting and GLOBALG.A.P-certified receive a price that is 25 percent higher than the price received by noncertified exporters and 150 percent higher than the price received by producers who market their produce domestically, Asfaw, Mithöfer, and Waibel (2009) show. Subervie and Vagneron (2013) find, controlling for various farmer characteristics, that GLOBALG.A.P.-certified lychee farmers in Madagascar receive, on average, a 15 percent higher maximum price than noncertified farmers. Hansen and Trifković (2014) show that farmers of Pangasius (catfish) in Vietnam who comply with GLOBALG.A.P. or BAP (Best Aquaculture Practices) standards, and who have a written agreement with a trader, receive a substantially higher average farm-gate price compared to farmers who do not comply or do not have a contract. Even when prices do not rise, guaranteed market access or prices still improve farmer welfare and may stimulate technological adoption. In the Nicaraguan vegetable subsector, Walmart paid significantly lower prices than the traditional market or domestic supermarkets, Michelson, Reardon, and Perez (2012) report. Michelson, Reardon, and Perez suggest that farmers accept a lower price because (1) Walmart covers the transportation costs and risks of sourcing the crop in the field, and (2) the price offered by Walmart is less volatile than the price on the traditional market. Similar results were found in Chile. Although ChileGAP- or US GAP-certified raspberry farmers obtain significantly lower prices for fresh raspberries on average, they also face considerably less price variation, Handschuch, Wollni, and Villalobos (2013) find. Likewise, for farmers in Hungary and the Slovak Republic, guaranteed market access was a key factor in their choice of value chain (Swinnen 2005).

Case studies from Eastern Europe in the 1990s and 2000s document the dramatic adoption of farm-level technology and productivity increases arising from vertical coordination schemes and triangular structures. Box 5.2 presents the findings for the sugar subsector of the Slovak Republic and the dairy subsector of Poland. Recent studies also document important productivity effects in Asia and Africa, including in the coffee and cocoa subsectors of Uganda (Bolwig, Gibbon, and Jones 2009; Jones and Gibbon 2011) and the lentil subsector of Nepal (Kumar et al. 2016).

Although most evidence on strong productivity effects is from high- and medium-value products, recent studies provide evidence of the farm-level effects of contract schemes in staple crops in poor countries. For example, various maize contract farming schemes in the Upper West region of Ghana increased the use of fertilizer, improved seed, and improved farming practices among participating farmers, boosting maize yields by 400–800 kg/acre, Ragasa, Lambrecht, and Kufoalor (2018) find. The scale of these schemes is large. Ghana has multiple maize contracting schemes; more than 10,000 farmers participate in the largest one. Similarly, in Benin, contract farming of rice increased input use and raised rice yields by 250 kg/ha, Maertens and Vande Velde (2017) find.

Spillovers and Indirect Productivity Effects

The productivity effects of value chain transformations are not limited to the products under contract. Several studies document how transferred technology has been applied to—and has increased the productivity of—crops that are not grown under contract. Box 5.3 presents two examples from Sub-Saharan Africa: the vegetable subsector of Madagascar and the castor sector of Ethiopia. The effects might not be limited only to farmers participating in the value chain innovations. Productivity in the entire agricultural sector can be affected as a result of horizontal institutional spillovers. Contracting systems that successfully stimulated improvements in farm technology in the sugar subsector of the Slovak Republic forced other processing companies to offer similar contractual arrangements to attract farms to supply to them, Gow, Streeter, and Swinnen (2000) show. This contractual convergence and subsequent wave of technological upgrading was not confined to a specific agricultural subsector (in this case sugar). Other subsectors that competed for the same resources (land and farms) started to offer similar contracts. Another interesting institutional spillover worth mentioning is that

BOX 5.2

Value Chain Innovations and Farm Productivity in Eastern Europe, 1990–2005

Liberalization, privatization, and the restructuring of farms and agribusiness caused major disruptions in the Eastern European agricultural sector in the early 1990s. Farmers' access to credit and inputs was constrained and output fell sharply during the early 1990s. By the mid-1990s, however, significant investments, both foreign and domestic, in the food processing and retail sectors were triggering major changes in agricultural value chains, introducing vertical coordination with farms and agricultural banks and stimulating investments and growth at the farm level.

One well-described case is from the sugar subsector in the Slovak Republic (Gow, Streeter, and Swinnen 2000). In 1993, the biggest sugar processor in the Slovak Republic—Juhocukor a.s.—was taken over by western investors. Soon afterward, Juhocukor introduced several contractual innovations to assist farms with purchasing seed, fertilizer, and chemicals. By 1995 Juhocukor had developed a triangular loan program with the main agricultural bank in the Slovak Republic to help farms obtain working capital and invest in machinery. These innovations stimulated large increases in productivity along the value chain. Farm-level sugar yields increased from 32.5 t/ha with 14 percent sugar content in 1992 to 45 t/ha with 16.5 percent sugar content in 1997. The company's sugar production more than tripled, rising from 24,700 t to 75,000 t in five years' time (figure B5.2.1).

FIGURE B5.2.1 **Value Chain Innovation Spurred Large Increases in Production and Productivity at the Slovak Republic's Biggest Sugar Processor and Its Supplying Sugar Beet Farms**

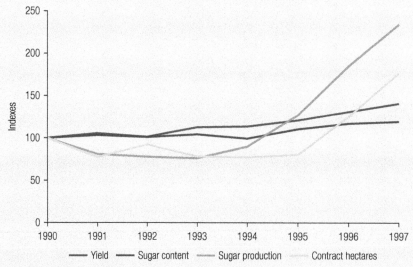

Source: Gow, Streeter, and Swinnen 2000.
Note: Data are for Jukocukor a.s.

(Box continues on the following page.)

Value Chain Innovations and Farm Productivity in Eastern Europe, 1990–2005
(*continued*)

FIGURE B5.2.2   **Milk Productivity in Poland Rose Steeply in the 1990s and Early 2000s**

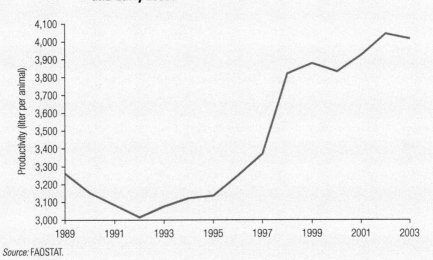

Source: FAOSTAT.

A similar story unfolded in Poland's dairy subsector (Dries, Reardon, and Swinnen 2004; Dries and Swinnen 2010). After productivity declined in the early 1990s, new investments in dairy companies were associated with extensive vertical coordination programs by dairy processors to help their dairy farmers overcome credit and technology constraints. A survey among dairy processors and dairy farms in northwestern Poland showed that each of the processors had introduced programs to support farms' access to feed, private extension services, and triangular structures with local banks to provide investment loans to farmers. As a result of these actions, farms quickly invested in modern dairy equipment (such as cooling tanks and better cows), and dairy productivity grew rapidly (see figure B5.2.2).

the financial institution that was involved in one of the value chain innovations later standardized and extended the successful contractual model into a range of financial instruments offered to the entire agricultural sector. Similar institutional spillovers have been observed in the dairy subsector of Russia (Serova and Karlova 2010) and the potato subsector of Peru and Bolivia (Devaux et al. 2009).[8]

Value Chains and Smallholders

The question of whether smallholders can benefit from value chain productivity effects has been widely discussed. Several theoretical arguments explain why companies would

Farm-Level Productivity Spillovers of Value Chain Innovations in Two African Countries in the 2000s

Value chain innovations that enhance farmers' access to inputs such as fertilizer for growing a contracted crop may increase the productivity of their other crops (such as staple foods) if those crops can benefit from the fertilizer use. One way this can occur is when improvements in soil productivity last beyond the growing season for the contracted crop. This is what happened in Madagascar's vegetable export subsector, in which almost 10,000 smallholders are involved in contract farming operations that provide technical training in making compost and weeding. By changing the way farmers operate, the value chain contracts resulted in strong increases in the productivity of rice (64 percent higher), Madagascar's major staple, Minten, Randrianarison, and Swinnen find (2009).

Similar improvements took place in castor value chains in Ethiopia, where a processing company distributed castor seed, herbicide, and fertilizer to more than 10,000 contract farmers and provided technical assistance. The productivity of staple food crops was 35 percent–52 percent higher on plots intercropped with castor, Negash and Swinnen (2013) find. These results suggest that the contract operation, although it focused on stimulating the production of a nonedible crop, also increased the productivity of food crops. These spillover effects on food productivity offset the impact on contract producers of having less land available to produce food crops

prefer working with relatively fewer, larger, and more modern suppliers. First, transaction costs favor larger farms in supply chains. Second, small farms are more constrained in making the investments necessary to participate in some value chains. Third, small farms typically require more assistance per unit of output. Empirical studies show that, however, companies do indeed work with surprisingly large numbers of suppliers, of surprisingly small size, for several reasons. Companies may have no choice if small farmers represent most of the supply base. In addition, farmers' willingness to learn may be more important than size in farmer-processor relationships. Small farms may have cost advantages in undertaking labor-intensive production activities. Moreover, processors may prefer a mix of suppliers as a risk management strategy (Maertens, Minten, and Swinnen 2012; Reardon et al. 2009).

Several empirical studies have documented that as standards increase, a decreasing share of export produce is sourced from small farmers. For example, studies find decreased inclusion of smallholders in food export chains in Kenya (Dolan and Humphrey 2000; Gibbon 2003; Jaffee 2003) and Côte d'Ivoire (Minot and Ngigi 2004; Unnevehr 2000). Subervie and Vagneron (2013) describe the rise of large exporter-owned lychee plantations in Madagascar in response to rising private standards. Maertens and Swinnen (2009) note a shift from smallholder contract farming to vertically integrated farming on large-scale plantations in the vegetable export subsector in Senegal as private standards gained importance, especially GLOBALG.A.P.

Schuster and Maertens (2013) conclude that the spread of private standards, especially production standards such as GLOBALG.A.P., in the Peruvian asparagus export sector has reduced sourcing from smallholders and that certified companies source significantly less from smallholders than noncertified companies. Some export sectors are even based completely on vertically integrated agroindustrial farming, without any inclusion of smallholder suppliers, such as the tomato export subsector in Senegal (Maertens, Colen, and Swinnen 2011).

Yet other studies show that smallholders continue to be included in modern value chains, sometimes exclusively. Several studies from Eastern Europe confirm that small farmers were integrated in modern agricultural value chains (see, for example, Dries et al. 2009; Noev, Dries, and Swinnen 2009). African and Asian smallholders also have been successfully integrated in several value chains. Madagascar's vegetable export subsector, which includes almost 10,000 smallholders, is based entirely on intensive contract farming systems (Minten, Randrianarison, and Swinnen 2009). Other examples of smallholders' substantial inclusion in high-value export chains through contract farming with buyers and exporters include the fruit and vegetable subsectors in Chile (Handschuch, Wollni, and Villalobos 2013); Thailand (Kersting and Wollni 2012); and Zimbabwe (Henson, Masakure, and Boselie 2005). Export horticulture chains in China rely almost completely on contract production by smallholders (Wang et al. 2009).[9] Gulati et al. (2007) show that smallholders overwhelmingly dominate many value chains in Asian countries through contract farming and innovative vertical coordination schemes.

Contracts are an important mechanism for reducing risk, but the terms of contracts will often depend on the negotiating power of the stronger contracting party. Well-managed contract farming can help farmers solve many bottlenecks while increasing profitability. Contract farming arrangements need to be subject to compliance with domestic labor laws and standards governing the use of inputs. The balance, or lack thereof, of bargaining power between large buyers and small producers is also central to forming contracts. Governments have an important role to play in addressing some of these challenges. Shaping a clear legal framework that reduces uncertainty in terms of nonperformance of the contract and strengthening dispute resolution mechanisms can encourage broader uptake.

Rural poverty reduction from value chain development and productivity growth may also occur without smallholder integration. An important—and somewhat overlooked—issue in the welfare analyses of agri-food trade is that poor households may benefit through employment effects. Empirical studies have documented that the development of high-value agroindustrial value chains creates substantial employment, as in the vegetable export subsector in Senegal and in the cut flower industry in Ethiopia (Mano et al. 2011). Employment in agroindustrial production and exporting companies is very accessible to the poor and can have a large positive effect on household incomes and on poverty reduction (Van den Broeck, Swinnen, and Maertens 2017). There seems to be a high demand specifically for female labor in these export sectors (Maertens and Swinnen 2012).

Cultivating Value Chains

Given the variety of benefits value chains can yield, this section also discusses ways to improve the agribusiness environment to enable and stimulate value chain transformation. It looks at the role of selective investments that aim to develop a particular value chain by targeting specific companies or farmers active in those chains. Here, the discussion distinguishes between (1) the overall enabling environment, (2) investments directed at lead companies to enable and stimulate them to develop their value chain, and (3) investments directed at key stages and links of the value chain that constrain its further development. The section concludes by outlining the role of public-private dialogue in enabling value chain transformation.

Overall Enabling Environment

The elements depicted in figure 5.1 remain fully relevant for value chain development, albeit with different emphasis. As discussed, value chains are more likely to emerge when the value of the crop is high and the transaction/contracting costs are lower.

Competition and Elimination of Distortions
The sine qua non of promoting value chains is getting prices that reflect the true value of the product in the relevant market. Simple remedies, like ensuring that commodity boards are not depressing prices to the farmers with the goal of ensuring affordable food in the cities, may not be so complex. Competition authorities can monitor and intervene if certain subsectors tend to become too concentrated or if cartels are forming. In addition, governments should be aware of how their own actions affect competition. Subsidies of inputs (such as fertilizer), state-owned enterprises, or selective support to companies, for example, can distort prices, create an unlevel playing field, and crowd out the private sector. More competition at the nonfarm stages of the value chain can induce more incentives for companies to contract with farmers (to secure supplies) and may improve contract conditions for farmers. As discussed, however, more competition may also increase the options for breaching contracts (side-selling) and—as companies anticipate this possibility—reduce the likelihood of increasing innovations and contracting within the value chain.

International Integration
For export-oriented value chains, domestic prices will reflect external prices filtered through the exchange rate. Ensuring that exchange rates are not overvalued and are stable requires competent macroeconomic management and navigating a host of

competing social objectives. Value chain transformations are often driven by a need for quality upgrading and/or guaranteed supplies. This process was particularly apparent after the economic reforms in Eastern Europe, where due to sudden and strong competitive forces and western European FDI, the demand for high-quality products was outpacing supply. Similar market developments are now occurring in Sub-Saharan Africa and other parts of the developing world, following the growth in high-value exports, urbanization, and a rise in domestic purchasing power. Sophisticated forms of vertical coordination are often introduced by companies that pay greater attention to quality standards.

Again, however, measures such as opening of the economy and liberalization may not uniformly encourage the emergence of value chains (Rozelle and Swinnen 2004; Swinnen, Vandeplas, and Maertens 2010). Price increases improve incentives to produce (direct effect) and improve the provision of inputs because private enforcement is possible (indirect effect). However, increased competition on the side of the buyers of farm produce may make enforcing contracts more difficult. The net effect of these two offsetting effects is not clear in advance. In Africa, the rise in commodity prices since 2007 has led to a dramatic transformation in cereals that has led to a rise in the rate in labor productivity from 1.7 percent to 5.9 percent, on average. The price increases caused a "double whammy" effect on productivity, Swinnen and Janssen (2016) speculate: it increased the profitability of investing in cereal production and it enhanced the capacity to enforce contracts—and thus access to inputs. In China, for example, the increase in centrally controlled prices combined with gradual liberalization of input markets led to vast increases in labor productivity. As box 5.2 shows, more disruptive pattern emerged in eastern Europe that resulted in productivity falls at first, with the disruption of state-provided input providers, but dramatic increases subsequently, with demand from western Europe leading to high demand for quality and hence higher value in the chains.

Contracting Environment

Improving the rule of law can radically lower the costs of dealings among distinct parties. Imperfect contract enforcement increases the risk of transferring knowledge and farm inputs to farmers, who then might divert the technologies or side-sell their produce. Holdups on the side of the buyer, such as delaying payment, renegotiating prices, or inappropriately rejecting produce after inspection, might lead to reduced investments by farmers (see, for example, Cungu et al. 2008). As it is generally either not possible or too costly to resolve contract disputes in courts, alternative dispute settlement institutions can play an important role in contract enforcement. Other measures can include increasing the transparency of contracts, supporting alternative dispute-settling arrangements, or training farmers in their rights/obligations as contractors.

Reforms in this area can be difficult, and involve increasing the capacity and independence of the state. To complicate matters, trust is often lacking as a base for business exchanges in many transition countries. High levels of corruption, a high administrative burden to comply with government regulations, and ill-defined property rights all are a drag on value chain integration. Companies try to create "self-enforcing contracts" by designing the terms of the contracts so there is little incentive to breach them, yet in many cases enforcement still fails. Even successful cases required considerable fine-tuning of the contracts or adjustments as circumstances changed. The right conditions for successful and self-enforcing contracting cannot be created without extensive knowledge of the sector and of local conditions.

Infrastructure

Rural infrastructure includes roads, electrification, irrigation, rail, and (air)ports, as well as public transport, warehousing, cold-chain facilities, designated trading areas, and information and communication technology (ICT). Though clearly important in delivering inputs and information, infrastructure deficiencies are particularly binding in the last mile to market. Reductions in delays and shipment times are particularly important for becoming included, as a country, in global agri-food value chains. Where there is potential for high–value added but fragile exports, such as in the Chilean fruit industry or Peruvian specialty vegetables chain, access to a reliable transport infrastructure including cold chain is critical. The emergence of a strong exotic fruits industry in the pacific coastal area of Colombia, where much poverty is concentrated and many ex-combatants live, has been inhibited by the difficulties of negotiating secure and reliable access to the Port of Buenaventura.

Investments Directed at Lead Companies to Enable and Stimulate Them to Develop Their Value Chain

Start-Up Finance

Firms that initiate the value chain innovation require significant financial resources, because interlinked contracting, prefinancing, and loan guarantees require large upfront investments or sufficient collateral. Thus, access to finance, as discussed, is a prerequisite for private-sector-led development of value chains. In addition to quality requirements, it is essential for the initiator of the value chain programs to provide access to finance.

Donors and governments can facilitate value chain transformation by (co)financing lead firms to introduce value chain innovations. Offering agribusinesses concessional loans or even subsidies/grants (for example, as part of public-private partnership or impact bonds) can also mitigate the investment risk induced by a (moderately) unfavorable environment.

A potential advantage of (co)financing lead firms for value chain development is that it can leverage private sector resources to achieve public objectives (such as the

Sustainable Development Goals). Not only can it crowd in much-needed private investment, but it can leverage the commercial relationships that the firm currently has with large numbers of farmers and/or consumers. (Co)financing lead firms for value chain development also carries risks, however. First, providing public finance to private initiatives to develop value chains might not be additional to initiatives that would have been carried out by the private sector on its own. In other words, the risk is that the firm does not behave differently than it would have done in the absence of public finance, which makes "additionality" of public funding a necessary condition for effectiveness.[10]

Second, public finance for private value chain development might create a relationship of dependence, especially if farmers are trained to comply with company-specific standards. As explained, if standards are company specific, it will be more difficult for the farmers, after having made the necessary investments, to profitably side-sell their produce to other buyers, giving the lead company less incentive to offer them a price premium.

R&D

Alternatively, governments can subsidize the establishment of value chains by underwriting relevant R&D. As discussed, either raising the quality of existing crop (as in the case of wine) or shifting to a higher–value added crop (moving from ordinary to Jasmine rice) will raise the benefit from forming a value chain. This necessarily will involve working on several fronts at once, but a successful model has been to foment research in the public sector that then makes is profitable for the private sector to organize the elements of the value chain. For instance, the An Gian Plan Protection company in the Mekong Delta of Vietnam benefitted from agricultural research underwritten by the state, but then organized the other markets to create a complete value chain.

Some nongovernmental organizations (NGOs) and multilateral organizations question whether, in general, the cultivation of large lead firms serves the interests of farmers. In reaction to these concerns, some private sector development programs, such as the Facility for Sustainable Entrepreneurship and Food Security, now demand the involvement of an NGO to represent the interests of farmers and wage laborers and to ensure the inclusiveness of the initiative. It is unclear whether NGOs are capable of fulfilling this role, however, especially if they are becoming financially dependent on these partnerships or if they also fulfill a role as a service provider within the scheme (by providing training to farmers, for instance).

Finally, as discussed in the previous section, selective investments in particular companies might distort competition in the market. This concern needs to be weighed against the potential for stagnation in the agri-food sector without the investments.

Policies Targeting Links of the Value Chain

Public investments can also directly target key stages and links of the value chain that constrain its development. What is new to these types of initiatives, compared to more traditional approaches, is that these investments are made in anticipation of high demand for high-quality agri-food products or, more actively, in close collaboration with downstream companies. Traders, processors, and retailers might, for example, commit to engage in buyer agreements (namely, contract farming) if farmers, with support from the public investment project, succeed in complying with its product and process requirements (box 5.4).

This type of value chain development is generally implemented by a governmental or nongovernmental organization and can include financial, technical, and organizational support to farmers and key service and input providers. Typical activities include building capacity of farmer organizations; representing farmers in coordination and negotiation activities with input distributors and potential buyers; training and certifying farmers so that they can comply with buyer standards; and setting up and supporting (micro)agribusinesses to provide key services and inputs to farmers (such as collection, storage, transport, and distribution of inputs). The immediate objective of these activities is either to reduce transaction costs between different stages of the value chain or to build the capacity of key agents in the value chain that are constraining its further development (typically farmers and input/service providers).

BOX 5.4

Examples of Multistakeholder Platforms to Stimulate Innovative Forms of Value Chain Organization

Multistakeholder platforms in the potato subsector of Bolivia and Peru, supported by the Swiss Agency for Development and Cooperation, led to several product innovations that have stimulated innovative forms of value chain organization to respond to the new quality criteria (Devaux et al. 2009). These initiatives reinforced the capacity for collective action, teamwork, and innovation, and led to higher farm-gate prices, increased revenue for farmers, and more stable markets. Horizontal spillover effects occurred as other value chain actors imitated products developed by the platforms. Owing to the program's success, policy makers and donors are increasing their support for future collective action for value chain innovations. A similar program in the potato sector of Ecuador had a positive impact on use of agricultural inputs, yields (kg/ha), and gross margins, Cavatassi et al. (2011) find.

A multistakeholder platform in Ghana's pineapple subsector has led to a triangular value chain system in which a finance institution provides farmers with credit to obtain the inputs necessary to comply with the standards of a modern processor. The processor, in turn, pays the farmers directly, after deducting the cost of the inputs to repay the loan from the financial institution (Kolavalli, Mensah-Bonsu, and Zaman 2015).

Traditional areas of public investment, such as research and extension, market information systems, veterinary services, and animal surveillance programs remain generally important, but they could improve their focus to reflect the developments (or lack thereof) in value chains. As discussed, private sector initiatives are particularly expected in high-value market segments, and private technology transfer is more likely for firm-specific technologies. For that reason, public research and extension should focus on those farms being excluded from privately initiated programs, those low-value market segments for which private solutions are unlikely, and those technologies that are not provided by the private sector. This focus requires agricultural research to be clearly targeted and adapted to local conditions.

Intensive and continuous dialogue between public and private actors is necessary for value chain transformation policy to be effective. Input from private actors is essential to identify the key constraints that bind further transformation of the value chain and to prioritize public investments. Moreover, public-private dialogue can be used to map public and private objectives and to identify areas for collaboration. Initiatives such as multistakeholder platforms (sometimes called "agribusiness clusters" or "value chain committees") can facilitate better coordination between value chain actors, identify common interests, facilitate knowledge sharing, identify new business opportunities, and act as lobby group for the common interest of members. Membership in these platforms is generally not exclusive to value chain actors and can include governmental and nongovernmental agencies and knowledge institutes (see box 5.4 for examples).

As discussed, the value chain offers a way of remedying many of the missing markets in credit, information, and risk diffusion. Hence, the conditions to promote their emergence requires working on two fronts: raising the profitability of the crop and reducing the transaction costs involved. Boxes 5.5 and 5.6 present two innovations that could help micro, small, and medium enterprises.

Improving Spillovers

Spillovers are not restricted to vertical interactions among elements of the value chain, but can also be horizontal, to other commodities or other sectors. Competing companies of firms that initiate a technology transfer program may introduce similar contractual arrangements, either to stay in business (as farms will otherwise shift to supplying other companies) or because it is profitable for them to do so once they observe the success of the innovations elsewhere—or both. Contractual convergence may go beyond sectors in which the transfer program was initiated. Other sectors that compete for the same resources (such as land) might offer similar contracts, or financial institutions might standardize the approach for other farms. In general, countries with institutions that facilitate learning from emerging success stories and diffuse their experiences are more likely to increase horizontal spillovers.

Blockchain at the Border: Exploring Whether Blockchain Can Help Rural Entrepreneurs and SMEs Boost Exports and Get Financing

Blockchain, for all the hype surrounding it, is still an abstruse concept for most policy makers and the theory behind it outstrips practice considerably. Through the Blockchain at the Border project, a World Bank team sought to explore what it might take to implement a blockchain-based project at scale. The project also sought to analyze the benefits and challenges of emerging technologies such as blockchain from the perspective of nondominant market players such as small firms and women-led firms and investigate whether technologies such as blockchain could make markets more inclusive. For the project, the team partnered with the Department of Customs in Vietnam and Nestle and focused on the coffee supply chain.

Key questions that the project tried to explore included whether first, blockchain can make it easier for rural entrepreneurs and small and medium enterprises (SMEs) to participate in international trade. International trade agreements frequently contain provisions designed to favor the participation of SMEs, but evidence suggests that their utilization is relatively low. One possible cause could be the complexity of trade regulations and the fact that most small firms do not have the knowledge, capacity, or access to legal resources to take advantage of these provisions. The project sought to explore whether blockchain could help simplify the business environment for them by making the rules and regulations more transparent, as well as by simplifying or eliminating the paperwork and bureaucratic procedures currently required for export.

The project also explored whether blockchain can make it easier for entrepreneurs and SMEs to access finance and new buyers. Small firms often find it difficult to prove or demonstrate their experience and skills in the markets they serve. The data are often held and controlled by large buyers or their intermediaries. The project sought to explore the possibility of blockchain-based solutions to hand control of data to small firms and help them turn this information effectively into a form of collateral. Such applications have been tested by other organizations, but not in the context of the supply chain.

Suggested benefits include transparency of rules and their application. Smart contracts are a potential tool to uniformly (and automatically) apply trade provisions and thus to reduce the legal capacity and manpower currently required to export—which most women-owned or micro or small enterprises do not have—as well as to limit the harassment of women at borders. Other benefits include greater visibility and access to networks. Public blockchains may make it easier for participants to manage and control their business identity and profile. This is likely to be especially beneficial to women-led firms that are often excluded from business networks and markets. Access to finance and ownership of property are issues that affect women entrepreneurs more than their male counterparts. Through the current prototype, the team managed to raise awareness about blockchain features, especially management of business profiles for banking purposes, that may facilitate greater access to finance, especially for women.

As expected, the private sector has taken the lead in applying blockchain solutions to improve logistics management in cross-border environments. However, the information captured by businesses for their own supply chain management can potentially be used to transfer goods

(Box continues on the following page.)

Blockchain at the Border: Exploring Whether Blockchain Can Help Rural Entrepreneurs and SMEs Boost Exports and Get Financing *(continued)*

across borders, define applicable duties depending on the goods origin and control for conformance to specific quality requirements. However, many questions about feasibility remain. Blockchain as a technology still has a long way to go. Any future solutions also need to leverage other technologies like the Internet of Things (IoT) and artificial intelligence (AI). In any case, the challenges that the project tried to address are not amenable to purely technological solutions. It appears that blockchain at the border has high potential to disrupt current trade facilitation practices and procedures, but the changes require substantial adaptation of national and international legal agreements.

Source: Prasana Das and Emiliano Duch, World Bank.

Pilot of Distributed Ledger Technology for Traceability and Payment in Haiti's Fresh Fruits Value Chains

Weak links in several agricultural value chains in Haiti currently impede linking micro, small, and medium enterprises to final buyers in more profitable markets, limiting inclusive regional development and sustainable growth. Without a traceability system for products and refrigerated transport and packing houses, Haitian producers cannot enter high-quality market segments, in which end users demand shelf life and want to know more about the origin of the product and its producer. Furthermore, small producers usually must sell their products immediately to intermediaries for lack of financing or technical capabilities, preventing them from capturing more value for their products.

The proposed solution uses a third-party cold logistics service provider to reduce spoilage, and a broker, equipped with distributed ledger technology, to connect Haitian farmers with buyers in the United States and Canada. The distributed ledger technology solution makes two key upgrades. First, it improves traceability along the value chain (such as for purposes of food safety, product liability, or rules of origin), which is always verified by third parties and includes a system of penalties for defective services. Second, it puts in place a fraud-safe system to ensure reliable, fast, and timely payments to the individual producer and all service suppliers along the value chain.

The government of Haiti, with the support of the World Bank and University of Wageningen, tested the prototype, with sample shipments to the United States, Canada, and the Netherlands, that were registered in a prototype distributed ledger. The results of the test were encouraging. First, spoilage rates were reduced dramatically (from as much as 60 percent previously), while shelf life and quality of produce improved due to better postharvest handling and temperature control. Second, farmers' revenue increased eightfold, as the technology helped eliminate

(Box continues on the following page.)

Pilot of Distributed Ledger Technology for Traceability and Payment in Haiti's Fresh Fruits Value Chains *(continued)*

inefficient middlemen resellers and reduce markups. Third, real-time data enabled all parties (including the government) to track merchandise throughout the entire value chain. In addition, consumers were able to obtain granular information about the product by scanning a QR code, such as who the farmer is, where the tree is located, the timeline from harvest to table, and the price structure. The government was developing the pilot scaled-up solution in time for the harvest in June 2019.

When implemented on a larger scale in Haiti, such technology has the potential to improve financial inclusion by giving rural smallholder farmers access to a financial service platform; contribute to poverty reduction among the rural poor, thus reducing income inequality between rural and urban zones (in the Haitian countryside, almost 70 percent of households are considered chronically poor, against a little over 20 percent in cities); increase fiscal transparency and tax compliance (tax revenue is easily tracked), potentially raising domestic revenue; generate some employment during the harvest season; and improve the skills of produce growers.

Going forward, a wider implementation of this program could involve addressing various challenges. These include the logistical management of a larger-scale program with domestic resources; having effective mechanisms in place to deal with system failure (for example, due to hacking); preventing intervention by interest groups (who may, for example, block shipments or transit until a "fine" is paid); and addressing any potential environmental consequences (such as mono-cultivation if the program becomes too lucrative).

Source: Prasana Das and Emiliano Duch, World Bank.

Concluding Remarks

The role of increasing agricultural productivity to eliminate extreme poverty and meet global food needs remains as central in a shifting climatic environment as when Jia Sixie synthesized his Chinese agricultural encyclopedia, *Essential Techniques for the Common People,* in 535 CE. This volume makes one kindred but central point: the key to achieving higher productivity growth still lies in increasing the generation and dissemination of new techniques and technologies. However, it also documents that the global effort in this regard is diminishing—the agricultural research gap is widening. In this sense, it is a call to action to increase the resources dedicated to these activities, and increase the efficiency with which they are used. Fortunately, the rise of private sector agents and digital technologies offers important new ways of facilitating this effort and ameliorating long-term market failures.

The analysis here builds on the now vast literature on agricultural productivity in several ways. First, it offers the first consistent estimates of the sources of agricultural output and productivity growth to date globally and by region. It documents that productivity growth has been low precisely in the regions facing the most poverty and greatest climatic challenges.

Second, locating this discussion in the context of recent advances in the broader productivity literature, it argues that the diagnostics pointing to the gains from reallocating factors of production have probably been overemphasized. Studies of optimal firm size have become more agnostic on whether there are large gains to be had by redistribution.

Third, building on these insights on reallocation, the volume then shifts the focus to within-farm improvements as the driver of productivity and the role of research and technological diffusion. With the goal of closing the agricultural research gap, it discusses the relative roles of public and private research agencies and the types of framework conditions required to make them effective and transformative.

Fourth, the discussion then explores complementary markets and factors necessary to ensure take-up of new technologies. The new thinking on the barriers posed by problems of information, finance, risk, and market access suggests that a comprehensive approach to the application of new research and adoption of new technologies is necessary if increased research spending is not to be pushing on a string.

The final analysis shows how the rise of value chains in agriculture radically changes that landscape of global agricultural production and marketing and offers new tools to resolve the various market failures impeding research and adoption of new technologies in the presence of weak government capabilities. In particular, it offers a framework for organizing the policy discussion and approaching the vast literature on agricultural policy. Throughout, the volume details how the advent of new digital technologies permits new forms of global coordination of research, less expensive and more tailored modalities of extension, flexible and low-cost financial instruments that can extend credit to heretofore unreachable small farmers, and more effective ways of managing and hedging risk.

The focus of this volume has been deliberately narrowed to issues of productivity in agriculture. Clearly, harvesting prosperity in the rural areas will require a more comprehensive vision that goes beyond improving efficiency, shifting to high–value added crops, and diversification, discussed here, to the larger transformation of the rural economy. This lies beyond the scope of this analysis, but clearly merits a complementary effort, as does the looming issue of climate change that threatens to undermine rural prosperity and will importantly condition future agricultural research and policy.

This said, the aspirations of this work are metaphorically captured by the Spanish/Mexican surrealist Remedios Varo in her painting, "Rebellious Plant," depicted on the front cover. The miracle of agricultural productivity growth has nourished people and lifted people out of poverty to a degree unimaginable to our ancestors. However, adapting agriculture to new and possibly dramatically changing contexts requires a sustained process of experimentation and scientific inquiry. Continuing this trend is vital in the final push to end global poverty and create fulfilling livelihoods for all.

Notes

1. For more on the program, see documents.worldbank.org/curated/en/818191468240888662 /Colombia-Rural-Development-Investment-Program-RDIP.

2. See Lacroix (1985); Zandstra et al. (1979); and Maloney (1983).

3. Food standards have increased sharply during the past two decades and now play a dominant role in world agri-food trade (Aksoy and Beghin 2005) for five main reasons, among others (Swinnen and Maertens 2007). (1) Food safety hazards in high-income countries have increased demand for food safety systems. (2) Rising incomes and changing dietary habits have increased demand for high-quality food. (3) Specific standards were developed to reflect ethical and environmental concerns related to food production and trade. (4) The growing trade in fresh foods—which are prone to food safety risks or subject to specific quality demands from consumers—heightened the need to regulate trade through standards. (5) The expanding role of large multinational food and retail companies heightened the importance of private standards for freshness, product quality, and food safety to prevent the high reputational damage and loss of market share arising from sales of unsafe food (Henson and Humphrey 2010).

4. Another common institutional innovation for overcoming technology and output market constraints, not discussed here, is collective producer organizations such as farmer associations and cooperatives. There are several explanations for why such organizations could enhance productivity. Notably, (1) collective marketing can reduce the risk of relationship-specific investments; (2) collective bargaining can increase output prices (increasing the return on technological investment) and reduce prices for equipment, inputs, and services; and (3) collective purchasing can give farmers access to lumpy technology, like harvesting machinery. Empirical evidence confirming these explanations is scarce, however.

5. HACCP stands for hazard analysis and critical control points. GLOBALG.A.P. is a quality control program that translates consumer requirements into Good Agricultural Practice (G.A.P.). See https://www.globalgap.org.

6. Interestingly, in the large grain-producing areas of the former Soviet Union (Kazakhstan, the Russian Federation, and Ukraine), extensive vertical integration has developed not so much to address product standards as to overcome farmers' constraints in financial and input markets (Gataulina et al. 2005). Large agroholdings sometimes operate on thousands of hectares. It is not clear to what extent these arrangements can be a model for large-scale investment in land-abundant regions in Sub-Saharan Africa. Vertical integration seems to be on the rise in Asia. In peri-urban areas of China, the Philippines, and Vietnam, for example, large-scale vertically integrated pig farms are emerging. These firms integrate different stages and activities of the supply chains in a single company. It is not uncommon for pig breeding, fattening, slaughtering, and meat processing to be integrated in one company. These are often very large companies that are financed through FDI and that rely on imported genetic material and technology. In some fruit and vegetable export subsectors in China, export companies and packing houses have moved toward procurement from their own vertically integrated farms, established on land leased from the government. Apple-exporting companies source 5 percent–20 percent of primary produce from their own vertically integrated farms, whereas onion exporters source 30 percent–70 percent, Miyata, Minot, and Hu (2009) report.

7. Not surprisingly, the adoption of technology and use of inputs are positively associated with output prices. For example, among Kenyan maize farmers, a 1 percent increase in the maize price increases the probability of fertilizer use by 5 percent and the amount of fertilizer used by

1.04 percent, Alene et al. (2008) find. Similarly, a 1 percent increase in the coffee price increases Tanzanian coffee growers' expenditure on chemical inputs (such as fertilizer and pesticides) by 1.25 percent, Winter-Nelson and Temu (2005) report. In Ethiopia, the adoption of fertilizer is negatively associated with the price of fertilizer relative to output prices, Zerfu and Larson (2010) find.

8. Various other studies investigate how value chain spillovers affect health, nutrition, and education. See, for example, Asfaw, Mithöfer, and Waibel (2010); Chege, Andersson, and Qaim (2015); Demmler, Ecker, and Qaim (2018); Meemken, Spielman, and Qaim (2017); and Van den Broeck, Van Hoyweghen, and Maertens (2018).

9. Many examples of smallholder inclusion in high-value chains come from horticulture. One potential explanation for this phenomenon is that horticultural crops tend to have high labor requirements for crop protection and harvesting, and smallholders have a competitive advantage in accessing cheap labor compared to large estate farms. Large farmers must hire labor to produce horticultural crops, but smallholders often use family or community labor. The advantage of family labor over hired labor is that it avoids the principal-agent problem. Consequently, smallholders might have a comparative advantage because they do not bear the costs of suboptimal levels of effort, supervision, and labor output monitoring.

10. See Heinrich (2014), which presents six necessary conditions that must be satisfied for additionality of private sector development initiatives.

References

Aksoy, M.A., and J. C. Beghin, editors. 2005. Global Agricultural Trade and Developing Countries. Washington, DC: World Bank. https://openknowledge.worldbank.org/handle/10986/7464.

Alene, A. D., V. M. Manyong, G. Omanya, H. D. Mignouna, M. Bokanga, and G. Odhiambo. 2008. "Smallholder Market Participation under Transactions Costs: Maize Supply and Fertilizer Demand in Kenya." *Food Policy* 33 (4): 318–28. doi: http://dx.doi.org/10.1016/j.foodpol.2007.12.001.

Asfaw, S., D. Mithöfer, and H. Waibel. 2009. "EU Food Safety Standards, Pesticide Use and Farm-Level Productivity: The Case of High-Value Crops in Kenya." *Journal of Agricultural Economics* 60 (3): 645–67. https://doi.org/10.1111/j.1477-9552.2009.00205.

————— 2010. "Agrifood Supply Chain, Private-Sector Standards, and Farmers' Health: Evidence from Kenya." *Agricultural Economics* 41 (3-4): 251–63.

Banerjee, A., E. Duflo, N. Goldberg, D. Karlan, R. Osei, W. Parienté, J. Shapiro, B. Thuysbaert, and C. Udry. 2015. "A Multifaceted Program Causes Lasting Progress for the Very Poor: Evidence from Six Countries." *Science* 348 (6236): 1260799–16.

Bardhan, P. 1989. *The Economic Theory of Agrarian Institutions*. Oxford, UK: Clarendon Press.

Barrett, C. B., M. E. Bachke, M. F. Bellemare, H. C. Michelson, S. Narayanan, and T. F. Walker. 2012. "Smallholder Participation in Contract Farming: Comparative Evidence from Five Countries." *World Development* 40 (4): 715–30. https://doi.org/10.1016/j.worlddev.2011.09.006.

Barrett, C., and M. Carter. 2012. "The Economics of Poverty Traps and Persistent Poverty: Policy and Empirical Implications." Working paper, Cornell University.

Barrett, C. B., L. Christiaensen, M. Sheahan, and A. Shimeles. 2017. "On the Structural Transformation of Rural Africa." *Journal of African Economies* 26 (Supplement 1, August): i11–i35. https://doi.org/10.1093/jae/ejx009.

Bell, C., and T. N. Srinivasan. 1989. "Interlinked Transactions in Rural Markets: An Empirical Study of Andhra Pradesh, Bihar and Punjab." *Oxford Bulletin of Economics and Statistics* 51 (1): 73–83.

Bellemare, M. F., and J. R. Bloem. 2018. "Contract Farming: A Review." Working Paper.

Bolwig, S., P. Gibbon, and S. Jones. 2009. "The Economics of Smallholder Organic Contract Farming in Tropical Africa." *World Development* 37 (6): 1094–104. https://doi.org/10.1016/j.worlddev.2008.09.012.

Carletto, C., P. Corral, and A. Guelfi. 2017. "Agricultural Commercialization and Nutrition Revisited: Empirical Evidence from Three African Countries." *Food Policy* 67 (February): 106–18. https://doi.org/10.1016/j.foodpol.2016.09.020.

Cavatassi, R., M. González-Flores, P. Winters, J. Andrade-Piedra, P. Espinosa, and G. Thiele. 2011. "Linking Smallholders to the New Agricultural Economy: The Case of the *Plataformas de Concertación* in Ecuador." *Journal of Development Studies* 47 (10): 1545–73. https://doi.org/10.1080/00220388.2010.536221.

Chege, C. G., C. I. Andersson, and M. Qaim. 2015. "Impacts of Supermarkets on Farm Household Nutrition in Kenya." *World Development* 72 (August): 394–407. doi: 10.1016/j.worlddev.2015.03.016.

Cirera, X., and W. F. Maloney. 2017. *The Innovation Paradox: Developing Country Capabilities and the Unrealized Promise of Technological Catch-Up*. Washington, DC: World Bank.

Cungu, A., H. Gow, J. Swinnen, and L. Vranken. 2008. "Investment with Weak Contract Enforcement: Evidence from Hungary during Transition." *European Review of Agricultural Economics* 35 (1): 75–91. https://doi.org/10.1093/erae/jbn001.

Cusolito, A. P., and W. F. Maloney. 2018. *Productivity Revisited: Shifting Paradigms in Analysis and Policy*. Washington, DC: World Bank.

de Janvry, A., and E. Sadoulet. Forthcoming. "Transforming Developing Country Agriculture: Push and Pull Approaches." Development Review Paper for *World Development*.

Demmler, K. M., O. Ecker, and M. Qaim. 2018. "Supermarket Shopping and Nutritional Outcomes: A Panel Data Analysis for Urban Kenya." *World Development* 102 (February): 292–303. https://doi.org/10.1016/j.worlddev.2017.07.018.

Devaux, A., D. Horton, C. Velasco, G. Thiele, G. López, T. Bernet, I. Reinoso, and M. Ordinola. 2009. "Collective Action for Market Chain Innovation in the Andes." *Food Policy* 34 (1): 31–38. https://doi.org/10.1016/j.foodpol.2008.10.007.

Dolan, C., and J. Humphrey. 2000. "Governance and Trade in Fresh Vegetables: The Impact of UK Supermarkets on the African Horticulture Industry." *Journal of Development Studies* 37 (2): 147–76. https://doi.org/10.1080/713600072.

Dries, L., E. Germenji, N. Noev, and J. Swinnen. 2009. "Farmers, Vertical Coordination, and the Restructuring of Dairy Supply Chains in Central and Eastern Europe." *World Development* 37 (11): 1742–58. https://doi.org/10.1016/j.worlddev.2008.08.029.

Dries, L., T. Reardon, and J. Swinnen. 2004. "The Rapid Rise of Supermarkets in Central and Eastern Europe: Implications for the Agrifood Sector and Rural Development." *Development Policy Review* 22 (5): 525–56. https://doi.org/10.1111/j.1467-7679.2004.00264.x.

Dries, L., and J. Swinnen. 2010. "The Impact of Interfirm Relationships on Investment: Evidence from the Polish Dairy Sector." *Food Policy* 35 (2): 121–29. https://doi.org/10.1016/j.foodpol.2009.11.005.

Dyer, J. H., and H. Singh. 1998. "The Relational View: Cooperative Strategy and Sources of Interorganizational Competitive Advantage." *Academy of Management Review* 23 (4): 660–79. doi: 10.2307/259056.

Eswaran, M., and A. Kotwal. 1986. "Access to Capital and Agrarian Production Organisation." *The Economic Journal* 96 (382): 482–98.

Gataulina, E. A., V. Y. Uzun, A. V. Petrikov, and R. G. Yanbykh. 2005. "Vertical Integration in an Agroindustrial Complex: Agrofirms and Agroholdings in Russia." In *The Dynamics of Vertical Coordination in Agrifood Chains in Eastern Europe and Central Asia: Case Studies*, edited by J. F. M. Swinnen, 45–71. Washington, DC: World Bank.

Gereffi, G., J. Humphrey, and T. Sturgeon. 2005. "The Governance of Global Value Chains." *Review of International Political Economy* 12 (1): 78–104. https://doi.org/10.1080/09692290500049805.

Gibbon, P. 2003. "Value-Chain Governance, Public Regulation and Entry Barriers in the Global Fresh Fruit and Vegetable Chain into the EU." *Development Policy Review* 21 (5-6): 615–25. https://doi.org/10.1111/j.1467-8659.2003.00227.x.

Gow, H. R., D. H. Streeter, and J. Swinnen. 2000. "How Private Contract Enforcement Mechanisms Can Succeed Where Public Institutions Fail: The Case of Juhocukor a.s." *Agricultural Economics* 23 (3): 253–65. https://doi.org/10.1111/j.1574-0862.2000.tb00277.x.

Gow, H. R., and J. Swinnen. 2001. "Private Enforcement Capital and Contract Enforcement in Transition Economies." *American Journal of Agricultural Economics* 83 (3): 686–90.

Goyal, A. 2010. "Information, Direct Access to Farmers, and Rural Market Performance in Central India." *American Economic Journal: Applied Economics* 2 (3): 22–45.

Gulati, A., N. Minot, C. Delgado, and S. Bora. 2007. "Growth in High-Value Agriculture in Asia and the Emergence of Vertical Links with Farmers." In *Global Supply Chains, Standards and the Poor*, edited by J. Swinnen, 98–108. Wallingford, UK: CABI (Centre for Agriculture and Bioscience International).

Handschuch, C., M. Wollni, and P. Villalobos. 2013. "Adoption of Food Safety and Quality Standards among Chilean Raspberry Producers: Do Smallholders Benefit?" *Food Policy* 40 (June): 64–73. doi: 10.1016/j.foodpol.2013.02.002.

Hansen, H., and N. Trifković. 2014. "Food Standards Are Good—for Middle-Class Farmers." *World Development* 56 (April): 226–42. doi: 10.1016/j.worlddev.2013.10.027.

Heinrich, M. 2014. *Demonstrating Additionality in Private Sector Development Initiatives; A Practical Exploration of Good Practice for Challenge Funds and Other Cost-Sharing Mechanisms.* Cambridge, UK: DCED (Donor Committee for Enterprise Development). https://www.enterprise-development.org/wp-content/uploads/DCED_Demonstrating-Additionality_final.pdf.

Henson, S., and J. Humphrey. 2010. "Understanding the Complexities of Private Standards in Global Agri-food Chains as They Impact Developing Countries." *Journal of Development Studies* 46 (9): 1628–46. https://doi.org/10.1080/00220381003706494.

Henson, S., O. Masakure, and D. Boselie. 2005. "Private Food Safety and Quality Standards for Fresh Produce Exporters: The Case of Hortico Agrisystems, Zimbabwe." *Food Policy* 30 (4): 371–84. https://doi.org/10.1016/j.foodpol.2005.06.002.

Henson, S., and T. Reardon. 2005. "Private Agri-food Standards: Implications for Food Policy and the Agri-food System." *Food Policy* 30 (4): 241–53. https://doi.org/10.1016/j.foodpol.2005.05.002.

Jaffee, S. 2003. "From Challenge to Opportunity: Transforming Kenya's Fresh Vegetable Trade in the Context of Emerging Food Safety and Other Standards in Europe." Agriculture and Rural Development Discussion Paper 2, World Bank, Washington, DC. http://documents.worldbank.org/curated/en/598771468753012002/From-challenge-to-opportunity-transforming-Kenyas-fresh-vegetable-trade-in-the-context-of-emerging-food-safety-and-other-standards-in-Europe.

Jaffee, S., and S. Henson. 2004. "Standards and Agro-food Exports from Developing Countries: Rebalancing the Debate." Policy Research Working Paper 3348, World Bank, Washington, DC. https://openknowledge.worldbank.org/handle/10986/14061.

Jones, S., and P. Gibbon. 2011. "Developing Agricultural Markets in Sub-Saharan Africa: Organic Cocoa in Rural Uganda." *Journal of Development Studies* 47 (10): 1595–1618. https://doi.org/10.1080/00220388.2011.579107.

Kersting, S., and M. Wollni. 2012. "New Institutional Arrangements and Standard Adoption: Evidence from Small-scale Fruit and Vegetable Farmers in Thailand." *Food Policy* 37 (4): 452–62. https://doi.org/10.1016/j.foodpol.2012.04.005.

Klein, B., R. G. Crawford, and A. A. Alchian. 1978. "Vertical Integration, Appropriable Rents, and the Competitive Contracting Process." *The Journal of Law and Economics* 21 (2): 297–326.

Kolavalli, S., A. Mensah-Bonsu, and S. Zaman. 2015. "Agricultural Value Chain Development in Practice: Private Sector-Led Smallholder Development." IFPRI Discussion Paper 1460, International Food Policy Research Institute, Washington, DC. http://ebrary.ifpri.org/cdm/ref /collection/p15738coll2/id/129473.

Kuijpers, R., and J. Swinnen. 2016. "Value Chains and Technology Transfer to Agriculture in Developing and Emerging Economies." *American Journal of Agricultural Economics* 98 (5): 1403–18. https://doi.org/10.1093/ajae/aaw069.

Kumar, A., D. Roy, P. K. Joshi, G. Tripathi, and R. P. Adhikari. 2016. "Impact of Contract Farming on Profits and Yield of Smallholder Farms in Nepal: An Evidence from Lentil Cultivation." Presented at the 2016 Annual Meeting of the Agricultural and Applied Economics Association, Boston, July 31–August 2.

Lacroix, R. L. J. 1985. "Integrated Rural Development in Latin America." Staff Working Paper 716, World Bank, Washington, DC.

Maertens, M., L. Colen, and J. Swinnen. 2011. "Globalisation and Poverty in Senegal: A Worst Case Scenario?" *European Review of Agricultural Economics* 38(1): 31–54. https://doi.org/10.1093 /erae/jbq053.

Maertens, M., B. Minten, and J. Swinnen. 2012. "Modern Food Supply Chains and Development: Evidence from Horticulture Export Sectors in Sub-Saharan Africa." *Development Policy Review* 30 (4): 473–97. https://doi.org/10.1111/j.1467-7679.2012.00585.x.

Maertens, M., and J. Swinnen. 2009. "Trade, Standards, and Poverty: Evidence from Senegal." *World Development* 37 (1): 161–78. doi:10.1016/j.worlddev.2008.04.006.

———. 2012. "Gender and Modern Supply Chains in Developing Countries." *The Journal of Development Studies* 48 (10): 1412–30. https://doi.org/10.1080/00220388.2012.663902.

———. 2015. "Agricultural Trade and Development: A Value Chain Perspective." WTO Working Paper ERSD-2015-04, World Trade Organization, Geneva. https://www.wto.org/english/res_e /reser_e/ersd201504_e.pdf.

Maertens, M., and K. Vande Velde. 2017. "Contract Farming in Staple Food Chains: The Case of Rice in Benin." *World Development* 95 (C): 73–87. https://doi.org/10.1016/j.worlddev.2017.02.011.

Maloney, W. F. 1983. "Integrated Rural Development in Colombia." Unpublished.

Mano, Y., T. Yamano, A. Suzuki, and T. Matsumoto. 2011. "Local and Personal Networks in Employment and the Development of Labor Markets: Evidence from the Cut Flower Industry in Ethiopia." *World Development* 39 (10): 1760–70. doi: 10.1016/j.worlddev.2011.04.024.

Meemken, E.-M., D. J. Spielman, and M. Qaim. 2017. "Trading Off Nutrition and Education? A Panel Data Analysis of the Dissimilar Welfare Effects of Organic and Fairtrade Standards." *Food Policy* 71 (August): 74–85. https://doi.org/10.1016/j.foodpol.2017.07.010.

Michelson, H., T. Reardon, and F. Perez. 2012. "Small Farmers and Big Retail: Trade-offs of Supplying Supermarkets in Nicaragua." *World Development* 40 (2): 342–54. https://doi.org/10.1016/j .worlddev.2011.07.013.

Minot, N., and M. Ngigi. 2004. "Are Horticultural Exports a Replicable Success Story? Evidence from Kenya and Côte d'Ivoire." EPTD Discussion Paper No. 120 and MTID Discussion Paper No. 73, International Food Policy Research Institute, Washington, DC. http://www.hubrural.org/IMG /pdf/minot_ngigi_2004.pdf.

Minot, N., and B. Sawyer. 2016. "Contract Farming in Developing Countries: Theory and Practice, and Policy Implications." Chapter 4 in *Innovation for Inclusive Value-Chain Development: Successes and Challenges,* edited by A. Devaux, M. Torero, J, Donovan, and D. Horton, 127–58. Washington, DC: International Food Policy Research Institute.

Minten, B., L. Randrianarison, and J. Swinnen. 2009. "Global Retail Chains and Poor Farmers: Evidence from Madagascar." *World Development* 37 (11): 1728–41. https://doi.org/10.1016/j.worlddev.2008.08.024.

Miyata, S., N. Minot, and D. Hu. 2009. "Impact of Contract Farming on Income: Linking Small Farmers, Packers, and Supermarkets in China." *World Development* 37 (11): 1781–90. https://doi.org/10.1016/j.worlddev.2008.08.025.

Negash, M., and J. Swinnen. 2013. "Biofuels and Food Security: Micro-evidence from Ethiopia." *Energy Policy* 61: 963–76. doi: 10.1016/j.enpol.2013.06.031.

Noev, N., L. Dries, and J. Swinnen. 2009. "Institutional Change, Contracts, and Quality in Transition Agriculture." *Eastern European Economics* 47 (4): 62–85. https://doi.org/10.2753/EEE0012-8775470404.

Ragasa, C., I. Lambrecht, and D. S. Kufoalor. 2018. "Limitations of Contract Farming as a Pro-poor Strategy: The Case of Maize Outgrower Schemes in Upper West Ghana." *World Development* 102 (February): 30–56. https://doi.org/10.1016/j.worlddev.2017.09.008.

Reardon, T., C. B. Barrett, J. A. Berdegué, and J. Swinnen. 2009. "Agrifood Industry Transformation and Small Farmers in Developing Countries." *World Development* 37 (11): 1717–27. https://doi.org/10.1016/j.worlddev.2008.08.023.

Reardon, T., C. P. Timmer, C. B. Barrett, and J. Berdegué. 2003. "The Rise of Supermarkets in Africa, Asia, and Latin America." *American Journal of Agricultural Economics* 85 (5): 1140–46. https://doi.org/10.1111/j.0092-5853.2003.00520.x.

Reardon, T., C. P. Timmer, and B. Minten. 2012. "Supermarket Revolution in Asia and Emerging Development Strategies to Include Small Farmers." *Proceedings of the National Academy of Sciences* 109 (31): 12332–37. https://doi.org/10.1073/pnas.1003160108.

Rozelle, S., and J. Swinnen. 2004. "Success and Failure of Reform: Insights from the Transition of Agriculture." *Journal of Economic Literature* 42 (2): 404–56. doi: 10.1257/0022051041409048.

Saenger, C., M. Torero, and M. Qaim. 2014. "Impact of Third-Party Contract Enforcement in Agricultural Markets—A Field Experiment in Vietnam." *American Journal of Agricultural Economics* 96 (4): 1220–38. https://doi.org/10.1093/ajae/aau021.

Schuster, M., and M. Maertens. 2013. "Do Private Standards Create Exclusive Supply Chains? New Evidence from the Peruvian Asparagus Export Sector." *Food Policy* 43 (C): 291–305. https://doi.org/10.1016/j.foodpol.2013.10.004.

Serova, E., and N. Karlova. 2010. "The Russian Federation: Review of the Dairy Sector." FAO Investment Centre Studies and Reports, Food and Agriculture Organization, Rome.

Subervie, J., and I. Vagneron. 2013. "A Drop of Water in the Indian Ocean? The Impact of GlobalGap Certification on Lychee Farmers in Madagascar." *World Development* 50 (October): 57–73. https://doi.org/10.1016/j.worlddev.2013.05.002.

Suzuki, A., L. S. Jarvis, and R. J. Sexton. 2011. "Partial Vertical Integration, Risk Shifting, and Product Rejection in the High-Value Export Supply Chain: The Ghana Pineapple Sector." *World Development* 39 (9): 1611–23. https://doi.org/10.1016/j.worlddev.2011.02.007.

Swinnen, J. F. M., ed. 2005. *The Dynamics of Vertical Coordination in Agrifood Chains in Eastern Europe and Central Asia: Case Studies*. Washington, DC: World Bank.

———. 2007. *Global Supply Chains, Standards and the Poor: How the Globalization of Food Systems and Standards Affects Rural Development and Poverty*. Wallingford, UK: CABI (Centre for Agriculture and Bioscience International).

———. 2016. "Economics and Politics of Food Standards, Trade, and Development." *Agricultural Economics* 47 (51): 7–19. https://doi.org/10.1111/agec.12316.

Swinnen, J., and E. Janssen. 2016. "Political Economy of Agricultural and (Regional) Trade Policies and Value Chain Performances in Sub-Saharan Africa." In *Political Economy of Regional Integration in Sub-Saharan Africa*, edited by P. Brenton and B. Hoffman, 13–48. Washington, DC: World Bank.

Swinnen, J., and R. Kuijpers. 2017. "Value Chain Innovations for Technology Transfer in Developing and Emerging Economies: Conceptual Issues, Typology, and Policy Implications." *Food Policy* 83 (February): 298–309. https://doi.org/10.1016/j.foodpol.2017.07.013.

———. 2019. "Value Chains and Agricultural Productivity." Background paper for *Harvesting Prosperity: Technology and Productivity Growth in Agriculture*, World Bank, Washington, DC.

Swinnen, J., and M. Maertens. 2007. "Globalization, Privatization, and Vertical Coordination in Food Value Chains in Developing and Transition Countries." *Agricultural Economics* 37 (s1): 89–102. https://doi.org/10.1111/j.1574-0862.2007.00237.x.

Swinnen, J., T. Vandemoortele, K. Deconinck, and A. Vandeplas. 2015. *Quality Standards, Value Chains, and International Development: Economic and Political Theory.* Cambridge, UK: Cambridge University Press.

Swinnen, J., and A. Vandeplas. 2011. "Rich Consumers and Poor Producers: Quality and Rent Distribution in Global Value Chains." *Journal of Globalization and Development* 2 (2). doi: https://doi.org/10.1515/1948-1837.1036.

Swinnen, J., A. Vandeplas, and M. Maertens. 2010. "Liberalization, Endogenous Institutions, and Growth: A Comparative Analysis of Agricultural Reforms in Africa, Asia, and Europe." *World Bank Economic Review* 24 (3): 412–45. https://doi.org/10.1093/wber/lhq017.

Ton, G., W. Vellema, S. Desiere, S. Weituschat, and M. D'Haese. 2018. "Contract Farming for Improving Smallholder Incomes: What Can We Learn from Effectiveness Studies?" *World Development* 104 (C): 46–64. https://doi.org/10.1016/j.worlddev.2017.11.015.

Townsend, R., L. Ronchi, C. I. Brett, and E. Moses. 2018. *The Future of Food: Maximizing Finance for Development in Agricultural Value Chains.* Washington, DC: World Bank Group. http://documents.worldbank.org/curated/en/593641523880972785/Future-of-Food-Maximizing-Finance-for-Development-in-Agricultural-Value-Chains.

Unnevehr, L. J. 2000. "Food Safety Issues and Fresh Food Product Exports from LDCs." *Agricultural Economics* 23 (3): 231–40. https://doi.org/10.1111/j.1574-0862.2000.tb00275.x.

Van den Broeck, G., J. Swinnen, and M. Maertens. 2017. "Global Value Chains, Large-scale Farming, and Poverty: Long-term Effects in Senegal." *Food Policy* 66: 97–107. https://doi.org/10.1016/j.foodpol.2016.12.003.

Van den Broeck, G., K. Van Hoyweghen, and M. Maertens. 2018. "Horticultural Exports and Food Security in Senegal." *Global Food Security* 17 (June): 162–71. https://doi.org/10.1016/j.gfs.2017.12.002.

Wang, H., X. Dong, S. Rozelle, J. Huang, and T. Reardon. 2009. "Producing and Procuring Horticultural Crops with Chinese Characteristics: The Case of Northern China." *World Development* 37 (11): 1791–1801. https://doi.org/10.1016/j.worlddev.2008.08.030.

White, J., and M. Gorton. 2005. "A Comparative Study of Agrifood Chains in Moldova, Armenia, Georgia, Russia, and Ukraine." In *The Dynamics of Vertical Coordination in Agrifood Chains in Eastern Europe and Central Asia: Case Studies*, edited by J. Swinnen, J. White, E. A. Gataulima, V. Y. Uzun, A. V. Petrinov, R. G. Yanbykh, M. Sadler, S. van Berkum, J. Bijman, L. Dries, and N. Noev, 5–44. Washington, DC: World Bank.

Williamson, O. E., 1985. *The Economic Institutions of Capitalism.* New York: Simon and Schuster.

Winter-Nelson, A., and A. Temu. 2005. "Impacts of Prices and Transactions Costs on Input Usage in a Liberalizing Economy: Evidence from Tanzanian Coffee Growers." *Agricultural Economics* 33 (3): 243–53. https://doi.org/10.1111/j.1574-0864.2005.00064.x.

Wollni, M., and M. Zeller. 2007. "Do Farmers Benefit from Participating in Specialty Markets and Cooperatives? The Case of Coffee Marketing in Costa Rica." *Agricultural Economics* 37 (2-3): 243–48. https://doi.org/10.1111/j.1574-0862.2007.00270.x.

World Bank. Forthcoming. *World Development Report 2020: Trading for Development in the Age of Global Value Chains.* Washington, DC: World Bank.

World Bank Group. 2016. "Linking Farmers to Markets through Productive Alliances: An Assessment of the World Bank Experience in Latin America." World Bank, Washington, DC.

Zandstra, H., K. Swanberg, C. Zulberti, and B. Nestel. 1979. *Cáqueza: Living Rural Development.* Ottawa: International Development Research Centre (IDRC).

Zerfu, D., and D. F. Larson. 2010. "Incomplete Markets and Fertilizer Use: Evidence from Ethiopia." Policy Research Working Paper 5235, World Bank, Washington, DC. http://documents .worldbank.org/curated/en/319431468035973728/Incomplete-markets-and-fertilizer-use -evidence-from-Ethiopia.